1968

THE ORIGIN OF MANCHU RULE IN CHINA

Frontier and Bureaucracy as Interacting Forces
in the Chinese Empire

THE ORIGIN OF MANCHU RULE IN CHINA

*Frontier and Bureaucracy as Interacting
Forces in the Chinese Empire*

BY

FRANZ MICHAEL

1965

OCTAGON BOOKS, INC.

New York

Reprinted 1965
by special arrangement with The Johns Hopkins Press

OCTAGON BOOKS, INC.
175 FIFTH AVENUE
NEW YORK, N. Y. 10010

LIBRARY OF CONGRESS CATALOG CARD NUMBER: 65-25880

Printed in U.S.A. by
NOBLE OFFSET PRINTERS, INC.
NEW YORK 3, N. Y.

To

OWEN LATTIMORE

PREFACE

This study of the Origin of Manchu Rule in China deals with a period of Chinese frontier history. The Inner Asian Frontiers of China—the mutual interrelationship of developments on both sides of the frontier—have been shown in a new light by Owen Lattimore's studies and writings. In this book I have tried to study this interrelationship through a most significant period. I have attempted to analyze it further; to show the importance of political organizations and institutions, of their growth and development, for the great processes formed by interacting forces in China's history. To study these forces rathen than to give an exhaustive description of the period has been my aim.

I have to be grateful for much friendly assistance. It is impossible to state here all that I owe to Owen Lattimore. He has been a teacher and a friend, never-failing in his advice, criticism and encouragement.

Dr. Karl August Wittfogel has had the great kindness to read the whole manuscript and to give me a number of most valuable suggestions and criticisms. He has furthermore allowed me to read and make use of the manuscripts of his own books on Liao history and on *Oriental Society in Asia and Ancient America,* both soon to be published. I wish to thank also Dr. A. W. Hummel for his kind permission to read various Manchu biographies from his biographical dictionary: *Eminent Chinese of the Ch'ing Dynasty* which he is preparing. My colleagues at The Johns Hopkins University have been most friendly in their advice. To Dr. Sidney Painter especially who has taken it upon himself to read and edit the text I am very grateful. Mr. David Lattimore has kindly read the proof.

This book was written while I was a fellow of the Walter

Hines Page School of International Relations at The Johns Hopkins University. The acquisition by the School of the private library of the late Erich Hauer, noted German scholar in the field of Far Eastern Affairs, has greatly facilitated my work.

FRANZ MICHAEL.

Baltimore, Md.,
September, 1941.

CONTENTS

CHAPTER I

INTRODUCTION

At the end of the 16th and during the first half of the 17th century the northeast frontier region of the Chinese empire was the scene of a most important political development. A frontier tribe, later known as the Manchus, succeeded in building up in a comparatively short time a state organization which eventually became strong enough to conquer China. In 1644 a Manchu emperor ascended the dragon throne in Peking, and China fell under the sway of the Manchu dynasty, which was to rule until the revolution of 1911 ended the imperial history of China altogether.

The fact that a comparatively small tribe on the edge of China should succeed in dominating Chinese history for almost 300 years cannot be explained simply by military achievements. A military power not based on an elaborate social entity could perhaps be a destructive but not a positive and constructive factor. Indeed the "barbarian" conquests of China were not such simple affairs as imagination sometimes has pictured them. We are inclined to think of these "wild horsemen" from the Mongol steppes or from the forests and mountain valleys of Manchuria as something like an irrisistable force of nature sweeping over the plains of northern China. The descriptions of their conquests deal mostly with the wars they fought, the battles they won, the towns they took before their triumphant entry into Chinese capitals. Little is usually said about the real process of getting hold of the country.

So intensive an agricultural society as the Chinese could, however, not be conquered by riding over the land. If the outside invaders attempted more than a pure looting raid, if they were to remain in China, not only to conquer but to rule it, to attract enough Chinese groups to open the way thereto, they had to possess more than a "barbarian" organization.

1

This truth was once told to the greatest nomad conqueror of all times by a wise and upright captured official. When Ghenghis Khan had destroyed in North China the Chin dynasty, his men had taken captive one Yeh-lü Ch'u-ts'ai, who had served under the defeated dynasty. Yeh-lü Ch'u-ts'ai was a descendant of the " barbarian " dynastic family of the Khitan (Liao). As an official of the likewise barbarian Chin dynasty he had been trained and had served under the Chinese form of administration. His whole life experience had thus been with barbarian groups which had never given up their tribal traditions, but which had had to adapt their control of their Chinese agricultural subjects to the Chinese way. This man more than anybody else would understand the necessity for any barbarian conqueror to use Chinese forms of administration in agricultural China. "You have conquered the empire in the saddle, you cannot govern it so," was this man's advice to the Khan of all Khans.[1] And it was he who in the Mongol service was instrumental in creating the administration which allowed the Mongols later to subjugate and rule all China.

The importance of the gradual formation of these administrative organizations, of the intermediate stages, has not received great attention in histories of China. Owen Lattimore was the first to point out that the successful barbarian invaders of China did not come straight from the open steppes or the depths of the Manchurian forests. Looting raids were sometimes a first form of attack, but for the real conquest and domination an organization was needed that made of the horsemen, or added to them, administrators versed in the control of agricultural country and rural labour.

Such an organization could not be improvised. It had to be built up and developed slowly before a serious attempt to gain rulership over China could be made. Nor could it be created under entirely different social conditions outside of Chinese society. The most important political aspect of

---

[1] 天下雖得之馬上, 不可以馬上治, see Léon Wieger, *Textes Historiques*, Vol. 2, pp. 1657 f.

these invasions was therefore an organization starting at the margin of the Chinese world and proceeding simultaneously with further penetration into China and organization of " tribal " auxiliaries in the trans-Great Wall " hinterland." The foreign dynasties which set themselves up in China, as the Liao, the Chin, the Mongols and the Manchus, had developed a mixed culture on the margin of the Chinese society and thus " grew " into China, before they overran her. Only thus were they able to gain control and domination of the country.

This is very different from the so-called " assimilation " of invaders in China. The theory of " assimilation " would indicate that the " barbarians " came in as children of nature and then were made Chinese. There is some truth in the fact that physically the different kind of life, the greater luxuries and a good deal of laziness changed the people of the invading group within a few generations. But politically the word " assimilation " is misleading. It was not a change after the conquest of China. The change was necessary before the conquest was even possible. Only by becoming " Chinese " in their political organization had the " barbarians " a chance of conquering the rule over China.

A political organization of this kind, however, could never be solely an accumulation of offices and institutions. The group undertaking this task needed political thought, ideologies, a conception of the state. Not only the institutions and manifestations of Chinese political life had to be accepted by the rulers to be; but also something of the Chinese beliefs had to prepare the conqueror's mind for his new role. Chinese philosophy and organization were thus reaching out to the border and preparing there forces for a penetration and conquest of China.

All this meant a process of development that would take time. The conquest of China was not a military question alone, it was not even in the first place a military question. It was a question of the growth of a political organization, a process of amalgamation.

The Manchu conquest of China was not only the last but

also the most important and longest lasting[2] of the frontier invasions into China. This conquest followed the pattern described above of a slowly growing political organization suitable for the rule over Chinese society. This organization was built up while the Manchus penetrated that part of Manchuria which had been since ancient times Chinese and agricultural. It was another case of learning Chinese administration on a small scale before subjugating China.

*   *   *

The phenomenon of invasions and conquests of China by so-called barbarians was of course only a part of the whole political mechanism of the Chinese world. And the Manchus in their penetration from the frontier into China made use of circumstances which could be found at recurrent intervals in Chinese history. In order to be able to discuss the complex state organization of the Manchus, we must therefore first, shortly at least, outline the background of the Chinese political system, in which the Manchus were to play a part.

The most outstanding characteristic of Chinese history is the chain of dynasties succeeding each other in a line, usually interrupted by years of strife and chaos. Out of the recurrent chaos of rebellion there arose always a new dynasty which, after a time, reestablished the former order. The political system as such was never much altered. The dynasties passed through the stages of a cycle which started with the consolidation of newly gained power and led with more or less regularity over a time of highest success into decline and fall.

Conservative Confucian political theory explained this change of dynasties in a static Chinese world by the "will of heaven." The Chinese agrarian society gave the state only the task of upholding peace and order. This was the responsibility of the emperor, the bearer of a "heavenly

---

[2] The life of the Manchu dynasty was at the end artificially prolonged by the intervention of the Western Powers, without which the Manchus would probably have fallen during the Taiping rebellion some fifty years earlier.

mandate." As long as the emperor possessed "virtue," he retained this heavenly mandate. But when flood, drought or disorder showed that this virtue had disappeared, he would loose the mandate. The people could then revolt, overthrow the dynasty and put on the throne another dynasty which would hold the heavenly mandate in its turn.

Foreign scholars, sceptical of the will of heaven, saw the reasons for dynastic decay chiefly in the corruption at court, the eunuch system and the degeneration of the imperial family.

A number of modern scholars have sought and found a further, deeper functional explanation to this periodical change of dynasties which was always accompanied by similar circumstances. The first modern analysis of this cyclical system was fomulated by K. A. Wittfogel [3] and taken up by others. A rich and complete analysis of these dynastical cycles can be found in Owen Lattimore's recent book: *The Inner Asian frontiers of China.*[4] We will try to give here a very short, necessarily oversimplified, restatement of the mechanism of cyclical dynastic change in China.

The explanation is found in the Chinese system itself. The Chinese agrarian society was controlled financially and politically by the landed gentry, the class from which the state drew its officials. The landed gentry and the officials, being of one and the same social class, the "scholar gentry," worked the agrarian taxation system at the same time for the government and their private interests. The two interests were of course of a conflicting nature. And the first weakening of central control would allow the private in-

---

[3] See K. A. Wittfogel's article "The Foundations and Stages of Chinese Economic History," p. 53. The idea was taken up by Wang Yü-chüan in his article "The Rise of Land Tax and the Fall of Dynasties in Chinese History." See also K. A. Wittfogel's description of the cycles in "Die Theorie der Orientalischen Gesellschaft," pp. 109-114. The fullest picture of the economic circle in oriental society in general and Chinese society in particular is given in Wittfogel's new book, *Oriental Society in Asia and Ancient America,* to be published this winter by the Oxford University Press. Through Dr. Wittfogel's kindness the author has been able to see various parts of his manuscript in advance.

[4] Owen Lattimore, *Inner Asian Frontiers of China,* Ch. XVII.

terests to win out. The officials, aside from other possibilities of exploitation, could exempt their own property from taxation. The increasing burden on the property of the rest led to indebtedness. Since the great landholding families which supplied the official bureaucracy also engaged privately in money lending, exorbitant rates of interest would speed up the development that brought more and more property into the private hands of men who held official positions and thereby also exempted it from taxation. The government finances naturally would suffer.[5] The central control would be further weakened. This situation, combined with the accumulation of great private fortunes, the neglect of public enterprises such as irrigation and flood control, resulting famines, the unrest among the suffering and exploited farmers, became the basis of rebellion of the discontented people. If the rebellious movement became menacing enough, it would find the support of parts of the leading class, anxious to protect their fortunes. When this happened in important economic or strategic areas, the rebellious group would have a good chance to succeed.[6] A new regime would be started by the victorious leaders with concessions to the farmer. A stronger, stricter control over officials would be exercised at the outset. But the system would not be changed and the ruling class would remain the same. Thus the game could start all over again.

From the point of view of this cyclical system the most interesting period is the time of the decline of one dynasty, when new forces, bandit leaders, political figures with little to lose and much to gain had a chance to build up a new government. This is also the time for successful invasions. K. A. Wittfogel in his *Probleme der chinesischen Wirtschaftsgeschichte*[7] has pointed out that the conquest of China, always tempting for the surrounding barbarians, was

[5] Wang An-shih's attempts at reform give a very illustrative view of his fight against such a development in the Sung time. See Williamson, *Wang An Shih*.
[6] See Chi Ch'ao-ting, *Key Economic Areas in Chinese History.*
[7] See K. A. Wittfogel, *Probleme der Chinesischen Wirtschaftsgeschichte,* p. 325.

naturally easiest at the time of political decay, of inner strife in China. Aside from the rumbling of Chinese inner revolts, which potentially would lead to new Chinese dynasties, there was also at such periods the possibility of outside conquest. Chinese rebellion and outside invasion became competitors for the prize of the dragon throne. Which of the two was in each case in a better position to succeed, depended on the political configuration at the time.

* * *

If one compares the development of outside barbarian groups with that of rebellious Chinese groups in this competition for control of China, one finds that they were by no means as different as one might be inclined to think at first. Both grew in a similar way, had to build up similar types of organizations and establish themselves at first each in certain definite regions, where they gained the base for further expansion, attack and final control of the country. The barbarians brought, of course, certain elements and political conceptions of their own with them. But, as already indicated, they had to adapt themselves to a Chinese form of political organization, had to use Chinese political instruments and, to a high degree, Chinese officials. They had to rule China in the Chinese way.

This fact has been somewhat obscured by the events of the recent history in China. The impact of the West has brought new factors into the political and social life of China. The arrival of Western merchants, industries, railways, gunboats and ideas upset and changed the usual course of events. China could with these forces be ruled in a different way. The security and unchangeableness of the Chinese system under whatever rule came to an end. To rule China meant no longer to have the benefits of agricultural taxation and live on it in the country. China, opened by force, became a "market" and later a possible reservoir of raw material and cheap labour. It could be controlled with the help of modern means of communication first from treaty ports and, as attempted to-day, even from outside the

country. If China wanted to survive as an independent society it had to defend itself against this new and different
menace. That could only be done by changing the Chinese
society, adapting it to modern conditions, creating something which China had not been before: a national state.
That meant not only a change of government. It meant a
revolution.

China had not known a revolution in this sense since the
beginning of its imperial history. There had been rebellions
and revolts, civil war, invasion and conquest, but the system always remained the same. The ruling group changed,
but not their political ideology, nor their method of government, nor the scholar-gentry class necessary for this type of
government. Now, however, a change of system became
necessary and a national union had to be formed of the
Chinese society. With the revolution of 1911 a first attempt
was made in this direction. It remained partial and was
altogether not very successful. But it destroyed the old form
and started a transformation which has since gone further.

With the necessity of transformation there came also the
necessity of a new ideology. As the conditions of the new
world for China had been created by the West, it was
also Western thought that influenced and started the
Chinese revolution. Western ideas of democracy and nationalism were used as propaganda by the revolutionists in
their struggle against the Manchu dynasty. This influence
was rather sudden and without sound preparation. It was
propagated in China by men, some of whom came from the
new merchant class of the treaty ports, though others were
modern representatives of the old scholar-gentry. Still others
like Sun Yat-sen represented the millions of Chinese who
had gone abroad as coolie laborers and petty merchants
during the second half of the nineteenth century, where a
few of them acquired great wealth—notably in Malaya.
Some of these new Chinese political theorists were rather
superficial in their "Westernism." Others were rather
superficial in their "Chineseness"; for while discrimination
against the Chinese living abroad kept them loyal to China,

the environments in which they lived were un-Chinese. Thus the theorists' knowledge of Western things remained often rather limited and was not always well digested, while their knowledge of Chinese tradition was sometimes not very profound. We find that certain modern, outspokenly foreign and hitherto non-Chinese ideas were not only applied to the time of the revolution, but that Chinese history became reinterpreted in the light of such new thought. In his *San Min Chu I*, Sun Yat-sen accuses the Manchus of having destroyed Chinese "nationalism" by introducing "cosmopolitanism." The revolutionists called the Manchus "alien intruders" and serious Chinese writers on political science have used many arguments to prove that the Manchus were not "rightful successors" to the Ming throne,[8] but only "conquerors" and therefore China had to be freed from them.[9]

All these ideas were of course modern and did not fit into the old Chinese world, the world of the time of these "barbarian" and "alien" invasions. Confucian state philosophy did not know the national state. It did not differentiate between nationalities or races. "When the barbarian enters China (i.e. Chinese civilization) he becomes Chinese" (夷而進於中國則中國之) states a Confucian saying. Besides, the majority of the "Manchus" at the very time when they moved into China were racially of Chinese stock, as we shall later see. They did not aim at anything else than at what the Chinese rebels of the same and other periods had aimed at, namely to establish a "Chinese" dynasty. That they used force and conquest was also not unusual. True, the emperor who held the heavenly mandate and followed the kingly way, was according to the orthodox interpretation supposed to have gained his position by his virtue rather than by the force of arms. But Chinese political reality could never do without force. No Chinese dynasty, from outside or inside the country, ever gained the throne without recourse to arms. In this way there was no

[8] As the Manchus themselves had claimed at the time for reasons of political propaganda.
[9] See Hsieh Pao-chao, *The government of China* (1644-1911).

essential difference between conquest from outside and from inside the country. Of course, like other invaders, the Manchus kept a part of their own traditions together with their adaptation of Chinese ways. We shall have to study this development of their organization. But as a general system they had to accept the Chinese way of life and Chinese civilization.[10]

If we study the organization formed by the Manchus before they seized power, we must then be careful not to bring in thoughts and conceptions of another time. It is the working of the cyclical and competitive forces in Chinese history, as described above that will interest us here.

*   *   *

From this view point the period with which we have to deal is of particular interest. The Ming dynasty was in decline. Peasant unrest and revolts created armies of bandits starting out from Shantung and from Shansi and ravaging the countryside in China. The rebellion swept to the capital and for a time it seemed as if a new Chinese dynasty might be established by its leader.

In the meantime the Manchus organized their frontier state. When finally the Mings fell and the dragon throne was in their reach, the Manchus were ready to grasp for it.

Both rebellion and invasion had then a fairly equal chance of success. The scale was tipped in favour of .the Manchus by the weight of several factors. They possessed a better organization and leadership. The Manchu success was only possible because of the base the Manchus had built in their

---

[10] The ideological fight between the Chinese revolutionists of 1911 and the Manchu dynasty was therefore not so much a struggle between Chinese and alien conquerors, as it was a clash between the forerunners of a modern Chinese national state and the representatives of the old Chinese Confucian tradition. It has even been said that the Manchu dynasty " was more Chinese-Confucian than any previous dynasty had been. Every member of the ruling family had a profounder Chinese education than the leaders of the revolutionary party, except of course the group of K'ang Yu-wei." See Haenisch, " Die gegenwärtigen chinesischen Wirren und ihre geschichtlichen Voraussetzungen." This statement has to be modified, however, by the realisation that even with their education the Manchus—as we shall see—never became quite absorbed into the Chinese life.

state formed at the edge of China. But, most important of all, the Manchu policy was, as we shall see, more "Chinese" than that of the Chinese rebel who was the Manchus' rival! So well had the Manchus come to understand and to apply the Chinese system of government that the country turned to them rather than to an unorthodox Chinese.

We shall try to analyse this development. In studying the genesis of the Manchu rule in China we shall show this transformation of a frontier force into a dynasty of the Chinese empire. We shall discover that this was not a simple one-line development. The Manchu acceptance of Chinese bureaucracy had been preceded and facilitated by a certain feudalization of the frontier regions. A dual process from within and without the Chinese agrarian frontier created a sphere of transition through which the Manchus could pass into China. Outward and inward forces opened thus in their interaction the way for a new dynasty.

This creative dual process was not limited to the Manchu period. It was a characteristic part of Chinese history. The case of the Manchus seems however particularly suited to demonstrate this development.

CHAPTER II

MANCHURIA AND ITS PEOPLES

The region where the Manchus founded their political organization was especially suited for the development of a frontier state through the interaction of bureaucratic, feudal, tribal or clan elements. It was by nature a region of contrasts where geographical conditions favoured different forms of human society and economy side by side—a frontier par excellence. This region's present name: Manchuria, is of Western origin and without equivalent in the Chinese language and is historically misleading. It seems to indicate a uniform country with a uniform people. This Manchuria was not.

The name Manchuria came into use only in connection with the conflicting interests of the Great Powers over a region in which the way of life in modern times has changed entirely, chiefly through the modern means of railway communications. Today Manchuria, although called by the Japanese "Manchukuo," has an overwhelming Chinese population which has spread rapidly along the railways over a great part of the arable land.

In past history, however, Manchuria was not a country with either definite borders or a uniform people, but rather an area of contact of different types of life and societies. There was the Chinese society, agricultural in its economy and bureaucratically administrated. There were the steppe nomads and stock breeders and the forest people, living in tribal or feudal organizations.

In recorded history the oldest and most mature part of Manchuria was the extreme south, southwest and southeast, which was old Chinese cultural ground. The lower plains of the Liao river, the narrow strip of plain along the coast line on the northwest of the gulf of Liaotung down to Shanhaikuan, the shores of the Liaotung peninsula and

12

the lower valley of the Yalu river lent themselves to an intensive irrigational agrarian economy comparable to that of North China. In this region there lived from neolithic times people with the same characteristics and the same mode of life as those in North China.[1] Their history was a part of Chinese history. Together with the rest of China they had advanced from early feudalism to the Chinese bureaucratic form of government of the imperial age.

Yet, though Chinese in its way of life, this region was geographically rather isolated from the rest of China, separated from it by mountains, steppes or the sea. For normal constant communication in terms of trade, taxes in kind, " barbarian" tribute missions passing through on the way to the capital, the coming and going of officials and other people there was but one narrow land route to be followed. That was the narrow strip of agricultural land between the gulf of Liaotung on one side and the mountains of what is to-day Jehol on the other. The narrowest point was the strategic pass of Shanhaikuan, where the Great Wall comes down to the sea and one enters China Proper. This road connected Chinese Manchuria with the rest of China. Other routes, further inland, leading from China through the mountain passes, steppes and grassland of Jehol into Manchuria were not practical for normal communications. The lack of cultivation along these routes made traveling or transportation of goods too difficult and expensive. These routes were good for mobile raiding parties and armies and were thus used by barbarian invaders. The Manchus themselves after their conquest of Chinese Manchuria made looting campaigns into North China over these passes. Until they had undisputed control of Shanhaikuan, they were, however, not sure of permanent access to China Proper over these Jehol routes alone.[2] All the more important appeared thus the precarious route through Shanhaikuan.

---

[1] Owen Lattimore, *Inner Asian Frontiers of China*, pp. 103 ff.

[2] Without the passage through Shankaikuan they could not keep connection with the conquered towns in Hopei and lost them again. See *K'ai Kuo Fang Lüeh*, Ch. XIII, p. 9. In this the Manchus differed from the earlier

The other important connection between Chinese Manchuria and China Proper was the sea route, in particular over
the comparatively short distance from the Shantung to the
Liaotung peninsula. This sea route created an interrelationship that showed itself in the origins of the Liaotung
people and their political connections. While in the Western
part of Chinese Manchuria many people had family links
with Hopei province, in Liaotung a great many Shantung
Chinese were to be found.[3]

With only one practical land route and otherwise sea
connections with China Proper the Chinese part of Manchuria was but an outpost of Chinese society and life. It
was vulnerable to attack and had therefore a particular frontier character.

Outside this Chinese basin and bordering on it were,
broadly speaking, two other types of peoples, societies and
economies in Manchuria. To the West and Northwest, in
the mountains and plains of Jehol and the Hsingan range
and beyond, the country consisted largely of rich grassland
and open steppes. The steppe society populating these regions in varying strength and political combinations was related to that of other parts of Inner and Outer Mongolia.
It was a nomad society of tribal peoples of Mongol or related origin. Their economy was based on the herding of
horses, sheep, cattle or camels on the pastures of the steppe.[4]
They lived in tents and their strength lay in the mobility
of their tribal groups.

Khitan and Juchen, peoples of Manchuria which formed the Liao dynasty
and the Chin dynasty which flourished in the eleventh and twelfe centuries.
(For a short valuation of their organizations see below.) Each of these
dynasties occupied and was partly based on the mountains and grass lands
of South and North Jehol, which regions at that time had some sedentary
population. They thus had direct access to the Peking-Tientsin plain and
were not dependent on the narrow Shanhaikuan passage. When the Manchus
were rising to power, however, Jehol was occupied by Mongol tribes, not
yet under full Manchu political control.

[3] Many of the Chinese in Manchuria who went over later to the Manchus
originated either from Hopei or Shantung. The rest were born in Manchuria, but the families had often Shantung or Hopei connections.

[4] For the difference " between the stockbreeders of Jehol and the steppe
nomads of Mongolia " see Wittfogel-Feng, *Liao*, section 1. (Compare note
9 below.)

There was, however, no fixed natural frontier between the last arable acre and the steppe. A gradual transition and diminuition of returns created a marginal zone of changing economy.[5] This zone would serve to allow a changing steppe group to grow into China, or for Chinese groups to break loose into the steppe, according to the political strength and configuration on the inside and outside.

This kind of interrelationship between the Chinese kind of society and that of the steppe and grassland Mongols existed in Manchuria as well as in other regions of the Mongolian border with China. In Manchuria we find the same mixed frontier groups as elsewhere along the marginal zone. The control of these zones would at times serve the Chinese to extend their domination far into the steppe.[6] At other times it would serve Mongols as stepping stones to gain control over Chinese Manchuria or China Proper. In between such periods there would sometimes develop in the marginal zone little hybrid states, feudal in their political organization, with walled towns and a mixture of agriculture and pastoral economy.

The Mongol groups of the steppes were, however, not the only frontier problem of the Chinese basin in Manchuria. To the north, northeast and east, in the forests and marshes along the Hurka, Sungari, Ussuri and Amur rivers and in the valleys of the Chang-pai-shan or Long White Mountains lived a variety of tribes of Tungus origin. They were primarily hunting and fishing nomads, yet differed among themselves considerably in their life and use of animals and equipment. In the north the reindeer was used, in the east we find dogsleds and canoes. But the main part of these tribes that came into contact with the Chinese world used— probably at first under steppe influence—horses. Their chief domesticated animal was the pig. Its major economic importance was reflected in the religious rites of the shaman-

[5] Owen Lattimore, *Inner Asian Frontiers of China*, pp. 480 ff.

[6] The beginning of the Ming dynasty was a period in which Chinese control extended far into Jehol. Compare T. C. Lin, "Manchuria in the Ming Empire." This fact can be explained by the marginal, partly sedentary, economy created in Jehol by the Liao and their Mongol successors.

istic tribes. They had also a certain amount of desultory agriculture. And we can even believe that this type of agriculture was " original " with them and not at first accepted from the Chinese. The Manchus, themselves one of these Tungus tribes, had in their own language a good number of words for agricultural products and implements.[7]

Like the steppe nomads these hunting nomads had intermittently been in contact with the Chinese basin of Manchuria. The mode of life and the political organization in the adjoining regions had consequently been considerably affected. Again as with the Mongols, intermediate small feudal states with a type of settled life, with a greater emphasis on agriculture, with strongholds and walled towns would originate and lead to political transformations. At times these little states would be under the political control of the Chinese. At other times, when Chinese frontier control became lax, one of them could become the starting point for a strong frontier power which in its turn would penetrate the Chinese basin in Manchuria or beyond it into China Proper.

The three different types of societies and peoples, the Chinese, the Mongols and the Tungus were in no way static towards each other. The whole of Manchurian history is a constant movement, a melting and a new separation of these elements. The traces of these contacts and transformations had, of course, been left in the characteristics, tradition and even racial stocks of the groups concerned. Groups from the steppe and the forests that had penetrated the Chinese basin and became settled there, remained after their political control was ended. Others left again, but took with them the knowledge of Chinese life and, most likely, Chinese adherents and slaves too. And sometimes Chinese that had penetrated the barbarian regions became " barbarian " themselves.[8]

---

[7] F. Otte, " Early Manchu Economy," gives a list of such words handed to him by E. Hauer.

[8] Thus we find among the Manchus clan names that indicate Chinese origin. Of one of the clans, Irgen Kioro, we know that it consisted of the

Out of all these elements states were formed. In the course of years they fell apart again. Some remained just little frontier states, others became the cradles of Chinese dynasties.

The economic basis for all political development was, however, always the Chinese agricultural, sedentary society. Any barbarian dynasty to be set up had to gain its economic power through the rich return in taxes from the Chinese parts of its frontier state. Sometimes North China—Hopei, Shansi (and Shensi) provinces of our time—would be the Chinese agricultural base of such frontier states. The Liao government for example, based upon the pastoral centres of Northern Jehol, gained its chief revenue and subsistence economy from these North Chinese regions.[9] But, leaving Jehol aside, for Manchuria and Manchurian political development it was the Chinese agricultural heart of the country, as described above that would serve as base fore economic political power.

Whoever held control over this agricultural center with its rich income was politically ascendant over the outlying regions. The agricultural basin of Manchuria within the range of soil and water that favoured the Chinese way of life was thus the key to any political organization of Manchuria. Its economy and settled society formed the dominating influence under whatever rule it lived. It could be conquered. But when the surrounding tribes wanted to penetrate the Chinese basin, they had to adapt their organization first to the Chinese form of economic life in order to

descendants of Sung princes who had been originally brought there as prisoners. See L. Gibert, *Dictionnaire Historique et Géographique de la Manchurie*, p. 357.

[9] The history of the Liao and their complicated system of half tribal and half bureaucratic administration has now been fully revealed with richest material in the volume *Liao* by Karl August Wittfogel and Feng Chia-sheng, the first to appear soon in the series *History of Chinese Society* brought out by the Chinese History Project at Columbia University under the direction of Dr. Wittfogel. Through Dr. Wittfogel's kindness the author has had the privilege of using the Liao manuscript before its publication. The economy of the Liao is dealt with in section II; the political institutions are given in section XIV of the Liao volume.

profit from and to exploit the productive power of the region. That meant the necessity of bureaucratic administration of the Chinese type. The regions outside thus remained always under the shadow of Chinese Manchuria; even if it was a Chinese Manchuria under "barbarian" rule. Of the three regions of Manchuria, the Chinese agricultural part was thus the political and therefore also the cultural center.

Yet strategically there was a hitch in this superiority. When the Chinese were strong, they could make from this region successful invasions of steppe and forest—as they did in the early Ming time. But even then the Chinese could not occupy these outlying regions because the latter did not lend themselves to Chinese economy and social life. When on the other hand the Chinese organization in the agricultural basin was weakened, the wealth and decisive political importance of this heart of Manchuria became an immediate incitement for outside groups to attack the region and to form there new political organizations.[10] All that the Chinese could do against this possibility was to attempt to keep the outside groups apart and thus prevent them from getting strong and dangerous. The policy of *divide et impera* was applied. A sort of vassalage relationship with each single small group was established and they were played one against the other to guarantee the balance of forces, in itself the guiding principle of Chinese frontier policy. There was a constant danger in this policy and it could only be upheld as long as the Chinese organization, always somewhat isolated from the rest of China, was strong and intact.

This difficulty of guarding outlying regions that could not be occupied was not limited to the Chinese in control of this agricultural center. Interestingly enough a "barbarian" ruler, once established there, would meet the same difficulty with regard to other barbarians. Whoever held this agricultural region, Chinese or conquerors, had to be strong enough to defend it and keep the outlying regions under some form of "remote control." The political organization

[10] No natural barriers or obstacles protected the settled Chinese region from such attacks. But palisade walls were several times erected as defense.

to cope with this problem would in each case be similar. The Chinese basin would have under Chinese or "barbarian" control a bureaucratic administration. The outlying regions would in each case be kept separated under feudal regimes.

Yet there was a difference in the "center of gravity" between Chinese rule that extended into the outlying regions and "barbarian" domination that had taken root in Chinese territory. In the latter case the "barbarian," though drawing his strength from the Chinese basin, had his origin in some part of the outlying regions. This home part, although feudal or tribal, would keep a predominant influence in the common organization. The dualism of bureaucratic and feudal form of government would thus be a greater problem with a barbarian group on Chinese soil than with a Chinese government. We have here a problem for which the Manchus, as we shall later see, found a more harmonious solution than former "barbarian" dynasties.

The history of Manchuria gives many examples of the combinations of these three Manchurian societies. Since ancient times a number of local states or kingdoms based on the settled agrarian life of a greater or smaller part of the Chinese basin had been formed by peoples from the outlying regions. The region of modern Hsinking, which was the focal point of the three different societies, and northwestern Korea were especially suited as main bases for such smaller states. The Huimai, the Kaokoli, the Muoho and the Pohai were examples of such kingdoms.[11]

In between, the Chinese regained their hold over Manchuria. The periods of the Han, the Sui and the Tang dynasties were the times of strongest Chinese control. But after the 10th century not only Manchuria, but at first northern and finally all China came under the domination of "barbarian" dynasties for almost half a millenium.

Two of these barbarian dynasties originated in Manchuria. The Liao came from the partly forested mountain valleys

[11] A comprehensive outline of Manchurian history is found in **Gibert,** *op. cit.,* pp. 51 ff. and 591 ff.

and plains of Jehol with their rich grazing grounds. The
Chin came from the eastern rivers and mountainous forest
regions of Manchuria. Both conquered Chinese territory
and established their economic power-center there; the Chin
in Chinese Manchuria, the Liao mainly in North China. The
development of their power naturally shows interesting
parallels to the later Manchu rising.

The Liao dynasty (907-1125),[12] formed by the Khitan,
a group of Mongol tribes in Jehol, established their state in
Jehol, Chinese Manchuria and parts of North China and
expanded from there chiefly into the Northwestern regions.
They not only subjected agricultural regions in North China
and Manchuria, but settled a great number of farmers,
particularly from Manchuria, on patches of land in their
own region of Jehol. They strengthened thus the marginal
character of this region which remained the strategical center
of power.[13]

The Liao used Chinese officials and introduced Chinese
administration.[14] But the administration of their own pastoral tribal world and of the subjected agricultural regions
and populations remained strictly separated. Their whole
territory was divided into five circuits with five different
capitals. Within these circuits the Chinese world[15] had a
bureaucratic system of town administration, prefectures and

---

[12] These dates have been chosen following Wittfogel's determination. The
year 907 was the time of the establishment of the hereditary dynasty. The
penetration into Chinese territory and the adoption of the dynastical name
of Liao came later.

[13] See Wittfogel-Feng, Liao, section I.

[14] See Wittfogel-Feng, Liao, section VIII. Compare also Liao History,
Ch. I and 74, p. 2a, with regard to the Liao's Chinese adviser Han Yen-hui,
who played a part under the Liao similar to that of Yeh-lü Ch'u-ts'ai under
the Mongols. He "founded towns, markets, fixed the border of the land,
allowed settlement to the people who had been Chinese subjects. He regulated the relationship between husband and wife, taught agriculture and
procured food for the people. Therefore it became rare for anyone to flee
or rebel. If the emperor T'ai-tsu could firmly establish his rulership, build
towns and palaces, establish law courts, arrange the relationship between
emperor and officials (sic!), take the title T'ai-tsu, stipulate laws and customs, it was Han Yen-hui, who had made all this possible." (Quoted from
Gabelentz translation of Liao history, pp. 9-11.)

[15] Including the P'o Hai of Manchuria.

counties, while the Khitan were governed under their own pastoral tribal system. A few feudal organized groups and frontier towns with military bureaucracy played a minor part.[16] It was a completely dualistic system, a politically and economically "amphibian empire," as Wittfogel calls it. This dualism created many difficulties. It kept the two parts of the state separated, mutually distrusting each other, with the various subject people always ready to throw off the yoke when occasion arose. The surviving tribal institutions and kinship cohesion were responsible for violent inner struggles all through the Liao period. These bloody inner fights were largely caused by succession questions and competition for the throne, due to the violation of the traditional tribal rules of succession. And this fighting weakened the strength of the Liao dynasty considerably.[17]

On the other hand the Liao, based on Chinese soil, encountered in their relationship towards the outlying regions the same kind of difficulties which a Chinese dynasty would have had. At the height of their rule their power ranged far to the northwest and north into Outer Mongolia and toward Turkestan. During this period it was revealed that a tribe of frontier origin which had acquired Chinese agricultural possessions, was subject to the same handicaps in frontier control as a Chinese dynasty. The wider its prestige in the steppe, the sooner the point of diminishing returns was reached in the control of frontier tribes.[18] The same was true for the Liao control of the Tungus frontier in Eastern Manchuria. Some unruly Tungus frontier people were settled in the "civilized" agricultural way under a native "governor." They were of the Ju-chen tribe and 150 years later themselves organized a powerful frontier com-

---

[16] "The Ch'i Tan were governed according to their national system, while the Chinese were governed according to their own system. The national system was simple and crude. In the Chinese system the usage of the traditional terminology was preserved." *Liao History*, Ch. 45, pp. 1 a-b, quoted from Wittfogel-Feng, *Liao*, section XIV, which describes in detail the political organization of the Liao.

[17] Wittfogel-Feng, *Liao*, section XIII.

[18] See *Liao History*, Gabelentz transl., pp. 120-2; Wittfogel-Feng, *Liao*, section XIII.

bination, penetrated further into the Chinese world, defeated the Liao in a prolonged struggle and inherited their
power and imperial position. Their victorious prince
founded the Chin dynasty (1115-1234).

The Chin rose thus on the "tribal" frontier of the Liao,
when the Liao state with its dualistic tribal-military control
over Chinese revenues developed a China-like vulnerability
to predatory tribalism.[19]

The Chin had a development similar to that of the Liao
before them. Their administration of the Chinese agricultural region of Manchuria followed the pattern of their
Mongol predecessors. They ruled Manchuria and North-
China from five different capitals under a quasi-Chinese
system of administration, while their people and army remained tribal-feudal as had those of the Liao. But with
their settlement in China and Chinese Manchuria they also
became subject to the difficulties of frontier control when
their power was weakened.

The Liao had come from the steppe frontier of Manchuria,
the Chin from the forest frontier. Now the pendulum was
to swing back to the steppe frontier again. In the steppe
domain of Mongolia a rivalry between Turks in the west and
Mongols in the east led to ascendancy of the Mongols under
their famous ruler Genghis Khan. He and his successors
defeated in several stages the Hsia kingdom in Northwest
China, the Chin Empire and the Sung Empire in South
China until Genghis' grandson Kubilai established in China
the Yüan dynasty (1280-1368). These Mongols (now in
the narrow sense of the word) had not originated in Manchuria.[20]   Their state was organized elsewhere.   Manchuria
had to be conquered only to cover their flank and exterminate
the Chin there. This fact explains that for Manchuria the

---

[19] The Chin were cousins to the later Manchus. The story of the early
submission of neighbouring tribes, the flight of one rival into the camp of
the Liao where he found support, etc., give a number of interesting parallels
with the later Manchu history.

[20] Ancestors of Genghis Khan had, however, been minor frontier employees
of the Chin.

rule of the Mongols meant " une période de décadence." [21] The country became badly depopulated with the exception of the steppes of Jehol. The majority of the administrative centers of the Chin was suppressed, because they were not needed when the Mongols established their capital at Peking. The administration, however, remained bureaucratic. Agricultural Manchuria became a province with seven districts or Routes, Lu (路), and the Capital in Liaoyang. But besides his civil administration the Mongol Yüan dynasty placed military units with feudal hereditary commanders and officers in all Lu.[22]

All three barbarian dynasties, the Liao, the Chin and the Mongol Yüan had thus administered the Chinese basin of Manchuria and conquered China under the Chinese form of civil bureaucratic administration. Their own military might was kept apart in feudal or tribal form. It was a dualistic form of political control! Tribal-feudalism and bureaucracy remained side by side in their government. Only the Manchus succeeded later in merging these two inherent factors of the Chinese world state and thus created a government that was a more complete and longer lasting fusion of frontier and Inner China than had been accomplished by any former frontier government in China.

For this task the Manchus could profit from past experiences and developments. The Manchus originated from a Tungus border tribe, the Ju-chen.[23] They were thus related to the founders of the Chin dynasty who had lived 300 years earlier. Their background was certainly not the original hunter and fisher society of the Manchurian forests. They were not only good horsemen, but their military suc-

---

[21] Gibert, *op. cit.*, p. 45.

[22] The so-called Wan Hu Fu (萬戶府). This was undoubtedly the same as the Mongol Tumen. Like the Chinese Wan, this means 10,000, but also multitude and was the major unit of Mongol military feudalism. These Wan Hu Fu were divided into upper, middle and lower for resp. 7000, 5000 and 3000 men. Their chiefs and other officers (Chen Fu 撓鎮) were hereditary. Compare Tze Yuan, Shen 51; see Hauer, *K'ai Kuo Fang Lüeh*, p. 617, note 52.

[23] Or Nu-chen.

cesses, like those of the Chin, owed much to their skill in mounted archery, an art that must have been developed by the steppe nomads. From the Chinese part of Manchuria these Ju-chen tribes had accepted a greatly extended agriculture and a life in walled towns. They maintained a flourishing border trade with the Chinese. And when their time came, the Manchu knew the historical lesson—that any strong frontier state had to be based on the agrarian center of Manchuria. Their task was then to blend their own organization with that of the Chinese state, attach the Mongols to it and thus form a unit of the three peoples of Manchuria. In this endeavor they found a new farther reaching solution of the frontier problem of the dual forces of feudalism and bureaucracy. It was the preceding Chinese Ming dynasty that had paved the way to this solution.

CHAPTER III

THE MING ORGANIZATION IN MANCHURIA

The history of both Chinese and barbarian dynasties based on Manchuria or ruling Manchuria indicates that control of the region as a whole always had a dual requirement: Administration and the main sources of revenue had to be based on the " Chinese basin "; but strategy always required a special military cadre of a separate and peculiar frontier character. These two requirements could never be coordinated in an entirely stable, integrated state structure. There was always a little extra weight on either the military requirement or the requirement of revenue and bureaucratic administration. This emphasis was bound, in the course of time, either to increase or to shift in the opposite direction. Either process led to conflict between the loosely coordinated but unintegrated and heterogeneous elements of the composite state. And when this conflict went far enough it led to the rise of a new dynasty, attempting to cope afresh with the old problems.

This did, of course, not only hold true for Manchuria. The problem was similar at other points of the Chinese inland frontier. Control over the regions of the frontier and beyond was a political and military necessity for China. These regions formed therefore an inevitable element in the conception of the Chinese Empire and in its system of government.

The Chinese Empire consisted really of two parts. Its center was the Chinese agricultural society. The administration of this center had become increasingly bureaucratic ever since Tsin Shih Huang Ti destroyed the feudal confederation of old and created the empire. Chinese society had by then outgrown the regional limitations under which a feudal system could work efficiently. The tasks of the government in irrigation, defense and other administration had become too general. The feudal lords had already ad-

25

vanced from the use of labour to taxes in kind, and now the bureaucratic state was ruled on a kind and money basis.[1]

Yet not the whole Chinese world had become bureaucratic. We have seen that the Chinese political influence extended beyond the confines of the Chinese agrarian society. This was necessary as a measure of protection if nothing else. But the people of the frontier and outside of it could not, in the tribal or feudal condition of their societies, be ruled in a bureaucratic way. This part of the Chinese Empire had to be controlled on a feudal basis.

Political philosophy, formed in accordance with actual conditions had to make allowance for this dualism. And Chinese political philosophy allowed, indeed, a very vast and general interpretation. Confucianism, the official state philosophy of the Chinese empire, was bureaucratic on the whole. Confucius, teaching during a period of dying feudalism and coming himself from obscure aristocracy, had aimed at an antifeudal bureaucracy, regardless of rank.[2] But while the aristocracy of old was destroyed and all power transferred to the emperor, China did not become an organized national state in our sense of the word. The emperor was really the constitutional expression, and indeed the only one [3] of a common culture. The Chinese empire was a great unity of civilization. From the Chinese view point theirs was the only possible civilization, which was far superior to any barbarian life outside. Yet this unity had to include barbarian regions. It was therefore all-embracing, and in its conception a world state. The people outside would share

[1] See Wittfogel, " Foundations and Stages of Chinese Economic History," pp. 40-51.

[2] The idea of Confucius as the prophet and creator of a non-feudal ideology with ethical training and qualifications of the new official in contrast to the military feudal virtues of old has been formulated by Wittfogel in his " Foundations and Stages of Chinese Economic History," pp. 49/50. The concept of Confucius as the creator of the philosophy " of the bureaucratic way of life in its most civil, most literate and most cultured form " is given more fully in Dr. Wittfogel's forthcoming book: *Oriental Society in Asia and Ancient America.*

[3] " L'empire n'a d'autre fondement que la vertu propre à une dynastie. Hors de l'empereur l'Etat n'est rien." Granet, *La Civilisation Chinoise*, p. 158.

in a "benevolent" way as far as possible in the benefits of this civilization. The emperor, entrusted with the heavenly mandate, was the son of heaven and the responsible mediator between heaven and the people on earth. These were then not only the Chinese, but also the neighboring nations through the medium of their rulers. The relationship between the Chinese emperor and the rulers of the neighboring states or small tribes was regarded as a vassal relationship, a feudal suzerainity.

The Chinese empire consisted thus constitutionally of two spheres. The regions with Chinese agricultural society, China in the narrow sense of the word, were administered bureaucratically under officials directly responsible to the emperor. The outer spheres were connected in a vassal relationship with the head of the Chinese civilization. At the frontier, as in Manchuria, these two different constitutional elements were in constant contact. We have already seen how they interacted in reality and still remained separated, dualistic, an unsolved problem.

It was this problem that the Chinese Ming dynasty (1368-1644) tried to solve in a new way. What the first Ming rulers had in mind was in particular a strengthening of the local defense of the agrarian regions against outside attacks. We have said before that these attacks were always possible when the weakening of central control would invite the frontier people to gain control of North China or the rich Chinese basin of Manchuria. We have described the weakening process itself as being caused by the officials of the scholar-gentry class, working for their own benefit rather than for the central government. The weaker the emperor's power became, the greater was the independence of the local gentry through its local wealth and influence in regional affairs. In theory the emperor was still omnipotent. But in practice the life of the local communities, or rather of the local ruling groups, became more and more autonomous.

The chief disadvantage of this tendency towards localization in Chinese political life was the fact that it was a localization of privileges more than of responsibilities. The central power was weakened by the enrichment of the local gentry, but not relieved of its tasks by local assets. This was especially true of the question of defense. Defense was traditionally the task of paid armies of riff-raff and a responsibility of the central government. A financial weakening of the central government naturally rendered more difficult the payment of large mercenary armies, although more needed in difficult times. The concentration of such armies largely in the capital made their upkeep particularly expensive. The scholar-gentry on the other hand owed its monopoly of administrative posts to its educational monopoly. For it the army, representing the central power signified an unwished-for supervisory pressure, against which "moral sanctions" were sought. Brutal force in contrast to the frailty of the scholar was stigmatized. And the soldier's profession became despised to the utmost by the leading class.[4] For the scholar-gentry there was more security in the administrative monopoly of their class, always needed, under whatever rule, than in the force of arms.

This unequal contest between the imperial power and the local classegoism of the gentry made the securing of the agricultural frontier against outside attacks particularly difficult.

There had been, in Chinese history, interesting attempts to solve this problem. The most important of them had been undertaken in the Sung period (eleventh century) by the statesman and reformer Wang An-shih.[5] It was the time when the last Chinese dynasty for over a century to come struggled against an ever more threatening northern invader. Wang An-shih's plan was to develop a militia army. The advantages of his plan were numerous. Financially the militia was much cheaper to maintain and would, and did indeed, allow a very substantial decrease of the much

[4] For the old and new type of Chinese soldiers see Olga Lang, "The Good Iron of the New Chinese Army," *Pacific Affairs,* March 1939.

[5] Compare Williamson, Wang An Shih. Wang's other important reform attempts—the most serious attempts ever made to reform the Chinese political system—cannot be described here.

more costly standing army. Militarily the fighting value of
the militia, supported by the best elements of the region,
was far superior to the hired riff-raff of the standing army.
The militia was furthermore at the spot to uphold the peace
not only against foreign aggressors, but also against the local
banditry.[6]

The militia scheme—like Wang's other reforms—was
strongly opposed by the bureaucratic class, because a
"healthy" militia would have created a new quasi-feudal,
embryo elite of men whose appeal was to their armed followers, not to the classics. Wang An-shih's reforms were
thus undone by his conservative successors, and fifty years
later the Sung were driven from all of North China. Finally
the South too fell under the rule of the invading power.

A somewhat similar reform was now tried again by the
Ming dynasty. The Ming took up again the idea of a local
military organization and thus knowingly or unknowingly
followed the example of the great Sung statesman. The
bureaucratic civil administration, as it had been developed
by long tradition, was maintained by the Ming for China
Proper. The country was subdivided in provinces, prefectures
and districts. But in addition to this civil administration, or
rather beside it, a special military organization was set up.
The Ming created the so-called Wei (衛) or military
guards.[7]

These Wei were regional military establishments, located
at strategic places in between the civil administrated districts. They were most important along the sea coast to

[6] The danger of this system was the possible strengthening of local political
forces, which might become independent. This was one chief objection of
the time and is a consideration that has to be kept in mind with regard to the
later Ming organization in Manchuria.

[7] Compare *Ming Shih,* Chüan 27, Chih 52, Chih Kuan (職官) 15, p.
7257. The name "Wei" was in use before the Ming, for instance for the
Chinese translation of the ordo of the Khitan by the expression Kung Wei
(宮衛). The meaning is however in this case that of a tribal, not a bureaucratic, military institution. Yet, institutions similar to the Ming Wei were
not unknown in former Chinese history for border protection. But they had
been frontier posts, never organizations of whole agricultural regions. To
study their development might bring interesting results.

guard against invasions by Japanese pirates and on the Northwestern frontier. They were also found in strategic places inland, especially to protect the imperial canal.[8]

These Wei were in themselves a complete military administration, so that the Ming bureaucracy was in itself dualistic. The civilian districts had a greater share in taxation, the military districts supported and controlled the troops. The Wei, consisting of about 5600 men, were subdivided into larger and smaller So (所) or posts, of 1120 and 112 men respectively.[9] The So consisted of two general banners (旗總) of 50 or more men and ten small banners (小旗) of 10 or more men each. These guards and posts were under the direct command of regional high commanderies and these in turn under the orders of the military board of the five armies at the capital.[10] The army was hereditary and registered.[11] We have thus a complete separate military administration of a regional kind.

This was the Ming administration of China Proper. In Manchuria the Ming went further than this dualistic system of intermediate civil and military administration. While in other parts of China these Wei were established parallel with and between the civil administration, in Chinese Manchuria only military districts were formed.

As we have seen, Manchuria had been greatly depopulated under the Mongols. When the Ming defeated the Mongol dynasty, a Manchurian Mongol leader, Nahach'u, surrendered after some fighting. His followers and their families, probably a mixed Mongol-Chinese group, some 200,000 strong, were settled in Liaotung and Liaohsi (east and west of the Liao valley) in the Chinese basin of Manchuria,[12] thus making the Mongol element in the weakened Chinese

---

[8] Compare *Ming Shih*, Chüan 27, Chih 52, Shih Kuan 5, p. 7257.
[9] Compare Chapter II, note 11: the military organization of the Wan Hu Fu of the preceding Mongol Yüan dynasty.
[10] Compare T. C. Lin, "Manchuria in the Ming Empire," p. 26.
[11] Compare *Ming Shih*, army system: ping 2, p. 7293, Chüan 89, Chih 65. See also Tze yuan, shen 159, compare Hauer, *K'ai Kuo Fang Lüeh*, p. 618, note 53.
[12] See Gibert, *op. cit.*, p. 49.

basin particularly strong. The Chinese hold over Manchuria seemed therefore somewhat precarious. To strengthen it, the Ming organized the whole region of the Chinese basin into military guards or Wei exclusively.[13] No other administration existed within the region.[14]

In Liaotung, the Eastern part of the Chinese basin, 25 guards were stationed at strategic points; nine of them along the coast and the rest at communication centers. The High Commander was in Liaoyang. One guard at Tung-ning, consisting of five and later of seven posts, was formed of settled Ju-chen immigrants,[15] a fact that may have facilitated the later quick submission of this region to the Manchus.

For the Western part, Liaohsi, the High Commandery was at Peking. There were at first twenty guards and posts in this region; the greater part of them was however in marginal pastoral territory.[16] They were soon given up to the Mongols.[17]

From the strictly civil point of view Liaotung and Liaohsi were regarded as parts of Shantung and Hopei provinces for those branches of administration that could not possibly be executed under military administration. Thus the candidates from Liaotung and Liaohsi for the examinations of the civil service had to go to Shantung and Hopei respectively.[18]

---

[13] Another measure was the building of a palisade wall to defend the Chinese basin against outside attack. In this the Ming followed other precedents.

[14] A short attempt at civil administration in Liaotung was given up again in 1373 after two years. This was before Nahach'us defeat in 1375. See Lin, *op. cit.*, p. 26.

[15] Near Liaoyang.

[16] Lin, *op. cit.*, pp. 27/8, with a number of further references.

[17] Lin, *op. cit.*, pp. 30/1, speaks of the vital strategic importance of the loss of these guards in and along Jehol under the Ming. The real reason that they disappeared is most likely to be seen in the economic conditions of the region. Under various Mongol rules this region of Jehol had remained politically a center of power, and efforts had been made to settle agricultural sedentary population wherever feasible. Now, with impaired importance of the region, the marginal agriculture must have greatly suffered and the maintenance by the Chinese of bureaucratically administered sedentary military guards must have become impossible in the long run.

[18] Compare for the whole organization Meng Sen, *Ch'ing-Ch'ao Ch'ien Chi*, pp. 12-18.

If the administration of the Chinese basin had thus gained a regional and frontier aspect, life itself had also changed its forms somewhat. In contrast to the steppe society the Chinese agriculture would be expected to use all cultivable land for the plough. Yet we hear that great pasturages in Liaotung were set aside for horse raising. Under emperor Taitsu the Ming had a bureau for horse inspection, and a little later in 1406 a bureau for horse breeding was established. Six divisions were under its control, each in charge of four stud farms, which meant 24 stud farms for Liaotung alone. In its best time Liaotung had over 400,000 horses registered.[19] The Ming wanted thus to become selfsufficient in the horse supply needed for frontier fighting and defense. But the sound of galloping hoofs and the military discipline of the communities of the guards and posts created a frontier atmosphere with dangerous outlooks. The frontier would thus be protected against looting or organized attack. But once the center of power, the imperial government in Peking, became weakened or disorganized and the ties binding the regional administration to the center loosened, the danger that these parts would break off would be hightened. The whole of Chinese Manchuria had become frontier zone.

More than that. With their Wei the Ming had created a type of administration that would stand in good stead for any barbarian group that hoped to penetrate Chinese ground. Their problem had always been to fit their society to the Chinese bureaucratic government. With the Liao, the Chin and the Yuan this had led to a dualism of administration. This dualism helped to bring about the fall of these dynasties as their frontier-barbarian states were undermined by over-bureaucratization. Under the Ming now this dualism was for the frontier region alleviated by these military bureaucratic guards, assimilating the feudal frontier. This projection of bureaucracy proved later too great a burden for the bureaucratic Ming state to carry. But the bridging of the dualism by the Ming with their regional military

---

[19] T. C. Lin, "Manchurian trade and tribute in the Ming dynasty," pp. 866 f.

organization facilitated the breaking off of these parts from China and, most important, it showed the barbarians a way by which their society could more easily be blended with the necessary Chinese bureaucracy! Indeed, the "Wei" of the Ming became the prototype of the coming Manchu banner organization! Even the term "banner" had already been used by the Ming, although for smaller units than the later Manchu banners. In this sense the Ming prepared the way for the later barbarian Manchu group to "grow" into China.

This "preparation" was not limited to the Chinese basin of Manchuria. In their policy towards the outlying regions the Ming created likewise the conditions which facilitated later transformation.

We have said before that the bureaucratic Chinese conception of the state allowed, nevertheless, a sort of feudal vassal relationship between the Chinese emperor and the kings or chiefs of neighboring states or tribes. The extent of such control naturally varied greatly in practice in Chinese history.[20] In Manchuria the first half of the Ming period meant a genuinely far-reaching Chinese control over the outlying regions. This control was exercised by division of the regions into districts with the same names for posts and guards, So and Wei, as used in the administration of the Chinese agrarian basin of Manchuria and also—in between civil administration—in China Proper. But these native guards and posts were, except for the name, something very different from the Chinese military bureaucratic organization at home. They were the subdivisions used to keep the native groups apart and prevent them from combining to form a dangerous power. The old principle of *divide et impera* was clad in a new garment.

The native guards and posts were not really military in character. They were a device to advance and confirm the native chiefs in their position as local lords and rulers. Not

[20] The existence of "tribute" to the emperor, or "presents" to the vassal princes did sometimes cover a relationship of Chinese ransom to prevent attack or looting expeditions.

only could one group thus be kept from controlling others, but the tribes themselves could be broken up into smaller units, each independent of the others and directly responsible to the Ming High Commanderies. It is noteworthy that the Manchus later copied the same method and applied it in subdividing the Mongol tribes, especially in Inner Mongolia.

The tribes recognized already the hereditary succession of leadership. The Ming succeeded—and this again was later imitated by the Manchus—in making this succession dependent on their confirmation. And this confirmation was not automatic. It had to be deserved and was only given for one grade lower than that possessed by the predecessor in the official hierarchy. The same rank as the predecessor had to be gained by merit. The possibility of supporting rival candidates remained also a strong deterrent.[21]

Various ways existed to secure the loyalty of the chiefs of tribes or clans to the emperor and the Chinese local government. Aside from simple confirmation of their position, this position could be made more dignified by bestowing upon them titles and outer signs of recognition. There were all sorts of ranks, appellations and names, of robes, caps, belts and other awards, attractive not only for "uncivilized" people.

Most important, however, was the title to the geographical region combined with the position. It was the bestowing of what really amounted to a fief. For, a policy of keeping these units permanently apart involved not only hereditary leadership. To break up the dangerous mobility of the frontier tribes it was necessary to attach them to a definite territory, to its land, jealously guarded by their chiefs against encroachment from other tribes.

The easiest way to create an attachment to the land was to promote agriculture. Yet that was not everywhere equally feasible. It would naturally be more difficult therefore, to

---

[21] Sometimes such strife between relatives attempting to gain the same vacant lordship would lead to further subdivision of a unit. Thus the Chienchow guard, the cradle of the later Manchu state, was in the middle of the fifteenth century divided into two "wings" because of the rivalry of local chiefs. Later it became united again.

break the mobility of the tribes in the steppe and grasslands where agriculture was difficult. This may explain the fact that the Ming were not able to uphold for long the separate guards they had established in Jehol and the Mongol steppes of Manchuria.[22] But the attachment to a definite territory under local rulers was more easily accomplished over the Ju-chen world including the mixed Mongol-Tungus region to the North of Kaiyuan. We know that the Tungus forest tribes had from of old a certain amount of agriculture. The history of Manchuria with its movement of peoples to and from the Chinese basin had increased this knowledge of agricultural life. On this basis the Ming succeeded in creating a great number of what amounted to little feudal states or lordships. For a while the Ming controlled not only the frontier groups, but practically all of the Tungus region.[23] Naturally, the further one went from the center of Manchuria, the less one would find settlements with influence of Chinese agriculture and town dwelling. The original hunter and fisher type of life would survive; and the peoples' dependence on the Chinese administration could never have

[22] The Manchu succeeded better in dividing the different Mongol tribes into Leagues and Banners, alloting to each definite regions for summer and winter pastures with mounts marking the intertribal border lines. The Ming had established first a number of guards in southern Jehol which were originally under the High Commandery at Taning. In addition the Mongol tribe of the Urianghai-Kharchin further north was divided into three guards. But after their support had been needed by the emperor Cheng Tzu in his coup d'état, the region of Taning was given up to the Urianghai and the military or quasimilitary administration withdrawn. The control of the Ming over the Mongol tribes was from this time on precarious.

[23] Following the example of the Mongol Yüan dynasty the Ming reached out even to the mouth of the Amur where they established the High Commandery of Nurgan for the control of the Ju-chen people. At the height of their power the Ming had divided the Ju-chen world into over 200 guards, posts, stations and camps. This included not only the so-called Hai-hsi Ju-chen (海西) in the region around Harbin and the Sungari river, and the Chien-chow Ju-chen (建州) in the region of Ninguta, Sanhsing and the slopes of the Ch'ang-pai-shan, but also the so-called Wild Ju-chen in the regions of the Ussuri and lower Amur. Yet a sign of decay appearing at the moment when their power reached its peak could be seen in the fact that one of the Ming commissioners who established this system was a eunuch. See also Lin, " Manchuria in the Ming Empire," p. 29.

been for long much more than nominal.[24] But the Ju-chen on the frontier of the Chinese basin easily accepted the territorial idea. They developed a number of small states with walled towns, agriculture and hunting.[25] For them the old tribalism with its hereditary nobility plus the new agricultural settlement on the land led to feudalism. In this combination of tribalism plus territory their feudalism resembled that developed in Europe after the fall of the Roman empire.

It is this feudal world which was the first step toward Manchu political greatness. Tribalism, feudalism, regional bureaucracy, is the scale of its development. And the Ming had created in the Chinese basin as well as on the frontier the favorable conditions for their growth.

Not only in the political field had the conditions been favorable. To keep the frontier states peaceful and friendly the Ming had allowed them the possibility of profitable trade. The trade, as all trade under the Chinese form of social life, was controlled by the Chinese officials. It was strictly limited to definite markets at regular times at determined places. The trade was barter and, in the first line, official. After the official trade had taken the best parts, a controlled and taxed private trade was permitted. The development of such markets was a good indication of the development and importance of the different frontier states. And the Manchus got a good share of them.[26] These markets,

---

[24] " They lived east of Ninguta along the coast and on rocky islands and were cut off from the Ming frontier and far away. They were subject in name only and nothing more." *Sheng Wu Chi*, p. 3a, see Hauer, *K'ai Kuo Fang Lüeh*, p. 616, note 28.

[25] See *Sheng Wu Chi*, same page.

[26] At first trade was started at the Mongol side with the steppe people. The first and following markets were chiefly horse markets, serving simultaneously the Ming need for cavalry horses. While the Mongol Urianghai had three horse-markets, the Ju-chen people had at first only one market at K'ai-yuan. But when the Chien-chow Ju-chen moved down to the east frontier of the Chinese basin in the Ch'ang-pai-shan mountains, a special market was opened for them at Fu-shun. When they became stronger three more markets were opened for this Juchen group. See Lin, " Manchuria, Trade and Tribute in the Ming Dynasty," pp. 866 f.

in which silk, cloth, salt, etc., were exchanged for horses, cattle, furs, ginseng, etc., were "not only economic assets but also accelerated the impact of Chinese culture—a fact most significant in the development of the political ambition and capacity of this tribe."[27]

It is, however, important to note that except for a very few commodities—the cheaper kinds of cloth, salt—trade was not in consumer goods, but in luxuries. Not being an exchange of necessities it was all the easier to control politically, channelling the profit into the hands of chiefs. On the Chinese side, aside from the profits made by the officials, some individual merchant would often become wealthy, but the merchant class as such did not become politically powerful.[28]

Aside from these markets another kind of trade grew under cover of the feudal system described above, and the Ju-chen-Manchus had their share in it. Like other native princes and vassals of the Chinese emperor they were obliged to send tribute to the court in Peking. This tribute was for the sender something like a privilege, as these yearly tribute missions became quasi-trade missions. In exchange for the tribute, the bearers received ample presents; and they were furthermore allowed to take other goods along for barter or selling. The tribute was a small price to pay for the glamour and the luxury trade of the Chinese emperor and helped to strengthen the finanacial position of the Ju-chen leaders and their knowledge of things Chinese.

The political balance could not be forever upheld by this dividing and placating policy of the Ming. The frontier tribes, developing under Ming support an organized state life, would use the first occasion of Chinese weakening to organize greater political combinations. In this frontier atmosphere the nucleus was formed for the Manchu power

[27] See Lin, op. cit., p. 870.

[28] This was the characteristic of all past trans-frontier trade. It never substantially influenced the Chinese economic system. There is therefore an enormous difference from the development of Western commodity and raw material (colonial) trade in the nineteenth century.

that was to gain the dragon throne of China. The Ming policy itself had created the condition from which the Manchus could profit for their necessary political transformation. The outgoing political tide of the Ming was followed by the incoming tide of the Manchus. We have so far discussed the background and conditions which enabled the framing of the Manchu organization. Now let us see the rise of the Manchu power and the building of their organization.

CHAPTER IV

THE RISE OF THE MANCHUS

We have described how the Ming dynasty attempted to render harmless the frontier tribes and to gain control over them. The Ming created for this purpose little feudal states to which they gave the same names of guards and posts, Wei and So, which they used for their own military regional units. One of these native feudal guards and frontier statelets, the Chienchou guard, became the cradle of the Manchu power. This guard was located on the east border of the Chinese basin in the Ch'ang-pai-shan, the Long White Mountains. Its capital town became Hsingking in the Ch'ang-pai-shan. At the end of the Ming period it had become one of a number of rival feudal frontier statelets.

The people that formed this small native state were a group of Ju-chen (Jurchid), a Tungus people already mentioned. To distinguish them from the Ju-chen tribes they were called the Chien-chou Ju-chen.[1] They were near relatives of the Ju-chen that had formed the Chin dynasty.[2] Under these names: as Chien-chou Ju-chen and soon making use of the traditional value of the name of Chin they

[1] The Chienchou Juchen group, as far as we can trace them back, had originated further north at Sanhsing, in the middle section of the Sungari river valley. They had migrated from there via the Hurka River and Ninguta to the Ch'ang-pai-shan and their location on the border of the Chinese basin, possibly reoccupying regions which their ancestors had held before them. Compare Owen Lattimore, *op. cit.*, pp. 117 ff. See also Chapter III, note 23.

[2] Owen Lattimore has pointed out that "Chienchou" may be a euphonic corruption from an original form Chintsu, "tribe of the Chin"; the fact that the name Chienchow was brought by this Juchen group down to the Ch'ang-pai-shan from its former homes on the Sungari corroborates this suggestion. See Owen Lattimore, *op. cit.*, p. 116, note 29. Owen Lattimore, *op. cit.*, (p. 115) describes the Manchu as deriving from "outlying tribal followers" of the Chin. Somewhat fantastic sounds Gorski's thesis that the founder of the Manchu power Nuerhaci was a direct descendant through ten generations from a prince of the house of Chin. See Gorski: "Ueber die Herkunft des Stammvaters der jetzt in China herrschenden Dynastie Zin und vom Ursprung des Namens der Mantschu."

39

started out on their historical career. Much later only, in 1635, shortly before their conquest of China did they adopt the new name " Manchu," [3] to indicate for propaganda reasons that they had started a new page in history.[4]

The origin of the Manchus, then, was in a small frontier group, numerically at first unimportant, but holding a favorable political and trade position and formed by the Ming into a feudal administrative unit. Like others of these feudal units, the Manchu-Chien-chou guard was not static. A great deal of inner and outer conflict kept the political affairs of these feudal units in constant movement. They each consisted of several kinship groups. And the loyalty of the groups—and even within the groups—to lords and overlords depended on the latter's power to organize and to protect the group. Small feudal families could withdraw their allegiance from one lord who did not prove strong and form an independent group or join another combination.[5] The Chinese attempted to stabilize the frontier. Yet any weakening of Chinese supervision could lead to separation or junction of families and clans and the extension of power and territory of one ruling group.

That was the case when after initial expansion the Ming lost finally any direct rule over the outer regions and had to resign themselves to playing politics. The frontier states could raise their heads, could fight among each other for predominance, and a strong leader could attempt the formation of a larger state. The setting was ready for any powerful personality with political ambitions.

[3] The etymology of the name Manchu is still doubtful. Gorski, *op. cit.,* sees in it a Juchen word with the meaning " chief," " superior," " master " (in contrast to serf), that was later only extended to the whole people. Hauer (*K'ai Kuo Fang Lüeh,* annex, p. 592) explains it as derived from Manjusri, in this case the personal name (as often with Mongols and Tungus) of an ancestor of Nuerhaci, called by the Chinese Li Man-Chu. This name was then later used when a new name was sought for the group.

[4] Gibert, *op. cit.,* p. 54, note 1; Owen Lattimore, *op. cit.,* p. 116. See also biography of Nuerhaci in A. W. Hummel's coming biographical dictionary, *Eminent Chinese of the Ch'ing Period,* which the author has been kindly permitted to see in advance.

[5] The Chienchou guard had been part of the time divided into a left and right wing, each under its own feudal chief.

It is interesting to see how in this and parallel situations in Chinese history such leaders arose. Owen Lattimore has pointed out that as a rule these men started from very precarious and small beginnings.[6] A ruler in safe control of a given group would not lightly start a struggle for supreme power and thus endanger his present position with the possibility of losing everything he had. The man who had nothing to lose, who had to fight even to establish himself in a position inherited by feudal law from his ancestors but menaced by others might be swept and forced by his first victory into the road of fighting and struggle that would finally lead to a throne.[7]

Naturally, the candidate for such an ambitious policy had to have not only great natural gifts of leadership, but would also need personal experience of the forces he had to counter and to make use off. A feudal frontier leader in Manchuria, in order to be successful, had not only to be able to deal with the other feudal groups, but he had also to know the Chinese world enough to handle it.

In Nuerhaci, the founder of the Manchu state, such a leader arose. Nuerhaci (1559-1626), was first a feudal lord in the Chien-chou guard. He knew the Chinese world by personal experience as he had been to the market at Fushun,[8] and had personally gone on tribute missions to Peking.[9] He had played the part of a sort of interpreter and had thus known the Chinese " colonial service." He must thus have been acquainted with the Chinese political conceptions and their methods. And it was Nuerhaci personally who later against the advice and will of his feudal entourage

---

[6] Owen Lattimore, op. cit., pp. 119, 540, 543.

[7] In the bureaucratic world the leaders of rebellions would similarly spring up mostly from the lower strata of the official class. Men who had failed in examinations, who had lost their job, been unfairly treated or even fugitives from justice would be potential leaders of rebellious bands. See K. A. Wittfogel, " Die Theorie der orient. Gesellschaft," p. 113, and Owen Lattimore, Inner Asian Frontiers of China," pp. 72, 540, 543.

[8] See T. C. Lin, " Manchuria trade and tribute."

[9] In 1590 Nuerhaci led more than 100 junior Juchen tribal chiefs to carry tribute to Peking. Compare Nuerhaci's biography in A. W. Hummel's Eminent Chinese of the Ch'ing Period.

insisted in moving his capital into newly conquered Chinese centers, emphasizing frequently the importance of the Chinese basin, of land and people and agriculture.[10]

In the feudal world he was born. But he was one of the men, characterized above, that had to fight at the outset for their very existence. Called to leadership after his father's death, Nuerhaci had to assert himself at first in his own domain against dangerous rivalry. He had to start from unbelievably small beginnings to gain the inherited position of leader. We read how he carried on petty fights with the help of just a handful of followers; of nightly attempts on his life which he, alone in his house with his wife and children, had to avoid by ruse and bluff.[11]

His rival, a Manchu nobleman known as Nikan Wailan, had caused in a looting raid on another town the death of Nuerhaci's father and grandfather. This raid had been executed with Chinese support. In order not to lose all authority, Nuerhaci had to avenge these deaths and to fight Nikan Wailan. But the latter was protected by the Chinese who tried to play the two rivals against each other. When Nuerhaci became too presuming, they threatened to support Nikan Wailan as chief of the whole guard. In destroying his rival Nuerhaci had therefore to oppose the Chinese officials of the frontier. He had to carry on a struggle that lead to the inclusion of smaller neighboring groups under his domination, until he finally crushed his adversary, whom the Chinese by then no longer dared to support (1586).[12]

Not only the Chinese were concerned about Nuerhaci's growing power. His feudal neighbors became equally alarmed. The most important of these neighbors were four little states at the north of the Chinese basin known as the Hulun group. They were called Yehe, Hata, Hoifa and Ula. They stretched from the forest frontier to the region where steppe and forest met near the Chinese basin. At least Yehe,

[10] K'ai Kuo Fang Lüeh, Chapter VII.
[11] K'ai Kuo Fang Lüeh, Chapter I (1584).
[12] Ibid.

the westernmost of them, had a strong percentage of Mongol blood.

This Hulun group, located in the strategic region where all three Manchurian types of society touched, was naturally very important for the Chinese policy and consequently supported if menaced. These Hulun states had now become jealous of Nuerhaci's growing power. The former disunity of the neighboring Chien-chou state must have been to their liking. The new successful ruler of the Chien-chou group found in them distrusting opponents. These opponents obtained the support of the Chinese and Nuerhaci was forced into further fighting. That does not mean that a peace loving ruler was forced to war by his bellicose neighbors and that thus all the wars were caused by Nuerhaci's opponents. The change of the local balance of power could not be carried out without natural resistance of the threatened rulers. At first Nuerhaci was on the defensive, defeating a combined attack of the Hulun states against his own territory.[13] Then he himself started after 1599 a program of counter attack and conquest in which he finally destroyed both his feudal adversaries and the Chinese power protecting them.

A look on the map shows us how Nuerhaci was able to defeat one after the other the Hata, Hoifa and Ula states. To destroy the most distant state of this opposing Hulun group, it was necessary first to clear his flank from the Chinese who supported his adversary. Only after Nuerhaci had conquered the Ming town of Fushun in 1618, had destroyed in the following year the powerful Ming armies sent against him, had taken the northern Ming towns of Kaiyuan and T'iehling, was he able to destroy finally the last of his feudal rivals of the Hulun group, the Yehe state (1619).[14] It was a dramatic moment, when the last feudal rival, Gintaisi, the leading prince of Yehe sought death in the flames of his burning castle. Manchu legend tells of a curse he hurled down from the tower to his enemies before his death, threatening that the Manchus themselves would perish one

[13] K'ai Kuo Fang Lüeh, Chapter II.
[14] K'ai Kuo Fang Lüeh, Chapters V and VI.

day by a woman from Yehe and that thus his clan would be revenged.[15]

With this victory Nuerhaci had gained the uncontested rule over the feudal frontier. But it was no longer a feudal frontier fight which he was leading. The preceding penetration into Ming territory gave Nuerhaci's advance an entirely different character. Already, in 1616, Nuerhaci had proclaimed himself Khan or emperor. He had taken the device T'ien Ming (天命) and had called his dynasty Hou Chin or Late Chin, to indicate that he was to take up the imperial claim of his racial ancestors, the Chin.

This meant that he no longer regarded himself as fighting in defense of his position, but had started on an ambitious program. At first Nuerhaci had had no such imperial ambitions.[16] But with his eating grew his appetite.

The fighting had carried Nuerhaci far into the Chinese region. He followed up this advance and moved further. In 1621 the Ming towns Liaoyang and Shenyang (Mukden) were conquered and with this the whole eastern part of Chinese Manchuria or Liaotung fell into Nuerhaci's hands. Most towns surrendered and the remaining strongholds were captured.[17]

The comparative smoothness and easiness of this conquest of the whole eastern part of Chinese Manchuria in a short time indicates that transformations on the Chinese as well as on the Manchu side had prepared this transfer of power. Some of these transformations have been indicated already. Others will be discussed in more detail in the following chapters. Here the general strategy of the Manchu rise must be traced.

Nuerhaci took immediate advantage of his conquests. They were for him not temporary invasions. He transferred his capital to Liaoyang and later to Shenyang, indicating

[15] Because of this curse no women from Yehe were taken into the imperial harem. The only exception over 200 years later was Yehonala, the famous empress Tze-hsi, who was, because of her reactionary policy, regarded by many as the final cause of the downfall of the Manchus in 1911.

[16] K'ai Kou Fang Lüeh, Chapter I, sentence before last.

[17] K'ai Kuo Fang Lüeh, Chapters VII and VIII.

that he was to establish himself in the Chinese basin for good, and to found there a new kind of state. At the same time Nuerhaci secured his right flank by alliances with Mongol tribes starting with the Kalka and Korcin, submitting others by force. When he then attempted to conquer the rest of Chinese Manchuria, its western towns and regions, Nuerhaci met for the first time defeat at the hands of the Chinese governor Yuan Ch'ung-huan. The defeat was caused in part by technical superiority through the use of guns that had been made for the Chinese by Western missionaries. But it also may have been influenced by the fact that here the Chinese organization was still more intact, while the Manchu transformation had not yet gone far enough to appeal to traitors in this region. Nuerhaci, himself wounded in the fighting and depressed over the failure of his further plans, died in 1626. His imperial temple-name is T'ai-tsu.

His ninth son and successor Abahai, imperial temple-name T'ai-tsung, carried on his father's plans. He tried to negotiate a peace with the Chinese governor Yuan, who had defeated his father. No agreement was reached, but the negotiations prevented Ming interference while Abahai attacked and subjugated Korea, securing thus his left flank. It is probable that the negotiations were only delaying tactics on Abahais' side. In any case immediately after the subjugation of Korea, he attacked Yuan again, but was again repulsed (1627). Frustrated in his frontal attack, Abahai or T'ai-tsung as we shall call him, extended further his alliances and campaigns in the Mongol world. From there he invaded North China in 1629/30 through the mountain passes of Jehol, avoiding the Chinese held towns of Eastern Manchuria and the pass at Shanhaikuan. But without this connecting link, the invasion could not lead to any lasting conquest, and the towns conquered in North China were quickly lost again. The campaign had one important result— the Manchus got rid of their strongest opponent, governor Yuan, who was falsely accused of treason at the court in Peking and imprisoned.

The coming years brought a slow conquest of the remaining Chinese parts of Manchuria with a simultaneous increase of Chinese troops and officials in the Manchu ranks and further transformation of the Manchu government. The hold over Mongol tribes was extended and another transitory backdoor invasion of China Proper, this time through Shansi, took place in 1632.

In 1635 T'ai-tsung called his people Manchu and his dynasty Ta Ch'ing to destroy all traces of former submission to China.[18] Tai-tsung now openly became a contender for the rule over China. In a new campaign Korea was forced to recognize this position, become a vassal and discontinue all relations with the Chinese Ming dynasty.

To strengthen their own racial group in the growing political structure, the Manchus undertook frequent raids and missions into the Tungus hinterland to fill their ranks with people brought from there by force or persuasion. From 1636 to 1644 the whole Amur region came under their control.

In 1639 another backdoor invasion of China Proper took place. And in the coming years the remaining towns of Chinese Eastern Manchuria fell one after the other. It was, however, not given to T'ai-tsung to live to see himself in Peking. He died in 1643. Only one year later inner disorder brought the collapse of the Ming and gave the Manchu regent Dorgon the chance to complete the work begun by Nuerhaci and place the third emperor, then a child, on the throne in Peking.[19]

The campaigns and alliances by which this Manchu victory was accomplished were only the outer signs of a process of state formation. These military and diplomatic accomplishments are recorded in detail with all the heroism and skill deployed in the historic records of the period. They are most interesting material. But the clue to this story

---

[18] K'ai Kuo Fang Lüeh, Chapter XXI. Ta Ch'ing was the dynastical name under which the Manchu were to rule over China until 1911.

[19] History given in K'ai Kuo Fang Lüeh and Tung Hua Lu. Valuable Outline in Gibert, op. cit., pp. 591 ff., and historical introduction.

of success is to be found in the remarks, scattered in between, on the transformation and political organization of the state. The real greatness of the statesman Nuerhaci and his co-operators and successors was the capacity to create out of different elements and constituents a new organization. The amazing success of a small clan, originally in control of one small frontier state, was due to the ability to blend their own type of life with the Chinese system of the frontier region.

CHAPTER V

THE MANCHU FEUDALISM

Feudalism can be defined as a system of relations between lord and vassal, based essentially on land which the vassal held as a fief. The lord recognized the vassal's rights of income and jurisdiction in this fief in exchange for services of a military and general political and financial character. Public functions and private property rights were thus combined in the vassal's fief, while in his relation to the lord public duties had become personal obligations.

In speaking of feudalism we are inclined to think of the European situation as it developed after the collapse of the Roman empire. In this disorderly time the central control over provinces and regions broke up into a number of local powers. The character of these local powers was far from uniform. Some of them were local troop commanders or civil magnates, others were the chiefs of Germanic groups whose invasion had helped to bring the collapse of the former order of things. They became attached to the land, and we know how this combination of the Germanic idea of tribal followership with the surviving territorial civilization created the basis of the central European feudalism of the coming centuries. The insecurity of the time forced free men and small farmers to seek the protection and support of greater landowners and lords and thus furthered the institution of feudal power. They received this protection in exchange for their services and dues. The lord organized from his feudal dependents a private army and extended his jurisdiction over all the inhabitants of his fief. The development was completed when the king recognized the situation and made the lords quasi-representatives of the state. A whole hierarchy of vassalship was then developed with mutual obligations of loyalty, protection and service binding all ranks.

48

When this feudalism as a political system was finally undermined in different degrees by a growing centralization of administration, its property relations survived much longer than the form of government.

In this European situation feudalism had thus been the result of a former bureaucratic administration breaking up and being partly superseded by tribal groups. In China, in the pre-imperial era before Tsin Shih Huang Ti, feudalism had been of a somewhat different nature. It had been a stage of development from a primitive to a more advanced form of life and not the result of a collapse of a former central order. Consequently it had seen a far more uniform development than in Europe with various deviating features.[1]

But the frontier feudalism of later time, such as the Manchu feudalism, was in its origin more similar to the European picture. The Manchu feudalism was also formed by a tribal society that had become settled on land with a growing importance of agriculture. It was the fringe of the Chinese agricultural bureaucratic system that became superseded by feudalism. The first public functions of the formerly tribal groups were executed in these regions in the form of feudal service and protection. Rival feudal leaders fought among themselves for predominance. And the chief who succeeded in gaining this predominance did so at the head of feudal supporters. He recognized their feudal position and extended it by rewards. The chiefs' own relationship to the neighboring bureaucratic Chinese government was also feudal. The Chinese emperor was the suzerain of the feudal king.

Later, when penetrating further into China, this feudal system was slowly undermined by the establishment step by step of an administration that dealt with the growing state tasks. And again, as also in Europe, when feudalism thus

---

[1] The Chinese dependence on irrigated agriculture with its necessity for the allotment of water rights and labor etc. necessitated even under feudal conditions a greater employment of clerks than in European feudalism. Compare Owen Lattimore, *op. cit.*, pp. 375/6. For the whole Chinese development see Wittfogel's " Foundations and Stages of Chinese Economic History,' 1935. Also *Liao*, section XIII.

became hollow, the property relations survived longer than the form of government.

Yet we cannot draw the parallel too far. The irrigated agriculture created a kind of feudalism that was very different from the Western form.[2] The kinship system introduced also a special element in the Manchu organization that differed from European conditions. And the military organization of the Manchus was a unique feature that greatly facilitated the smooth transformation from feudalism to bureaucracy.

*   *   *

Manchu feudalism had its chief root in the development of frontier agriculture on a smaller scale than the intensive irrigational agriculture of the Chinese type. Human labor was needed, however, for this agriculture too. For a militant group this labor would be subject labor of war prisoners or subjugated peoples. The outstanding and leading Manchus became nobles and their work was done for them by serfs. Serfs were used not only for agricultural labor, but also as artisans and for the manifold activities in housework and accounting.[3] These serfs were not real slaves to be sold at

[2] The greater care necessary for the cultivation of land results in a different position of the serf in irrigated agriculture and eliminates statute labor on the lords fields, replacing it with dues in kind. See Wittfogel, " Die Theorie der Orientalischen Gesellschaft," pp. 96 f.

[3] For the same reason as in note 1 slave labor in the Roman sense is unpractical in irrigated agriculture. See Wittfogel, " Die Theorie der Orientalischen Gesellschaft," pp. 96/7. Otte, op. cit., compares the Manchu system with the high stage of home production as found with the Greeks and Romans. He follows Werner Sombart's analysis of the Greco-Roman economy. And he proposes to use Sombart's term " oikoseconomy " (Oikenwirtschaft) also for the Manchus. He cites Bücher's description of oikos economy: " All the bondage workers of a rich Roman house consisted of two groups, the familia rustica and the familia urbana. The familia rustica was for productive requirements. . . . The familia urbana may be divided into administrative personel and indoor and outdoor personel, serving the master and the mistress of the house." There is doubtless a parallel with the subdivision of the bondserfs of the Manchus. In the household they had also a small number of slaves. This comparison seems, however, not too helpful and cannot be carried further. Otte himself mentions that the Manchu serf could not be "sold in the open market." This fact together

will and with whom the master could deal as he liked. The master was on the contrary responsible to the chief for the welfare and adequate care of all the people under his control including the serfs.

But not all the Manchus were nobles, or as to that, serfs. A great number were free men, who were the followers of Manchu nobles; men who at the outset of the Manchu rise did not control serfs themselves.[4] Their number was constantly reinforced by newcomers from the Juchen hinterland.

At the head of this group of feudal nobles was an overlord as chief of the state. We have described how Nuerhaci had become the feudal chief of the Manchu state. His position had a double sanction. He had inherited his rule from his father, an inheritance which by the way did not go by necessity to the eldest son but to the most worthy of the sons' generation. The inherited position was, secondly, confirmed by the Ming emperor through the Chinese officials.[5] This confirmation was given by appointment and the conveyance of a seal, the sign of office. But the loyalty to the emperor of China as suzerain depended on the political situation and became later only nominal.

For his feudal group Nuerhaci was as chief and overlord the highest source of governmental power. And when he took the title of Khan (1616), Nuerhaci indicated that he extended his power over all the other feudal groups too. He had become the head of the feudal hierarchy of the frontier. But this feudal power of Nuerhaci and his successors was modified by a special factor: the clan, the original nomad-tribal family compact that had been carried over into the feudal society. And as with former barbarian dynasties,[6] the conflict between the monarchical and the

with the master's responsibility for the well-being of his dependents indicates the feudal relationship of the serfs in the case of the Manchus with their oriental irrigated agriculture in contrast to the monetary or "capitalist" system of antiquity.

[4] But had a chance to acquire them. Compare the many gifts of prisoners given to simple men in the army as mentioned in the *K'ai Kuo Fang Lüeh*.

[5] See *K. K. F. L.*, Chapter I, p. 1 f.

[6] See our Chapter II on the struggle in Liao history within the ruling family. (Wittfogel-Feng, *Liao*, XIII.) We use here occasionally the term

clan group principal of control showed itself in early Manchu history. It will be discussed at a later time.

In the historical narration of the Manchu rise can be found a number of evidences for this feudal organization. The importance and wealth of a lord or nobleman depended on his ownership of land, horses, cattle and his control of serfs. There was apparently no obstacle to the rise of a free man by merit to the position of nobleman. And the nobleman would be ambitious to extend his position. Consequently the reward given by the chief to the nobles would be in this line. In the narrative of these rewards, important enough to be mentioned in the annals, one can therefore best check the structure of the feudal organization.

The material for these rewards would be gained by wars and raids into the neighboring territories, particularly the Chinese region.[7] But the story of the Manchu rise relates at first a number of fights within the narrower Manchu group itself. It was a fight for control, not for booty. That remained the same when feudal neighbors became involved. These fights would not lead to subjection of formerly free people of the larger Tungus family. When such related people or towns were conquered in the petty fights of Nuerhaci's first years, as a rule the opposing leader or leaders were killed, and the group joined under the rule of Nuerhaci. The serfs and possessions of the nobles that had been killed may have been gained by the conqueror. But on the whole their social structure remained intact. Sometimes even the opposing leader was forgiven after his defeat, when Nuerhaci either did not yet feel strong enough to include the group outright, or when he really expected a loyal, submissive attitude.[8]

" clan " for kinship-group. In the Liao volume, Wittfogel has shown that the Mongol-Tungus tribal world did not know " clans " in the strict sense of the word, but rather loose kinship groups. For certain purposes, however, Wittfogel uses the term " clan," and we follow his example. The problem for the Manchus will be dealt with later in Chapter VII.

[7] Compare Cheng Hsiao-Chin's report in the conclusion of Chapter I, *K. K. F. L.*

[8] Examples in *K. K. F. L.*, Chapter II.

Thus when the Hata were conquered, their chief or "beile" ("beile" was the Mongol and Juchen-Manchu word for chief), Menggebulu by name was at first only deprived of his position, but received financial support. Later, when rebellion was feared, he was killed. But when the Ming interfered, his son Ulgudai was restored to power and married to a daughter of Nuerhaci, in order to keep him loyal. The Hata nation perished, however, in the political strife between their neighbors on both sides and their plight was made worse by famine. Their remnants joined the Manchus. When Ulgudai sought refuge with the Manchus, he received from Nuerhaci "fields, houses, families, clothes and all sorts of utensils." [9]

Once the control over the Manchu tribes was firmly established and the fight carried further into the neighboring Chinese regions, more and more is reported of booty in the form of prisoners and animals.[10] Submitting people were still taken in without change of their status. But prisoners were divided among the men of the army.[11] Thus the state grew by a growth of the feudal organization. Nobles, who were successful in war or who came to submit received new fields, families and serfs in smaller and greater numbers. Free men who distinguished themselves were treated in the same way. Serfs were given as rewards, serfs were taken away as punishment. Ever again the narrative mentions something like: the ruler "presented him of men forty families,"[12] "he gave them official posts, and to each slaves and servants, cows and horses, fields and huts, clothes and utensils,"[13] "he presented each of the eight heads with 20 men and women, 10 horses and 10 cows, . . . fields, huts . . .,"[14] "the chiefs who had come for homage, were divided into two classes for the reception of gracious gifts; those belonging to the first class received 10 men and women,

---

[9] *K. K. F. L.*, Chapter III, Hauer, p. 33.
[10] *K. K. F. L.*, Chapter III at several occasions, Chapter IV and from then on frequently.
[11] *K. K. F. L.*, Chapter IV, Hauer, pp. 47/8.
[12] *K. K. F. L.*, Chapter V.
[13] *Ibid.*   [14] *Ibid.*

10 horses and 10 cows and 50 garments; those of the second class 5 men and women, five horses and five cows and three garments; fields, huts and utensils were made available." [15] These examples could be further extended.

The constant reservoir of captured people, prisoners of war and animals was divided up among the chief's own group and those feudal groups who came to join under Manchu leadership. The state grew by the junction (Kuei 歸) or submission ("pacification") of more and more feudal groups. Through addition of booty in serfs and animals, through the new cultivation of more and more land, it became richer and stronger. On several occasions the necessity of grain storage was mentioned by Nuerhaci.[16] Already the importance of a strong population was clearly realised and emphasized.[17] The constant campaigns into the Ju-chen hinterland, bringing easy laurels to some Nuerhaci's relatives and other nobles, were chiefly organized to gain greater manpower of the same racial stock. The policy of increasing the population was further stressed by the official measures—including financial support—to secure wives for all men without families.[18] The task of finding wives for the serfs was also part of the responsibility of the nobles.

This feudal state slowly expanded into the Chinese agricultural basin were it came to face new administrative problems. This eventually meant the end of feudalism as the political basis of the state. But at first this penetration, bringing a tremendous increase in manpower and agricultural production, brought feudalism to a head and created a powerful group of leading nobles. The position of a noble in the group depended on his income. The size of the income was determined by the control of land and labor gained as rewards for his services. In time a scale of such income was developed. In a speech to discontented Chinese

[15] *K. K. F. L.*, Chapter VI (people of the Hurha).
[16] Hauer, *K. K. F. L.*, pp. 10, 42, 53; *K. K. F. L.*, Chapters, I, III, IV, etc.
[17] *K. K. F. L.*, Chapter IV, Hauer, p. 52.
[18] *K. K. F. L.*, Chapter III, p. 41, when over 1000 girls and women were given in marriage.

followers in 1634 T'ai-tsung mentioned that the Manchus had no official money salaries like the Chinese, but had built up a whole system of rewards, where the highest officials (or nobles) had over a thousand serfs, the others less by degrees, according to their rank.[19] On this occasion it can then be learned from the statement of T'ai-tsung that not only the Manchus (Juchen) and Mongols, but even Chinese officials deserting to the Manchus were rewarded in a similar way. Their highest families had not less than 1000 serfs while those of the lowest class had at least 20.[20]

It is very difficult to determine to what degree exactly Chinese in Manchu service were incorporated into this feudal system. We shall deal in the following chapter with the introduction of bureaucratic government by the Manchus. And it will be seen that Chinese and the Chinese basin in Manchuria after its conquest were governed by the Manchus more or less in the Chinese (military) bureaucratic form. But there are also a number of indications that Chinese officials in the Manchu service had likewise become feudal masters and had acquired a great number of serfs and servants in personal bondage. Something of this development may have taken place before the desertion of these Chinese into the Manchu camp.[21] Yet one cannot say that such feudalisation before the Manchus took over had gone far enough to change the essential character of Chinese military bureaucracy. The latter was still strong enough to be respected by the Manchus at the time of the first important desertion of a Chinese official.

In May 1618 the Chinese commander of Fushun, Li Yung-

---

[19] *K. K. F. L.*, Chapter XVIII, p. 3.

[20] *K. K. F. L.*, Chapter XVIII, p. 5. It should be remembered, however, that in the T'ang period the Chinese aristocracy in China, holding many official positions, was still supported by taxes figured on the basis of a number of families ranging from 300 up to 10,000 according to the aristocratic rank of the official.

[21] The easiness of these desertions after the first military successes of the Manchus has been mentioned before (Chapter IV, p. 44). An indication, mentioned in *K. K. F. L.*, Chapter XV, page 23, that the Liaotung Chinese had become more feudalised than the rest of the Chinese basin will be discussed in Chapter VI, p. 73/74.

fang had surrendered to the Manchus, setting an example
to be followed by many later. He and the Chinese people
of the several towns and places that surrendered with him
were transplanted into Manchurian territory. But their administration remained allegedly bureaucratic, and "higher
and lower officials were appointed according to the regulations of the Ming." As an indication of the beginning
of the feudalization of these Chinese one may adduce perhaps
the fact that Li Yung-fang, who remained their highest
official, received a grand-daughter of Nuerhaci as wife.[22]

The first direct mention of feudal status for former Chinese officials under the Manchus was in July 1619. After the
further Manchu penetration into Chinese territory, a number of Chinese lower military officials surrendered, following
the example of a Mongol formerly in the Chinese service.
The Mongol received 100 men, 100 cows, horses, sheep, 5
camels, silver and cloth. The Chinese officials according to
rank from 40 to 50 men, 40 to 50 horses, cows and sheep,
1 to 2 camels, silver and cloth. In addition they were all
given "women, servants, cows, horses (for their men?),
fields, huts and utensils."[23] This then was clearly a beginning of feudal positions for Chinese officials in Manchu
service, a development that in 1634, the year of the above
mentioned speech of T'ai-tsung, had gone so much further.

Up to then a great number of Chinese had surrendered.
Some rebellious troop leaders had come of their own accord.
In the first case of troops surrendering the rank and file was
partly divided among their own former officers and the rest
was given to the Manchu nobles.[24] A quasi-feudal relationship must have been thus developed in these cases among
the Chinese themselves. In the case of the rebel leaders it
developed in the group itself without any such assignments.
One has thus the picture of Chinese quasi-feudalism within
the Manchu organization.

It is, of course, open to speculation how much by this

[22] See annex, Li Yung-fangs biography.
[23] *K. K. F. L.*, Chapter VI, p. 86.
[24] *K. K. F. L.*, Chapter XV; Hauer, *K. K. F. L.*, p. 295.

process Chinese were converted to a feudal way of life, or to what extent Manchu feudalism became diluted by taking Chinese into its body. Apparently most of the Chinese officials had serfs belonging to them, working for them, who could be inherited by their descendants. Yet, when they came to the Manchu side, they brought with them their idea of offices and administration, of which the next chapter will deal. Genuine feudalism means, however, a lifelong and bequeathable position of government and control over dependent people on agricultural land in exchange for loyal followership. It seems that the Chinese officials never had enjoyed quite this position. Their administrative position was not hereditary,[25] and in most cases they could not only be transferred, displaced or promoted as in any bureaucratic system, but their governmental functions were altogether delegated and not original. They acted under the orders and control of several government offices and not as feudal masters.

On the other hand these newly created government offices that came with the Chinese and of which the next chapter will deal, undermined also the feudal position of the Manchu nobles. For them too the administrative job became more important than the original feudal position. What remained was the benefit of the work of serfs, not the political control. In this latter benefit the Chinese members of the Manchu group seem to have participated. But it was no longer genuine political feudalism. Thus Chinese bureaucracy with feudal characteristics and government controlled Manchu feudalism met each other half way.

The growth of administration that finally ended the political importance of feudalism did not come only from outside. The greater the power of the feudal lords and their control over people and land became, the more they needed themselves a growing administration in their own fiefs. Diversification of activity became necessary and clerks were

---

[25] Compare annex, the end of Li Yung-fangs biography about the career of Li's sons.

needed that could deal with the new tasks confronting the nobles who had become great landowners.

It has been mentioned already that the serfs were not only used for work in the fields by their masters. Many of them were warriors for most of the time. But others helped also in administration, were artisans, or even scholars. This diversification was encouraged by the ruler. Nuerhaci ordered the Manchu clan nobles to use their people in the right way. Whoever was efficient in war should not be forced into other services. For secret state affairs careful and thorough people should be used.[26] This division of work seems to have been particularly used to create a class of clerks. When later the state needed learned men for its growing bureaucratic administration, it found them among the serfs of the feudal nobles. Thus an examination of (Confucian) scholars was ordered: "The Beile and Manchurian, Chinese and Mongol families, who possess scholars as their property shall have those examined. For each chosen they shall be compensated with another man." [27]

When bureaucracy developed in the Manchu state there ·was thus a competition between central government and feudal masters for the control of the essential services. At the outset the necessary national or common tasks were divided among the leading nobles by assessment of the labor or expenses involved. A description of some assessments of services and products for national tasks was given in T'ai-tsung's own words on the occasion of his admonition to discontented Chinese officers mentioned above. The regular services were shared by all, with the Chinese complaining of a comparatively high burden. To demonstrate that the Manchu did not get off lighter than the Chinese, T'ai-tsung enumerated in detail the Manchu nobles' services rendered in campaigns, for guards, for communications, for artisans and clerks, the delivery of products like horses, corn, game,

---

[26] K. K. F. L., Chapter V, p. 4.
[27] K. K. F. L., Chapter XII, p. 12.   This edict was published in 1629. Hauer in his translation omits the word "Chinese." Yet the inclusion of Chinese families among those possessing scholar "serfs" is another important evidence of "feudalism" among the Chinese in Manchu service.

the relinquishment of land etc.[28] These assessments were assigned to the Manchu nobles exclusively whenever war, the inclusion of new groups, embassies, news communication, patrol and other military preparation made them necessary.

The method of assessment for public purposes and the responsibility of the nobles for their people remained even after a more complicated central administration had been created. The latter was ingrafted on the feudal basis without immediately dissolving it. As the feudal lords had developed their own clerical administration, a certain friction between feudal and public interests frequently arose. The central government under the ruler would attempt to limit and keep in check the great power of the feudal lords so that it would not become dangerous for the unity of the state. One way of doing this was to see that they used their own power only in a way that would not be harmful to the public interest. The state regarded their position of control over people as much a responsibility of the holder as a privilege. Those who had neglected the people they had to care for were punished.

In particular this conflict of interests became apparent in the case of the leading feudal nobles, "beile" as they were called,[29] who were mostly princes of the imperial clan. It is told how they were kept from private jurisdiction.[30] They had to be admonished not to take private booty,[31] not to abuse their domain administration or to be idle or pleasure seeking. They were stopped from exploiting their dependent people too crassly by excessive forced labor.[32] In time of famine they were ordered to give corn to the needy, free

---

[28] *K. K. F. L.*, Chapter XVIII, p. 4.

[29] The term "beile," as has been mentioned before, is a Mongol-Manchu word for chief. The word is the same as the Turkish "boila" (prince) and has even come into Slavonic languages. See T. Marquart, "Die Chronologie der alttürkischen Inschriften." Leipzig, 1898, S. 41. (Quoted from E. Hauer, (Prince Dorgon). In the case of the Manchus the title was given to the outstanding members of the imperial clan, after Nuerhaci had taken for himself the title Khan or Emperor. According to the later court order a beile was a prince of third rank.

[30] *K. K. F. L.*, Chapter V, pp. 7/8.

[31] *K. K. F. L.*, Chapter VIII, p. 28.   [32] *K. K. F. L.*, Chapter XX, p. 14.

if necessary,[33] and not to enrich themselves by storing grain,[34] not to raise corn prices for their own advantage and exploit thus their position as the greatest grain producers to the public disadvantage.[35] These limitations were mostly but the economic sphere of a struggle for the control of the state that was chiefly fought out in the field of political and military affairs. Particularly through the new military organization the feudal power was broken.

Originally all feudal lords had in military affairs the command over their followers and serfs and led them in war. But with the growing army a military organization that was based on greater unity became necessary. Thus Nuerhaci created the Manchu banner organization.[36] Most, but not all of the feudal characteristics of the army disappeared with it. Some of the so-called Niroo, subunits of the banners, remained under the command of hereditary leaders.[37] And some of the subdivisions were formed by complete groups of bondserfs of the leading nobles of the imperial family.[38] And furthermore feudalism or tribalism survived of course in the main part of the auxiliary Mongol troops. But with these exceptions the army which we will describe in detail later, became bureaucratic in its organization.

But the political control of the army did not yet belong to the newly developing central government, for each banner of the army was at the outset given to a prince of the imperial family. These princes or beiles came to control thus not only great numbers of serfs and land, but also temporarily in an hereditary feudal way the otherwise bureaucratic military banner organization. This gave these few princes

---

[33] *K. K. F. L.,* Chapter XXII, p. 18.
[34] *K. K. F. L.,* Chapter XXII, p. 18; XXIV, p. 4.
[35] *K. K. F. L.,* Chapter XXIV, p. 5.
[36] See next chapter.
[37] Compare Chapter III, section on Manchurian banner organization, обстоятельное описание происхождения и состояния маньджурскаго народа и войска в осми знаменах состоящаго. (Russian translation of *Pa-ch'i T'ung-chih*).
[38] The so-called Pao I (包衣). See later Chapter VI, note 14.

a feudal position of extraordinary political might, as the banners were the Manchu people's organization for peace and war. They came, however, to this position as members of the imperial clan and not because of their feudal power. A third element, the clan power, was thus reintroduced into the general struggle between feudalism and bureaucracy for the organization of the Manchu state. This question of the political control of the banners by members of the imperial clan will therefore be discussed later in connection with the importance of the clan element in the Manchu state. First we shall describe the banner organization itself, as the banners were the institution in which the question as to what clanism, feudalism and bureaucracy would play in the Manchu state, was decided. The bureaucratic system prevailed, and with this the next chapter will deal.

CHAPTER VI

MANCHU BUREAUCRACY

When the Manchus penetrated from the valleys of the Long White Mountains into the larger plains of the Chinese basin the feudal organization no longer sufficed as the integrating factor of the state. Feudalism was effective as long as the community lived on scattered patches of agricultural land in separated mountain valleys. The agricultural plains did not have any natural frontiers for the separation of feudal powers; the common tasks of defense, of irrigation and flood prevention became larger, and a centralized system to allot services and expenses for the whole community became indispensable. This of necessity lead to a weakening of the authority and responsibility of local lords and chiefs in favor of a system of departments or bureaus carrying on the business of government by appointed officials.

It has been stated before how former dynasties which came from the frontier had to deal with this problem of developing in the place of the powers of the local chiefs an administrative apparatus that would be directed from a central government. The difficulty of this transformation and the ensuing dualism have been mentioned. The Manchus did not encounter difficulties to quite the same extent. Their transformation from feudalism to bureaucracy, though not without frictions, was smoother than it had been in the past. What made it smoother was the kind of military organization which the Manchus set up early in this development: the banners.

These banners had their model in the military district organization of the Ming, the Wei, described above. Nuerhaci's farsighted adaptation of a similar organization for the Manchus was the most decisive step of the Manchu penetration into China.

At the outset it was certainly not clear to Nuerhaci how far his start would carry him in the end. Had he only planned to secure for himself his fathers position and the chieftaincy of the Chien-chow district, he could have carried on with the feudal system. But his initial successes and the resistance he had found made him envision the ambitious scheme of creating a strong frontier power including his neighbors. Once started there was no given limit to this extension. His ambition grew to the vague and limitless claim of founding a great " Yeh " (業), family realm or state. This aim surpassed the capacity of the inherited feudal system. With it in mind Nuerhaci founded the banner organization even before the penetration of the Chinese basin had begun.

The first step was taken in 1601, immediately after the inclusion of the first neighboring people, the Hata. " As the number of followers had grown extensively" Nuerhaci divided the army into new units.[1] And these units showed the first definite signs of bureaucratic administration.

The history of the Manchu army can be traced back into the pre-feudal time. In this period the kinsmen from villages or boroughs marched together on hunting trips or campaigns. A group of about ten men chose their own leader by taking out an arrow. The word " Niroo," Ju-chen for arrow, became thus the name for the military unit.[2] The name " Niroo " remained when this elective system disappeared in the feudal period. The feudal lord acquired his position by birth, and smaller feudal lords would follow the leadership of a major chief.[3] However, a major feudal chief like Nuerhaci, did also appoint commanders over Niroo units. The first such appointments are reported from the year 1584, when two

[1] *K. K. F. L.*, Chapter III, p. 6.

[2] *Ibid.*

[3] The system was, however, rather flexible and it happened frequently that followers left their chief to join the group of another chief or even aspired themselves for the chieftaincy. Compare the story of Nikan Wailan, who had been the follower of Nuerhaci's father, before his connivance with the Chinese and rivalry to Nuerhaci. *K. K. F. L.*, Chapter I, p. 3. Compare also the attitude taken at this occasion by the descendants of the Ninguta Beile.

former enemy warriors received the command over 300 men each.[4] Appointments of this kind indicated that the feudal followership was beginning to be transformed into an army with appointed officers. In 1601 the whole Manchu army was divided into Niroos of 300 men each with appointed officers who received the title Commander of a Niroo or Niroo-ejen.[5]

These appointments marked a new kind of government. This becomes even clearer from the fact that the new military organization was initiated by a registration of people. Shortly before the families of the newly subjected Hata had been registered in records.[6] And on many occasions from that time on we read that newly subjected families were grouped together and recorded, so that we can conclude that these records were a general institution for all the people. The recording meant evidently a direct central control over all the people regardless of allegiance to feudal lords. The recording then was connected with the military organization when in the coming years larger units were formed. Five Niroos were called a " Jalan " and placed under 'one higher commander. Five Jalans formed a " Banner," the military unit for which the Manchus became so famous. At first the army consisted of four such banners. In 1615 the development was completed by the creation of four more banners, so that there were now eight in all.[7] Together with the Banners came the banner lists, the records in which all the members of the banners, their names, appointments and all personal affairs were noted. In peace and war these banners became the administrative organization of the Manchu people, and through the appointed officers this people followed the rule of a central bureaucracy.

It has been said that this banner organization of the Manchus was something new and different from the system used by either Mongol or Tungus former invaders of China. How then did the Manchus happen to come by it? The

[4] *K. K. F. L.*, Chapter I; Hauer, *K. K. F. L.*, p. 13.
[5] *K. K. F. L.*, Chapter III, p. 6.
[6] *K. K. F. L.*, Chapter III, p. 5.   [7] *K. K. F. L.*, Chapter IV, pp. 16 f.

answer is that Nuerhaci had before him the Chinese military guards and posts instituted under the Ming. The army he created resembled the Ming system in so many ways that it can hardly have been accidental.

Like the Wei of the Ming, the banners became a civil as well as a military organization for all Manchu people. The registration of the banner people in banner lists reminds one of the registration lists of the Chinese Wei as mentioned above. Here like there a military bureaucracy dealt not only with command in war time but with civil affairs as well. The men of the Chinese Wei lived in assigned regions where they produced enough to support themselves. The banner units became settled in the same way. As a matter of fact the settling of peoples in military units at strategic places with the additional task of cultivating new land became one of the basic policies of the Manchus.

Yet there was a difference between the Chinese and Manchu policy. The Chinese Wei were organized regionally. Each Wei formed a certain district bordering on others. In this regional attachment lay a danger of local policy with local interests that would facilitate a breakup of Chinese control in times of crisis.[8] The Chinese, organising a free settled agricultural population for local defense, had to run the risk of such regionalism. The Manchus were in a somewhat different position. It is most likely that the Manchus with their surviving feudalism were more aware of the danger of regionalism. They were also very much more mobile. Agriculture was still being extended and new land brought under cultivation. It was thus neither necessary nor desirable to give one group exclusive control over a newly included region. And it became a policy to settle in a certain place not one complete military unit, but rather fractions of several military units. The peoples of the same banner became thus scattered in several regions, and in a

[8] Thus after the fall of Liaoyang, which was the capital of a Wei, all the remaining towns of this Wei, over 70 in number, surrendered likewise. And the history of the fall of Talingho and the Manchus' dealing with the Chinese officers that surrendered in this town shows that they were regarded as one political clique with one interest.

given region people of several banners could be found. On one occasion it is for example reported that ten people of each Niroo were settled on land to be newly cultivated, each group in a village with sixteen officials and eight clerks to place to account the entries and expenses.[9] The banners did thus have their agrarian basis as had the Chinese Wei, but they were more scattered than their Chinese counterpart.

As for the rest, the parallel can be drawn rather closely. The banners organized the whole Manchu people in peace as well as in war. Production, taxes, services and assessments of the people became regulated in this frame. A staff of clerks figured out the amount of work and production within the banner units themselves and for the general public purpose.[10] The banner was simply the administrative unit of the state,[11] as the Wei was the administrative unit for the Ming. Both banner and Wei were bureaucratic in administrative form, both selfsupporting, both primarily military, but both of necessity included the civil, economic and other activities of the people registered in the unit. Even the use of a flag as sign for a unit occurred on both sides, the Chinese and the Manchu, although this was certainly nothing so very unusual. In the Chinese organization the smaller units were called banners. Each " Post" consisted of two " general banners " and ten " small banners." [12] The Manchu used the term banner for the largest unit.[13]

Still, if the Manchu banner formed a parallel to the Chinese Wei and—as we think—was largely copied from it, the Chinese and the Manchus had come to a similar thing

[9] *K. K. F. L.*, Chapter IV, p. 12.

[10] Serf service was thereby in no way excluded, as the economic basis of feudalism survived. Each official or officer, for instance all the Niroo commanders, had their serfs to work for them.

[11] Compare A. O. Mayer's Chinese Government, No. 28, on the banners.

[12] 總旗 and 小旗. See Hauer, *K. K. F. L.*, Chapter I, note 53, with a description of the Ming system quoted from Tze Yuan Shen, 159.

[13] The use of a real banner as sign for the lead of the army was known to the Manchus already at the time of their first wars against the Hulun states. One black silk banner was carried with the army as a rallying and also a religious symbol. Thus one reads that Nuerhaci offered a great sacrifice to this banner at the beginning of a campaign. *K. K. F. L.*, Chapter IV, p. 2.

from two different approaches. The Chinese Wei was a partial devolution from normal bureaucracy, the Manchu banner the beginning of evolution towards bureaucracy. If the two met in the middle of the road, their different origins explain their differences in character. The officers of the banners were officials who could be replaced and promoted, and a staff of clerks was needed for the accounting and the division of the services. But at the same time there remained in the banner certain feudal and clan relations and elements. Most of the high officials chosen to command and administer the banner must have been the leading feudal lords, a high percentage of them from the imperial clan. Their serfs were included in the banners, so that one finds free Niroos and serf Niroos side by side.[14] The still more important question of the political control of the banners played an important part in the struggle between imperial clan and emperor for power and will be dealt with later.

The banner administration was created as a preparation for the coming struggle before the Manchus crossed the frontier region and invaded the Chinese basin. This preparation included other institutions of a bureaucratic state. While the banners and their officials represented the local administration, the central government received also appointed secretaries of state. In 1616 the offices of five High Government Secretaries and ten Executive Secretaries were created. The state secretaries had been raised from the "ordinary people" and placed in their high position.[15] They were the predecessors of the later six Pu or ministries copied from China. Their functions were however not only those of ministers, they also acted as court to decide legal cases.

The final challenge to China was made in the same year, 1616, by the acceptance by the ruler, "on the demand" of his nobles and officials, of the title of emperor and the founding of a dynasty. It was a Chinese type of dynasty, with a Chinese name for the period of the reign: T'ien Ming–

---

[14] The so-called "pao i," 包衣, compare Mayer, *The Chinese Government*, No. 379.

[15] *K. K. F. L.*, Chapter XIV, p. 7.

Heaven Ordered; with a Chinese title for the dynasty: Hou Chin or Late Chin, indicating that the dynastic claim of the former Chin dynasty was taken up again.[16] The inauguration speeches were full of allusions to the Confucian conception of the state.[17]

With an emperor ruler, two grades of bureaucratic state secretaries as central government, and the territorial military organization of the banners a bureaucratic Manchu state had thus come into being, ready for a fight with Chinese Manchuria.

The Manchu feudal nobles were however at the outset not trained for bureaucratic administration. The Manchus had therefore not only to imitate the Chinese system, but also to use Chinese for their administrative posts. There were many such posts to be filled and more and more people were needed for them. In many instances the ruler was searching after talented men for his growing administration.[18] And he was pointing out that not kinship or social position but talent were to be taken as conditions for appointments; an emphasis clearly necessary at the time of transformation from feudalism and clanship to bureaucracy. But the "talented" Manchus were not enough. And thus Chinese serfs of the feudal lords were taken for this purpose. It was mentioned in the last chapter that scholar-serfs were thus exchanged against other men.

This draft of scholar-serfs indicates the beginning of a system that could have led to a slave administration as built up by the Osmanlis in the Ottoman state in the 14th century[19]—a system where the actual administration was

[16] The dynastical name was Hou Chin—Late Chin, in reference to the Chin dynasty of the Juchen that had reigned over Manchuria and Northern China from 1115-1234. The name was in 1636 changed into Ta Ch'ing, the name under which the Manchu dynasty ruled over China until 1911. In the dynastic histories we find the name Manchu instead Hou Chin for the early time. We know, however, that this is a falsification started in 1636 in order to disconnect the Manchu dynasty with the defeated former Chin, and to start with a clear sheet. Compare Gibert, *op. cit.*, p. 60.

[17] *K. K. F. L.,* Chapter IV, pp. 2 ff.

[18] *K. K. F. L.,* Chapter IV; Hauer, p. 54, etc.

[19] Compare The Osmanli in Toynbee, a *Study of History*, Vol. III, pp.

in the hands of trained alien people who were serfs, or in the case of the Osmanlis rather slaves, and therefore absolutely dependent upon the ruler.[20] For the Manchus this system was, however, only a start that did not develop further. With the later inclusion of greater groups of Chinese—no longer as prisoners but as part of the nation on equal terms—the Chinese official assured himself a position with his own rights similar to the one he enjoyed under the Chinese rule. The Manchus wanted to win the Chinese over. This they could not do by the formation of a slave administration. They needed the help of experienced Chinese officials on terms which these officials could and would accept.

This broader policy towards the Chinese which in its result decisively changed and shaped the new Manchu state came with the invasion of the Chinese basin. It was a deliberate far-sighted policy of Nuerhaci and was a development which we want to follow up in detail with regard to its important initial step.

The first attack on the Chinese basin in 1618 was not meant as an occupation. The aim was the destruction of the Chinese town of Fushun that barred to the Manchus the approach into the Chinese basin. After this aim was achieved the Manchus withdrew again from Chinese territory because they were then not yet strong enough to hold it against the expected Chinese counterblow. But they gained something more than the destruction of the town. The Chinese major in command of Fushun, Li Yung-fang, surrendered with the people of his town, and the people of the smaller towns Tungchow and Mahatan and a number of other boroughs and military posts followed his example.

It was the first such desertion on the Chinese side, and it was to set an example for many Chinese officials to follow in the years to come. The story of Li Yung-fang seems

22-50, with references to Lybyer, *The Government of the Ottoman Empire in the time of Suliman the Magnificent.*

[20] With the Osmanli the fighting forces themselves consisted of such alien slaves.

therefore of particular interest.[21] Li Yung-fang, a native of T'iehling in Liaotung, had been at his post at Fushun at least since 1613, that is five years before the Manchu attack. In these years he must have become well acquainted with the Manchus. Besides his official position in which he had to handle Chinese frontier policy, the regular markets at Fushun gave ample occasion for such acquaintance. And considering the nature of Chinese officials and Chinese trade, he had probably become personally interested in the profit of trade. It must also have been interesting for him to watch the developing bureaucracy of the Manchu administration.

In 1613 Li had exchanged letters with Nuerhaci about the aggressive policy of the Manchus against the Hulun states. Nuerhaci had come in person to hand over a letter. Li received him honorably. There is no record of oral discussion at the time, but most likely there was some personal contact.

When the Manchus marched against Fushun in 1618, a letter was dispatched to Li intimating a capitulation. There was the statement that Li "had been always an intelligent man with a sound grasp of present requirements," hinting at former understandings between Li and the Manchus. The letter offers Li admission on par into the Manchu state organization. "Our state has always had a generous appreciation of talented men. And if somebody is gifted and quick in administration, we elevate him, appoint him and bind him by marriage," the letter went on. And Li was told that he would keep his position and would find protection in the Manchu state. The protection would be extended to the Chinese people under Li. The alternative was death, terror and destruction for all. Again there was the sentence: "But if you fight, how can our arrows know who you are?"; an indication that they would take good care to kill him.

This was the type of letter sent later on many occasions to wavering Ming officials. On the Manchu side it showed a determined policy to build a larger state. It was not

[21] See his life in *Erh Chen Ch'uan*, I, translation given in annex here.

simple, crude, barbarian invasion, but a well planned political strategy that carried Nuerhaci into Chinese Manchuria.[22]

Li Yung-fang surrendered after initial fighting. It would have been his duty as a Chinese official to die for his emperor if he could not resist the attack. That he surrendered instead is an indication that there was enough motive to do so. He had held his post for several years in succession and had almost certainly acquired local interests in trade and property, which, if left to him, would enable him to remain somebody of importance even without the shadow of the Chinese empire behind him. And the development of the Manchu state with its growing bureaucratic banner and central organization would give him such a chance and a career similar to one in Chinese service. A purely " barbarian" society would scarcely have outweighed the shame of treason for the Chinese official. But the development of the Manchu state had prepared the ground for surrender. Li became a loyal supporter of the Manchu power and resisted all attempts of loyal Chinese officials to win him back to the Chinese cause.

To gain this kind of support the Manchus had to make concessions and to accept the Chinese way of doing things. The slave administration of which certain beginnings existed could not serve this purpose. A new element entered the Manchu state: The Chinese subject and the Chinese official class. At first this element was not very numerous. One thousand families were taken with Li Yung-fang from their former homes into Manchurian territory. But this number was to grow steadily. And with the later conquest of the Chinese basin, the Chinese population must have finally outnumbered considerably the Manchus and Mongols in the Manchu state in Manchuria.

[22] It is for instance interesting to note that after the capture of Fushun Nuerhaci permitted the Chinese merchants from other parts of China that had been in this town when it was attacked, and who were thus captured, to return home. They received money, presents and the Manchu political claims were made known to them before they left. This shows indeed a very farsighted propaganda policy of Nuerhaci. See *K. K. F. L.*, Chapter V; Hauer, *K. K. F. L.*, p. 67.

The Chinese factor changed slowly the original character of the Manchu state, which became more and more predominantly bureaucratic. When Li Yung-fang and the 1000 families were taken in, land, huts, horses, cattle and implements were given to them and they were settled near Yenden in the Chinese way. That is, "as formerly under the Ming, higher and lower officials were appointed," Li Yung-fang, raised to the rank of general (banner-general!), remained their highest commander. He received further the promised Manchu princess as wife and was thus connected by marriage with the Manchu clan.

From that time on one Chinese group after another joined the Manchu state. Most of them were the people and officials of newly conquered towns and regions. Some were Chinese rebels or bandits escaping from China Proper to the Manchu side. But the latter were also groups that originated in Chinese Manchuria.

It should be remembered that the change made in the Manchu state was not quite as sudden and epoch making as it may seem at first. Along the frontier the Chinese had become less Chinese by acculturation to the Manchus; just as the Manchus with their banner organization and bureaucracy had become somewhat acculturated to the Chinese. The change was thus gradual, but nevertheless it was fundamental in its final affect. Formerly the state consisted of the clan people and their serfs. But after the attack on Fushun captured or newly subjected Chinese were not all distributed as slaves or serfs among the leaders, officers and men of the banner army. Instead they were registered as "free subjects." [23] Chinese officials were confirmed in their former positions when they surrendered. In other words the Chinese form of political existence, civil and military bureaucracy, was taken over by the Manchus.

This seems to be a contradiction of what was said before

---

[23] The Chinese term is "Min Hu" (民戶). Compare, for instance, *K. K. F. L.*, Chapter IX, p. 6, where it is used in contrast to "Hu K'ou" (戶口) "people"; and Chapter XI, p. 13, where it is used in contrast to "Nu" (奴), slaves.

about the feudalism and the scale of serf control introduced also for the Chinese officials by the Manchus between 1618 and 1634. The contradiction disappears, if it is realized that the two developments went side by side without a clear line of demarcation and sometimes with one overlapping the other. It may well be that the followers or "subjects" of a Chinese border official had actually become something like his "tribe." It may be, on the other side, that the feudalisation existed more in words than in fact. In the language of imperial addresses the control of Chinese officials over a certain number of families could have been compared to the feudal lordship of the Manchu nobles over their serfs simply in order to emphasize the equality of treatment and position of Manchu and Chinese leaders under the Manchu regime. Nuerhaci as well as his successors were always anxious to emphasize this equality in order to prevent desertions and a breakup of their conglomerate state. Statements of the equality of position of the Chinese and Manchu leaders should therefore be taken *cum grano salis.* The Chinese officials may have often been set over a number of families without the same domination as the feudal lord. And it may even be that both the official-subject and the lord-serf relationship were modified towards a middle course by their juxta-position.

Even so, there remain clear cases both for Chinese feudalism and for preservation of Chinese bureaucracy. For the former the Fifth Chapter has given examples. For the latter there is proof in the frequent recording of the registration of Chinese as "free subjects."[23] Sometimes both Chinese feudalism and bureaucracy appear in the same scene. An interesting case of this kind is recorded at the fall of the town of Talingho in the Chinese basin.[24] On this occasion many Chinese officers and men had surrendered to the Manchus. Of these the higher officers were assigned to the eight banners, four to each banner.[25] Over 100 lower officers

[24] *K. K. F. L.,* Chapter XV, p. 23; Hauer, *K. K. F. L.,* p. 288.
[25] They thus became most likely feudal lords with regard to their standing and income while remaining officials in position.

were assigned to former Chinese officials already on the Manchu side, for reception and care. Then the chronicle goes on: "Their men were separated according to their origin from Hotung or Hohsi.[26] The men from Hohsi were reunited with the old Chinese people in the eight banners.[27] Those men from Hotung that had deserted from Liaotung were given back to their masters. Those without masters were given to competent officers for placement." Hotung or Liaotung, the eastern part of the Chinese basin was nearest to the Manchu feudal world, while Liaohsi or Hohsi, the Western part, was further away and nearer to China.[28] The fact that the men from Hohsi after capture by the Manchus became free banner men, while those from Hotung were handed back to former masters or otherwise divided up, would indicate that a differentiation existed already under Chinese rule. In Hohsi—nearer to China but at the same time next to the Mongol regions of Jehol—the Chinese conception of life as "free subjects" had not only survived but been strengthened by the freer life of the neighboring Mongol tribes.[29] While in Hotung—at the edge of the Manchu world—feudalisation had developed already under Chinese rule. Thus the Manchus in taking in the Chinese accepted this difference.

Yet we know of other cases of Liaotung Chinese who became "free subjects" and bannermen under the Manchus, so that we cannot conclude more from the above example than that Chinese feudalism had been stronger in Liaotung than in Liaohsi. And the phenomenon of Chinese feudalism side by side with Chinese bureaucracy in the Manchu

[26] Hotung and Hohsi, same as Liaotung and Liaohsi, means the two parts of Chinese Manchuria: East and West of the Liao River (Ho—river).

[27] This sentence, in Chinese: 以河西人‧歸于八旗舊漢民內, which is so important, is omitted in Hauer's translation!

[28] It was the region where the Ming had established the horse pastures mentioned in Chapter III.

[29] The military frontier bureaucracy of the Wei may in this case have been influenced by the tribal Mongol world, where cattle property gave greater individual freedom. We mentioned before in Chapter III that under the Ming a mixed cattle-agricultural economy had penetrated the Chinese basin of Manchuria from the Mongol side.

state is better understood if we think of the different geographical regions from which the Chinese partisans came. But the chief importance of the Chinese in the Manchu state was that they furthered bureaucracy and the bureaucratic development and diminished the feudal element in Manchu society. Once the institution of the Chinese "subject" was generally accepted in the Manchu state, it seems that even a retrograde motion of the former distribution of Chinese as serfs happened occasionally. Thus one reads: "As Taitsung now feared that with longer duration of the distribution perhaps oppressions or ill treatment might happen, he ordered that there be given according to the rank of the Manchurian officials, to each Pei Yu—the Tsoling of today—(the commander of a Niroo) only eight strong men (of a certain group of formerly captured Chinese villagers who had been distributed as serfs) to be at his disposal. The rest were to be settled separately in villages, registered as subjects, and placed under selected honest and correct Chinese officials." [30]

Thus the Chinese forced their standards on the invader. True, some became "Manchus," but the majority retained while obeying their new masters the Chinese idea of government. Far from being slaves, they could call themselves at the court "ch'en," officials, while the Manchus as a sign of the feudal origin of their obedience addressed themselves as slaves, "nu," in their relationship to the emperor; a distinction which remained after the conquest of China Proper right down to the revolution in 1911.

It was not so difficult for the Manchus to integrate the Chinese into their state. The Chinese Wei, formed for the frontier, had served as model for the Manchu banners. When now the Manchus conquered the Chinese basin, it was comparatively easy to include the Chinese into the Manchu organization. The Chinese formerly belonging to a Wei

[30] K. K. F. L., Chapter IX, p. 6. On the other side the Chinese officials were held responsible for the well being of the group they administered. A simple method was used to find out the efficiency of their administration. If the number of families and people under their care had increased, they were promoted, otherwise degraded or punished.

became now, under the same or newly appointed officials, units of the Manchu army. They became banner units. At first there was only one Chinese banner unit, then two, then four and finally eight, which then became attached to the eight Manchu banners.[31] A separate Chinese unit could thus be found in each Manchu banner.

At the same time the Manchu army itself, that is its Manchu units, became sprinkled with Chinese. Though acculturated to the Manchu life, they must also have had a diluting effect on the original Manchu society and feudal life. Captured Chinese were divided among the Manchu Niroos, and high officers without their Chinese men were placed in Manchu banners.[32] If one remembers that there was constant intermarriage among these groups, it really becomes difficult to say just how many genuine Manchus were left outside the imperial clan itself.[33]

In this form Chinese influence and the growth of the banners made the banner administration more complex. The officials were frequently admonished to practice a careful performance of their duties.[34] But a greater number of officials was needed. In 1626, after Nuerhaci's death, the new emperor reorganized the banner command with one chief, two assistant chiefs for civil affairs and two inspecting secretaries each.[35]

Not only the banner administration needed such an enlargement. The ever increasing size of the Chinese population and the resulting growth and bureaucratization of the banners demanded an extension of the central supervisory bureaucratic authority. The example again was the Chinese administration, now with so many Chinese officials in the Manchu ranks even easier to adopt. In 1631 the Beiles and high officials decided in a meeting to establish the 6 Pu

[31] *K. K. F. L.*, Chapter XVII, p. 319; XXI, p. 391; XXIV, p. 452; Chapter XXVII., Hauer, *K. K. F. L.*, p. 489, and Chapter XXXI., Hauer, *K. K. F. L.*, p. 554/5. Mayer's *Chinese Government*, No. 379.

[32] *K. K. F. L.*, Chapter XV, p. 23, see above, note 25 f.

[33] Compare Chapter IX, note 5.

[34] *K. K. F. L.*, Chapter VIII, Hauer, *K. K. F. L.*, pp. 120, 137/8, etc.

[35] *K. K. F. L.*, Chapter IX, Hauer, *K. K. F. L.*, pp. 146 ff.

or ministries, patterned and even named after the example of the Chinese imperial government in Peking. They were the ministries of civil affairs, finances, rites, war, justice and public works.[36] Each had one head, who was in each case a member of the imperial clan, and each had Manchu, Mongol and Chinese directors and advisors. The censorate, the three secretaries' offices and the Mongol office completed the imitation of the Chinese system.[37] The Manchu administration had become essentially an image of the Chinese bureaucratic system.

This account of the bureaucratic development of the Manchu organization should not be concluded without reference to another effect of the Chinese influence on the growing Manchu state. The Chinese officials going over to the Manchus brought with them not only their knowledge of organization but also their respect for rules, discipline and the idea of "Staatsraison," to which a feudal noble had to get accustomed. An incident in the life of Li Yung-fang, the Chinese officer who was the first to surrender to the Manchus, may serve to stress this point.[38] This man, once on the Manchu side, remained loyal to his new master. With the exception of the defense against the first great Ming counter attack right after the battle in which he surrendered he took part in the fighting against his former Chinese comrades and in the campaigns against the Chinese basin. The Ming officers sent many letters asking him to return. He handed them to his new ruler together with the messengers. His most active participation in the shaping of events was, however, in the campaign against Korea. The Manchu emperor had directed that Korea be brought to submission, but treated fairly and mildly. The political aim of the campaign was the assurance of the flank of the new Manchu state. The trained Chinese official must have seen and understood this, in contrast to at least one of the leading Manchu lords of the imperial clan who could not think beyond his

[36] *K. K. F. L.*, Chapter XIV, Hauer, *K. K. F. L.*, pp. 258 ff.
[37] *K. K. F. L.*, Chapters XXI, p. 392; XXII, pp. 403-4; XXV, pp. 469-70.
[38] See annex.

personal enrichment in an old time looting raid. After the
Manchu army had penetrated Korea, the king of Korea was
ready to submit to and fulfill the proposed conditions. The
Manchu Beile Amin, however, wanted to march on for loot
and the plunder of the capital. With reasonable arguments Li
Yung-fang gained the support of the other Manchu leaders
to the proposed agreement with the king. But Amin reviled
him with the words: " You Chinese slave(!), why all this
talk? I should kill you." Yet Li Yung-fang's moderation won
out, although Amin had to be satisfied with an extra agreement and extra booty, a fact that left for some time a bitter-
ness in the new Manchu-Korean relations. But the Chinese bureaucrat had won over the feudal nobles to the
advantage of the Manchu state.[39]

Most of the important bureaucratic head positions were
kept by the Manchus for their own people. But Chinese
secretaries and councilors introduced the Manchus to this
new type of government. The Chinese tradition and experience was thus gained for the young state. A deliberate
policy of integration was undertaken by the outstanding
Manchu leaders. First among these leaders in the sixteen
thirties and forties was Prince Dorgon who helped to build
this administration. When the ministries were created, this
man became minister of civil affairs, certainly the most
important administrative post in the Manchu organization.
As such he had the best opportunity to become acquainted with
the new problems of administration facing the Manchus
and to gather able men around him. The most capable of
the surrendering Chinese were always placed in his service
and became his advisers.[40] When T'ai-tsung died, Dorgon
became regent for the third and still young Manchu emperor
and as such led the Manchu armies in 1644 into Peking and
to the conquest of China Proper. It was a Chinese adminis-

---

[39] The Chinese officials seem to have often emphasized this state philosophy. And the Manchus, somewhat angry over the poor Chinese participation
and heroism in battles, accused them of not holding these rules themselves.
Compare K. K. F. L., XXIV, pp. 451-2.
[40] K. K. F. L., Chapter XV, Hauer, p. 288.

trative policy that he had acquired in Manchuria and which he could apply to the whole of China after the conquest.[41]

Feudalism had given the Manchus their first integrating power. The acceptance of bureaucracy in the banner and central administration made them a state. It was the Chinese system, Chinese officials and Chinese ideas that enabled the Manchus to conquer China.

---

[41] Compare Dorgon's biography in Ch'in Ting Tsung Shih Wang Kung Kung Chi Piao ch'uan 欽定宗室王公功績表傳. Translated by Hauer in Ostas. Zeitschrift, Neue Folge, III. Heft 1, pp. 9 ff.

CHAPTER VII

THE CLAN ELEMENT IN THE MANCHU STATE

The Vassalage of the Mongol Tribes

Traditional history has dealt with the Mongol and Tungus tribal people as consisting of a number of clans. The clans, the enlarged exogamic family groups of agnati, with clan names, bound together by shamanistic clan spirits and common ancestor worship were supposed to be the economic and political units that formed the tribes.[1] This traditional interpretation can apparently no longer be upheld without modification, after new light has been thrown on the question by the analysis of Liao society by Wittfogel and Feng. This analysis shows that the word "clan" should not be injudiciously used.[2] Aside from the ruling families the Liao had no clans in the strict sense of the word. Their loose exogamic kinship groups had no clan names, were broken up and reformed after a few generations and did not form that "historical and magic unity" which the clan was supposed to be. Wittfogel avoids therefore the name "clan" and speaks instead of "kinship groups" or "lineages" to express the idea of certain loosely knitted temporary family units. On the whole he discovers a "clanless" tribal society with the peoples in Inner Asia in general. Only certain ruling groups—two in the case of the Liao—assume the shape of veritable clans, although they also have been formed "synthetically." Dealing with these with regard to their general social structure rather than their kinship components the term "clan" is applied to them "preliminarily and tentatively" by Wittfogel, although otherwise they are called "lineages."

Applying these results to the Manchu society it can be said

---

[1] Shirokogoroff, *Social Organization of the Manchus.*
[2] Wittfogel-Feng, *Liao*, section VII.

80

that the Manchu " clans " were in their formations also somewhat vague. The lower people had no clans of their own but
joined the group of leading nobles. For the noble families
there where, however, a number of clan names.[8] And the
imperial house " Aisin Kioro " had a clan history surrounded
with a number of legends. True, they were made up later
to give the family the necessary standing in Chinese eyes.
Ancestor worship was also started for political reasons.
But the effect remains the same; and, granting that the clan
structure of the Manchus was loose, not original and limited
to the upper groups, it still seems justifiable to apply the
term clan in these cases, as we are interested more with the
political structure than with the kinship problem.

Of course the size of such a clan group or the question
through how many generations it would hold together, would
depend on the economic and political feasibility. If the
group became too large it would break apart and a new
clan or new group would be formed with new symbols.
How large a kinship group could become before it was split
by division depended a great deal on outside circumstances.
Exhausted hunting grounds could result in a division of
hunters' groups, etc. Two kinds of political circumstances
would, however, tend to keep clans, although large, to
gether. Firstly, if a group was threatened by outside danger,
it would most likely remain united in its fight for survival.
And secondly, if a group ascended to political leadership and
became a political power, families that otherwise might have
split off would in this case hang on to share in the spoils
of victory. If a nomad group, therefore, succeeded in building up a successful frontier state, a large clan would be
leading the group. For the clan relationship was not broken
up by the development of feudalism. The fact that the members of the clans advanced from free hunters or nomads to
the position of the control over serfs and landed income

[8] The *Pa-ch'i Man-chou shih-tsu t'ung-p'u* （八旗滿洲氏族通譜）
comprehensive genealogy of the Manchu clans, printed in 1745, contains
such a list. I am indebted to Dr. Tang Chao-ying of the Congressional
Library in Washington with whom I had several discussions on the character
of Manchu clans.

did not destroy the bond of the clans. On the contrary clan unity strengthened all clan members, who profited by it likewise.

Not only the leading group upheld its clan bond, the other people also kept their clan associations, as far as they had formed clans before they joined the new state. As the clans had their own authority, a dualism of political control with the feudal and bureaucratic state authority resulted that could create difficulties. This dualism was of real importance only in the case of the leading clan, the clan of the ruler of the new state.

The clan authority was a rather democratic affair. Clan meetings, where the clan head—usually a representative of the senior line—presided, decided on clan affairs. With the growth of the political power of the state, the members of the leading clan would naturally endeavor to extend this "democratic" principle to the control of the whole state— in other words to share in the government. Monarchical and clan power were thus in competition with each other, with a number of inherent dangers for the political stability and unity of government.

The possible danger of disunity would become more evident with the second generation after the establishment of the state. In the first generation was the man who had created the power, who with his qualities of leadership and energy had led his group to success and victory. Naturally his authority as ruler over the state and even within the clan would be comparatively uncontested. The very fact that he emerged and gained control of a larger following was the condition and beginning of the clan's success.

But to gain his success this first ruler would have to depend on the help and cooperation of his clan, as it would take time to develop a political organization. When this first leader died, it would be difficult for his successor to assure himself against the personal ambition and rivalry of important men of the clan who had become entrenched in their positions during the first period. A struggle between the idea of monarchical power and that of clan autonomy or even among different persons for supremacy would often ensue and would lead to results disastrous for the state. Only if the ruler of a frontier state could assert himself against the clan could he organize a centralized power strong enough to survive or penetrate further into China. The problem of stability depended on the elimination of the clan members' political power by the ruler, because otherwise this power would inevitably lead to the breaking up of unity of the state as numerous examples of frontier history show.

One difficulty for the ruler in such struggles was the strength of the clan tradition. The ruler had to be careful and diplomatic in his dealings with the clan members. He could not act against the clan as such; he would have to single out certain persons and act against them with the consent of the rest of the clan. The elimination of clan influence was thus at best a slow process. Even if rebellions of clan members occurred and were put down, it was—as frontier history shows—sometimes impossible or at least difficult to eliminate the rebellious relatives, brothers, or others too nearly related to be harmed even after defeat.[4] Many former frontier dynasties in Chinese history had been greatly weakened or caused to fall by such internal conflicts.

The most critical period for possible conflicts arising from this situation was that following the death of a ruler. Division of power between important and influential clan members could lead to competition between rival candidates.[5] The

[4] In Liao history, in the beginning at least, rebellious brothers of the ruler had to be defeated several times with heavy losses for the Liao people on both sides without the leading brothers suffering at first bodily harm. The wife of one brother, however, coming from another kinship group and regarded also as the *spiritus rector* of the rebellion was hanged. Later such clemency disappeared. Compare Wittfogel-Feng, *Liao*, XIII, also Gabelentz, Liao translation, pp. 12-13.

[5] The possibility of fighting for the succession is of course a general danger for all regimes without a fixed order of succession. If the clan tradition made such fights possible, it also had a certain restraining effect. The clan also bound its members together by their common interests. This can be seen in comparison with the Ottoman state where many sons and possible successors were born in the harem of the ruler without any restraint of clan tradition as a check on their personal ambitions. To avoid fights between heirs, the Osmanlis therefore ruthlessly killed all of them except the successor, once this successor had been determined. Compare Toynbee, *op. cit.*, p. 33, note 1.

general tradition of succession in Manchu clan leadership was particularly unfortunate in this connection. It determined that the new ruler be chosen out of the men of the next generation, but by the men of the older generation.[6] Who actually had the say in such elections depended not only on personal influence, but more generally on the age of the two generations involved. The age relationship of the two generations depended again on the age the former ruler had reached. If this ruler had died young, his generation would still be in the active age, while the next generation had not come to influence. If the ruler grew old, his generation had in practice possibly already lost some of its influence to the younger generation. In any case there was much occasion for rivalries and jealousies that could become fatal to the group.

With the Manchus this danger never became so grave that it broke the restraining check of political institutions and of group unity. The Manchus were thus spared the worst aspect of divided rule and control. But there remained the problem of the elimination of clan influence and power in order to give the ruler the absolute authority needed for a lasting centralized bureaucratic government over Chinese territory and people.

Nuerhaci had brought his family into powerful positions, for he had naturally needed the support of the outstanding men of his clan. Yet he had, interestingly enough, sought the support chiefly of the younger generation where his traditional authority prevented any danger of rivalry. His sons and nephews and their descendants who received the titles of beiles and beises[7] came to share in the new power. The banners were organized, as has been said, on a bureaucratic basis. But the ruler's family as a privileged group was given control over them and also participation in the administration. At first four family members—three sons

---

[6] This general tradition was in the first Manchu succession after Nuerhaci's death changed by Nuerhaci's institution of the Hosoi Beile described below.
[7] The title beile has been described above, Beise was one grade lower. Later Chinese princely titles were introduced.

and one nephew—were chosen to control one banner each, at the time when there were only four banners. Three other sons and one grandson of Nuerhaci were chosen for a similar position when the other four banners were created. This control was given to them to remain hereditary in their families. Each of the men had gained this position at least partly on his own merits as companion in arms of the ruler. But it implied forthwith a tremendous power, as each was to control his banner's whole economy. This position necessarily gave the bearer an extraordinary standing in the council of the nation. The eight leaders thus created became known as the four senior and for junior beiles.[8] Not the whole clan, but eight outstanding members of the clan shared thus in the rule of the state. They gained their position as trusted junior members of the clan, but as their position was hereditary, they became in reality great feudal lords. Only the bond of the clan, the bond of the common interest of the group, could keep these nobles from misusing their position.

To eliminate or diminish the danger of feudal autonomy of these most important pillars of the Manchu state their position was made more formal and at the same time more pseudo-bureaucratic when they received in 1622 the title Hosoi Beiles.[9] This formal appointment to govern the eight banners as the "eight houses of the Hosoi Beile," as they came to be called, transformed clan power into an institution

---

[8] 四大貝勒, 四小貝勒. The four senior beiles were Daisan, Amin, Manggultai and Abahai, often named singly because of their importance. Compare *K. K. F. L.*, Chapters V, 68, IX etc.

[9] 和碩貝勒. *K. K. F. L.*, Chapter VII, p. 23. The word Hosoi itself has been explained in different ways. It is probably the genetive derived from a Manchu word Hoso meaning corner. Pelliot and Hauer following him translate it as "apanage," meaning that the Hosoi Beile were great apanaged princes. Haenisch states however that Hoso or Hosoi can in no dictionary and in no particular connection elsewhere be found with the meaning "apanage." He thinks it to be a Manchu translation of the Chinese word fang (方), corner, which appeared in the Chinese official title Fang Po (方伯) "count of the corner," of old origin and still used under the Ming for provincial treasurers. As a word of feudal origin but with later beaucratic meaning it would lend itself indeed to use as a title for the important Manchu leaders. If Haenisch's opinion is correct, it would be another instance of Chinese influence in the shaping of the new Manchu state. Compare Haenisch, "Hosoi Cin Wang," *Asia Major*, II, 590.

of the government. The Hosoi Beiles formed also the highest council of state. Nuerhaci had used high dignitaries before to help him with the growing administration. His government secretaries and executive secretaries, appointed in 1616, have been mentioned already. They were his technical advisers. In political questions, however, he had to rely, before his descendants grew up, on the help and advice of a few older companions in arms.[10] Now he found in the younger generation of his clan a group of men for this assistance. Already in 1621 he had started the practice of having the four senior Beiles take monthly turns as the administrative head of national affairs—a sort of temporary Prime Minister.[11] This practice was continued, and in addition the council of the Hosoi Beile was created. The clan was thus permitted to share in the ruling power. But at the same time the misuse of this power by individual members of the clan for their own ends was made difficult. The participation of the Hosoi Beiles in this council meant a check on their control of the individual banners. According to Nuerhaci's will the council should lead to an active participation of each in state affairs. Anyone who could not or would not take part in shaping the policy would lose his position, which another young clan member would receive instead. Nobody would be allowed to go on trips solely on his own responsibility and without informing the others. And, most important of all, " all questions shall not be discussed privately by one or two men, but commonly deliberated in a meeting of all. If a report is presented to the throne, all together have to appear for the report." [12]

The appointment of the Hosoi Beiles and their council transformed the clan element into a quasi-bureaucratic insti-

---

[10] *K. K. F. L.*, Chapter VII, p. 111, where Eidu and Fionggon were mentioned as old generals with the title " assistants in government." (車甫國政).

[11] *K. K. F. L.*, Chapter XII, p. 5.

[12] *K. K. F. L.*, Chapters VII and VIII, p. 1. This transformation of clan nobles into a quasi-bureaucratic institution did not go too smoothly, as the beiles had to be frequently admonished not to follow their own selfish interests, but to think of the common welfare. *K. K. F. L.*, Chapter VIII, p. 137, etc.

tution. Together with the "professional" officials and the dignitaries they formed the government of the ruler. Most of the ruler's edicts and statements were addressed to all of them. And in military campaigns the Hosoi Beiles shared the command with other deserving leaders.[13]

But the most important function of the Hosoi Beile was to begin only after Nuerhaci's death. According to Nuerhaci's wish they were to elect the successor to the throne.[14] And this they did.[15] They elected with little delay or difficulty Nuerhaci's eighth son, Abahai, as successor.

With this change of ruler, the position of the Hosoi Beile became automatically different and of much greater importance. When Nuerhaci had given the clan, through the institution of the Hosoi Beile, a great share in political control, he had himself nevertheless remained the uncontested and outstanding leader of the nation. The Beiles had been the assistants of the ruler but in no way his equals. They had to obey him not only as officials, but also as clan members, as he belonged to the older generation.

With Abahai, the new emperor, this was completely different. He was of the same generation as the Hosoi Beiles with one exception. He himself had been one of them. He was the fourth of the senior Beiles. The three other senior Beiles were furthermore of higher age. Although there was in Manchu life a recognized tendency toward inheritance by junior sons, the seniors nevertheless deserved a certain respect. For Abahai, therefore, the powerful position of the Hosoi Beiles in the banners and in the central government meant simply a limitation of his own power and control as ruler. The question of the clan power versus monarchical power became an issue. Nuerhaci had with his institution of

[13] Compare the campaign against Korea, which, however, is only one of many examples.

[14] *K. K. F. L.,* Chapter VII, p. 116. By this regulation the general clan tradition was given up for the election of Nuerhaci's successor. (Compare note 4.) The Hosoi Beile were of the same generation or even younger than the successor. After Abahais' death it was again the older generation that decided the election.

[15] *K. K. F. L.,* Chapter IX, p. 3.

the Hosoi Beile meant to give the clan through them a preponderant influence after his own death.

The ceremony of the inauguration of Abahai showed the difference. It was really a clan affair. An oath was taken by the clan members and the ruler in which they mutually vowed each other loyalty.[16] "Brothers and brothers' sons" was the term under which in both oaths the family community was named and mutual support was promised. Abahai—or T'ai-tsung with his temple name—promised to honor his elder brothers and elders and to love his younger brothers and their sons and to follow the right way. The clan oath ended with the words "if we are unanimously one house and have no concealed and bad thoughts, Heaven and Earth shall both give us benevolent help." [16]

The new emperor's first position as *primus inter pares* of his clan rather than as an autocratic ruler could be recognized in several ways. The way he talked to his elder brothers on their return from successful campaigns,[17] the way they were seated at receptions at his right and left side instead of below him,[18] indicated the respect he owed them. The Beile Amin showed in his undisciplined actions how little he cared about the emperors authority. Even in later years the elder Beiles' voices had to be heard in military campaigns.[19]

But slowly T'ai-tsung succeeded in wresting the power from the hands of the clan and in particular from those of his elder brothers and in building up his own authority. For this purpose the development of a bureaucracy, needed for so many other reasons, was also a useful weapon. This development served thus not only the general administrative needs of the state, but also T'ai-tsung's personal aim to create a monarchical rather than a clan government. The success of his policy was decisive for the further greatness of the

---

[16] *K. K. F. L.*, Chapter IX, p. 5.
[17] *K. K. F. L.*, Chapter IX, p. 23.
[18] *K. K. F. L.*, Chapter X, p. 1.
[19] *K. K. F. L.*, Chapter XII, pp. 206-7, where the elder Beile disagree with the Emperor and have to be persuaded; an incident that creates general misgivings.

Manchu state, as the survival of the clan power would most likely have ultimately led to the same kind of inner cleavage with which former frontier states had to cope.

T'ai-tsung began his policy immediately after he came to the throne in 1626 with a reorganization of the banner administration. At that time two of the banners were under his own control, as he had not complied with Nuerhaci's last wish, that one vacant banner should be given to T'ai-tsung's brother, Ajiige.[20] T'ai-tsung kept this banner for himself in addition to his own banner. Aside from this he introduced for all the banners a larger staff of administrative officers. The authority for the banners remained for a while with the Hosoi Beiles. But the actual command and administration came more into the control of a staff of officers, of which the highest took part in all consultations with the ruler on banner affairs and other government business, led the march of their troops in campaigns and had to examine and hear all banner matters. The lower officers were divided into civil officials who decided the law cases and dealt with administration, and military officials who led their units in military training and campaigns.[21] Thus the position of the Hosoi Beile was weakened at the very source of their power, while the bureaucratization of the banners went one step further.

Another step was taken by T'ai-tsung in 1629, when the three remaining senior Beiles were deprived of their position as head of the administration, which they had held in monthly rotation since Nuerhaci's time. Under the pretext that the elder brothers should not alone be troubled with this work, the younger brothers and nephews were ordered by T'ai-tsung to take the job instead, sharing it between themselves in monthly turns.[22] With the handing over of this post from the seniors to the juniors, T'ai-tsungs authority must have been strengthened.

After this, T'ai-tsung began to get rid of these superior

[20] See Abahai's biography in A. W. Hummel, *Eminent Chinese of the Ch'ing Period.*
[21] *K. K. F. L.,* Chapter IX.   [22] *K. K. F. L.,* Chapter XII, p. 5.

elders altogether. Of the three, Amin, T'ai-tsung's cousin, soon gave cause for discontent. His disregard of the emperors orders in the Korean campaign has already been described. Amin had then not succeeded in looting the Korean capital as he had hoped. But he had done nevertheless a bit of looting of his own and made his special treaty with the king of Korea. At that time T'ai-tsung did not apparently feel strong enough to act. He received Amin on the return from this campaign with all honors. But three years later, in 1630, Amin, then in command of the rear guard of the Manchu army in a campaign in China, misbehaved again. After a brutal and entirely unnecessary slaughter of the civilian population, he deserted his own troops, who suffered heavy losses in their retreat. Weakened in power, he was on his return put into prison where he died 10 years later. His banner was given to his brother Jirgalang. T'ai-tsung had got rid of the most violent of the senior Hosoi Beile.[23]

Two years later, in 1632, the two remaining elder Hosoi Beile, Daisan and Manggultai gave up their seats at each side of the emperor at receptions. The pretext was some misbehavior of Manggultai.[24] The two elder Beile were in future to sit flanking the approach to the emperor's chair. With this new seating order disappeared the last outer sign of a limitation of T'ai-tsung power by elder or other clan members. A year before, in 1631, the six ministries had been introduced, a step by which the whole administration was put on a bureaucratic basis by the emperor, who controlled it. Manggultai was, after his death in 1633, posthumously accused of treason and his banner was taken from the control of his family and placed under the direct control of T'ai-tsung, who thus had direct control over three of the eight banners.[25] T'ai-tsung thus succeeded without any real opposition in asserting himself as a monarch and in ridding himself of the major restrictions of the clan element.

[23] K. K. F. L., Chapter XIII, Hauer, K. K. F. L., p. 240.
[24] K. K. F. L., Chapter XV, Hauer, K. K. F. L., p. 290.
[25] A differentiation between the three "superior" banners and the five "inferior" banners was thus introduced.

When T'sai-tsung died in 1643, the clan regained importance. T'ai-tsung's efforts had weakened the clan influence in government, but had not resulted in creating any other council for the highest state decisions that were at the same time clan affairs, such as the succession. The Hosoi Beile had lost their position in favor of the bureaucratic ministries. But no arrangement had been made for the nomination of the successor. As a result, the discussion after T'ai-tsung's death involved a large group of leading clan members and officials and led to a conflict of opinion that was overcome only after 17 days of debate, and not without leaving some misgivings.[26]

The strong man of the time was prince Dorgon. It has been described before how Dorgon as head of the ministry of the interior had been appointed to the most important and decisive post in the new bureaucratic administration. As actual organizer and creator of the new bureaucracy he became the exponent and champion of the new form of government. As such he would have to carry the brunt of the clan animosity against limitation of clan power in favor of the monarchical idea. As Dorgon was rather self-willed and not free of personal ambition, this animosity became rather bitter and led after his death to the deprivation of all his former titles and rank and the degradation of his memory. Only later Manchu history rehabilitated him.[27]

Prince Dorgon was the fourteenth son of Nuerhaci and the younger brother of the second Manchu ruler T'ai-tsung or Abahai. Under his brother's rule Dorgon had revealed himself to be not only an excellent organizer and administrator but also an extremely gifted military leader.[28] When

[26] See Gibert, op. cit., also Hauer, " Prince Dorgon," see note 7.

[27] The very interesting life of Prince Dorgon can be found in Ch'in ting tsung shih wang kung kung chi piao chuan, 欽定宗室王公功績表傳, translated by E. Hauer in Ostasiatische Zeitschrift, Neue Folge III, Heft 1. The following details were taken from this biography.

[28] His title, Jui, Manch. Mergen, means clever, indicating that he gained his military fame more by strategy than being a dare-devil. Yet he did not avoid personal danger, so that once his entourage was blamed for not taking better care for his protection against risks. He was rather self-willed and of independent judgement. Once Dorgon disobeyed, probably for good reasons,

Dorgon's brother, the emperor T'ai-tsung died, Dorgon because of his talent and training would have been the man
to take over the rulership himself. But as he was of the
same and not the next generation, he could not, according
to clan tradition, become emperor himself. There was nevertheless a conspiracy in his favor, which he, however, revealed to the clan, so that the conspirators received capital
punishment. He accepted the election of the emperor Shun-
Chih, the twelfth son of T'ai-tsung, a five year old child,
while he himself and Jirgalang his cousin Hosoi Beile and
head of another clan faction, became co-regents and shared
the actual power.

This was a compromise solution. It revealed the fact
that none of the leaders of the older generation, including
Dorgon himself, were willing to renounce their own power.
Therefore a young child was put on the throne with no voice
yet of its own. Haoge, the eldest son of T'ai-tsung and
already a grown up man, had been another candidate. But—
in Dorgon's words—"the princes and high dignitaries all
said: ' If the Su Ch'in wang (Hagoe) is placed on the throne
we all shall have no standing.' "

Of the two new regents, Dorgon was the real power. He
set to work to weaken the clan influence and particularly to
destroy the power of his antagonists in the clan. Even if he
was not free of personal ambition, his policy resulted chiefly
in the strengthening of the central bureaucratical power of
the state and the emperor.

Shortly after Dorgon's appointment as regent he decreed
that the control of the princes, beiles and beises, (in other
words of the clan nobility) over the six ministries should
end. He also gained preeminence over his co-regent Jirgalang. The latter instructed the dignitaries of the court and
ministries to report government affairs first to Dorgon and
to place his name first on documents. All this happened in
the same year, 1644, in which Dorgon led the Manchus
to Peking, placed the boy emperor on the dragon throne and

military orders of his ruling brother. He was punished with the loss of one
unit of his warrior serfs. Dorgon accepted this punishment without grudge.

established the Manchu power over China. The military and diplomatic skill displayed by him in this successful undertaking was amazing and served, of course, to strengthen his position in the state.

In the coming years he built up the Manchu power over China. He strengthened further the power of bureaucratic institutions; and it was not in contradiction with this policy if he at the same time undertook the elimination of his opponents in the clan. Personal ambition and state policy went well together in his case. In 1647 Dorgon succeeded in getting rid of the Co-regent Jirgalang, who was deposed "because while building his palace he had tresspassed the rules and had used bronze lions, turtles and cranes without being entitled to them." A further degradation of Jirgalang came later on the accusation that he had, in 1644, privately conspired to make Haoge emperor and that he had omitted to promote officials in the imperial yellow banners, while on the other hand the blue banners of his faction had been permitted to take the front positions when the Manchus had entered Peking. These trifling accusations were of course only pretexts and show simply a clan rivalry which Jirgalang never forgot and which made him after Dorgon's death the leader of the group that demanded Dorgon's posthumous degradation.

In Jirgalang's place Dorgon chose his own younger brother Dodo as co-regent, but this was in fact not more than a nominal limitation of his own power. In the year 1647 Dorgon also got rid of his former rival candidate, Haoge, who was imprisoned and was said to have been poisoned. The fact that Dorgon took Haoge's former wife into his own house did not make this story any better.

These and other acts of personal arbitrariness resulted in overshadowing for some time the fame of this perhaps greatest of the Manchu leaders. He had been responsible not only for the march on Peking but also for a policy that immediately accepted and confirmed the majority of local Chinese officials in their positions, preventing a chaos that would have allowed a stronger Ming opposition. He honored and buried the Ming emperor slaughtered by the bandits and thus gave his authority an appearance of Chinese legality. But he also abolished immediately all extra taxation that had been the cause of unrest and rebellion. He thus accepted and strengthened the bureaucratic administration found in China, and he did not permit the Manchu imperial clan to interfere with this administration. In 1649 he warned the Chinese officials against permitting such interference: "If princes or palace dignitaries interfere in goverment affairs of the ministries or in the promotion or degradation of Chinese officials in the capital or in the provinces, they will be punished without further ado and regardless of whether they were right or wrong. If promotions of officials become necessary I shall promote, and if degradations are necessary I shall degrade. Should we perhaps, like at the end of the Ming, listen partially to the words of third persons or promote and degrade wantonly? Regarding summons by princes into their palaces of officials not under their orders, the fault is with the princes. If the officials obey the summons, the fault is with the officials. If summons should become necessary, the princes must first report to the throne and get permission."

Dorgon thus established the authority of the throne and prevented the development of powerful rival clan leaders. If he served at the same time his own ambition for power as the regent and if he assumed certain tokens and characteristics of imperial position such as robes, a greater number of bodyguards, palaces, etc., there is no proof that he aspired for more and hoped to gain the throne for himself, as his enemies said after his death. On the contrary his actions against attempts of others to place him on the throne indicate that he was a loyal supporter not only of the monarchical idea, but also of the existing monarch and the order of succession. If he was jealous of his position as regent, he was certainly the best qualified man for this position, and his efforts really completed the work of the foundation of the Manchu dynasty that had been begun by Nuerhaci.

The final elimination of the power of the imperial clan

came only later under the emperor K'ang-hsi, when the imperial clansmen became excluded from any administrative office of high political importance. The institutions of government, once established to replace clan and feudal control, were then even cleared of the persons that belonged to the clan. And these persons were deprived of all but the enjoyment of a privileged social position with a great income. And from the past there did not survive much more than the distinction of the girdle, yellow or red according to the nearness of relationship to the emperor, which Nuerhaci had allowed the members of the imperial clan to wear, and a sizable income for the members of the imperial family. It was the completion of a long development of struggle against the clan power, a struggle of which the outcome in favor of the monarchical order was decisive for the Manchu success.

There was, of course, in the Manchu social structure, not only the imperial clan. A number of other clans are known, but only the imperial clan, the clan of the ruling group, was of great political importance and a real problem. For the rest the clans survived as social institutions without however greatly affecting the new organization of the state. The clan heads—Mokunda—still held their positions, which were indirectly connected with the banner to which the clan belonged. The company commanders of the banners received recruiting lists from the Mokunda. In clan affairs the Mokunda was even the higher authority. Officers, as members of the clan, had to obey the Mokunda's orders in clan affairs, had to come to clan meetings, and could be punished if they did not. All orders and regulations of military authorities were announced for the knowledge of the clan members through the Mokunda. There was thus cooperation between military organization and the clans.[29]

In civil affairs, the Mokunda was held responsible in cases concerning clan members. Only in very serious cases did the authorities act directly. The Mokunda had limited jurisdiction inside the clan. The interclan relations, on the other

[29] Shirokogoroff, *Social Organization of the Manchus,* pp. 53, 55.

hand, were taken over by the state. The clan element thus remained together with feudalism and bureaucracy a part of the Manchu state's social organization.

* * *

During the process of building their state, the Manchus greatly changed their society and political life. From forest tribes, they changed to feudal lords and bureaucrats and accepted Chinese political organizations and ideologies, integrating them with their own. Various elements were thus integrated to a new growth on a preeminently Chinese basis. Yet not everything included by the Manchus in their state, was integrated to the same degree into this organization. The Mongols became a part of the Manchu state, but their world remained far less affected by social and political development. The Chinese life transformed the Manchus, and the frontier could also be transformed in its life. But the conditions beyond could not be changed for those people who remained in the steppes. The tribal society of the Mongols did join the Manchus but remained for the most part unchanged. The Mongols became allies under Manchu control rather than an integral part of the new state organization. Some resisting tribes were broken up, destroyed and the remainders included into the Manchu banners.[30] Some other tribes had by themselves moved into the frontier region and changed their society.[31] But the steppe society as such could hardly be changed.

This steppe society has been described in different ways. It has usually been called feudal. If this word is to be used, one has to keep in mind that it would have one meaning with the Manchus as described above, and another meaning when applied to the Mongols. The Mongol nobles of the

---

[30] *I. e.*, the Chahars and Tumets.

[31] Thus the Easternmost Mongols, who were also not conquered by the Manchus but had rather " allied " themselves after defeat, had already a certain amount of agriculture, carried on for them by Chinese tenants. The Khitan with their economy of cattle breeding in Jehol had also developed some agriculture there (see Wittfogel-Feng, *Liao,* section II). Compare also the mixed Mongol.-Manchu-Chinese composition of the Yehe state.

steppe aristocracy had serfs, but without agriculture they lacked the strict attachment of one noble household to a definite piece of land, the distinguishing characteristic of true feudalism. Without this connection with the land, the status of the serf or dependent man could be " freer" than with agrarian feudalism. With the latter the man meant for the lord nothing but his labor. If he wanted to run away, he could not take the land with him. But the property in the steppe was movable cattle. And the man with cattle was worth more to his lord and to others. The power of one lord therefore never became as exclusive, as if it would have become had it been based on territory, and the strength of the groups or the clans were proportionally greater.

There was also in the steppe a certain attachment to the land; the mobility was not unlimited; summer and winter pastures made up a definite territory for each group; but it was the whole group, not the single lord, to which this territory belonged. The Mongol society will therefore here be called tribal rather than feudal, following a distinction proposed by Owen Lattimore.

The Manchus could not change much this tribal social structure of the Mongols. They could only follow the Chinese example and rule the Mongols through the latter's spiritual and secular leaders. It was a vassal relationship, such as the outer regions always had had to the Chinese dynasty. It contained, however, for the Manchus the same dangers of attack from beyond the frontier as the Chinese had had to face, the danger of agglomeration of power under one leading clan. To avoid it the Manchus applied to the Mongols the same policy of *divide et impera* that had been applied by the Chinese Ming to the Mongols and the Manchus. They fixed the boundary for each Mongol tribe more rigidly than it had been done before, increasing the territorial limitation of mobility.[32] They gave the hereditary princes the sanction of imperial appointment and limited their power and the power of their families by the introduction of more

[32] *Ta Ch'ing Hui Tien, Li Fan Yuan* contains the lists of tribes, their boundaries, the chiefs and their positions.

bureaucratic leagues, whose heads could only be appointed by the emperor. They thus kept apart a number of tribal leaders. These leaders, the ruling Mongol class, were bound by a vassal relationship to the Manchu court.

This vassalage had a double importance. Firstly, it allowed the Manchu court a control and voice in Mongol affairs, so that even official imperial representatives could be placed at several major places in Mongol country as residents and political agents.[33] But during the rise of the Manchus these vassalages had a second, primarily strategic, importance for the Manchu campaigns in China. Not only were the Manchus assured against flank attacks by the Mongols, but they had in the Mongols auxiliary troops of considerable value. The Manchu army thus consisted not only of bureaucratic banners but also of feudal or tribal auxiliary troops. The necessity of keeping this heterogeneous army together under one discipline caused the Manchus to announce for this army before a campaign certain " instructions for the army in the field." [34] These disciplinary rules, stating how to behave against the enemy soldiers and people in conquerred territory, were not always simply decreed; they were sometimes sworn to by the whole army with a " yueh " (約), a compact, here of feudal character. The Mongols and their army thus formed a feudal-tribal annex to the Manchu state.

The state with which the Manchus conquered China, was formed on a bureaucratic Chinese basis with certain feudal characteristics and clan cohesion integrated into it, and a tribal Mongol vassal annex. It was based on a military banner organization copied from China but with feudal fragments and was ruled by the Manchu imperial clan and the emperor.

---

[33] The so-called Amban. Under the Manchu emperor Ch'ien-lung in the eighteenth century this control found its greatest extension.

[34] K. K. F. L., Chapter XII, Hauer, K. K. F. L., pp. 201, 207, 211; XVI, pp. 296, 300; XVIII, p. 345 etc.; XXXII, p. 584 etc.

CHAPTER VIII

THE MANCHUS AND THE CHINESE EMPIRE

We have discussed the several elements out of which the Manchus formed their political organization. The bureaucracy of China and the feudalism and clanism of the frontier and beyond became interacting and counteracting forces that integrated themselves into the Manchu state. It is, of course, only in theory that one can view them apart. In reality they formed a whole. They were, in their interaction, the forces that constituted the larger Chinese state system of China Proper and the outlying regions. The Manchu state was growing in the Chinese world at the edge of the Chinese empire. Its development can only be understood in its relationship to the Chinese empire, as it was—though a conquering force—still a part of China all the time.

At first the Chienchow guard and its head had owed a vassal allegiance to the Chinese emperor. From the view point of Chinese state philosophy there could be only one emperor,[1] set over all the earth, over people and vassals. The fact that the Manchus enlarged their original feudal territory and conquered more and more of Chinese Manchuria, would therefore not change the position of the Chinese emperor as head of the world state and representative of the heavenly will. But it would upset the "inner" arrangement and cut the bond between the emperor and the rebellious vassal. The emperor would have to use force to put the vassal in his place. This use of force was, according to the Chinese conception, not war of wars but punitive campaigns against rebellion. The Ming attempted such campaigns against the Manchus. But all their attempts to crush the growing Manchu power, first by an offensive into Manchu

[1] The Chinese explanation by natural phenomena can therefore be said to be that: there can be only one emperor on earth as there is only one sun in heaven.

99

territory or later simply by seeking to stem the Manchu tide by defense, failed.

There would of course have been also the possibility of "appeasement." The reestablishment of peace and order in the empire meant not of necessity a return to the *status quo ante*. The recognition of the Manchu conquests and the acceptance of the Manchus as a larger and more powerful frontier state within the empire would have been in theory quite possible. Indeed the Manchu rulers made a number of attempts to come to terms with the Chinese. There were periods of truce and of intercourse between the Chinese officials of the frontier and the Manchus. But there was never a settlement or peace. The formidable military state of the Manchus with its miniature imitation of Chinese state organization was too dangerous a competitor for world rulership to live with peacefully. The Chinese demanded the lost territory back. And the Manchus refused this demand, as they saw in the new land their most valuable possession.[2]

From the Chinese emperor's side there was thus a vacuum in the relationship with the Manchus. In a letter of the Ming emperor to Chinese frontier officials the statement was made that the Manchus were originally dependent;[3] but their present status remained open. They were simply rebels.

From the Manchu side the idea of vassalage was not given up for long. Nuerhaci had started out as the vassal of the Chinese emperor. And after the wars with the Ming had started, he and his successor did not give up the fiction for quite a time. Only at the very end of the struggle, when in 1636 the title of the Manchu ruling house was changed from Hou Chin to Ta Ch'ing did the struggle with the Ming become for the Manchus openly one between two equals.[4]

---

[2] 1627. *K. K . F. L.*, Chapter X, pp. 164, 166.

[3] 滿洲原係我屬國·

[4] It must be remembered that the Chin had never been rulers over all China. Of course, the tenor of the Manchu communications to the Chinese court and officials did show all during the periods of fighting and truce a strong arrogance. Compare the exchange of letters 1627, *K, K. F. L.*, X, but in these letters the Ming dynastical name was placed highest, indicating recognition of Ming suzerainty.

This veiled situation for the preceding time was possible as the vassalage of the Manchu ruler to the Chinese emperor did not—at least for the Manchus—exclude the possibility of fighting. The vassalage relationship, the "Meng" (盟) which had been sworn to locally by the Manchus and the Chinese frontier officials could be violated by either side. It has been disputed whether under the ancient Chinese feudal system the vassalage based on the Meng could be regarded as a two sided legal act, a contract.[5] The feudal frontier chiefs like the Manchus certainly regarded their vassalage as a two sided contract with obligations for the Chinese emperor, their suzerain, as well as for themselves. Violations of these obligations on the side of the emperor by his officials, were taken as a pretext to justify the Manchu war or feud with the Ming. The justification was given in the "seven great complaints" listed by Nuerhaci before the first attack on Fushun and repeated later as often as was thought necessary.[6] The seven great complaints were really a feudal declaration of war. They were directed against alleged violations of the overlord vassal relationship by the emperor's officials.

In many utterances of the Manchus this overlordship of the Chinese emperor remained recognized in theory. "The words of the emperor can, of course, not be opposed" said Nuerhaci during early negotiations with a Chinese frontier official about possession of fields on the frontier which he refused to give up, threatening the emperor with the possible nuisance value of his little country if not satisfactorily

[5] O. Franke, "Zur Beurteilung des chinesischen Lehenswesens," believes that there existed only a one-sided obligation on the side of the vassal prince.

[6] K. K. F. L., Chapters V, p. 64; X, pp. 156, 162, etc. The seven great complaints were:

1. Violation of frontier and murder of Nuerhacis' father and grandfather.
2. Assistance given the Yehe.
3. Arrest of envoys, freed only after extradition of ten men, killed by the Ming on the frontier.
4. Assistance in marrying a Yehe girl, engaged to Nuerhaci, to a Mongol.
5. Ming soldiers prevent Manchus from harvesting contested fields.
6. Threatening letter in support of the Yehe.
7. Prevention of the incorporation of the Hada in the Manchu state and general assistance to the Yehe.

treated.[7] Later he claimed on several occasions that the position given by heaven to the ruler of the great country (China) imposed an obligation to fairness in the rule of the world.[8] The lack of this fair treatment and of neutrality of attitude in border strifes was the chief tenor of the seven complaints. Nuerhaci promised nevertheless several times to be obedient to the " great country," if he should only be recognized in his standing, that is, as being superior to the Chahar Mongols, who were then his enemies.[9] But he refused to return any of the territory he had conquered, advancing the argument that it belonged anyhow to the emperor as suzerain.[10] As this was said at the time of the first Manchu invasions into China Proper, it was a rather ironical recognition of the emperor's overlordship. Yet the idea expressed was in tune with the Chinese state conception.

The letters in which such statements were made did not reach the Ming emperor or come from him. It was a correspondence between the Manchu ruler and Chinese frontier officials. In the beginning the Manchu power had been too unimportant to be honored with direct communication with the emperor, except of course for the tribute missions to the court in Peking at regular intervals.[11] These ceased, however, with the fighting. And the court, unwilling to make any concessions to the dangerous frontier vassal, thought it beneath the dignity of the emperor to answer in person the rebel Manchu ruler. It was a constant complaint of the latter that he did not have direct contact with the emperor. His attempts to overcome the official barrier and his remarks on the question indicate that he felt realy offended. Once he succeeded in capturing the letter from the Ming emperor to frontier officials and in an attempted reply he did not deny his dependence.

This fiction of the Manchu state as a vassal of the Chinese

[7] *K. K. F. L.*, Chapter IV, p. 51. (帝之言自不可違.)
[8] 天建大國之君郎爲天下共主.
[9] 自當遜爾大國爾等志當視我居察命爾之上也.
[10] 且當天下之地盡爲爾朝廷所屬.
[11] See Chapter IV.

empire was given up only after 1636, when the Manchus set up a new dynasty under the name of Ta Ch'ing. The former title Hou Chin, taken in preparation for the first attack on the Chinese basin, had meant more the establishment of a feudal state than a claim to the rulership of the world, which " the " emperor was supposed to have, as the Chin had, in their period, only ruled North China. Until 1636 the Manchu policy was still disguised. The " Ta Yeh,"—the great realm—which was spoken of so often by Nuerhaci and his successor as something to be established could mean a feudal state and could mean more. With growing power the concealed reservation of gaining the Chinese throne—if possible—may have come to Nuerhaci comparatively early. But only after 1636 did the policy and intention become unmistakable and quite open. The change in attitude can be clearly seen in the relationship with Korea.

It has been related before how the king of Korea had been brought early to submission in order to secure the flank of the Manchus. He had become a Manchu vassal. But the Ming still remained for Korea, as a matter of course, the highest authority in the hierarchy. In 1636, however, after the change of the Manchu dynastic title and the new claim to world rulership, Korea was again informed. The king of Korea was asked to give up the year designation of the Ming and to accept the Manchu calendar instead. The king of Korea, fearing Ming vengeance, was afraid to take this step, and had to be forced by a new Manchu campaign to hand over the seal he had received from the Ming emperor and thus to break his former loyalty.[12] From a feudal ruler the Manchu chief had advanced to the claim of being the head of the Chinese system, the emperor of the world.

That meant that the Manchus had accepted the idea of the Chinese world state, and wanted to use it to further their own political ambitions. Indeed they had started out with the Chinese conception of the known world, as they had been from the beginning a part of it. The more they penetrated

---

[12] K. K. F. L., Chapter XXI, p. 398, and XXIII.

into Chinese territory and the more bureaucratic administration they had to introduce, the more Confucian ideology can also be found in the statements of their rulers. Erich Hauer has remarked that already the first two Manchu rulers, Nuerhaci or T'ai-tsu and his son and successor T'ai-tsung speak " like Confucian Sages." He sees in this the beginnig of a development which led to the disappearance of Manchu culture and their submergence in the " higher Chinese culture." [13] This statement is wrong both with regard to the Manchu background and with regard to the result of the development. Seen from the viewpoint of general political philosophy, Confucianism was the only possible state conception the Manchus could develop. There was no Manchu political world. The Chinese state was the known world state of their time and Confucianism the recognized state philosophy far beyond the borders of China proper. The Manchus built up their state at the edge and inside the cultural, economic and even the political frontiers of China. They used chiefly an economic system of organization. The adoption of the Chinese conception of the state was essential.

Thus the Manchu rulers referred to the model period and emperors of Chinese antiquity to create an ideology justifying their own attitude. They spoke of the favor of heaven, which has no " private interests," [14] of the virtues of the emperor; of the people being his children whom he has to save from water and fire and of many other metaphors taken from Chinese political ideology. The people were supposed to flock to the Manchu state because of the virtues and care of the Manchu ruler. And his virtue finally enabled the emperor to receive and hold the mandate of heaven, to extend his sway over t'ien-hsia, the earth. All this was expressed in Chinese Confucian thought and wording. The Manchus introduced also the Chinese state and ancestor cult. And to make this state philosophy the common knowledge of their young political leaders, the Manchu rulers promoted

[13] E. Hauer, introduction to translation of *K. K. F. L.*
[14] *K. K. F. L.,* Chapter V, p. 2.

the translation and reading of countless Chinese Confucian books, and the education of the young Manchus in their ideas. The Chinese had based the education of their officials on the knowledge of the writings of the ancient philosophers. They had thus created the scholar-gentry class. The Manchus were on the way to follow suit.

This application of Chinese philosophy, the talk about virtue and Tao, the principle of harmony with nature, even the fiction of the suzerainty of the Chinese emperor sustained through the time of the fight against him, must seem at first view pretty much like a farce if one compares all this with the reality of a very ambitious and carefully planned scheme of expansion and military conquest. Yet one must not forget that behind the philosophical language of Chinese states ethics there were always hidden very real political processes. It was always but an idealization of reality. And when the Manchus used these terms and language, it simply showed their realization and acceptance of Chinese political realities. While building up a Chinese administration, the Manchus needed the Chinese ideology.

But if the Manchus found it necessary to accept Chinese phraseology and ideology as justification for their political life, they did not accept everything that had the nimbus of Chinese antiquity. T'ai-tsung stated: "In the chronicles of Chinese literature there are many beautiful words which are useless even after detailed study." And he ordered his officials to choose from the histories of the Sung, the Liao, the Chin and the Yuan dynasties those sections for collection and translation, which portrayed the country as flourishing through diligent work aimed at a well ordered government and as declining in opposite circumstances or set forth the deeds of military leaders and the influences of clever men and scoundrels, of loyal servants and flatterers, on the interests of the state.[15] Even the Chinese phraseology itself was indeed in Manchu minds and mouths something different. They were warriors and behind many of their Chinese quotations one can sense an attitude which did not

[15] *K. K. F. L.*, Chapter XX, p. 9.

agree with the original meaning. Virtue was not the mature following of the Tao, the path of nature, in the terms of Mencius; it was not the winning of others by example. It was a very military virtue. When once the Chinese complained about their heavy burden and unfair treatment in comparison with the Manchu nobility, they were told that the Manchus had earned this position through their merits in the war. They did the fighting, they ran the risks. And a rather martial interpretation was thus given to the philosopher's words: "If the head of the family can maintain the worthy man, he will obtain a Kuo; and if the prince of a Kuo can maintain the worthy men, then he will obtain the rulership of the earth." [16] Not the sages or philosophers, but the warriors were the worthy men for the Manchus.

The Manchu rulers also claimed to have the Tao or heaven's support. They believed that it was necessary for a ruler to have it. But when they compared their own virtue and " goodness " with the virtue—and Taoless Chinese emperor we realize that this Tao was nothing but a political slogan. The excuse for the attack on the Chahar Khan was that " he has no Tao." [17] And the military meaning of this Tao becomes clear when they professed: " Whoever has it, has military success, who does not have it, fails in the field." [18] It was perhaps more honest when T'ai-tsung said on the occasion of his proclamation as emperor: ". . . by keeping peace inside and grabbing outside a great empire is rising . . . ." [19] The Manchus using Chinese state philosophy were thus certainly not true disciples of Mencius.

As has been seen, the Chinese bureaucratic administration and the Chinese " children subjects " were only a part of the original Manchu state. There was another, feudal, frontier half of it, also with its own tradition. The Manchus fell

---

[16] 有家者能養賢, 則取國而可得。有國者能養賢則取天下而天下可得。K. K. F. L., Chapter XVIII, pp. 5 ff. Compare also Chapter V, p. 55.

[17] K. K. F. L., Chapter XXIV, p. 4.

[18] 蓋聞古來用兵征代。有道者昌。無道者廢·

[19] K. K. F. L., XXI, p. 15.

heirs to his feudal militaristic thought which had been shaped in their own society. From the Liao and Chin history the Manchus knew the importance of military strength in gaining and later in keeping the throne. They had before their eyes the warning example of those other frontier peoples who had been spoiled by the comfortable life in China and thus had been defeated. They did not want to become " assimilated." But what they feared was not the dangerous influence of political theory or political organization. It was the danger for the physical strength of the race. The Manchu writing was created under T'ai-tsung's remarkable direction; it served to translate quantities of Chinese literature and philosophy into the national language, but among them also the histories of the Liao, Chin and Yuan. And T'ai-tsung, shortly after he accepted the new dynastic name admonished his Manchurian nobility never to forget the old art of mounted archery. It was a memorable scene when he gathered his princes, beiles and Manchu dignitaries around him and ordered a notable to read to the assembly from the history of the Chin, the kin of the Manchus. What was read was the edict of the Chin emperor Shih-tsung who warned his people not to imitate Chinese names and manners, to conserve the old straightness and simplicity and not to become extravagant and luxurious. After the reading T'ai-tsung spoke of the warning example of the history of the Chin, who did not heed their emperor's advice. They gave up mounted archery for wine and women, and their empire was destroyed. T'ai-tsung demonstrated that in Chinese dress the Manchus could not fight; yet, their fate depended on their military qualities.[20]

The Manchus thus felt themselves a part of the Chinese empire. Not only their organization but their ideology was of this Chinese empire. But as they came from the outer sphere of this empire, their ideology had a particular feudal frontier aspect in addition to the traditional Chinese thought. In

[20] *Tung Hua Lu* 6, pp. 18-19. For text of the Chin edict see Wieger, *textes historiques*, II, 1635.

this sense a dynasty that originated at the frontier was different from a dynasty originating in China proper.

There was still another difference between the two kinds of dynasties in the whole state-founding process. When a dynasty in China had "lost the heavenly mandate," it was not the same thing whether a rebel of inner China, a man from the people, founded a new dynasty, or whether a frontier ruler took over. In the first case there was no interposition, no half way. The founder of the Chinese Ming dynasty had not first established his own state. Li Tse-cheng, the rebel, who caused the downfall of the Ming and attempted to become emperor himself, could only be emperor or robber. The ministries and titles he created had never existed in law when he failed. The Chinese conception did not allow any intermediary state between a bandit and a successful usurper founding a new legal order.

This was different with a feudal frontier state such as the Manchus had established. At the frontier such feudal states were not only permitted but were the rule. Nuerhaci laid first a foundation (基) for a feudal state, a Kuo. He planned a Ta Yeh, a great state. The slow laborious process from the foundation upward has been frequently emphasized. At the beginning Nuerhaci did not even aim further than the establishment of a frontier state.[21] But the "state in the state" could be a preparation for the conquest of the larger Chinese state and was in this way an advantage for the frontier ruler over his Chinese rival in the competition for a vacant throne.

[21] Even the historiographs of the *K. K. F. L.* who wrote under order of the emperor Ch'ien-Lung over a hundred years after the establishment of the dynasty had to recognize this fact. See epilogue of Chapter I, *K. K. F. L.*

CHAPTER IX

CONCLUSION

In the development of the Manchu state organization as outlined in the preceding chapters can be seen an example of Chinese frontier history. The frontier always played an important part in Chinese history. Chinese control over outlying regions or outside penetration into Chinese agricultural country made this frontier alive. A zone was created through which outgrowing and ingrowing developments alternated in the course of time. These developments formed the background for Chinese expansion or barbarian invasion, which were both not simple military affairs, but complicated processes of transition.

Such an ingrowing process was the formation of the Manchu power. The conditions of the frontier region had prepared their start. It had been preceded by a military bureaucratic organization of the frontier by the Chinese Ming dynasty. The organization of the " Wei " by the Ming was an expansive Chinese move that was not only followed by the countermove of Manchu penetration but created a particularly favorable condition for this countermove. While former invading barbarians had to labor with the dualism of their own feudalism and the necessary bureaucracy in Chinese territory, the Manchus found in the Ming "Wei" a model organization that could be imitated for Manchu purposes and prevented the dualism for the Manchus.

On this model the Manchus built their banner organization. They created a state on a military bureaucratic basis, a state that grew in size, importance and institutional organization. This growth has been studied here in its elements. The transition from nomadism through feudalism to a bureaucratic state has been described with particular emphasis on the Chinese influence in the new edifice which the Manchus erected. The transition led to an interesting mixture

109

of political systems. An attempt has been made to describe one by one the various elements shaping the Manchu state. This dissection of a conglomerate body seemed necessary in order to point out the elements that with different emphasis at different times gave the Manchu state its form. Yet, one must not forget that the creation of the Manchu organization was a whole and indivisable process, a process of unification, adjustment and balancing that demanded no little statesmanship from its conceivers and originators.

⁓The process began in the Ju-chen-Manchu region with a growing feudal power that swallowed its neighbors one by one. The first bureaucratic organization, the banner, was modeled after the Chinese Wei, on the other side of the border. But soon this border disappeared, the Chinese basin was invaded and became the new basis of the Manchus state. Chinese officials entered the state and the bureaucratic element of the frontier variety became the determining factor. The feudal element, although it never disappeared, lost in importance. The official position won the first place over the feudal income.

⁓The other element of major importance was the position of the imperial clan. Clan power has always been of importance and often dangerous for the stability of states in frontier history. With Nuerhaci's ascendancy his clan had also been swept into power. After Nuerhaci's death the clan emerged more prominent and powerful, until the clan influence was slowly eliminated again in favor of the imperial power through the growing bureaucracy.

⁓Geographically based on the Chinese agricultural region of Manchuria, the whole Manchu state tended thus more and more towards a bureaucratic Chinese form of organization. The conception of the state, developed simultaneously, showed the same trends. As the state grew in the margin of China, the ideas grew in the margin of Confucianism. The military virtues of the warriors, the pride of the feudal nobility of the frontier, the clan cohesion, remained for some time at least. But the thought turned more and more to China and to a Chinese kind of rulership over the

Chinese world. At the same time the policy towards the other frontier, the Mongol world, was similar to, though perhaps more efficient, than the Chinese colonial policy. The Manchus, having started at the Chinese frontier, were ready now to play their part in the affairs of China Proper.

*   *   *

The period of Manchu growth was a period of decline for the ruling Chinese dynasty, the Ming. Corruption and weakness at the court, famine and rebellion in the country showed that the Ming cycle was nearing its end. There was a chance for a new dynasty to establish itself, to end corruption, cut down the personal profits of the official class and reestablish order. The question was whether the new power would come from the border or from within China.

The only border power ready to move in was the Manchus, who saw their chance and who had worked and prepared for this time. But they had to compete with the Chinese bandit leader Li Tse-cheng,[1] who tried to establish a new dynasty from within. It is interesting enough to compare Li's background with the Manchu organization, for neither of the two competing powers had at the outset a decisive strategical advantage over the other. The decision in favor of the Manchus indicated rather that something in their organization and political conception must have been stronger than their rival's preparation for his attempt at the throne.[2]

Li, born in northern Shensi province, had started out as a robber and bandit and never forgot his past. In the twenties and thirties of the sixteenth century Li had been the leader of small and large bandit groups as they sprang up at the time in the famine stricken regions of northwestern China.

[1] See the life history of Li Tse-ch'eng in *Ming Shih*, Chapter 309, translation by E. Hauer in *Asia Major*, July-Oct., 1925.

[2] In the introduction to his translation of Li Tse-ch'engs biography Hauer declares that the horrors of civil war made the "tormented Chinese salute the Manchus as liberators" and thus made it possible "that a handful of half civilized Tungus could occupy by 'coup de main' the imperial throne of a giant empire." It is difficult to see how Hauer, who had at the same time completed the translation of the *K'ai Kuo Fang Lüeh* could interpret the Manchu conquest in this way, doing so little justice to the Manchu state.

With his bandits Li had raided unsystematically Shensi, Shansi, Honan, Hupeh, Szechuan, Kansu and even Anhui provinces. It was an up and down bandit fortune without any higher aims. Finally Li was cornered in South Shensi and brought near to suicide or surrender. But he considered the matter, ordered his group to kill all their family adherents and women, leave the baggage and move as a light cavalry force into Honan and Hupeh. There he found in 1639 in the basin of the Han river a new base of operations as famine brought him new followers and success. Sustained by this important region the former bandit developed political ambitions and conceived the idea of becoming emperor himself. Members of the scholar class, a " Dr." Niu and a " Dr." Li Chi became his advisers. The slaughtering technique was abandoned and a political organization undertaken.[3] Hsiangyang on the Han river became Li's first capital. Offices and designations of rank were created such as Prime Minister, Left and Right Chancellors, Presidents, Councillors and secretaries of six ministries, established according to Chinese tradition. Commanders were placed at strategic places and governors appointed over the districts controlled.[4]

From this base Li penetrated Shensi and Shansi[5] and broke through the pass of Nankou, attacking Peking. He

[3] Honanfu in the north, Ichang in the south had been conquered and added to the territory that was now to be politically organized.

[4] Many of the offices remained, however, pseudo appointments on paper only and the controlled districts were somewhat scattered.

[5] Before this move an important council had been held. Three routes of march came under discussion. One was to move through Honan straight up to the capital, Peking. It was the shortest and straightest way of attack but certainly the most exposed and unsafe one with only the small base in the Han valley as starting point. Two other possibilities offered themselves. One was to move down the Yangtse valley and first gain control of the rich economic area of the lower Yangtse to cut Peking off from its rice supplies and income from this key economic region. The third possibility was the strategic approach. The proposal was to move into Shensi and Shansi where probably connections from bandit times would help the conquest. This last way was chosen by Li. Strategically it was the best decision, but it indicated that strategic considerations led to the neglect of economic stability. Li did not seek this stability as he did not want to compromise with the ruling group.

conquered the city, drove the last Ming emperor to suicide and thus seemed to hold the palm of victory in his hand.

In the contest with the Manchus Li had thus the advantage of having reached the prize first. Whether he would be able to hold it would depend on his basic strength compared with that of the Manchus. Li's strategic position was rather strong, as he held, with the Han basin, Shansi, and the Tungkuan pass and the mountains of Shansi, all the military key positions to the control of North China, except the Manchurian border.

That Li finally failed was due to his weakness in the economic field and the fact that he did not really gain the support of the leading Chinese class, the scholar-gentry and its members in high political and military offices. Li remained a rebel, a hater of the ruling class, of the landlords and the gentry. Of course, he had very little time to gain political stability and to turn from a rebel into the guarantor of peace and order. Five years was all the time that Li used to organize his attempt at founding a dynasty, and the whole conquest of Shensi, Shansi and Peking happened in the last of these five years. Compared with the slow process of Manchu development, one must recognize the disadvantage of the inner Chinese rebel who had to march to quick victory. But even so he could have succeeded after he had gained control of the capital. What he needed was the support of people with decisive influence and administrative experience and in particular of the men in the decisive military positions. This support he could only gain if he turned from being a rebel to a protector in principle of the scholar-gentry class and the system of Chinese bureaucratic administration under it. But Li could not make in time his peace with the system in China. After his new start in Hsiangyang he followed for a time the advice of his scholar-councillors for a new constructive policy of trying to gain the support of all groups. But the bloodthirst of the bandit, looter and slaughterer he had been soon broke through again. Probably no Chinese rebellion was ever a soft affair, but the death and destruction Li left in his path—if one can believe his official biography [6]—was unusual, largely undid his military achievements and deprived him of the value of his own bases.

What was more important, Li's attitude cost him the sympathy of the group on whose support he depended and in particular of the man who held the strategic key position at the frontier. This man was the Chinese general Wu San-kwei, the commander of the troops at Shanhaikuan. He refused to go over to Li, and when Li marched against him, he called for the help of the Manchus and together with them defeated Li's armies. By doing so, however, he opened the gate of China to the Manchus, who took Peking and established their own dynasty there. Wu San-kwei had thus decided the struggle in favor of the Manchus. It was his act that gained the Manchus their first victory at Shanhaikuan.

The treason of Wu San-kwei to the Chinese cause has been dramatized in history. Much has been made of the touching story of his personal grief over the loss of his sweetheart who had been taken by a commander in the army of the bandit Li Tse-cheng.[7] But there was a deeper explanation. In contrast to Li, who persecuted the official class, the Manchus had in their organization made use of Chinese officials in leading positions. They had in no way disturbed the system of the official class, the position of the landlord and the gentry. On the Manchu side there was for Wu therefore a life and career in the traditional Chinese style, while he could await only with concern Li's future

---

[6] See note 1.

[7] The history narrates how this girl that had been promised to Wu San-kwei had been taken by one of the underlings of Li Tse-ch'eng. Wu therefore is supposed to have made common cause with the Manchus because of his outraged love, and finally he indeed regained the girl in battle. See Wu San-kwei's biography in *Erh Chen Ch'uan* (also translated by Hauer). Owen Lattimore has pointed out that behind this touching personal story was hidden the fact that Wu came from a family in Manchuria where his father before him had held high office, a more important fact than his personal motives. With regard to his personal motives it can also be said that Wu did indeed regain the girl through his choice of action (would there not have been also another way?) but also caused the death of his father who had been taken as hostage by Li Tse-ch'eng and was killed when Wu turned against Li.

political plans. Many Chinese officials before Wu had already found a profitable career on the Manchu side, especially such Chinese officials, who, as also Wu himself, came from the Chinese basin of Manchuria.

Wu was probably even some time before he actually went over to the Manchus not unfavorably inclined towards this new power in Manchuria. Thus he had remained inactive at Shanhaikuan, when the Manchus raided China through Jehol. When the decisive hour came, the choice was for him, as his letters to the Manchus indicate, really between order—as he understood it—and the protection of his interests, which he then could find only on the Manchu side, and disorder on the side of the rebel Li. He choose the Manchus.

This choice was a first indication of how Chinese the Manchus had become, if a Chinese official would prefer them to a Chinese rebel. In the sense of the traditional Chinese system of government, the Manchus were more Chinese than Li Tse-cheng. That became even more apparent after the first victory at Shanhaikuan and the opening of the road into China for the Manchus. The officials in North China, particularly in Shantung province, were quick to surrender. It may be remembered, as we stated before, that Shantung had been the province from which had come many of the families that had immigrated into Manchuria. And with the possession of Shantung the Manchus gained control of the imperial canal and with it the approach to the grain taxes of the Yangtse valley.

The Manchus attempted even to use the argument of their conservative loyalty to the Chinese system with the remnants of the Ming in South China.[8] Here, however, they found resistance, which was later broken by the force of arms.

Li Tse-cheng, on the other hand, could nowhere rally his forces again to an effective stand. He was chased from defeat to defeat all the way back to whence he had come, from Shansi to Shensi and, after a vain attempt to break into Sze-chuan, he was finally driven into the Han valley,

[8] See the argumentation in Hsieh Pao-chao, *op. cit.*, against the "legality" pretended in the exchange of letters with the Ming. See Chapter I, note 8.

from where he had started. His power simply collapsed
and he withdrew into the Kiukiang mountains south of
Wuchang. There he was killed by farmers into whose hands
he fell on a foraging raid. Li's inability to draw any new
strength from his bases after his first defeat, his collapse
that came as quickly as his former rise to power, indicate the
loose background of his whole adventure and the lack of
support from regional sources that could command tax income and manpower.

The Manchus' newly gained power and rule, on the other
hand, was "Chinese" enough to be acceptable to the
Chinese. Thus, as a result of their largely Chinese organization and with the support of a majority of Chinese officials
and soldiers, the Manchus occupied the throne in Peking as
the new Ch'ing dynasty. It sounds very Confucian and Chinese, when one reads the Manchu proclamation that the
"wheel of the world" had turned, the decline of one dynasty had made room for another, the Ming had lost the
heavenly mandate. "Through heaven's favor and the new
emperor's blessing" the Manchus had conquered Peking.[9]

Yet it was not the same as if the robber Li had become
"fit for society" and had succeeded or as if another Chinese
leader had established a new dynasty. The difference was
discernible from the proclamation of the emperor which
read: "Consequently one has elevated our old state to receive the new mandate."[10]

This sentence expressed the fact that the Manchus had
marched into China not as a dynasty alone, nor as a simple
barbarian horde, but as a state organization. The state which
they had organized in Manchuria they now transferred
into China. The state was not a "foreign nation" that conquered China. It was a partly foreign frontier organization
which the Manchus brought. The banners, as has been said,
had Manchu, Mongol and Chinese units. Even in the Manchu
units only little more than half the people were of Manchu

[9] 天眷及皇上洪福巳克燕京 *Tung Hua Lu*, Shun Chih 2, p. 26.
[10] 逐舉舊邦誕膺新命 K.K.F.L., end and *Tung Hua Lu*, Shun Chih, *ibid*.

or Juchen origin.[11] And intermarriage made it difficult to say how genuinely Manchu they were. But it was still a separate political organization, a state.

Would the Manchus, now in control of China, dissolve this organization or transform it by the inclusion of the whole Chinese government in its frame? They did neither. They " elevated the state to receive the new mandate."

The Manchus accepted the Chinese administration in China as they had formerly done in Manchuria.[12] They confirmed all surrendering officials in their posts, only introducing a stricter control with the threat that from then on no corruption would be tolerated. They emphasized, as they had frequently done in Manchuria, that they would not make any racial distinctions among their subjects. Chinese, Manchu and Mongol all were to be equally cared for.[13] But to organize all China in the same way as Manchuria was of course impossible. What suited the frontier did not suite the whole of China.

But the original organization was nevertheless still of importance. Any reorganization that would bring the whole of China into the Manchu state, or, rather, would dissolve the Manchu state into the government of China, would destroy the balance which the Manchus held in their frontier organization. It would also destroy the source of their power, aside from the fact that it would be a new difficulty to integrate the noble Manchus with the state.

Hence the Manchus kept their banner organization. The central government, established in their Manchurian capital, was also kept independent. Five of the six ministries in Mukden were maintained as branches of the new ministries

---

[11] Haenisch, *op. cit.*, points out that of the banner families of that time only little more than half were of Manchu or Tungus origin. The handbook of the banner organization of 1735 counts 1,100 families, about 250 of whom were of Chinese, 200 of Mongol, 40 of Korean origin. All these had intermarried with the exception of the purely Manchu imperial house and a few noble families.

[12] Only in Southwest China did they nominate three great vassal princes, who were later abolished after a suppressed rebellion. The vassal princes were deserving Chinese partisans, one of them Wu San-kwei.

[13] 同屬朝廷志子. *Tung Hua Lu,* 3, p. 4.

of the central government in Peking, the ministry of the interior being the only exception.[14] Manchuria thus remained under the central control of Peking a frontier state and the basis of the Manchu banners and their power.

The banners had at first been the Manchu state. Now they became a state within the state. The frontier state was elevated and its people became a sort of hereditary privileged group. Units of the banners were strategically distributed over the country and their commanders ranked higher than the officials of the administration without having themselves administrative functions other than those connected with the life of their subordinate banner people.[15] The function of the banners had thus changed. They became a centralizing and controlling factor, strategically located as they were over the provinces and around and in the capital. This distribution was perhaps the most important factor in the greater and stricter centralization which the new dynasty brought at the outset.[16]

In this survival of the frontier state in partly new form, could be seen also the main difference between a Chinese dynasty originating from an inner rebellion in China and a dynasty that had organized its power on the frontier. In this regard the frontier power was different from the rebellious Chinese force. It has been stated before that in contrast to the rebellion which either won or failed and did not know any intermediary status, the frontier had its own *raison d'etre* regardless of whether it succeeded in gaining or even attempted to gain the throne. If it did succeed, however, it could not entirely denounce its own *raison*, even after taking over the throne of all China.

This difference was felt on both sides. The privileges of the banner people, of whom so many were Chinese them-

[14] These branch ministries in Mukden were abolished only in 1907.

[15] The comparison with party troops in totalitarian states is tempting.

[16] Many other reforms indicate this centralization, for instance the excellent system of postal communication which the Board of War organized. Post stations had existed under the Ming, but their functioning had greatly deteriorated like many other government functions. A censor could even propose their abolishment for economies sake! (Hauer, *Li Tse-ch'eng*, p. 444.)

selves, irked the Chinese people more than those of the
" alien race " of the Manchus.[17] The un-Chinese part of the
organization seemed "barbarian" to the Chinese and indicated the frontier origin.

Against this reproach the Manchus set their noble des-
cent. Already Nuerhaci had indicated that the Manchus
as proud seigneurs and vassals were of higher standing than
the ancestor of the Ming dynasty who had been a monk.[18]
In the introduction of the *K'ai Kuo Fang Lueh* the famous
emperor Ch'ien Lung took up the same idea. He stated that
none of the racially Chinese dynasties could have the authority of the Mongol or Manchu dynasties, for all the
others had come from the common people of China. Mongols
and Manchus had been noble vassals. In his heart the Manchu felt superior to the Chinese, felt something of the pride
of his feudal military past.

The Manchus never became completely absorbed into the
Chinese culture. They remained the privileged group of
conquerors; the group which retained part of the military
and feudal past all through its history. A Manchu would
always have his bowl of rice, a small pension at least, paid to
the member of the conquering group by the conquered people. The Manchu warriors still practiced archery when the
modern guns and gunboats of he West had already forced
another civilization on China.

On the throne in Peking the Manchus thus remained tied
to their past history. And in this history the frontier had
interacted with the Chinese tradition. In their Chinese
bureaucratic organization the Manchus never quite lost the
frontier touch. But the frontier, with its own characteristics, formed also a part of the general scenery of China's
political history. The great idea of Chinese civilization em-
braced also the frontier development. Even the Manchu
superiority could not conceal the fact that it was the Chinese
civilization which had to be recognized as their political and
ideological standard by the Manchus too.

[17] Haenisch, *op. cit.*
[18] *K. K. F. L.*, Chapter XXII, p. 16.

ANNEX

Li Yung-Fang. *Erh Chen Ch'uan*, book 1, pages 42-49.

Li Yung-fang was a native of Tiehling in Liaotung. In the 41st
year Wan Li of the Ming (1613) he defended Fushun with the
rank of major. At that time the Yehe Beile Gintaisi and Buyanggu
sent a Mongol to the Ming and informed them as follows: " The three
states of the Hata, Hoifa and Ula have been already completely conquered by the Manchus. If they attack us now again, their intention
is to attack forthwith the Ming." The Ming ordered the major to
strengthen at once the troops of the mountain passes, and to prepare 1000 men with fireweapons in order to defend the two Fang
and Hsi-towns of the Yehe. Then they sent a messenger to our
ruler and said one should not attack, but reestablish friendly relations
and dismiss the troops.

When T'ai-tsu had received the letter, he wrote the Ming: " In
the past the Yehe, Hata, Ula and Hoifa, the Korcin and Sibe,
Guwalca, Juseri and Neyen, the countries of nine tribes have in
the year Kwei-si (1593) assembled their troops in order to attack
us. We collected troops for defense and heaven disapproved of
injustice. Our troops had a great victory, beheaded the Yehe Beile
Bujai and captured the Ula Beile Bujantai, who was sent back again
into his country. Then in the year Tingyu (1597) a horse was
slaughtered and an alliance sworn over the blood. One became connected by marriage and was not to forget the good relationship.
Who would have thought that the Yehe would disavow the old
alliance? They regretted that they had promised the girl and did not
give her away. With regard to Bujantai, I have treated him with
favour. He has paid for decency with hatred. Therefore I have punished him, annihilated his army and taken his country. Now Bujantai
has fled to the Yehe. The Yehe have received him and did not hand
him over to me. Therefore I now chastise the Yehe. With regard to
the Ming, what mistrust or hatred should arouse in me the wish that
we attack each other? "

After he had conceived the letter he went with his followers
to Fushun; at this Li Yung-fang went three miles out of the town
to welcome him. He led him to the training ground. After T'ai-
tsung had handed over the letter, he returned.

Not long after the Ming general Chang Ch'eng-yin placed signposts and made it known that the districts Ch'ai-ho, Sanch'a and Fu-an, situated within the borders of our soldier settlements, could not be harvested. The governor Li Wei-han furthermore kept our envoys Kangguri, Fanggina and others, in order to revenge the people captured and killed for passing over the frontier. In the 4th month of the third year Tien Ming of our dynasty, that is the 46th year Wan Li of the Ming (May 1618), T'ai-tsu announced to heaven the seven great complaints. Then he brought up the army to fight the Ming.

To Li Yung-fang he communicated in a letter the following order: " You have sent troops over the frontier and helped the Yehe with protection. Thus I have called up the army and am coming. You are in Fushun only a major. Even if you fight, you will certainly not win. Now I order you to capitulate. If you surrender, my troops will penetrate to-day deep into the country. If you do not surrender you delay the time of our invasion. You have always been an intelligent man with a sound grasp of present requirements. Our state has always had a generous understanding of talented men. And if one is somewhat gifted and quick in administration, one elevates him, appoints him and binds him by marriage. And all the more with a man like you one must show special esteem and place him in the same rank with our first dignitaries. If you do not fight, but surrender, I shall let you keep your former office and shall care benevolently for you. But if you fight, how can our arrows know who you are? You will find death in the shower of arrows. If one has no chance to win victory, of what use then is death? Besides, if you come out of the town and surrender, our troops shall not penetrate into the town and your officers and men will all remain unharmed. But if our soldiers invade the town, old and young, men and women, will face terror and ruin; that will also be of no advantage to you. Do not say that we make empty threats that must not be believed. Think. If I could not take such a small town, what purpose would it serve to call up the army? If you miss your chance and do not make up your mind, regret will also be of no avail. If the high and low officers, and soldiers and the people in the town surrender the town and submit, then their parents, wives and children and all the families shall be protected and also not be separated. Is that not wonderful? To surrender or not, think it over well, and disobey not my words in the indignation of the passing hour, so that anger should destroy this possibility and a chance be missed."

Yung-fang received the ruler's letter. He knew that a great army had come. In his official attire he stood at the south gate of the town but ordered his troops to prepare all for defense. In a moment our troops put up the scaling ladders and climbed on to the wall. The defenders were thrown into disorder and terror. Then Yung-fang mounted his horse and came out and surrendered. When our banner dignitary Adun led him before the emperor, he threw himself down and remained long on the ground to accept his fate.

The people in the town surrendered as did the two towns Tung-chou and Mahatan and also over 500 castles and posts. Whoever prepared defense and did not surrender in spite of the ruler's order was killed.

Chang Ch'eng-yin from Kuangning with lieutenant-general P'o Feng-hsiang from Liaoyang, the lieutenant-colonel P'u Shih-fang from Haichow, the major Liang Ju-kuei and others came to help with over 10,000 troops; they all were killed in battle.

The ruler ordered Fushun to be destroyed and the conquered people of 1000 families to be grouped and settled in Hsinking. As formerly under the Ming, high and low officials were appointed. They were placed under Yung-fang, who was made deputy general and appointed to govern the subjected people. He was married to a daughter of the Beile Abatai, the seventh son of the ruler.

In the seventh month of this year (1618) he took part in the campaign of the ruler against the Ming. Lieutenant-general Tsou Ch'u-hsien of Tsingho was asked to surrender. Ch'u-hsien did not obey. Together with the lieutenant-colonel Chang Pe he was killed in battle at the head of 10,000 men. The town was then conquered.

In the 4th year (1619) the ruler went with the whole army against the Ming town T'iehling. In the 6th year (1621) Mukden and Liaoyang were taken. Yung-fang took part in these campaigns, earned merits and was promoted to the grade of general. The Ming governor Wang Hua-cheng and the frontier generals continuously sent messengers to entice Yung-fang away. He arrested these people with the letters and informed the ruler. He was commended and granted pardon from capital punishment three times in advance by imperial command.

In the first year T'ien Tsung (1627) the Ming general Mao Wen-lung was established on the islands off the shore of Korea. The Beiles Amin and Jirgalang and others, the high officials Yang-guri and Namtai together with Yung-fang were ordered to lead the troops against Korea. The emperor ordered them to ask Korea in a proper way to submit, not to take everything, but to act according to occasion and with fairness. Then they conquered at first Jehou in Korea. They sent troops that attacked T'ieshan and drove Mao Wen-lung away. Then Tingchow in Korea was stormed. In Tingchow they took prisoners and killed a great number of people. Then the army reached the town of Ping-yang. The officials and the people had all run away. The Tatungkiang was crossed. The king of Korea sent envoys with a letter to meet them. The Beile received the letter, in which several times excuse for former disrespect was offered. They granted that he should send a trusted high official to apologize and conclude an alliance; then they would lead the army back. The army reached Huangchow. Li-tsung sent a mounted messenger with the information that trusted high officials were already on the way to swear an alliance. But the Beile Amin wanted nevertheless to attack. Yung-fang said to all the Beiles: "We have received the highest command to be fair. In the recent exchange of letters with Korea we said that we would lead the troops back if a trusted high dignitary should come, apologize and swear an alliance. If we now break our former word, it is unjust. One should rather remain here for a while and wait." All the Beiles agreed with his words. Only Amin shouted furiously at Yung-fang and said: "You Chinese slave. Why all these words? I should kill you." Then they marched on Pingshan. Li-tsung thereupon sent trusted high dignitaries and his younger brother the Yuan-ch'ang-chün Li Chüeh. After their arrival Amin said to all the Beiles. I have always had a desire to see the capital and the palace of the Ming emperor and of the king of Korea but have never seen them. As we are now so near the capital of Korea, how can we turn back without going there. We must move to their hole and then see further. The Beile Yoto, Jirgalang, Ajige and Dudu were all of the opinion that one could not do this. At last, as Yung-fang had formerly advised, they sent the lieutenant-general Liu Hsing-tsu and others to conclude the alliance and turned back.

In the 5th month of the 8th year (1634) all officials were rewarded for their performances. At that time Yung-fang, who had received at the time of his surrender the rank of a Viscount of the third class, received his rank as hereditary without discontinuation. In the same year he died. He had nine sons, who served in the blue Chinese banner. All received official appointments. The second son had the rank of a high official. He became state secretary and governor-general. The third son, Kang A, was a high official and moved up to the position of a general. The fifth son Kang Yen was hereditary Viscount and became lieutenant-general. All had descendants.

BIBLIOGRAPHY

(Note: No claim is made to give an exhaustive bibliography of the subject. The books and articles named are only those mentioned and quoted in the text.)

CHINESE HISTORICAL TEXTS:

K'ai Ming. Erh Shih Wu Shih, Ming Shih. (開明. 二十五史, 明史).
The K'ai Ming edition, Shanghai, of the "twenty-five Dynastic Histories," Ming History.

Huang-Ch'ing K'ai-Kuo Fang-lueh. (皇清開國方略.)
History of the foundation of the Manchu Empire. Imperial ed. with Emperor Ch'ien Lung's facsimile introduction of 1786, quoted *K. K. F. L.*

Shih-Ch'ao Tung Hua Lu. (十朝東華錄.)
History of the period of government of 10 emperors of the Manchu dynasty. 1583-1861.

Ta Ch'ing Hui Tien. (大清會典.)
"Institutions" of the Manchu Empire. Peping, 1818 ed.

Pa-Ch'i T'ung-Chih. (八旗通志.)
Description of the eight banners, fourth year Ch'ien-Lung.

Pa-ch'i Man-chow Shih-tsu T'ung-p'u (八旗滿洲氏族通譜). Comprehensive genealogy of the Manchu clans, 1745.

Wei Yüan, Sheng Wu Chi. (聖武紀.)
History of the Wars of the Manchu Emperors.

Man-Han, Ming Chen Ch'uan. (滿漢明臣傳.)
Biographies of famous Manchu and Chinese officials under the Manchu dynasty.

Erh Chen Ch'uan. (貳臣傳)
Biographies of officials who served under two dynasties (the Ming and the Manchu).

TRANSLATIONS

Huang-Ts'ing K'ai-Kuo Fang-Lüeh, Die Gründung des Mandschurischen Kaiserreiches, übersetzt und erklärt von Erich Hauer, Berlin und Leipzig, 1926.

"Li T'ze-ch'eng und Chang Hsien-chung, ein Beitrag zum Ende der Ming Dynastie," translated from *Ming Shih,* Chapter 309, by Erich Hauer, *Asia Major,* Leipzig, July-Oct., 1925, April, 1926.

"Prinz Dorgon," translated from Ch'in Ting Tsung Shih Wang Kung Kung Chi Piao Ch'uan, by Erich Hauer, *Ostasiatische Zeitschrift,* Hamburg, *Neue Folge,* III, Heft 1, p. 9.

"General Wu San-kuei," translated from Erh Chen Ch'uan by Erich Hauer, *Asia Major,* Leipzig, Oct. 1927.

"Beiträge der frühen Geschichte der Manchu-dynastie. 1) Prinz Daisan,

2) die Prinzen Anim und Manggultai, 3) Prinz Jirgalang," translated from Ch'in Ting Tsung Shih Wang Kung Kung Chi Piao Ch'uan by Erich Hauer, *Ostasiatische Zeitschrift,* Hamburg, 1926.

Обстоятельное описание происхождения и состояния маньджурскаго народа и войска в осми знаменах состоящаго, organization of the Manchu banners, translated from Chinese ed. of 1739, St. Petersburg, 1784, in 12 volumes.

Geschichte der Grossen Liao aus dem Manchu übersetzt. Liao History, translated by H. C. von der Gabelentz, St. Petersburg, 1877.

BOOKS AND ARTICLES

Chi Ch'ao-ting, *Key Economic Areas in Chinese History.* London, 1936.

Otto Franke, "Zur Beurteilung des chinesischen Lehenswesens," *Sitzungsbericht phil. hist. Kl. 1927,* Berlin, 1928.

Lucien Gibert, *Dictionnaire Historique et Géographique de la Manchourie,* Hongkong, 1934.

W. Gorski, "Ueber die Herkunft des Stammvaters der jetzt in China herrschenden Dynastic Zin und vom Ursprung des Namens der Mantschsu." *Arbeiten der kais. russ. Gesandtschaft zu Peking über China,* Berlin, 1858, 1st Vol., p. 347.

Marcel Granet, *La Civilisation Chinoise,* Paris, 1927.

E. Haenisch, "Die gegenwärtigen chinesischen Wirren und ihre geschichtlichen Voraussetzungen. *Vergangenheit und Gegenwart,* Vol. 18°, 65-82.

E. Haenisch, "Hosoi Cin Wang," *Asia Major,* Leipzig, II, 590.

Hsieh Pao-chao, *The Government of China (1644-1911),* Baltimore, 1925.

Hsiu I-shan, *Ch'ing-tai t'ung-shih.* (清代通史.) History of the Manchu Dynasty, 2 Vols, Shanghai, 1932.

A. W. Hummel, *Eminent Chinese of the Ch'ing Period,* biographical dictionary, in preparation.

Olga Lang, "The good Iron of the New Chinese Army," *Pacific Affairs,* XII, New York, March, 1939.

Owen Lattimore, *Inner Asian Frontiers of China,* New York, 1940.

―――, *The Gold Tribe, "Fishskin Tatars" of the lower Sungari.* Memoirs Amer. Anthropological Soc., No. 40, 1933.

T. C. Lin, "Manchuria in the Ming Empire," *Nankai Social and Economic Quarterly,* Tientsin, Vol. VIII, No. 1, 1935.

―――, "Manchurian Trade and Tribute in the Ming Dynasty," *Nankai Social and Economic Quarterly,* Tientsin, Vol. IX, No. 4, 1937.

J. Marquardt, *Die Chronologie der alttürkischen Inschriften,* Leipzig, 1898.

Willian Frederik Mayers, *The Chinese Government,* 3rd ed., Shanghai, 1896.

Meng Sen, *Ch'ing-Ch'ao Ch'ien-Chi* (孟森, 清朝前紀). A study of the ancestry of the Ch'ing Dynasty, Shanghai, 1930.

Friedrich Otte, "Early Manchu Economy," *Chinese Economic Journal,* 1927.

S. M. Shirokogorov, *Social Organization of the Manchus,* Shanghai, 1924.

Arnold J. Toynbee, *A Study of History,* 6 Vols., London, 1934-39.

Wang Yü-chüan, "The Rise of Land Tax and the Fall of Dynasties in Chinese History," *Pacific Affairs,* IX, New York, June, 1936.

Léon Wieger, *Textes Historiques, Histoire Politique de la Chine depuis l'origine, jusqu'en 1912,* 2 Vols., Hien-hien, 1922.

Henry R. Williamson, *Wang An Shih, A Chinese Statesman and Educationalist of the Sung Dynasty,* 2 Vols., London, 1935-37.

Karl August Wittfogel, *Probleme der chinesischen Wirtschaftsgeschichte,* Archiv für Sozialwissenschaft und Sozialpolitik, Tübingen, 1927.

———, "The Foundations and Stages of Chinese Economic History," *Zeitschrift für Sozialforschung,* IV, Heft 1, Paris, 1935.

———, "Die Theorie der Orientalischen Gesellschaft," *Zeitschrift für Sozialforschung,* VII, Doppelheft 1/2, Paris, 1938.

——— and Feng Chia-sheng, *History of Chinese Society,* Volume *Liao,* to appear soon.

———, *Oriental Society in Asia and Ancient America,* to appear soon.

CONTRACTOR COMBATANTS

CONTRACTOR COMBATANTS
Tales of an Imbedded Capitalist

CARTER ANDRESS

THOMAS NELSON
Since 1798

NASHVILLE   DALLAS   MEXICO CITY   RIO DE JANEIRO   BEIJING

Published in Nashville, Tennessee. Thomas Nelson is a trademark of Thomas Nelson, Inc.

Thomas Nelson, Inc., titles may be purchased in bulk for educational, business, fund-raising, or sales promotional use. For information, please email SpecialMarkets@ThomasNelson.com.

Page design by: Walter Petrie

Library of Congress Cataloging-in-Publication Data

Andress, Carter, 1963–
    Contractor combatant / Carter Andress.
      p. cm.
    Includes bibliographical references and index.
    ISBN 1-59555-089-5
    1. Iraq War, 2003– 2. Andress, Carter, 1963– 3. Contractors—
Iraq—Biography. 4. Contractors—United States—Biography. I. Title.
DS79.76.A54 2007
956.7044'3092—dc22
   [B]   2007013015

Printed in the United States of America

07 08 09 10 11 QWM 5 4 3 2 1

Contents

ONE

Ripping Off Uncle Sam in Iraq

The orange desert swayed from side to side, from horizon to distant horizon, as we corkscrewed into Baghdad International Airport (BIAP). I was in Flying Carpet's thirty-seat prop jet (soon to be pictured in the *Wall Street Journal*); and as I looked down at the terminal complex below, my stomach churned. Soon I would be working in one of those buildings. The terminal was the ultimate symbol of America's presence in Iraq, and I could imagine a target painted on every rooftop below.

I had come to the Middle East not so much for the modest salary I would be drawing, but for the adventure and for the opportunity to serve in what some experts were already calling World War III. I had been trolling Monster.com and had run across an ad by Custer Battles (CB) calling for "security men." I googled the company and found that it was a "security" outfit whose services included cargo delivery and convoy protection. I also discovered that an old buddy of mine, Scooter, a former CIA agent, was on the board of directors. So I gave him a call.

After some catching up, I said, "Scooter, I see your people are looking for security men. Is this something I should be interested in?"

"No," he said. "Working as a guard on the perimeter of Baghdad Airport would be a waste of your time and talents. Give me a couple of days to see what I can do for you."

Sure enough, he got back to me a couple weeks later.

"We've created a job for you," he said, "one that will take advantage of both your military and civilian intelligence experience. It'll be dangerous work, but not excessively dangerous if you operate low profile. The pay isn't too good, but I can assure you the place is full of future business opportunities for Americans who get in on the ground floor."

The more I listened, the more I realized this opportunity would draw on all my skills and background as an entrepreneur and former infantry officer. Scooter knew that I had been trying to get into the fight since Afghanistan, when he attempted unsuccessfully to help me join the CIA's paramilitary branch in late 2001.

"That sounds very interesting," I said. "But first I'll have to discuss this with Tanya. We have two children now—a girl, eight, and a boy, four. They'll figure prominently in the equation."

"I understand," he said. "I hope you'll come aboard. We can use you."

I liked the idea of serving in Iraq, where America's chips were on the table. The events of 9/11 haunted me. Maybe for me this would be payback time. It was a tough decision, but in the end, Tanya and I agreed it would be worth the separation. I could come home now and then, and after a year we would be in a position to invest in our own business again, with my international security bona fides burnished. Too many positives. Manageable negatives. I interviewed, was offered the job, and took it. Now, as we approached the landing field, I was about to find out if I had made a good career move or a fatal mistake.

The pilot, a young Jordanian, hewed his tight turns inside the perimeter of the huge aerodrome in order to keep from flying over the outskirts of Baghdad, where the bad guys might seize the opportunity to come after us with a man-portable, surface-to-air missile. A little over a month earlier, the insurgents had nearly knocked a DHL plane out of the sky. If it hadn't been for the skill of the pilot—who used engine power alone to guide the rudderless Airbus A300 back down to the runway—the plane would have dropped to earth like a concrete mixer. They say the pilot never flew again. When we finally touched ground, still in one piece, and rolled to a stop, I understood a little of how he must've felt.

In fact, not much flew into BIAP those days. The airport used to be called Saddam International, and you could still see the faded outline of the dictator's name in four-foot letters across the main terminal's facade. The U.S. military used the south side of the airfield; and everyone else, including my new employer, Custer Battles, LLC, conducted air ops on the north side. The only nonmilitary planes landing were a very few charter flights: Flying Carpet from Amman, Jordan, or Beirut, Lebanon; AirServ for humanitarian organizations; the twice-daily flights on Royal Jordanian Air (flown by South African mercenaries); and giant Russian cargo planes flying in from Dubai, United Arab Emirates.

3

The cargo planes would be my focus. I would be managing Secure Global Distribution (SGD), Custer Battles' logistics subsidiary—run out of BIAP—trucking goods nationwide in Iraq for USAID, U.S. Army, General Dynamics, Halliburton, and other U.S. contractors. We delivered anything the transport planes hauled in: brand-new Ford SUVs; luggage; medical supplies; office equipment, everything from huge rolls of carpet and conference tables to paper clips and staples; even school supplies, including books, blackboards, boxes of pencils, and reams of paper.

Our specialty was shipments to the hot spots of the insurgency in the now-infamous Sunni Triangle, where ambushes and roadside bombs were as routine as breakfast. While I was with CB, we never missed a delivery, despite the fact that we operated daily in the same battle space where the insurgents regularly shot at and bombed the U.S. military.

I deplaned with another CB employee, Frank, who was returning from Christmas leave in Texas. Frank had been in Iraq long enough to qualify as an expert in staying alive, a subject I hoped to master. He was a Mexican American, slight of build, but I noticed that the muscles in his arms were lean and hard. He told me later that he graduated from college on a track-and-field scholarship awarded for his speed in the mile. I was glad I'd kept in shape.

"I'll show you your office first," he said. "Then we'll drive into Baghdad and you can unpack and meet the rest of the staff."

Custer Battles had offices at the airport, in one of the passenger terminals, which overlooked the 3,300-foot runway where the cargo planes landed. My second-floor office in Terminal C was directly over the commercial shipping operations on the other side of the looping, two-deck airport passenger departure and arrival ramps. The plate-glass window at the entrance to the building was shot out during the invasion, and a contract security guard from Nepal, one of the renowned British Army-trained Gurkhas, stood watch during working hours, monitoring foot traffic into CB's offices.

Custer Battles operated in Iraq because they had won the contract to provide security for Baghdad International Airport in the early chaotic days after the U.S. invasion in the summer of 2003. My role now was to help the company expand its services into the most dangerous spots, which were increasing in number given the growing Iraqi insurgency. While no delivery was completely safe, CB was carving a niche for itself by doing the jobs that others wouldn't touch. I knew the dangers before I accepted the job, and I'd come anyway.

We walked up the steps to the second floor, and I followed Frank down the corridor until he stopped, fished some keys from his pocket, found the right one, and unlocked the door.

"Here's where you'll be working," he said.

I stepped inside and looked around. It wasn't the executive suite at Microsoft, but it had three fine new desks, with swivel chairs and a long, brown real-leather sofa. The carpet also looked new, except for a couple of divots caused by what looked like bullets.

I asked what made them.

"Accidental discharge," he said. I didn't press him for details.

"Now, we'll go downstairs and get you armed. I have hidden my MP5 [submachine gun] in the locker in our office. That's all I'll need."

I followed him down the second-floor hallway, where he opened a steel door with a hefty padlock and led me into the company security office and armory. There I met the Officer of the Day, who immediately started moaning about missing weapons. Apparently, while everyone was away on Christmas leave, one of CB's now-departed American managers had stolen a couple of light machine guns, some sniper rifles, pistols, ammunition, computers, and over $50,000 in petty cash.

"We've only got an M-4 assault rifle that belongs in the Gurkha checkpoint guard rotation," the OD said. "You'll have to return it tomorrow morning."

He took one down from a rack and tossed it to me. I held the rifle in one hand to feel the weight.

"It's a shorter version of the M-16 I carried in the U.S. Army Infantry," I said. "It's a good weapon."

"Yes," he said, "but you'll need something more permanent than that."

"Like what?"

"Well, like an AK-47 and a pistol. We'll get you those tomorrow."

"What about body armor?"

"All we have is this." The OD handed me a lightweight Kevlar-like vest with thin metal "chicken plates" that would barely stop a 9mm pistol round, not to mention the omnipresent AK-47 high-powered rifle bullet. The next week I would confiscate for my own use a level 4 polymer-plated vest from a commercial shipment that CB was trying to sell. This armor would stop five AK rounds in a row to the chest or back, with serious bruising to the wearer of course, but with no penetration. Nevertheless, the lack of adequate body armor and weaponry on my first day in country did not inspire confidence in Custer Battles.

As we headed out to Frank's bulletproof gray BMW 728 in what used to be the rental car lot, I asked, "Where will I be living?"

"We have a company executive safe house in the middle of Baghdad," Frank said. "It's about fifteen miles from here—the former Syrian ambassador's place. It's nice, just this side of a palace, in the upscale Mansour district."

The living quarters sounded great. I'd expected barracks and army cots. Frank slipped behind the wheel of his BMW sedan, and I settled into the passenger seat. Soon we were hurtling down Airport Road as a viscous darkness descended on us. Ahead we saw the feeble lights of Baghdad. I sat next to him, cradling my assault rifle, riding shotgun, remembering my days as an Army Ranger. Obviously I'd be able to put all that Ranger training to good use. It was beginning to dawn on me that we were in the middle of a shooting war— and I was a combatant.

Frank was a former United States Marine Corps (USMC) Force Recon swimmer, so we had some things in common. As we bounced along the highway, he told me about running the logistics operation. He had been in country since the preceding November.

"January is a good time to be in Iraq," he said. "Right now the weather's rainy and cool. Unless you grew up in Death Valley, you can't imagine how hot it will get in the summer."

Before my tour was over, I found out. And the weather wasn't the only thing that heated up. The year was 2004, and the insurgency was shifting into high gear, with the worst yet to come. For example, at that time, Frank could still drive around Baghdad all by himself. He could even go to the bazaars with the Arabs because he looked like an American Indian, not an Anglo-Irish like me. Even after the reign of terror intensified, Frank was OK in Baghdad just so long as he didn't speak.

Soon enough the danger escalated. American civilians began to disappear from the streets, only to show up on al Jazeera TV, arms and legs bound, surrounded by masked men brandishing swords. Even when finally tanned by the desert sun, with my thick brown hair and full Taliban-style beard, I stood out as a non-Iraqi, though Iraqis were never quite sure where I came from. Once a former special counter-terrorist policeman—one of our Egyptian clients—raised that question, and when told America, he shook his head, refusing to believe it.

As we passed four or five Arabs waiting to cross the otherwise empty highway, Frank told me matter-of-factly, "You have to keep a sharp lookout, especially when you're driving along Airport Road. The insurgents' modus operandi is to wrap their heads with a *shmag* just before they strike. That may give you a few seconds warning."

"What's a shmag?" I asked.

"A checkered cotton scarf that's usually either red and white or black and white. Normally it's worn to protect your head from sun and sand, mostly by men who come from tribal areas outside Baghdad. You'll sometimes see shmags on workers in the city. Of course, in attacks they're used as masks, worn over the face with a slit left open for the eyes."

We rode in silence for a while, the gates of the airport receding behind us, burning red with the fading light from the afterglow of the set sun. Palm trees, motionless in the breezeless night, lined both sides of the road and grew in clumps in the wide sand median. Beyond the edge of the four-lane highway, low white walls lined the outskirts of residential suburbs with names such as *al Jihad*. Ahead, Baghdad was a silhouette against the darkening sky.

Baghdad. The very name conjured up visions of flying carpets, minarets, muezzins, and the 1,001 nights of Scheherazade. What I saw ahead in the distance looked like the typical Islamic Middle Eastern urban skyline—off-white stucco, flat-roofed office buildings and houses interspersed with cylindrical towers of mosques that all reflected the moonlight in a yellowish hue. As we drove through the dimly lit downtown area, I could see that this was a different world.

Even the newer hotels and the few commercial high-rises had facades that were Islamic in their intricate, wrought-iron design. The pointed arch was ever present, defining every possible doorway, window, or opening. I had the impression that the builders of this city had made few compromises with the Western world.

Some of the Arab men walking down the street were dressed in what Frank told me was a *dishdasha*—a one-piece robe made of wool or cotton basically unchanged in style since before Christ's time. Their red-and-white-checked shmags were held in place by black bands.

"Are they always dressed that way?" I asked Frank.

"No," he said. "Most of the men in Baghdad dress in pants and collared shirts. The city is more modern."

"What about the women? I don't see many on the streets. What do they wear?"

"Mostly *abayas*, those long, black full-body dresses. Some

cover their heads and faces. Some don't. Some of them wear Western clothes. I've seen a few in jeans and T-shirts."

We slowed to a crawl, hung a right, and stopped on a short entrance ramp formed by three-foot-tall concrete vehicle barriers on the left and right. The black iron gate was manned by two African guards with AK-47s and a Gurkha with an MP5. The Nepalese stepped forward, greeted "Mr. Frank" happily, and then opened the gate for our BMW. Once inside the gate, we were at the top of a sloping drive-way leading downward to a garage under the huge house. I thought, *Man, the security here is light!* There was literally no stand-off distance from the street to protect from car bombs or rifle fire. I looked up as we stepped out of the car and saw Saddam Tower looming just across the dark street. The building was 205 meters tall and mounted a multifloored glass observation deck topped with a radio antenna. I made a mental note that this would be an excellent landmark for navigating since the tower, the tallest structure in the capital, was visible from almost all of western Baghdad.

"You're home," Frank said.

The Gurkha at the gate, I later learned, was named Deal, a dark, short, and stocky man (as the high-altitude moun-taineers from the Himalayas tended to be). He offered to take care of my luggage but went away empty handed. All I had was my carry-on from the flight into BIAP and one duffel bag. Because the Flying Carpet plane did not have much lift capacity, we had shipped all of our check-in bags via taxi SUV from Amman, Jordan, across the seven-hundred-mile-wide Syrian Desert to Baghdad. At a rest stop at Trebil, the Jordanian border post with Iraq, someone stole my fully packed hanging bag. I knew it had to been an inside job—

probably an employee of the local Amman-based company that CB had carelessly hired for the trip. From then on I bought my clothes at the military PX at BIAP.

We entered through the twelve-foot-tall, heavy oak-paneled double doors with massive iron-hoop knockers and walked down the seventy-foot-long hallway paved with glazed blood-red tiles and bordered by intricate, ceiling-high wood lattice. To the left, we passed a sunken room, lined with plump sofas. Several men sat there, drinking whiskey and Heineken beer, some Middle Easterners, some obviously Americans.

"You'll be working with those guys," Frank said, "but there'll be plenty of time to meet them later."

"I want to hit the ground running," I said.

"Don't worry," Frank said. "You will. We have our daily staff meeting at 7 a.m. tomorrow. General Baumann [Custer Battles' in-country manager] believes in getting started early."

Frank showed me to my room, located just off a sitting area at the end of the hall. It was deep and wide, with a king-size bed in the back. The outside wall was lined with curtained windows. A set of French doors opened onto a steel-barred porch overlooking a series of walled gardens in the neighboring villas, all of which seemed even larger than the CB house. This was quite the neighborhood, probably the richest district in all of Iraq. My room was actually part of a suite of four rooms. The sitting parlor had a desk with stacks of paper on it, a couple of chairs, and two more doors leading on one side to a huge powder-blue bathroom with a sunken tub big enough for three. The other door beside the desk led to what I found out was the general's bedroom. They had put the new guy in the master bedroom, probably so the general could keep a close eye on him. The mattress was soft, the night cool, and I knew I would sleep soundly on this bed.

As I settled in, Brigadier General Charlie Baumann, U.S. Army, retired, poked his head in the open door. He was a small, upright man with wispy white hair crowning a balding head. He was well over sixty, and I guessed that this was the last hurrah for the Old Man—his last war. Charlie, as I later came to call him, had commanded an infantry platoon in Vietnam and had just spent several years in Africa. First he'd been in Liberia, where he had to evacuate his wife and cats when that country fell into chaos. Then he went to Sudan to head up an unarmed observation team monitoring the cease-fire between the Muslim Arab government and the Christian and animist African rebel south.

With his grandfatherly demeanor, I instantly took a liking to the man, though I was concerned that I had not received a newcomer's survival course; I had expected a little more concern for security from an old army commander. But I guess since he knew I had been a U.S. Army Infantry Officer and Ranger, he figured I could take care of myself.

I was also left somewhat in the dark about my job. My boss was my old friend Scooter, the ex-CIA man, who was elsewhere, roaming the world, and General Baumann could tell me little about my job, since it was outside his scope. That night the general simply said, "If you need anything, let me know. Oh, and keep me updated. I understand you'll be over at Secure Global Distribution at the airport."

"Yes, sir. I'm to run the company in Iraq. We're going to expand our operations, and I need to bring in some new business."

"Oh, I thought that was Frank's job."

"Frank will be working for me, focusing on ensuring that trains run on time, so to speak. He's really done an excellent job to date. I have a lot of respect for his success, but we need to get systematic in our approach in order to be sure we're ready to expand. For example, Scott wants us to get to work on setting up an airline from Dubai to BIAP."

"That would be great. You can only fly in commercial now from Amman."

"Right."

"By the way," he said with a thin smile, "enjoy your accommodations. Normally that bedroom is for the company directors. When one of them shows up, you'll most likely be moving over to the Green House. It's about three miles from here, and a little less spectacular, but you'll be comfortable there."

This brief encounter increased my uneasiness about the way Custer Battles did business. Everything seemed haphazard and ad hoc, like the weapons and body armor issues and no in-country brief. That evening I decided to take an unguided tour of the ex-Syrian ambassador's residence, which they called the Mansour House. As I walked from room to room, I was struck by its Middle Eastern opulence. I wondered if Suleiman the Magnificent had lived in greater luxury. I looked up to see a twenty-five-foot-tall dome formed by a multihued tile mosaic inlaid with gold. The dome capped an indoor fountain ten feet across. The servant quarters, which I later learned housed fifteen, were almost as well-appointed as the rooms at the Helmsley Park Lane. And the kitchen could have served a five-star Parisian restaurant.

All the American guys in khaki cargo pants, holstered pistols, and slung assault rifles intermingled cacophonously with

Arab and Filipino staff inside, and the Sudanese and Gurkha guards outside. I headed toward the front door by the fountain, along the lattice-work between the formal dining and sitting areas and the informal sunken front room off the kitchen. Just as I walked past the sunken room, in strode a tall, dark Lebanese with broad shoulders and a movie-star face.

"My name is Mohamed Darwish," he said imperiously as he stretched out his well-manicured hand. "Welcome to Baghdad; you must be Carter over at SGD."

"Yes. Scott told me that you're a director of Custer Battles Levant based out of your hometown of Beirut. He said I should always listen to you closely. You know what's going on because you worked here earlier, even under Saddam during the 1990s."

"Yes," Darwish said, "as long as you didn't say anything political you were all right. Business was good."

I immediately sensed that his character was highly questionable: the fact that he didn't mention the ongoing UN sanctions against the regime during the time when "business was good" concerned me. Also, he was also the only man I met in Iraq who outright scared me. Not as man to man, because his good looks were almost effeminate, but I got the feeling he might have you killed at the drop of a hat. He lived in the room above mine when he was in country.

The next morning, I was feeling the eight-hour time difference. As I groggily downed my coffee and eggs in the villa kitchen, I met some members of the team. Mar, the Filipino head cook who would be with me my entire time in Iraq, came up and asked where I was from. With an infectious smile, Deal—Frank told me he was the best of all the Gurkhas working for us—laughed with me about my missing luggage.

14

Mazin, the general's Iraqi driver—a bear of a man who, I learned later, was a bit of the mafia don among CB's Iraqis—came in and welcomed me to Baghdad with a wide grin, showing his large white teeth. The outward hospitality and sense of camaraderie made me feel at home, which is where I now was.

Shortly before meeting time at 0700 hours, I slipped into the dining room and took a seat unobtrusively at the twenty-place table located on a raised dais. Across the huge room I could see at least thirty Louis 14th-style chairs and sofas. I now understood why ambassadorships were fought over by contributors to presidential campaigns. You lived like royalty at state expense.

The dining room table slowly filled up with the rest of CB's managers for the staff meeting. They had to grab extra chairs. I was impressed by the size of the meeting: you had facilities and maintenance managers, the head dog handler, the BIAP security chief, the training director, the ops center manager, and several other managers from various security contracts the company had secured. This was a major operation employing over a thousand people: Iraqis of all ethnic groups and sects, Americans, Nepalese, Filipinos, Turks, Lebanese, and the odd Australian and Brit.

The meeting was so overwhelming for me that I remember little of it, other than General Baumann introducing me by simply saying, "He's going to be working with Frank over at SGD."

I mumbled something about my plans for SGD and that I really looked forward to working with everyone. Not my best performance. I was still in culture shock and knew how to keep my mouth shut. Two people at the meeting stood out, however. One was Gordon, a former major in the Australian

SAS—maybe the toughest spec ops outfit in any military—who had run around during the invasion with a frosted-white red beard in Taliban-style, doing who knows what for who knows whom. The Australian was the best Western security man I met in Iraq.

The other was Nate Hill, a strikingly athletic-looking African American and retired first sergeant with the 75th Ranger Regiment, the premier airborne light infantry unit in the world. He did something with training but hated his job. An Atlantan, he later asked me if he could transfer to SGD when our operation looked to be on the ascent. That's when I found out how badly they treated him on the security side of CB. He would later quit the company the same week I did. That week he had worn dark sunglasses in protest during Baumann's daily, in-door briefings. No one else mentioned them, but I said, "Nice shades," and he just laughed.

The Iraqis and Gurkhas were open and friendly. The Americans were all polite, but reserved. I had the feeling that, as far as they were concerned, I was on probation. Iraq was a dangerous place. Their lives might depend on how well I performed. They weren't about to give me their respect easily. I sensed I would have to earn it. And I did—one man at a time.

After the staff meeting, Frank and I were in his car on our way to the airport. As we were driving along, he gave me my first lesson in survival.

"Probably the most likely threat we face," he said, "is friendly fire. Because we are not openly identified as being with the American military, and because we are driving Iraqi vehicles, there's a good chance we can be shot up by U.S. forces. Make sure to stay out of their way. As soon as you get near them, quickly identify yourself as an American. Our side can be jumpy about pulling the trigger if for some reason they feel directly threatened and you pass by just then."

Frank knew what he was talking about, as I found out a few days later when an Iraqi police officer shot my Iraqi driver, Fadhel, in the face with an AK-47 assault rifle. I had been in country only a week. He was coming to pick me up in the morning to take me from the Green House, where I had moved to get out from under Baumann's feet, to our offices at the former Saddam airport. Although the name had changed, the airport was now the ex-dictator's home, orange jumpsuit and all. Saddam was being held in a U.S.-run prison inside the BIAP perimeter.

At the time Fadhel was shot, I was again at the daily meeting for key CB staffers. The insurgents set off a suicide car bomb next to a police recruiting station, slaughtering over fifty men standing in line. I heard the explosion and, more terrifyingly, felt the shock deep in the pit of my stomach.

Fadhel attempted to drive around the mass chaos immediately after the explosion, looking for a way to come and get me. The car bomb had exploded by the road between his house and mine. Apparently he failed to follow the orders of an Iraqi police officer (IP) to stop, but only after a U.S. Army soldier had already waved him by. The IP officer shot Fadhel in the face through the window of the company Mercedes.

You can't blame the IP for being nervous—one car bomb often begets a second for maximum effect on the follow-on first responders. I heard the news of the shooting via cell phone about fifteen minutes after the explosion. The blast—the equivalent of over one thousand pounds of TNT—had rattled the windows of our building and made me wonder what the hell I was doing here in Baghdad. When the call came through saying that an IP had shot Fadhel in the face, I thought for sure he was dead, or at least severely wounded.

As I drove to see him, I remembered that only the previous day I had asked Fadhel, "Do you want a pistol? I need to get a permit for you from the company."

Fadhel—a Shia Arab of about forty with a slack paunch so common among Iraqi males his age—said emphatically, "Yes, I need one. To protect you and car. Many *ali baba* [thieves] out there." Fadhel could string together just enough English to make himself understood.

"Well, do you have any knowledge of weapons, such as prior military experience?" Then it all spilled out.

Fadhel said quietly, "I flew, you know, planes that attack other planes?"

"Fighter jets?"

"Yes, for Iraq during war with Iran. Shot down."

"Wow, did you end up in a prisoner of war camp?"

He paused, but I could see that he wanted very much to tell me something. "No, I crash land on Iranian side of the border but in area where there were Iraqi troops. I came back angry from war, got drunk one night. Insulted Saddam. The Iraqi security forces found out and threw me in Abu Ghraib prison."

"For how long?"

"Two years."

"Did they torture you there?"

"Yes."

So getting shot in the face was just another unpleasant incident in his life. The bullet hit the windshield, then his nose, and split in two pieces, both of which lodged under his right eye. Fortunately most of the Iraqi cartridges were not of the best quality. With good ammo, he would have been dead. No real damage though. The U.S. Army doctor who operated on him was a plastic surgeon. When I saw Fadhel at his home a couple of hours after the operation, he offered me tea without a single sign of shock in his demeanor or eyes. We joked afterward that he now looked better than before.

———————

A couple of weeks after my arrival, Secure Global Distribution got a call from Kellog Brown & Root (KBR), Halliburton's logistics arm serving the U.S. military nationwide in Iraq. KBR wanted us to go pick up an airplane engine at Anaconda airbase in Balad, about fifty miles north of Baghdad, for shipment back stateside for repair. This was my chance to see what it was like out on the Iraqi road beyond the capital.

I now would learn in practice the one lesson that, for a year and a half, carried me and my business successfully forward in the war zone of Iraq: you don't want to use Americans and American-type vehicles for convoy security. It's not worth the potential cost in lives, since all you do is attract the wrong kind of attention. I learned that from Scooter, who had advised me about operating low profile when we got together just prior to my leaving for Baghdad.

Frank knew the deal as well, so we traveled in a rust-colored Mazda 626 hatchback manufactured at least ten years earlier. We were followed along by an old, beat-up Volvo Scania truck with a self-mounted crane, driven by Abdul, who, gaunt and dressed in rags, claimed he owned the Scania, though he probably "confiscated" it from the

Iraqi government when the regime fell. Our best English-speaking Iraqi employee, Bashar, drove the Mazda. I sat in the back, now carrying a Soviet-designed, Iraqi-made AK-47 and an old 1965 Belgian-made Browning 9mm pistol (the only one available, with the continuous shortage of sidearms in Baghdad). Frank sat in the front, with a German-designed, Iraqi-made Heckler & Koch MP5 that he loved, his dark hair, as always, in perfect place. Even in Iraq he was a fashion horse.

"It's stylish, isn't it?" he said to me one day, pointing to his weapon manufactured outside Baghdad. I preferred the AK for its stopping power, even though it was bulkier in the car than the MP5, a glorified pistol.

Bashar, a handsome, smooth-faced thirty-year-old Shia, noted as we departed, "We are going to drive right by my hometown—Dujail. As a matter of fact, you have noted it as a way point on the map to check in with our sat phone to the op center at BIAP."

"How about that," I said. I realized that Frank had chosen him because he was already familiar with the route. I had wondered why Bashar risked his life to work with us, but I found out with his next words.

"Yes, the town is named after the river you call the Tigris, we call it *Nahr Dijla*. My hometown sits on a bend of the Tigris and is famous for trying to kill Saddam. When I was about eight years old some of the people tried to shoot him when he came to visit. We are a Shia town located in what you Americans call the Sunni Triangle. After the failed ambush on the road leading into Dujail, Saddam's security came and took away hundreds of the people, never to be seen again, including some of my relatives. But we are proud that at least we tried to kill the tyrant."

This failed attack took place July 8, 1982, and the dictator's response was the first crime against humanity put before Saddam in Iraqi court after his downfall and capture and the charge for which he was executed December 29, 2006.

Soon we entered Anaconda, the massive base that housed several thousand, and found a long hangar lined with U.S. Army reconnaissance planes. Abdul, the truck driver, swung out the boom and lifted the one-ton General Dynamics turbo-prop onto the truck. Our miniconvoy of two vehicles then headed back to Baghdad International Airport in order to ship the engine to the United States for repair. When we left Anaconda, it was getting dark—not in our plan. But, then, everything took longer than you projected in Iraq.

We made good time on the highway, only to be held up in a traffic jam where the U.S. Army had blocked the road after a bomb exploded by a Bradley infantry fighting vehicle. This was the pattern on Iraqi highways. We sat in the traffic jam for two hours. There was no place to run. We would have to stand and fight if attacked because we could not leave the one-and-a-half-million-dollar engine behind. That was not an option. Fortunately because nighttime had arrived and our Mazda and old Iraq-worn truck attracted no untoward attention, we waited in peace, surrounded by hundreds of Iraqis deep in the Sunni Triangle. Who knows what would have happened if we, like so many other Western contractors, had been driving around in all-new vehicles, straight from their Detroit factories. Eventually, the army unblocked the road and we drove to BIAP where we were relatively safe.

Most of my time was taken up with the convoys and deliveries. In addition, I was organizing my office in preparation for a planned expansion. The Custer Battles home office in Rhode Island, however, had also told me to do an accounting of SGD's inventory as soon as possible. I dreaded the task, which would be tedious and prolonged. Little did I know that it would also lead to the loss of my job and the downfall of the company itself.

Preparing myself to tackle the job, I sat at my desk and stared at the new sickly yellow polyester carpeting that already had its first and second bullet holes from an accidental discharge (AD). I promised myself two things when I came to Iraq: one, not to get kidnapped; and two, not to have an AD. Thankfully, I achieved both goals and returned safely to my wife and two children back in Maryland. In places full of poorly trained people with weapons, ADs were more common than stubbed toes.

After staring at the bullet holes, I finally got up, walked across the hall, and entered the SGD office set up for our local Iraqis and the lone American security manager.

The back door of the staff office was new. Carpenters had recently built the partition, maybe a week before my arrival to Baghdad. On the door a printout said, "MX Program, *authorized personnel only.*" The money exchange (MX) program to trade in Saddam dinars for "Bremer" dinars was a top U.S. priority early on in Iraq. CB won the life-support project providing logistical and feeding services to the security force of three hundred Fijians guarding the money exchange. I opened the MX door and walked in.

"Hey, Derek, how're you doing?" I said. It was a casual greeting, friendly but impersonal. Derek was an air force reserve major, but not on active duty. He was serving as CB project manager for MX. He seemed startled by my sudden appearance and said in a low voice, "Hey, Carter, what can I do for you?"

"I'm just trying to gather up info on the inventory for SGD, per the home office. I need to see all documents that list SGD in some way. They tell me you've got them."

He was uneasy, nervous. He hesitated for a moment then shook his head. "Carter, I don't think you want to look at these."

I was puzzled. What was going on here? I sized him up and decided to be hard-nosed. "I've got to have them, Derek. Please. Now. I'm just doing what I was ordered to do."

Again he hesitated, then shrugged his shoulders. He walked over to the file cabinet, pulled out a couple of manila folders with papers, and handed them to me.

"Here. These will get you started. But there are more."

"I need all of them. Now."

He thumbed through the files and pulled out two or three additional folders.

"I think that's everything."

I took the folders into the outer office and copied them, then gave the originals back to Derek. He took them without a word. I suspected from his attitude that I wasn't going to like what I found.

The first name I noticed on the invoices and leases was Ihab Bashier, which immediately disturbed me because he was too junior to sign the document. Ihab was a rare straight shooter. The twenty-three-year-old Sunni Arab spoke English fluently with a British accent and was as dapper as a 1920s dandy, cravat and all. The young Baghdadi courageously and without fail worked as an SGD convoy commander for deliveries to and pickups from Ramadi and other high-threat areas, but his signature should not have been on these papers. When I later asked Ihab about the signature, he said Joe Morris, a CB director and former West Pointer who Custer fired before I showed up in Baghdad, had told him to sign it without allowing him to read it.

The more I looked, the more concerned I became. I was certain that one signature was a ghost employee. Another name I recognized heightened my suspicions: George Boustany, a Lebanese Maronite "local buyer" employee who worked for both CB and SGD. George was a big, strapping Arab, about six foot three, with jet-black curly hair and eye glasses that did not soften his thuggish look. Boustany was also directly associated with Darwish, whom I already did not trust. Earlier, I had heard rumors that Boustany was involved with stolen vehicles.

Sure enough, as I looked through the records of vehicle purchases, I noted that there were no registration papers for over a hundred vehicles bought for SGD. Money—U.S. government money—was paid out, but to whom? I knew George had bought these cars, trucks, and heavy equipment; and the more I thought about it, the more I realized there was only one logical explanation for the lack of any paperwork: somewhere along the way, the vehicles had been stolen. At the minimum, George, and by direct extension, CB, had become caught up in the lawless aftermath of the American occupation of Baghdad.

I was particularly struck by ten leases executed in the

name of SGD for extraordinary amounts of money and signed by either Boustany, who was under suspicion, a ghost employee, or a very junior employee. The leases in question were for twelve 5-ton trucks, dated September 16, 2003; three forklifts, dated October 1, 2003; six flatbed trucks, without a date; seven shuttle buses; and so forth. These were backup for CB invoices for work done on the MX Program to the Coalition Provisional Authority (CPA), the U.S.-run, UN-authorized governing agency for the occupation of Iraq.

Leasing the equipment was perfectly acceptable in the time-and-materials contract for MX. However, failure to disclose that CB owned the leasing company, SGD, and over-billing on the equipment allowed CB to double dip on profits illegally and to keep the equipment as well. The leases listed SGD as a Cayman Islands' limited-liability company with headquarters at an address in Beirut unknown to me and also to Frank, who I asked about the address right after I had had time to look closely at the documents Derek had given me. The Beirut agent for SGD was one of a very few Iraqis I had fired, a gofer who could not have had the authority or wherewithal to do any business in Lebanon. I was sickened by what I uncovered.

The issue of George Boustany's involvement with the leases, however, really set me on edge. George and Frank were running the roads together every day, and I knew Frank counted him as a friend. I liked Frank and thought I'd better let him know what I had uncovered. Earlier, when I'd brought up the stolen vehicles issue, Frank immediately went to his friend and told him we had discussed this matter. This led directly to a confrontation between me and Boustany.

The warning I had passed on to Frank came from General

Baumann and consisted of the stolen vehicles issue and that the Pentagon's Defense Criminal Investigation Service (DCIS) was making inquiries about George's relationship with Mohamed Darwish. A few days after I arrived in Iraq at the beginning of January, Darwish exported billions of new Iraqi dinars onboard a Flying Carpet plane into Lebanon without proper paperwork. He was then detained for a week in Beirut, but was never prosecuted, as far as I know. This high-profile incident precipitated the interest of DCIS and a number of articles in the *New York Times*, including one with a photo of the plane I flew into BIAP on.

A couple of hours after I'd relayed to Frank the stolen vehicles warning about George, I was inside the fence of CB's "Camp Bristol," which housed the Filipinos and Nepalese and fed all employees at BIAP—over a hundred CB people. During lunch, I looked across the chow hall and saw Frank and George talking. A few minutes later, I left. As I was on my way out and at the threshold of a prefab aluminum building, George came up on my shoulder. I heard him moving too quickly through the swinging double doors behind me and wheeled to face him. He said firmly, "Carter, what did you say to Frank?"

I was silent for a moment while my employee puffed up his chest and tried to stare me down. I replied only after he had blinked and looked away for a moment. "General Baumann told me that I should watch you because the Defense Criminal Investigation Service was raising questions as a result of your involvement with Darwish. I've also heard talk that you bought stolen vehicles. I've been trying to invoice them. I've found no registration at all for over a hundred vehicles in the MX program that belong to SGD. Where are the papers?"

George's eyes glazed slightly, and he said, "I brought all the papers from Kuwait. I never bought stolen cars."

"George, you're forgetting the local vehicles you started buying in Baghdad three months after the invasion."

"I never bought any stolen vehicles for CB." He strongly defended himself, but he no longer carried the threat of physical violence in his tone.

I thought, *In the midst of chaos and at a time when the people were taking back from a dictator's government what it had taken from them for decades, who cares if they made some money off Saddam's former property?* Citizen looting wasn't worth our trouble—or the Coalition's. However, in a company financed with U.S. government funds, this could mean trouble. Of course, I had no proof—other than the lack of standard papers of any kind for scores of SGD vehicles—only rumors that grew out of war and its chaotic aftermath.

I decided to launch my own investigation and found that several of the white CB Isuzu Troopers were traceable to an Iraqi police compound stripped bare during the looting. Also some forklifts were stolen from Iraqi Air, repainted, and leased to the MX program by CB.

Not a week after our discussion about the stolen vehicles at the chow hall, I discovered George's name on some of the leases, and I went to him immediately.

"Carter," he said, "there is no way I signed that document." He was almost pleading, afraid now that he might be charged with war profiteering, a serious crime in post-Saddam Iraq. He knew that the Defense Criminal Investigation Service (DCIS) had opened a criminal inquiry into Custer Battles because of alleged fraud with the MX program. He did not want to get caught up in that net.

"No, no, no," he kept saying when Frank and I talked with him about his signature.

"Are you ready to sign a statement to that effect," I asked him. He said he would, and he did. The signature did not match those CB and SGD had on file for George. He argued convincingly that his name had been forged, most likely by a former CB director dismissed from the company in December, a month before I arrived. The fact that a nonexistent employee had signed another of the leases suggested someone else was involved, so I came to believe that, though he was a shady character, George was telling the truth.

———

During this investigation, I was living in the Green House. It was really two buildings, twin townhouses with white marble-façades, linked by a flat roof with green-tiled eaves (hence the house name) and with a common front courtyard. It was located in a neighborhood controlled by CB's Kurdish guard force near the CPA main gate.

I had a room in the back, and the quarters were considerably less spectacular than those at the Mansour House. The room contained two narrow, single-mattress twin beds with a tiled bathroom opening into a tiny courtyard. Every now and then I would have a visitor who would sleep in the other bed. For a couple days, Ken Wortman, a retired Special Forces (SF) "A" Team sergeant from Tennessee, racked out there. Ken operated the long-range security detachment for the company, running the hundreds of miles of roads paralleling the twin high-tension power lines. These lines stretched north on a western and eastern slant respectively out of Baghdad and onto the Turkish border. The CPA had contracted with Washington Group International (WGI), a multibillion-dollar U.S. construction giant, to reconstruct the dam-generated power lines feeding the Iraqi capital. WGI subcontracted the project security to Custer Battles.

One night, I came back to my quarters from our BIAP office. There was a 12-gauge pump shotgun on the sofa in my room that I had never seen before and no Ken to be found that evening or the next. All his tactical gear and personal stuff were gone. I asked Frank what happened.

"Ken and J. P. [one of the security managers for the power lines] got mad at Baumann, chewed him out, and Baumann fired them. Put them out on the street in front of the Green House with no body armor and no guns."

"What? . . . How could the company do that to an American? And why did they get in an argument with Charlie?"

"Over money and project control. You know CB pays the lowest of any company in Iraq. They hardly ever pay the bonuses they promise either. Custer himself had guaranteed Ken the WGI project management slot and then didn't give it to him."

A few days later, two former SF sergeants and now CB security men stumbled into the Green House after getting blown up by an antitank mine while driving around in their pickup for the power lines project. Fortunately the massive explosion intended to take out a 70-ton M1 main battle tank split the Toyota in half, and the CB-rigged armor plate welded to the back of the front bench seat protected the two ex-Green Berets from the full blast force. After the two spent a couple of days in Baghdad, CB sent them back north to work. Two weeks later the U.S. Air Force had to mede-vac them both out of Iraq to Germany where they were treated for brain swelling, a delayed consequence of the explosion. CB never sent them to the hospital for a full examination before they returned to duty. The company leadership did not seem to care about people, only cash flow. The more I saw of Custer Battles, the more the weaknesses became evident.

After my interviews with Boustany, Ihab, and Frank, I took the fraudulent documents to Baumann. He seemed shocked and said so. But I heard nothing further on the subject from the in-country manager until we all would meet three weeks later in Beirut at the end of February to answer the questions I had raised with Baumann in a CB senior managers meeting with Scott Custer and his attorney.

Right after I gave the leases to Baumann in early February, however, Amy Clark arrived on the scene. She was a peppy, short, brown-haired thirty-year-old the home office had sent to do an internal audit of the MX finances. Her presence was an indication that the CB rear staff was starting to feel the heat from Baghdad. She went right to Frank to ask about SGD and MX—not to me because the money exchange operations had ended successfully before I arrived in Iraq.

Although the CPA had already told CB it was investi-gating their MX invoicing, the program could not be closed officially until the inquiry concluded. Right before I heard that Amy Clark was going to interview Frank, I gave her the fraudulent leases and invoices, saying that I found them in the MX files and thought she might be interested. She said this was the first time she had seen them.

Frank's desk was right across from mine as Amy asked him, "Do you know anything about this truck? For example, did you know that CB leased it to the U.S. government for $15,000 a month?"

"Yes, that truck is probably not worth $15,000 cash. I have a picture of it."

He rummaged around in his desk and produced a photo of a ratty, run-down 5-ton truck at least a decade old. She was visibly shaken.

"Did you draw up any invoices for SGD to CB for the MX program?"

"No, but one day at the Mansour House I saw Scott Custer holding the two invoices you have there. I believe they were blank at that time, with only the header filled out with the SGD name."

She was a company troubleshooter, sent there to fix what was broken and bury what couldn't be fixed. But she must have concluded fixing the situation was impossible, because a few days later Amy was gone. She had left for "a quick vacation to Amman, Jordan." She didn't come back to Baghdad until a year later, running a Romanian-registered front company named Danubia Global Incorporated that had taken over some of CB's Iraq contracts.

A few weeks later, Baumann, Pete Miskovitch, Mohamed Darwish, Custer, and I sat around a long mahogany table in Beirut and listened to CB's attorney, a tall, girl-next-door-pretty brunette named Anne Marie from Rhode Island. She told us, the key CB managers in Iraq, that Scott Custer sitting next to her was "not going to jail." Her implication—the whole operation had been clean.

I looked over at General Baumann sitting across the table.

He cleared his throat. "I believe from seeing the MX leases and invoices in question that there is evidence of fraud."

The room was silent. Custer—his sweaty face twitching from the strain—said nothing, probably because his lawyer had warned him to keep quiet. She, too, was silent in the wake of the general's blunt accusation.

I kicked Pete Miskovich under the table. Miskovich, a muscular, dark-haired construction investigator, had taken Major Derek's spot at the MX program. Derek, the air force officer who had provided me the original evidence back at BIAP, had fled the company and secretly turned state's witness against CB. Pete was a former Miami, Florida, police detective who used to enjoy "lemonading" people—so known because of the sour look on handcuffed suspects when Pete abruptly stopped, slamming their faces into the steel mesh between the rear seat and the officer driving. He was now closing out the internal MX program investigation mandated by CB's attorneys as a sort of prophylactic against future fraud charges.

Pete looked directly at Custer at the other end of the conference table and said, "My investigation concludes the same; there is fraud in the MX program."

Custer glared at me from the other end of the table, and I knew then that I had to submit my two-weeks' notice as soon as we returned to Baghdad from Beirut. I had been the whistle blower, the guy who wouldn't shut up, who told too many people about the waste, fraud, and abuse. The investigation had widened, and the company was making headlines worldwide.

The international press was covering the story extensively since it put the United States, its "military-industrialist complex," and its combatant contractors in the worst possible light. Because it savaged America and Americans, I was angry with the company ownership that had created this mission-weakening furor. I was further enraged in Beirut when I saw Scott Custer denying the clear-cut evidence of his greed and dishonesty.

Money in huge blocks of cash—hundred-dollar bills in shrink-wrapped hundred-thousand-dollar bundles labeled with U.S. Treasury strip codes—can distort a venal man's perspective. Hundreds of millions of dollars flowed into the streets of Iraq out of the Coalition Provisional Authority. Most of this cash was captured Saddam money now administered by the U.S. government-operated CPA. Over $50 million of it went to CB, and now the boys couldn't account for its flow through the organization. Much of their illicit profits—gained through leasing schemes and other such illegal actions, including forgery—they deposited offshore, in Beirut, the Cayman Islands, and then, apparently, Romania.

After the meeting, I was worried that those investigating the scam might airbrush Custer Battles' major fraud and allow Scott Custer to slip through the net. I was particularly concerned about Pete Miskovich's report. On several occasions, Miskovich had avoided taking copies of the fraudulent invoices I had offered him. He looked at the documents and listened to me describe them, but he would not take possession of the incriminating evidence. Back in Baghdad before the meeting in Beirut, he had even said his report was going "to stay on the surface." That sounded like a cop-out to me.

In the taxi back to the hotel from Beirut's best Japanese restaurant, I brooded about Miskovich's report. He had not gone to dinner but had stayed back to complete his paperwork and get to sleep early. Finally I decided to confront him. I went into the Hotel Bristol, found his room on the sixth floor, and banged on his door.

No answer.

"Pete, Pete, wake up!"

Finally, Miskovich opened the door, groggy from sleep. "Jesus, Carter. What happened?"

"Man, you've got to nail Scott Custer. I am going to kick your ass if you don't. Custer and Battles need to go down. These bastards are war profiteers. You know it. I showed you the documents. You acknowledged the fraud! A war profiteer is akin to a traitor in my book. This scum doesn't care about the mission, about the Iraqis, or even about the soldiers dying out there. You have to nail them in your report."

He nodded.

"OK," he said. "Now let me get some sleep."

The Miskovich internal company report on CB's involvement in the MX Program (dated February 28, 2004) concluded:

> [A] broader issue of criminal intent has become evident. In just the ten lease agreements purported to be signed by George Boustany and Ihab Bashier accounts for approximately $2,000,000.00 in alledged (sic) services provided by and through Secure Global Distrubition (sic) and Mideast Leasing Corporation. The documents are prima facie evidence of a course of conduct consistent with criminal activity and intent.

As soon as I received the report, I forwarded it and the copies of the fraudulent leases and invoices, through an intermediary, to the U.S. military's Defense Criminal Investigation

Service. The assistant U.S. attorney for the Eastern District of Virginia responsible for the CB matter, an FBI agent, and the lead investigator from DCIS interviewed me in December 2004. Subsequent to my interview DCIS banned CB and its principals from all government contracting. This ban excluded them, in theory, from doing work in Iraq, as almost all business there required U.S. government funding and approval somewhere down the line.

My last days at CB were spent collaborating with other employees who were preparing to jump ship. Almost half the management staff left in March and formed at least four new companies in Baghdad. Most of the other half thought hard about leaving as well.

I concluded that, having learned how contractor combatants operated, I wasn't about to pack up my tent and silently steal away. There was honest money to be made here, as well as an opportunity to serve the interests of my country. I had already taken advantage of my time in the Soviet Union to start an international business where I had run my own vodka import company for over ten years beginning in 1991. I was an entrepreneur staring at a rare opportunity. But I had to move quickly.

TWO

Business in Baghdad

I quickly discovered that I wasn't the only one bailing out of Custer Battles, nor was I alone in my desire to stay in Iraq, carry out the mission, and maybe make some serious money after the company's imminent collapse. Several managers, past and present, had the same idea. They agreed that Scott Custer and Mike Battles were clearly guilty of indictable offenses. In fact, a jury found the company guilty of civil fraud; and while U.S. District Judge T. S. Ellis III threw the conviction out citing a legal technicality, he also said that ample evidence existed to demonstrate that the company had submitted "false and fraudulently inflated invoices" (see Renae Merle, *Washington Post*, "Verdict Against Iraq Contractor Overturned," August 19, 2006).

Soon they would no longer be allowed to do business in Iraq. Or so we reasoned. All their contracts would be shut down, and we would all be out of work and tarnished by association. Even before I gave notice, several of us had talked about setting up new companies so that we could stay on in Baghdad.

The most vocal in this group was Pete Baldwin, who had been CB country manager before I arrived in Iraq. When the company brought in General Baumann, Pete had been demoted and was merely running the Facilities and Maintenance Department. Forty-four years old, bespectacled, and balding with a soft paunch, he was a former construction executive from Jacksonville, Florida. He lived across the patio from me at the Green House with his Filipino wife. In casual conversation, we discovered that he used to date the older sister of my fraternity brother at the University of the South, so the two of us were connected.

Baldwin, who had seen me out hustling new business for Custer Battles, told me one day just prior to the Beirut meeting, "This company is going under. I've told Custer to come clean, but I don't think he'll do it. Here, look at these."

He showed me a series of e-mails he'd sent to both Custer and Battles. The messages dated from late 2003 to the previous week and warned about fraud in the MX program.

"I can't go on like this," he said. "Particularly since Scott and Mike don't give a damn about their employees. So I'm forming a new company with an Iraqi named Namir Almufti. He owns the construction company that built Camp Bristol and the MX camp at BIAP. He'll put up the money. He's a millionaire, and he believes in me."

I was impressed and told him so.

"You know, there aren't many guys here who understand sales the way you do," he said. "Most everybody in Iraq is a security man, a knuckle dragger. I'm betting you'll leave Custer Battles in the near future. If you do, I'd like you to join me. Namir's funding will ensure that we have body armor, weapons, and vehicles. I am going out to look at our houses next week. We'll get to work on insurance for you and everyone else immediately."

That last bit of information worried me. To Americans in Iraq, insurance was more important than food, clothing, and shelter. In the United States, people preferred not to walk down Main Street without at least health coverage and a $250,000 term-life policy, but millions did it. In Baghdad, insurance was like breathing. I already knew enough about death and maiming to understand the heightened risk in this part of the world. If I joined Pete's company, I'd be looking at a window of no insurance, a scary thought to a man with a wife and two kids.

I knew the most readily available insurance came with a U.S. government contract, which mandated Defense Base Act insurance for all DoD contractors working outside the United States. But first you had to have a Pentagon contract, which Pete's company could not obtain at the beginning. They would have to go to the marketplace for the coverage—a costly proposition. (The company ended up paying about $1 million a year premium in 2005 for the sixty non-Iraqi employees who weren't covered by DoD contracts: Americans, Filipinos, Ukrainians, Nepalese, Fijians, Lebanese, and so forth.)

After working for Custer Battles only two months starting at the beginning of January 2004, I put in my two-weeks' notice the day I returned from the CB Beirut meeting. I faced three choices: one, to bag Iraq and go home to my family; two, to go to work for Pete Baldwin with no insurance; or, three, to take advantage of another opportunity offered me—the Afghanistan country manager for a company called EGL Logistics. Frank, who left CB the same week I did, was to take over EGL ops in Iraq and Afghanistan. When he offered me the job, I told him I was interested.

At first glance, number one was the most enticing—to head back to my wife and children in the United States and forget about Custer Battles and all the sheikhs and imams and suicide bombers in the Middle East. However, I never seriously considered this alternative. I wasn't about to admit defeat, particularly with the U.S. mission in Iraq unfulfilled and the potential for business opportunities so apparent.

My first choice was working with Pete—until we sat down and had a serious talk. As he outlined the company structure, I realized that all the top positions were already filled by an Old Boys network—the guys who had come to Iraq with Pete in 2003. As I understood the job he offered, I would be the business development officer, maybe little more than a door-to-door salesman, drumming up clients for the new company, which was to be called American-Iraqi Solutions Group (AISG).

"What about ownership?" I asked. "Will I get a piece of the pie?"

He frowned.

"That's a tough one," he said. "We've already carved up the pie. If you got ownership, all the other Americans who didn't get shares would want them also. That would be a hard sell."

I shrugged my shoulders.

"It'll be a hard sell getting me aboard without insurance or a share in the company."

While we shook hands and agreed to talk further, I was

already turning my attention to EGL. The multibillion-dollar outfit served as the air-freight carrier for KBR in Iraq and Afghanistan, where they had no permanent in-country American manager. The company had approved the offer Frank had made. I was set to go to Afghanistan. The money was good; and I would be my own man, with a group that offered a long-term employment perspective—and a first-rate insurance package.

I called my wife, Tanya, to talk about the move.

I said, "This job in Afghanistan has three offices: one near Kabul, one in Kandahar, and one in Qarshi, Uzbekistan. You and the goobers [our two kids] could move to Qarshi, and we could see each other every month, or maybe more."

Tanya, a Russian from Kiev, knew all about that part of the world, which had been part of the now defunct Soviet Union.

"Qarshi!" she said. "That place is a hell hole in the middle of nowhere! Uzbekistan is a poor country. They *hate* Russians in Uzbekistan! What would we do every day?"

Then she said in a quieter voice, "Do what you think is best and we'll follow, but Qarshi is not a great idea."

Tanya was all set to go abroad. She loved to travel. She was finishing her second Ph.D. in theoretical mathematics (her first doctorate is in chaos theory, and the second, "weird spaces") on scholarship at the District of Columbia's George Washington University. Tanya was already setting up with her advisor how to finish her dynamical systems dissertation via the Internet—having already finished her class work. So moving halfway around the world posed no threat to the completion of her doctorate. Qarshi was bad for the reasons she said, and because it was a decaying former

Soviet border-zone town, with heavy metal in the water and cholera in the hospitals.

So much for EGL. Telling myself that Baghdad was the place to be—the center of the action for world transformation—I decided to go with AISG. After some bare-knuckle bargaining, I negotiated a contract with a big upside if I could deliver new clients—and shares of the company over time. I'd always had the soul of an entrepreneur, having started my own vodka import company several years earlier. But this was the ultimate business challenge: another start-up company, this time in a war zone that was getting more dangerous by the day.

The business plan for AISG called for the company to undertake construction work for the Department of Defense in Iraq. With Namir's established Iraqi general contracting company with thousands of skilled employees as our prime subcontractor, and Pete's experience in construction, we believed that the company could win contracts with the big U.S. firms that the Pentagon had tasked with the multibillion-dollar challenge of reconstructing Iraq. My job would be to get those contracts. The company HQ would be in a cluster of houses in downtown Baghdad—the center of the reconstruction mission, but with the downside, of course, that I couldn't bring my family along for the ride. We all—my wife and children included—shared in the struggle. I wondered almost every day if the sacrifice was worth it. The separation by far was my greatest stressor. But the job turned out to be about the smartest move I ever made.

However, I didn't think so during those first hectic weeks. It's been said that every successful business enterprise begins in failure. That proposition may not be universally true, but it certainly describes my beginnings with AISG. My first attempts to solicit clients were at best frustrating and at worst life-threatening. With each failure, however, I learned a lesson, and I tried not to make the same mistake twice. I was lucky. Some contractor combatants made the same mistake once and went home in body bags.

I remember particularly one hot afternoon in front of the Green Zone's (CPA's base in Baghdad) Checkpoint 12, the exit from the ever-more dangerous Airport Road. It was on the same day the U.S.-run Coalition Provisional Authority surrendered sovereignty to the interim Iraqi government. I was out inspecting a piece of property, which I had obtained for AISG from the CPA in its waning days, with Sasha, a Ukrainian Spetsnaz built like Arnold Schwarzenegger I had brought to Iraq to work VIP security contracts. A former captain of the bodyguard of the president of Ukraine, Sasha could shoot a cigarette out of your hand with a pistol at twenty-five meters. That day I was driving my quite-common, gray, four-door BMW sedan with tinted windows. Sasha was crouched in the back for all-around security. We intended to use the land as a storage area for a USAID security contract I had won a month earlier. Immediately adjacent to the Green Zone, the acre-size plot was located just outside Checkpoint 12.

Normally I traveled around Baghdad alone, but Sasha was with me because we needed to inspect the property, and I wanted security while taking pictures and marking the boundaries with GPS. The day was a sizzler, well over 120 degrees, without a cloud in the sky. It was so hot that I blistered my hand when I momentarily leaned against a cast-iron pipe. That was to be the least of my worries.

We had exited our property in front of what later turned out to be a diplomatic convoy of five SUVs returning from BIAP. The State Department contract security men from MVM, Inc., of Alexandria, Virginia—there to protect the convoy—saw our BMW turn onto the road ahead and figured we were about to ambush them.

Suddenly, in the lead vehicle a man's head and torso emerged from the window of the passenger side. He was pointing a weapon at us.

Sasha screamed, "*Aftomat! Aftomat!* [assault rifle]."

With a quick glance in the rearview mirror, I saw an AK-47 pointed straight at the back of my head. *Crack!* The back window fell away like a curtain and a 7.62mm bullet went flying by, missing Sasha in the back seat and then my head by mere inches.

They're shooting at us! my brain told me, something my gut already knew.

I quickly shoved my 45 Colt pistol toward the window, steering with my left hand, looking for a windshield, a tire, a human target.

Sasha likewise swung into action. He rested his left elbow on the car's backseat shelf, steadily aimed his AK out the blasted-open rear window and *crack, crack, crack . . . crack, crack, crack . . .* he methodically hammered holes through the front windshield above the steering wheel of the lead SUV. Sasha, a former Soviet sniper, placed over twenty bullets in an eighteen-inch shot-group while we weaved along Airport Road at eighty miles an hour.

At that moment, we were in a one-vehicle-wide alley created by fourteen-foot-high concrete blast walls leading up to a U.S. Army checkpoint. Realizing that I couldn't shoot from

44

that angle, I decided to focus on driving. As Sasha continued to hammer away, I dropped my pistol and grabbed the steering wheel with both hands and swerved through the S-turn chicanes like we were on a crazy carnival ride.

Having "auditory exclusion"—quite common in firefights—neither Sasha nor I heard the multiple bullets whipping by our car. I had instinctively hewed the BMW toward the inside of the blast walls. Suddenly, it was over! Sasha's pinpoint shooting had disabled the lead vehicle, which had crashed into a blast wall. The other attacking vehicles were left behind, jockeying to get around the wrecked SUV, unable to get an angle on us.

In a strange, sped-up, brain-created bubble of silence, I looked back at Sasha who had now stopped shooting and asked him in Russian, "Are you OK?" We both started to shout and laugh, congratulating ourselves on surviving the ambush. In combat, the brain, if trained in a pliable way, will speed up the thought processes, thereby slowing down all perceptible action. This process helps you think more clearly during combat.

Little did we know that two cars had maneuvered around the wreck and were closing on our tail. I looked ahead and saw a U.S. Army M-1 tank, the bunker, and the guard tower protecting the entrance into the fortified Green Zone. They were coming up very fast. Though I had slowed down, we were still going over sixty miles an hour, so I started to step on the brake.

Then a sudden fear gripped me. We were now in danger of being shot by friendly forces at the checkpoint. At that moment, I heard a high-pitched *zing*, then realized that a 7.62mm rifle round had flown right by my ear, less than two inches away. A hole appeared in the windshield. I stomped on the accelerator of the BMW once again. (We later found out that over sixty bullets missed our vehicle for the two shots that hit us.)

As the sports sedan lunged forward with increased speed, I ducked down, thinking, *Better the devil we know than the one we don't.* I grabbed my DoD badge hanging around my neck and stuck it out the window and began to shout, "*Amerikanets! Amerikanets!*" in Russian, as if I were still talking to Sasha!

We proceeded to roll at highway speed through a high-security military checkpoint authorized to use lethal-force to ensure identification, inspection, and search. When I looked up again, we flew by a U.S. soldier crouched down in the checkpoint bunker waving us on as the car hurtled over and past the mandatory stop line. Immediately ahead, the commander of the M-1 tank was unlimbering his turret-mounted .50 caliber heavy machine gun, preparing to engage a target.

Little did I realize at the time that the army was shooting up the following vehicles that had attacked us, after noting numerous incoming rounds that missed our vehicle and hit the soldiers' positions at the checkpoint. Thankfully the GIs recognized us because I had used this entrance into the Green Zone day after day. It certainly paid off, being friendly to these brave frontline soldiers who never knew if the next vehicle to approach would be carrying a mass-casualty car bomb.

The lesson I learned from this incident: Don't just guard against your enemies. Watch out for your friends as well. Everyone in Iraq was jumpy and quick on the trigger. Even if they were sorry afterward, when they shot you, you would still be just as dead.

————————

We lived in a district of Baghdad where doctors and other professionals made their homes in large, sand-colored stucco houses with flat roofs, and in a part of what the army calls "the Red Zone." The Red Zone was actually almost all of Iraq, because it was any place not protected full-time by the U.S. military. The vast majority of Westerners, however, lived in the Green Zone (the five-square-mile area around the U.S. occupation headquarters), or various fortified places nationwide where U.S. or other Coalition forces stood guard twenty-four hours a day. As a result of our location out in the city, there was nothing really between us and the insurgents but our walls and internal security assets, so we called our three-mansion compound surrounded by fourteen-foot blast barriers "Fort Apache." We were definitely located in enemy territory just like the original Fort Apache of the Indian wars in the American West. The largest mansion in the compound was a former interior minister's residence. This was a huge home of about fifteen thousand square feet showcasing a central atrium with a thirty-foot ceiling. The atrium became our operations center.

Our company was in the Red Zone primarily because movements were not controlled by army checkpoints. The U.S. military exhibited a tendency to close and open at will the entrance to and from the Green Zone, thus constantly interfering with business travel. Yet we were all still prisoners to a certain extent, trapped in vehicles riding from one safe place to another. We employed several Baghdadi drivers, translators, gardeners, and mechanics. With diverse ethnic and religious backgrounds, they served as our eyes and ears on the city's happenings and moods.

All of our Iraqi coworkers risked their lives and those of their families in order to work with us, the so-called invading crusaders. Therefore we were not completely isolated from Iraq, unlike most Western civilians here. We hardly had the opportunity, however, to see the vast historical heritage of ancient Mesopotamia or to get out among the people, other than on our secure construction sites where we worked with hundreds of locals.

The question that continually nagged at me as we launched our start-up company in Baghdad was this: how could we survive financially in the harshest business environment possible where all the funding was controlled by the high-barrier-to-entry bureaucracy of the U.S. government? A few years earlier, when I was building my vodka business, I had had as much trouble with U.S. bureaucrats as I did with the KGB.

Fortunately I found a partial answer when AISG received help with its financing from Namir Almufti. He had owned a construction company and had done business with Custer Battles, but now wanted to work with us because he believed we were better motivated and more ethical than CB. Namir understood how CB had operated because, as he told us, the company had seized numerous opportunities to cheat his construction company.

Simply by supplying the government with evidence of corruption, I and the rest of AISG had gained a reputation for integrity. In the chaos of postwar Baghdad—where the playing field was full of con men and double dealers (some of them Americans)—our actions set us apart. All we had to do to get ahead was to live up to our reputation as straight shooters.

Namir was my first Iraqi friend. A man of imposing dignity, he came from a prominent Sunni family and owned a successful construction company. He was short and stout with a prominent Roman nose underscored by a thick, bristly, salt-and-pepper moustache that was *de rigueur* for all Iraqi men. I always suspected that the nose had entered Namir's bloodline a couple of millennia ago, in Caesar's time.

He was a serious man, unconcerned with the minutiae of life, incapable of small talk. He and I would sit around the sixteen-place mahogany dining table at our main house in Baghdad and discuss only subjects of great import. I always felt driven to plumb the depths of this man at every opportunity, as if I had foreknowledge that our time together would be brief.

One night, sitting at the dinner table with other members of AISG, we got into a discussion of Iraqi politics. I knew a little about his personal history; and since I respected him more than anyone I had met in the country, I was interested in his views on just about everything.

He opened the door by explaining to me why he and other Iraqis supported American intervention: "America represents the future," he said, "the future of the world. Iraq must move into that future, and who better to help her than America?"

This remark gave me an opening. I said, "Namir, I heard today that a member of your family was mayor of Baghdad."

"Yes," he answered with a pained expression. "My first

cousin was mayor of Baghdad. Saddam executed him in the late 1980s when he got too popular."

"Is that why you never joined the Baath Party?"

I wanted to understand how the Sunni had reached such a high level of influence in Iraq without belonging to the monolithic party that had ruled the nation since 1963 and from whose ranks Saddam had emerged. I had spent time in another totalitarian state, the Soviet Union, where no important leadership position in the country could be achieved without membership in the Communist Party. So had it been different here?

"Yes, I despised them for what they did to my cousin," he said in answer to my question. "But it was only partly because of that. In addition, the more I saw of the brutality and corruption of the regime, the more I wanted to stay apart from it. This is why I never rose to be number one at Al Fao [the state-owned military construction firm]. They only allowed me to be a deputy director."

"What do you see for the future in Iraq?" I asked.

"I think you Americans are pushing this democracy process too hard. The Iraqi people are not ready for this. They need a strong man to control them. America should install a strong man to rule and to get us on our feet again economically."

"Who will control that man, if he goes crazy with power like Saddam?" I asked. "This is the reason for democracy. You must have the rule of law, where no man is above it."

The rest of our people at the dinner table were suddenly silent, taken aback by my challenge to the man who was bankrolling our operation. They underestimated him. He obviously appreciated the discussion since he was trying to come to grips with tremendous changes in Iraq, as were all of us—American as well as Iraqi.

He leaned forward. "But what about the violence? The Iraqis need to be better educated before they are ready for democracy. In Baghdad and other major cities, yes. But once you get out into the countryside, you find too much ignorance, superstition."

"First of all," I said, "the violence must be overcome through counterforce. Almost all mature democracies emerged from some type of war. Thomas Jefferson wrote, 'The tree of liberty must be watered from time to time with the blood of patriots.' Those that now fall in battle against the forces of tyranny don't die in vain."

Namir, who had a tremendously mobile face, smiled broadly, a smile not of agreement but of understanding. He clearly found the debate of interest.

"Furthermore," I said, "India, a country at a much lower state of development than Iraq with a much more complicated ethnic make-up, has maintained a successful democracy for several decades. Iraq, with its tremendous middle class, educational system, and potential wealth, can and will have democracy, if we stand together."

"*Na'am*, yes," said the great man quietly, as we all got up to leave the table.

The same reputation for honesty that helped us with Namir also helped us gain our first big client, one who would not work with Custer Battles because of the fraud issues that were already public knowledge. However, knowing that we had turned our backs on CB, the Louisiana-based construction company wanted to work with us. That client was a prime subcontractor to Parsons, one of the seven "super prime" contractors in Iraq. Each super prime had won control over major reconstruction funds worth several hundreds of millions of dollars. We just wanted to be a subcontractor. We had never dreamed we could be a prime to the U.S. government in Iraq. The sectors where Parsons had won access included Oil Infrastructure, Military Base Reconstruction (Taji), Public Works & Water, Buildings, Education & Health, and Security & Justice. The total amount available in these sectors for Parsons was over $1.8 billion. The other super primes were KBR, Bechtel, Fluor, Perini, Washington International, and Contrack International (a supposedly Washington DC-based outfit, but actually an Egyptian-owned company. The Egyptians contracted to do $325 million in roadwork, but they eventually packed up and fled, failing to complete the work because they feared the insurgents.)

The government also awarded contracts to various companies as part of the $18 billion in congressional supplemental funds for Iraq reconstruction. There was even an award of $70 million for improving Iraqi seaports to an Alaskan Indian-owned corporation, the ultimate minority set-aside.

The vast majority of Parsons' work in Iraq was construction; and with Namir's company on board, we felt confident we could bring the Iraqis to the table to do anything required. This became our theme: "We are over 95 percent Iraqi, and that should be the underlying drive of reconstruction—to employ Iraqis to rebuild Iraq." We quickly rounded up engineers and architects who had built dams and skyscrapers, as well as skilled craftsmen of all types: plumbers, surveyors, electricians, carpenters, and laborers who could do any job on a construction site. We also hired a staff of Filipino engineers to help bring the Iraqis up to U.S. standards, a competence the Philippines educational system imparted to all its certified professional engineers.

As a first project for Parsons, we helped build a camp, a glorified trailer park in the Green Zone, for Parsons personnel—a crusty bunch of construction types who, to the man, were leery of heading to any job sites outside the fortified area. Then came the first real opportunity for major construction: a superstructure rebuild for the mining and industry headquarters in eastern Baghdad.

The site lay on the edge of Sadr City—the Shia slum and breeding ground for the anti-American Mahdi army of Moqtada al Sadr. He was the son of an ayatollah executed by Saddam, and for whom the slum was named. As we began the job, the Mahdi army was about to launch the first of its two uprisings against the "Occupation"—a factor that complicated our first major project opportunity.

Baghdad was heating up, as illustrated by the following excerpts from an April 14, 2004, intelligence report issued by the CPA to DoD contractors:

Three Russians and five Ukrainians were kidnapped 12 April in Baghdad. An Iraqi guard was also captured along with the employees. The incident took place at 1900 hours while the men were relaxing in the garden of the house they rented in the Dora neighborhood of Baghdad. 15-20 people with guns and wearing masks forced them onto a bus the kidnappers had arrived in. One hostage who complained about being an elderly person and having four children was released that day.

Media sources have indicated that the remainder was released earlier today.

Yesterday, 13 April twenty students from Mustensyria University in Baghdad went to a nearby CF [coalition forces] base complaining that an armed militia were coming onto the campus and causing problems. The ICDC [Iraqi civil defense corps] responded and searched several buildings and recovered 9 AK assault rifles and 1 pistol as well as pro Sadr literature.

U-S troops arrested a representative of Moqtada al-Sadr. The arrest came as the aide to the cleric attended a meeting of tribal leaders at a Baghdad hotel today. Hazen al-Aaraji was detained as he entered the conference hall at the Palestine Hotel. His bodyguards tried to prevent the arrest, but stepped aside when confronted by the soldiers. Troops took him to the neighboring Sheraton Hotel before he was taken away.

Reports continue to indicate that leaflets and pamphlets threatening Iraqis co-operating with the coalition authorities are being circulated in Baghdad. Leaflets and other propaganda have been reported in Adhamiya, Sadr City, Mahala, Rasheed and Mansour.

A group called the National Islamic Resistance 20th Revolutionary Group has declared the BIAP road a war zone and all vehicles moving on it are legitimate targets. This has been evident for some time now. It is the first time I have heard mention of this group.

Other Areas

Four Italians working as private security guards for a U.S. company in Iraq were reported missing Tuesday, with reports they were kidnapped by insurgents. The Italian foreign ministry said its civilians worked for the U.S.-based DTS Security Company and were first reported missing Monday. The Italian news agency AGI and other reports said the four were taken hostage in Fallujah, 35 miles west of Baghdad.

It has been widely reported in the press that Moqtada al-Sadr has pulled his forces back in An Najaf due to the conceived impression of imminent attack by a build up of U.S. forces to the north of the city. The U.S. have sent down a column of 2,500 U.S. troops backed by tanks and heavy artillery in an 80 vehicle convoy which has already been attacked by a roadside IED [improvised explosive device] and small arms fire on Monday night, north of An Najaf.

U.N. Secretary-General Kofi Annan is cautious about a return of the United Nations to Iraq, saying violence in the country is a major constraint in the foreseeable future. Annan told reporters at U.N. headquarters that even the small team now in the country, led by top adviser Lakhdar Brahimi, has been hampered in helping form an interim government and eventual elections.

Locals report that Moqtada has issued a fatwa saying that all Iraqi employees of coalition forces will be killed. Another report says that CPA has ordered all local employees to go home.

I was certain we could handle the Parsons job and said so. However, the focus on Moqtada and his Mahdi army began to worry me as we set out to do a site survey of a ten-story superstructure overlooking Sadr City. A Japanese construction management firm had built the Minerals and

Industry building in the late 1980s. The steel structure held excellent integrity even after looters had burned it all the way to the girders during the chaos after the regime fell.

This was to be a multimillion-dollar job—a real break-through for us. At this early stage of our growth, we had begun to feel that we could do anything—take on jobs that others were afraid to tackle, fight off the insurgency with our Kurds and other imported shooters, and build whatever needed building. We were like the legendary Seabees of World War II: we could build and we could fight.

However, our situation was hardly comparable. The Seabees had planes, tanks, and off-shore artillery to support them. We had nothing more than hand weapons and bags full of grenades. Our enemies were trained in combat and, in many cases, better armed. The M&I building would teach us a lesson we would never forget.

Our project manager (PM), Robert, was a Parsons sub-contractor willing to take risks. He claimed to have been a British spy who—after crossing from Oman sometime during 1970s counterinsurgency operations—had killed a border guard in Yemen with a knife. Iraq attracted all kinds—many of them little more than big talkers with yellow stripes down their backs—but this guy was the real thing, willing to put his life on the line by showing up at potentially dangerous job locations. He came with us to assess the damage done to the M&I building.

As we drove us to the site, I could see no U.S. Army types along the way. We were on our own: just me, a retired Special Forces sergeant (Ken Wortman, formerly of CB, and now our construction manager and seriously out of his depth because of a lack of construction experience), the ex-spy project manager, and Brahim, our Iraqi driver and part-time AISG arms procurer. The Sadr City Shia would fearlessly obtain for us AK-47s, PK medium machine guns, rocket-propelled grenades (RPGs), and WWII U.S. Army–issue .45s—the weaponry necessary to arm ourselves and our guard force for operations in the Iraq war zone.

Even though I was not yet in the operational chain of command, I controlled the client who controlled the contract, which required security support from us. We pulled into a side road, passed through a partially ripped-out fence, and stopped in an abandoned parking lot next to M&I. I said to Brahim, "Stay with the car, *rejaan*, *Ahooya*, please my brother."

"*Zen*, good, Mr. Carter, I drive well here, yes?" He pulled out the AK he had stashed beside him in the front seat and took up position by the white and orange 1990 Chevrolet Caprice, an Iraqi taxi we often used to move around town.

"Yes, thank you, Brahim."

That pleased him, but I wanted him to know that I regarded him as something more than a chauffeur.

"Maybe I drive next time, OK?"

Brahim laughed. "Yes, like you did at BIAP. You strong man, strong man!" he stated emphatically, remembering when he followed me back to BIAP to turn in my vehicle to CB for the last time.

We had been cruising along at about seventy miles an hour, Brahim following me in my SUV down the fast lane of the six-lane Terminal Road. We were already inside the U.S. Army-secured perimeter of Baghdad International Airport—probably the safest place in Iraq for Westerners—when suddenly, without looking back, the driver of a huge

40-ton army ammo carrier in the middle lane had abruptly swerved in front of me, crossing the fast lane, completely cutting me off. In an instant, I had to stomp on the accelerator and turn the car into the median, missing the edge of a fifteen-foot-deep ditch by an inch. Suddenly I was airborne at eighty-plus miles an hour.

"You quick," Brahim said, making a sharp turning motion with both his hands. "I thought you were dead. I close my eyes. When I open them up and the truck moves by, I see you . . . far ahead. *Alhamdullilah*! [Thanks be to God]."

The incident became an adventure we shared, a bond between us. He would often bring it up, just to remind me that he had been there and was working by my side at a time of great danger. At that moment, standing in the shadow of the M&I building, we both understood that we were friends.

Brahim stayed at the car and watched our backs and our avenue of escape as we entered the gutted structure. Everyone had on body armor and weapons, but we had no additional support as we climbed the stairs to the top of the building, just a steel skeleton, exposed from all sides since there were no walls.

We ascended floor after floor through the debris-clogged stairwells. The fifty-five-year-old, ex-spy Robert began to feel the exertion in the rising midday heat. This was a young man's game. I took his body armor and placed it over mine.

From one side we could see out across the city to the west and the comforting Green Zone, but from the other three sides we saw only the teeming, ramshackle Shia slum of two million or more souls, a large portion of them angry enough to blow us away.

As I looked out at this vast and menacing wasteland, I felt

like Custer—not Scott but George Armstrong at Little Big Horn—surrounded by murderous hostiles. Would the Mahdi army—positioned on three sides—allow us to reconstruct this important landmark? In my heart I wanted this badly. I knew we had to try. The job could be a big contract. As I stood there, I could almost feel Sadr City slipping around us on either side, closing in for the kill. I was suddenly aware that even at this height we could be picked off by a lone sniper.

After we assessed the problem, we descended the concrete stairs and walked back to the car in silence. Nobody put into words what we were all thinking. The building could be restored, but anyone who tried it now could be inviting disaster. The construction business was not going to be a piece of cake. That was a lesson I learned that day.

Several weeks after our site visit—and after the Sadrist uprising had begun—rockets hit while crews were doing preliminary work on the M&I building for our client, who had to admit there was no way anyone could reconstruct that building until Sadr City was under control. That finally happened a year later, and some other subcontractor got the job. The project value: $60 million.

The word came down from Ken one morning in late April that Fluor Corporation, one of the largest publicly traded construction companies in the world, needed some minor construction work done just north of Baghdad. The site was Taji, and Fluor officials generously offered to let us do a site survey and bid on the project. During lunch that day, as usual Namir showed up and asked what was happening. I figured he would turn up his nose at a job that wouldn't feed a good-sized dog.

"Namir," I said, "Fluor wants us to bid on constructing a brick generator building. It's a very small job; but if we can get in with Fluor, it will make us less dependent on Parsons. Plus, Fluor is a huge company with jobs all over Iraq, all over the world."

Namir seemed upbeat. He said, "Good, good. We will go together tomorrow with a couple of my subcontractors and do the site survey."

I was honored. Namir, with twenty-five years experience in building bridges, hospitals, and power plants, was going with me on an all-day site survey for an $11,000 job! We got up early the next morning and met at the AISG compound in Baghdad, ready to set out for the north gate of Taji, wherever that was. I had never been to that particular checkpoint. We were still a raw team, and the new U.S. military bases had changed so much that even our professional Iraqi drivers were confused.

Three of us climbed into a 1999 white Suburban. I was driving. Namir was in the passenger seat, and a Kurdish bodyguard was perched in the back, cradling an RPK light machine gun. We would form a caravan with an extra SUV trailing our Suburban in case of breakdown and a Toyota Land Cruiser filled up with subcontractors.

I cranked the car, and the other vehicles likewise cranked up. I sat there for a moment, engine idling, then broke down and admitted I didn't know where we were going.

"Namir, do you know where the north gate to Taji is?"

"No," he said. "Taji was the largest army base in Iraq

under Saddam. Almost all the entrances are to the east off Route 1."

"Of course, so it must be straight up Route 1 off to the right, after the major checkpoint called Gunner Gate."

"Perhaps, but I built roads all over that base; there are many miles after the first gate. We will see," Namir said.

We were still in downtown Baghdad, so I used the Iraqna (the new Egyptian-operated network) cell phone to call our construction department and ask for directions. After a couple of rings, Ken answered. I identified myself and told the ex-Special Forces trooper I needed directions.

"Where are you going?"

"The north gate to Taji."

"No problem," the voice said. "All you have to do is . . ."

The voice faded. We were out of range of the last cell tower north of the capital. I had no satellite phone. AISG did not issue me one, nor did I ask—a mistake. For several hours we wandered in the desert like Moses looking for the Promised Land. I drove round and round, crossing over the median eight times on Route 1, with the trail security SUV and Toyota Land Cruiser with Namir's people following. We bounced from the north gate to the base entrance, where we conferred with the guard unit. We left and drove up and down the dangerous highway to Tikrit, hometown of Saddam. Bewildered, we returned again to the north gate—twice.

Finally, we entered the base and spoke to the officer in charge, a bright, young second lieutenant with very squared-away sergeants. He looked to be about twelve years old, but he had a head on his shoulders. He got on the phone, contacted U.S. Army Taji ops center, and gave them the name of our Fluor contact. A miracle. Someone from Fluor at the base knew him. It turned out that our Fluor contact was not even at Taji, but was still in Fluor HQ in the Green Zone—back in Baghdad from where we'd come.

Namir, who watched me with patience the entire day, said, "There will be better days ahead, Carter."

"Well," I said, "we had a nice tour of the countryside, didn't we?"

Then I remembered the subcontractors, who had been trailing around behind us all day. I owed them an explanation, or—at the very least—an apology. I walked back to the Land Cruiser and saw two stone-faced engineers. Both had gray facial hair, the first sign of experience in the Middle East. They had gone round and round with us all the live-long day, even risking their lives by following so closely behind an obvious American at the wheel of an obviously U.S.-made SUV. They didn't speak English, and I didn't speak their language, so I could hardly explain.

I grabbed each man's hand individually and repeated over and over in Arabic, "*Afwan, koulesh afwan,*" in what I hoped would at least be interpreted as "I am sorry, very sorry. Please excuse me."

I climbed behind the wheel of the SUV one more time as dusk settled on that fruitless, frustrating day. Namir turned to me and said emphatically, "You have fixed it all! You have fixed it all for them, and me! You know not what you did, what and how you said it. That makes up for everything in my culture! They will now be ready to work with you again."

And they were—because the infidel crusader had humbly asked their forgiveness—and in an honest attempt

62

to speak in their language. At this point, I knew that Namir respected me for trying to do the right thing. This was the key to the door of Iraqi hearts: mutual respect. However, I learned two lessons that day: one, in Iraq, know where you're going before you start out, because if you don't, you may never get there; and two, make sure that the person you're supposed to meet is going to be at the location. Missed sales calls on the battlefield were unnecessary risks. You minimized your travel to what the job required, because only stupid Americans would joyride around Iraq—and stupid Americans were too often dead Americans.

Those first weeks I was lucky, but I was also a quick study. In a few months, the business development struggles were over, and AISG was one of the hottest prospects in Iraq.

THREE

A Routine Service Call to Taji

Once the company was up and running, I found that my duties had expanded far beyond my original job description, which was to be a salesman and generate business. I continued to play the rainmaker with increasing success. However, I was also straw boss, chauffeur, gunslinger, counselor, and father confessor.

I found myself on the road constantly, overseeing reconstruction and making routine deliveries to sites that other contractors would drive fifty miles out of their way to avoid. "Routine deliveries," by the way, were by no means uneventful, as one service call to Taji will illustrate.

We were on an Iraqi road in the midst of an increasingly violent insurgency. I was working a relatively routine communications job at a new Iraqi army base only fifteen miles north on the most dangerous highway out of Baghdad. The road was not a full-scale battle zone featuring hand-to-hand combat but a place of sporadic small-scale attacks. These attacks happened every day during this period. In a one-week span from April 29 to May 3, 2004, on this stretch of Route 1 there were sixteen such incidents involving bombs, rocket-propelled grenades, and small-arms fire.

Until that first day, I had only driven past the aftermath of an IED ("improvised explosive device"—normally command detonated). I had not actually experienced the impact. A few days earlier, we had just missed an IED explosion that wounded a KBR trucker in a U.S. Army-escorted convoy. By the time we arrived, we saw only swirling red smoke, marking the spot where a Black Hawk medevac helicopter had just landed.

On this trip, we were headed up from our offices in Baghdad to do the final installation of a satellite-linked VoIP system. I was behind the wheel of a 1999 Hyundai two-tone gray and silver Galloper four-wheel drive with tinted windows. I also had Fatah, an Iraqi Kurdish Pesh Merga (Kurdish partisans whose name can translate as "Ready for Death" or "Those Who Face Death") riding in the back seat with a drum-fed RPK machine gun. He served as my shooter. Following me in a red four-door Jaguar was our Iraqi Arab Internet guru, Ahmed, a tallish, aristocratic-looking man who resembled an American Indian chief. He had no training in this technology, but he seemed to make it up as he went along—a good man and very sharp. With Ahmed was his telephony expert, Jabaar. We were totally low profile, looking just like a couple of cars among a lot of vehicles heading up the dusty Iraqi road.

The Kurds stood alone in Iraq as clear-cut friends of America. They appreciated the role America played in freeing them from a dictator who had attempted genocide against their nation, a persecution that had included the use of chemical weapons. These fearless mountain warriors from the north constituted the only Iraqi ethnic group to fight with the Coalition against the Saddam regime.

Years of constant warfare had ingrained in the Pesh Merga that they were the baddest hombres in the valley (in their own minds). If they let anyone attack them (or their American charges) and escape, such a feat would damage their reputations and bring shame upon their families and the Kurdish people, in toto.

After decades of persecution and conflict from all sides, the average Pesh Merga awoke every morning thinking about killing an Arab, an Iranian, a Turk, or for that matter, several of each. In Arab Baghdad, the Kurds from the north possessed few friends, since communicating in Kurdish is very different from speaking Arabic. Also, the Kurds in Baghdad had no families the insurgents could kidnap. All of the above made for a loyal soldier.

My company's primary security force was wholly Pesh Merga. We had over fifty of them living with us in our compound in central Baghdad, providing us with house security and bodyguards. We all went to sleep every night confident in the knowledge that we had Pesh Merga watching over us on the rooftops and at our gates. They might not be trained to Western standards, but we knew they would not run away from a gunfight but shoot back. Possibly even more important, the Kurds would not sell us out.

This was maybe my fifteenth trip to Taji. Taji was a small, ugly, debris-strewn market town located on a patch of monochrome desert next to what was the largest army base in Saddam Hussein's Iraq. The once-modern, four-lane highway left Baghdad past the old north gate and proceeded up the flat desert terrain past a huge, smoldering garbage dump. The highway at this point was lined one-row deep with stunted, desert oaks that failed to mask the unyielding, desolate landscape beyond. You could get up to speed on Route 1, the primary north/south Iraqi artery, but if you weren't careful you would come across a bump in the road or a massive pothole that would send your head through the car roof. When driving, we spent more time watching the road immediately ahead than anything else. Yet we also had to keep looking out the rearview mirrors for the insurgents, coming up to spray our vehicle with bullets in a drive-by, hit-and-run ambush.

With those possibilities in mind, we were cruising along Route 1 to Taji. I was jamming to the Baghdad rock 'n' roll station. I was wearing a level-four, bulletproof vest with front and back ceramic plates, holding a cocked Czech CZ85 9mm pistol in the right hand and driving with the left. On the passenger floorboard sat my Yugoslav-manufactured Kalashnikov automatic rifle and a bag of Soviet-designed, Egyptian-made hand grenades. As we hurtled down the road, we could smell the burning garbage through the cracked side window.

The Iraqis were maybe the best drivers in the world and, at the same time, the worst. The Baghdadis, as the citizens of the ancient city call themselves, possessed a unique feeling for the outer limits of their own autos and the presence of other vehicles around them. Until you had been on the road with these drivers—who seem to operate bumper cars with an impenetrable cushion of air around their rides of about one inch or less—you couldn't imagine how nerve-wracking an experience it was. The Iraqis floated their cars all over the road. Evidently the lines meant nothing. When Fadhel took me home from the airport the first time, he was weaving the car down the highway. I thought he was drunk or just plain incompetent. The locals drove four abreast on two lanes of traffic. They snaked in and out of the lines in sweeping, erratic curves. Oftentimes Baghdadis drove the wrong way down the street, using the sidewalk, shoulder, and crossing the median, jumping the curb. The curbs in Baghdad were worn to nothing. One of the more concrete signs of progress in the capital was the new, brightly painted curbs along Al Kindi Street, our neighborhood's main boulevard.

On several occasions I had gotten caught in a traffic diversion from four lanes to one. It reminded me of beans sliding down a funnel. This predicament became highly stressful because the cars got so close that they were inside each other's side mirrors. The passengers flipped the protruding mirrors open and closed as they maneuvered through the packed chute of cars. You had no choice but to flow forward, trusting that these excellent Baghdadis would remain excellent behind the wheel. They had a canny, almost surreal, sense of the 360 degrees around their cars. Whereas we Westerners operated inside angles and straight lines, the Arabs saw curves and circles, at least when they drove.

About seven miles out of the city, weaving our way down the highway—because only foreigners drove straight between the lines—we ran into a massive traffic jam. We wended our way to the front, going down the wrong way on the highway. We couldn't really move about well (using the shoulder of the road or going over the median) because the trailing Jag had no ground clearance. I spotted a U.S. Army Stryker armored vehicle ahead, off the side of the highway, sitting alone amidst a crazy montage of local vehicles where not one car or truck was pointed in the same direction. Leaving Ahmed in the Jaguar behind on the hard pan immediately next to Route 1, I maneuvered the Galloper over the rutted, dried mud toward the Stryker to ask the GIs what was up.

The soldiers, standing in the rear well of the eight-wheeled behemoth manning machine guns, eyed our approaching Iraqi-style four-wheel drive nervously.

I leaned out the window and shouted above the din of the traffic jam, "DoD, DoD contractor!"

After he heard my accent and saw my smiling American face, one of the soldiers said to the other, "Hey, what the hell is this? That guy's U.S."

Then he looked at me, waved, and said, "OK, you can come closer."

I flashed my U.S. Department of Defense badge, the official get-out-of-jail free card in an occupied Iraq where the only laws enforceable for a Pentagon contractor are those of the U.S.A. After the soldiers quickly looked at the plastic photo ID, I asked, "What's the holdup, brothers?"

The fresh-faced, albeit dust-covered kid with hard eyes visibly relaxed when he realized he was dealing with the familiar—another American. "IED . . . on the shoulder of the road ahead. EOD is on the way." That, too, was familiar.

"Explosive Ordnance Disposal is going to disarm it," he said.

I asked, "How long till they are finished?"

But the soldiers were now scanning the crowd, doing their security jobs. So I got no answer and drove back up onto the road.

After the word from the Stryker crew, we quickly put distance between the army vehicle and us. I guided my SUV back up on the highway to link up with Ahmed in the Jag. Together we moved farther into the crowd and stopped. I didn't see any Iraqi police. This was an all-American show around the IED. Locals began to approach us—a crowd from the hundreds of cars and trucks trapped by the army cordon around the bomb. They just wanted to chat with us, their new neighbors.

This was the main highway north from the Iraqi capital and onto the Turkish border. A lot of commercial traffic made use of it. The number of cars on the highway was amazing, considering the ongoing conflict. The latest statistics showed that since the fall of Saddam, over five hundred thousand additional cars had been imported into Iraq: various old Japanese compacts, new Korean SUVs and minivans, Mercedes and BMW sedans, Scania tractor-trailers, Ladas from the old Soviet days, and the odd Chevrolet Caprice, one of the most common types of taxi in Iraq. This was good in many ways, especially from our security standpoint, because it meant more fish in the sea where we were hiding.

Brisk breezes propelled dust everywhere. Iraq was various shades of dust, sandy, or brown, no matter whether you were talking about the architecture, the pavement, the people, or the landscape. Even the date palm fronds were coated with a consistent khaki green.

We were stopped in a swirl of omnipresent dust blowing off the cracked tarmac of the highway. Ahmed began to act jittery.

Getting out of his Jag, he approached my car window on foot and said, "People are starting to notice you and us." Meaning they would notice that he was with me: the American.

"Oh," I asked, "are they not happy to see an American *kafir* [infidel, unclean nonbeliever] on the road with them?"

Ahmed further allowed, in his understated way, that "this is not a good area. Bad people who don't like Americans are all over the place here. Saddam loyalists. They are trying to cut off the highway."

Fatah, whose head was spinning as if on a swivel stick trying to maintain 360-degree observation, grunted, "*Der balik* [careful]," not at my irony, but at the numerous potential dangers. And we as a team were very few.

Acknowledging Fatah, IT guru Ahmed continued to worry me through the passenger window. With his forehead creased and the edges of his mouth turned down in a deeply concerned look, he finally advised, "We should move further to the front where there are American soldiers. It will be safer."

A bit surprised, I asked, "You really feel safer next to the big target, the U.S. Army?"

The Pesh Merga, a slim, dark twenty-five-year-old with an easy smile and the eyes of a man thirty years older, nodded his head vigorously in agreement.

I leaned back and said to Fatah, "*Sirchow!*"

He answered with gusto, "*Sirchow!*" This translated into "You are in my eyes" in Kurdish and roughly meant "Attention!"

Back when I was first in country, we had Kurds in blockhouses guarding the dirt roads around our house. I had asked Fadhel, my driver, what to say to alert them to our friendly presence. He had thought for a moment, and then said,

"*Sirchow*." That one word had become my standard greeting for the Pesh Merga. Now it was in common use around our company as a greeting for everyone, Kurdi or not.

After the exchange with Fatah, I turned back to Ahmed. "OK, let's move."

Ahmed, a Sunni Arab, agreed, saying, "Yes, it will be safer. No one will approach us then." Ahmed had worked a couple of years in England. He had said in the past that only the Americans could ensure fairness in the Iraqi judiciary because he didn't trust his own people.

Taking my Iraqi colleagues' advice, I headed up front. I would not normally have done this, since I liked to stay away from the U.S. Army because it often drew fire. The soldiers also might have shot us by accident. From afar, there was really no way for them to know that we were an American operation. That was the negative side of the low-profile approach. This was a serious risk: to be shot by friendly forces, like the Iraqi policeman who shot Fadhel or the South Africans who shot up my BMW.

Finally, with Ahmed's Jaguar trailing, we made our way to the very front of hundreds of vehicles. The passengers were all out of their cars and trucks in the highway, wandering around in the intensifying heat of a clear, blue May morning. The soldiers tried to talk to the Iraqis in a friendly way, but everyone was keeping his distance. No one wanted to get shot. I was alarmed, though, when I looked over to the side of the road and saw that Iraqis had surrounded a lone G.I., barely visible except for the top of his helmet and flashes of desert camouflage through occasional breaks in the throng. The average Iraqi wanted no part of this insurgency and wasn't openly hostile toward American soldiers.

The crowd milling about the lone soldier appeared quite friendly, and he eventually returned to a closer proximity with his unit. However, we knew there were people out there—the *erhabi* (terrorist) and the much-feared *entehari* (suicide bomber)—who would seize the opportunity to kill or kidnap an American.

The *entehari* was almost without exception a radical jihadist foreigner allied with al Qaeda, usually from another Arab country. Thankfully it was not in the Iraqi character or culture to blow oneself up. Iraqis enjoyed life too much. We were not the Israelis, and this wasn't the Palestinian West Bank. Nevertheless, the presence of these terrorists reminded me—and every other Westerner for that matter—not to go jogging or have a cappuccino in a café out in the Red Zone.

While more and more Iraqis and their vehicles surrounded me, I was sitting there, inching forward, pressing up against the U.S. blockade. I began to think that maybe I was overexposed and that this was not a good idea, being ass-to-cheek with the army. Everyone here now knew that we were somehow associated with the military. At a closer look—"*Shinu Hathe* [What's this]?! That driver in the Galloper doesn't quite look like us. . . . He's *Amriki* too!" Even with the tinted windows, they could see me through the windshield. They'd seen me waving at the soldiers when I pulled up, seen the GIs acknowledge that we were friendly. Then I started wondering why the hell I'd even made this service call . . . or for that matter, why I was in Iraq.

I had left the loves of my life—my wife and two beautiful children—to come to the war zone. I really had believed after I left the army, where I served as a Ranger and an infantry officer fourteen years earlier, that no more big wars loomed ahead for the United States. The Soviet Union had collapsed. There were no more dragons to slay. Then we invaded Afghanistan and Iraq. This would be my war, even though it would not be as a soldier but as an armed businessman, a contractor combatant, helping to reconstruct Iraq.

I remembered watching TV with rage and shock as the World Trade Center Towers came down in New York City, dumbly sitting there with my six-year-old daughter. I had just missed driving by the Pentagon attack on my way to work. (The consequent traffic jam forced me to turn around and go home.) That more recent memory then segued to a seminal discussion with my father from several years back when I took him to the National Vietnam War Memorial for his first time. As we walked up the incline after passing the full length of the black marble wall inscribed in gold with the names of Americans who had died in the war, I asked, "What do you think?"

His voiced rasping with emotion, my father answered, "The country let us down—all those who served over there."

This shocked me because I had always viewed him as the truest of blue Americans with the deepest faith in our country. So I said with hesitation, "You have really held that in a long time, Dad. It's hard for me to believe you just said that."

"Yes, it's painful, but those that didn't go to Vietnam also missed the greatest adventure of our generation."

Rotating my head like a praying mantis, trying to scan every direction but to the front where the soldiers joked watchfully, I thought, *Here we are in Baghdad. Wow. No one could have predicted two years ago that I would be living in a war zone.*

We had done it. Just as the movie *Field of Dreams* predicted: "Build it and they will come." The U.S.A. had constructed a killing field for terrorists, and they were coming. We had forced al Qaeda to react. We—the hated Americans, target Number One—were right next door, in one of the holiest lands in all of bin Laden's perverted version of Islam. The borders were open. They had to get us out of here before they could even think about wasting energy attacking us in America. But here in Iraq, they were not facing men, women, and children, unarmed and unaware, on their way to work or vacation or wherever. They were facing soldiers and people who came prepared to fight.

Awareness of our precarious situation jerked me back to reality. We were sitting like shooting-gallery ducks, stuck in a traffic jam on the most dangerous road out of Baghdad. I was next to the big target—the U.S. military, surrounded by who knows what kind of insurgent opportunist. There was even time for a planned attack. We had been stuck there for almost two hours. I was getting more and more nervous by the moment, as were my friends, Ahmed, Fatah, and Jabaar the IT telephony specialist—not exactly the trained and experienced security crew you might choose to be on your side in a firefight.

Fear at the visceral level was an ever-present part of working in Iraq. You never knew what would happen next. Every time you went to sleep at night or got in your car to drive to work, in the recesses of your mind you thought, *This could be it. Be prepared.* You checked your weapons, kept the faith, and moved on. Whether taking one of your people to the hospital with a gunshot wound, having bullets zing close by your head, or seeing a GI blown up, the sense of impending violence traveled with you always. You had to consciously suppress that anxiety and drive on with the mission. Subliminal fear was your constant companion. Unlike with soldiers, no one kept an exact record of the number of contractor casualties in Iraq, but at this writing it exceeded 330 killed and many more wounded, out of the estimated twenty thousand in country at any one time (see icasualties.org).

Why was I even doing this? We were working an IT project for Parsons, one of the largest construction management firms in the world, with $2 billion in contracts to rebuild Iraq. That's why. But this project was only worth $100,000.

I told Ahmed, "I'm not even supposed to be the project manager. Why am I doing this?"

Ahmed asked, "What happened to Darryl, who used to be in charge of the project?"

"You mean Darryl, the redneck fiber-optic expert? I guess he couldn't work with you because you make it up as you go along. He fled the country last week."

"Yes, I must admit," the Internet entrepreneur said, "the level of patience to work with the Iraqis, especially on something that we have never done before, could push anyone over the edge."

I agreed. Fortunately, I'd been working in Ukraine since the fall of the Soviet Union. I knew what it was to make something happen when you felt like you were working underwater. Political and historical inertia heavily resist forward motion. Who in Iraq had ever done VoIP through a direct satellite connection before the U.S. invasion?

"It's tough to learn the technology on the job," I said.

"True," Ahmed said. "Everything I know now, I learned

after the Americans invaded Iraq. The Internet means freedom, and we had no freedom under Saddam."

I was filled with admiration. "You learn fast, my brother. No doubt."

As anyone could see, doing business in Iraq was not for the faint-hearted. The security situation mandated so many precautions and preparations that it had drastically slowed down work. We were still caught up in developing the necessary infrastructure for Parsons project management (such as our Taji IT work) and had to finish before we could start building something for the Iraqi people. The Parsons people couldn't even move without a twenty-four-hour notice to their security contractor. The security firm then had to provide armored cars and armed protection teams made up of former Western Special Forces soldiers to accompany Parsons engineers to and from the job site.

Not only were these security precautions time consuming, but they were also quite expensive. Each of these highly skilled security operators cost Parsons up to a $1,000 a day. As a result, Parsons engineers and construction managers were holed up in the Green Zone, reconstructers of Iraq doing little—if any—reconstruction, seldom leaving their secure enclaves. These cautionary measures made it very difficult to build roads, dams, clinics, schools, power stations, etc., particularly when these projects were scattered about the countryside in a nation the size of California.

What we needed were more Seabees—the U.S. Navy combat construction teams that ran the project management office during the Vietnam War without problems in an even hotter environment than Iraq. In other words, what we needed were construction types who shot back when shot at and didn't fear to tread wherever the work took them. In contrast, Parsons by corporate policy prohibited its employees from carrying any weapons at all. Therein lay the niche for our company. We were a logistics/construction operation that moved about freely with our own internal security capabilities. Our ability, or more precisely, our willingness to react flexibly was the reason I had come to be stuck on the road to Taji with just one security man (other than myself) and a couple of Iraqi IT experts. What a niche!

Although lost in existential angst and frustration at not being able to get on down the road and complete the job, I was nonetheless alert. I looked to my left front and something caught my eye. All of a sudden, off to the side of the road, past the bomb and between the parallel railroad-track berm and Route 1, appeared a four-vehicle convoy of brand-new, shiny Ford Expeditions. The SUVs—full of American security men and clients wearing military-style Kevlar helmets—headed straight toward us. It was standard operating procedure for Western contractor security ops, therefore completely high profile. Windows open, weapons hanging out, they approached us sitting at the center front of the seemingly endless pack of vehicles. The lead vehicle needed for us to move to get by, so the convoy could continue on its trip south to Baghdad. We had nowhere to go because the median was too high for the Jag. I was not getting separated from Ahmed.

I looked out the window at the soldiers standing in front of my car and raised my hands in a gesture of "what to do?"

The young sergeant in charge smiled sympathetically and called out, "Pull forward toward the rear of the Humvee."

We moved up behind the truck, armored-up with

makeshift steel plates. I motioned the convoy forward, mouthing, "Come on."

The contract security operators were obviously surprised to see me, a lone American traveling Iraqi-style on the road. The lead driver said, "Thanks for letting us pass."

I said, "No problem. Nice day at the beach, eh?"

The security guy laughed. "Sure is."

Then I closed the joke. "I'm still looking for the ocean, must be near with all the sand and palm trees."

They were very cool. The expatriate bodyguards passed by, weapons poking out the windows but consciously not pointed at me. These operators were professionals: decent guys with smiles on their faces, but their movement technique was way too high-profile.

When selling our security approach to potential clients, I always referred back to a conversation I had with one of my retired Green Berets colleagues when I came up with the shark-and-two-swimmers analogy.

"You know how I see our security approach?" I said, as we all sat around the dinner table one evening at our house in Baghdad.

"You mean our 'low-profile modus operandi,'" the retired SF sergeant said, using words he just got out of the dictionary.

"When a shark attacks while you're swimming in the ocean with your buddy, what do you have to do to survive?"

Sergeant: "Kill the shark!"

"OK, that might be difficult, but to survive realistically, you don't have to swim faster than the shark, just faster than your buddy."

"Some friend you are!" the sergeant said.

I tried to explain it less metaphorically: "Because

Westerners all travel around in similar-style, brand-new American and Japanese SUV multivehicle convoys, it is much easier for us. We are able to slip below the bad guys' radar in our older, local, Iraqi-purchased, different-model vehicle movements of three or less cars."

The rule of low-profile movement in Iraq was try to blend in—don't stand out, stay in the flow of traffic, don't show that you are an American, and try to look Iraqi. One of my colleagues, J. P., while working on the Washington Group International power-line project protection up in north central Iraq, drove around in an old Nissan pickup with a live sheep in the back. This worked well until he went home on vacation for a couple weeks and came back to find his Pesh Merga security guards had barbecued his camouflage.

As noted before, don't show your weapons unless absolutely necessary. We were civilian contractors moving around Iraq, taking care of business, not the army out hunting the insurgents. We had no close air support, no real quick reaction force to come riding to the rescue. We were not going to intimidate the bad guys. We certainly couldn't intimidate a command-detonated IED, the most effective and frequent form of insurgent attack.

Drive various model vehicles that look like the rest of the thousands of other local-type transportation. Keep your distance on the highway so as not to appear part of a convoy. These two techniques tremendously lessened the chance of getting shot at or bombed by the various anti-Western elements present in Iraq. Tactical dispersion, keeping proper distance so a large portion of your element does not fall prey to an ambush or explosion—this tactic was key to increasing the odds of survival. Natural tendency pulls one close to your compatriots—strength in numbers and proximity. The marines had a big problem with this rule; they kept getting blown up in bunches. The bottom line: discretion is the better part of valor.

Contrary to my standard low-profile tactics, we now sat very much exposed. Concerned by this exposure, I stuck my head out the window.

I asked the sergeant in charge of the roadblock, "Can we go out on the route the Western contractor convoy just used?"

The young leader dressed head to toe in body armor and desert camouflage and wearing Ray-Ban wraparound sunglasses responded, "Sure, but EOD is about to blow the bomb."

"OK," I said, grasping the self-evident, "we'll wait. How far away is the bomb?"

He responded casually, a grin on his face, "About a hundred yards."

"What? That's not far for shrapnel to travel!"

The soldier saw the startled expression on my face and told me, "Pull up right up behind the Humvee."

I moved even closer, getting bumper to bumper with the armored Humvee mounting a big .50 caliber machine gun ready to rock 'n' roll, and called Ahmed on our walkie-talkies. "Get right behind me with the Jag."

Ahmed answered immediately, "Sure. What's going on?"

"They're about to blow the IED, so now we'll be better protected."

"Alhamdullilah," he prayed aloud.

Ahmed looked a bit paler than usual through the rearview mirror. I sat back in the Galloper to wait, and once again noticed how clear and azure the sky looked. Not a contrail disturbed the purity of the blue. Ahead of the explosion the army helicopters, Little Bird gun ships, and Kiowa surveillance choppers had stopped buzzing about the scene like angry hornets.

Time took on a bizarre quality in Iraq, telescoping and magnifying simultaneously. Today flew by, but you couldn't remember what happened yesterday, which seemed like a long time ago at the end of a distant, dim tunnel. A day is a week and a week is a month.

Boom! The bomb went off. Even though forewarned, the instant still came as a surprise. The explosion was so powerful that the sound painted the inside of our skulls with echoes. I felt the shockwaves pass through the armored Humvee and the Galloper and reverberate in the very marrow of my spine. The aftershocks tingled from head to toe. The vehicle briefly shuddered in an almost liquid manner, disturbed at a molecular level. This was a large bomb. A mushroom cloud of intermingled black and tan, smoke and dust, rose several hundred feet into the sky, marring the blue purity I had just been enjoying. The soldiers stood around laughing. An Iraqi standing next to a tractor-trailer off behind us started screaming. Somehow he had been hit by a piece of shrapnel from the blast. The nearest soldier rushed up to the injured man and shouted, "Medic!" Then a crowd gathered around the infantryman, who was leaning over to check on the wounded Iraqi. The next call went up, "Security!" as the soldier began to feel threatened. He was now completely surrounded by locals. A GI ran to his vehicle and called for medevac on the radio.

Viewing the scene as if from afar, I thought, *That's damn*

good of the army to treat this Iraqi at a U.S. combat hospital and carry him there on a helicopter. The truck driver will probably get his first ride ever on an aircraft. While observing the scene to my rear left, the sergeant standing next to the Humvee motioned us to drive forward with a smile on his dust-covered face. He shouted, "Move out!" the instant the all-clear was called. We slowly puttered up the wrong way on the highway. We made a wide arc to avoid the EOD personnel. They were examining their handiwork on the IED formerly situated where we would have driven two hours earlier, if the army had not discovered the bomb. After being within a hundred yards of the explosion, it was not hard to imagine what the impact would do to us at close range.

We got to the other side of the road. Ahmed followed so closely on the trip across no-man's land between the halted traffic heading north and south that the Galloper seemed to be pulling the Jag on a tow bar. However, once across, there was nowhere to go because the oncoming traffic blocked the highway from shoulder to shoulder, ditch to ditch. I steered to the far left shoulder and waved a request for an old panel truck packed with an Iraqi family to let us pass. After a moment's hesitation, the driver guided the truck out of the way. The Iraqis are basically a friendly and polite people who are quite used to crazy traffic situations.

Behind the truck sat a low-slung, metallic-blue, pin-striped BMW sedan with two wild-looking men standing outside the car with hair going everywhere, dressed in sort of Mexican-looking ponchos. They weren't getting out of the way. I looked at them again; and even with their full, tangled beards and long hair, I saw that the men were Americans for sure. No question. One man, I swore I recognized. (I never did figure out who he was.)

Rolling down my tinted window, I waved again and said, "Please get out of the way."

The one near the driver's side called out, "Nuh uh," and shook his head. I guess he thought he would get away with pretending incomprehension.

I responded, my voice rising, "Hey, I'm just trying to get to Taji." Obviously I was talking with them in English, and they must have seen I was an American.

The man I thought I recognized signaled me back angrily with a clenched fist, mouthing, "We're not moving," with added body language for me to get out of the car because he was going to kick my butt!

I started to get out of the car, my patience about to snap, mumbling, "Let's go, if you really want." He saw my movements through the windshield—opening the door and beginning to step out.

This would be really funny, I thought. Two Americans brawling on Iraqi Route 1 in the aftermath of an explosion with a potentially hostile audience of hundreds of fed-up locals.

One cowboy whipped out an MP5 submachine gun and the other went into the car and grabbed an AK-47, but the jerk-driver began to back his BMW out of the way.

I drove by, saying to the driver, half sarcastically but also honestly appreciative, "Thanks, brother. We're all in this together."

He stared at me like he wanted to kill me. I had no idea who those punks were. They looked like CIA—but definitely cowboys.

Once past the angry cowboys, the only way for us to get anywhere was to cross over the median, since the oncoming traffic was stalled. The army allowed us to cross the area before anyone else, mainly to get me, the American, out of the danger zone. I saw an opening. I launched the Galloper over the curb into the dirt median with a big dip in the middle and flew over the other side onto the northbound lanes heading toward Taji.

I looked back at the red Jaguar. It was up on the median, rocking back and forth like a seesaw. Uh oh. Frustrated Iraqis surrounded us, and they probably all knew by now that we were with the Americans. The Jag was stuck.

I had no other choice but to stop the SUV on the side of the road and jump out of the Galloper, holster my pistol, and do what felt like a world-class forty-yard dash. I shouted at Ahmed the whole way to get back in the car and drive as he flailed about, trying to push his auto off high-center. He got into the car. His 140-pound buddy, the telephony expert, was still trying to push. Sprinting up, I squatted under the rear bumper by the stuck tire of the full-sized, leather-upholstered saloon car. Fatah was coming quickly from behind, bandoliers of ammo crisscrossing his chest and holding a drum-fed machine gun with a bipod hanging off the barrel. We weren't attracting any attention now, were we?

I lifted the rear of the car with such force that the VoIP specialist just stared at me, eyes bulging. Nothing like pure fear gets the adrenaline pumping. In my mind, I kept hearing the advice of my ex-Special Forces friends: "Do not ever get out of a car in Iraqi traffic." The Jag slid away with a bump. I ran back to my ride and off we zoomed to our service call, which went smoothly, though we finished a couple of hours later than planned. Ahmed and Jabaar actually got the Internet phone to work, and we made a call to Pasadena, California—probably the first ever from Taji. This was business, Iraqi style.

And routine.

FOUR

Fort Apache

From the beginning I liked the Iraqis and was determined to understand their culture and to establish good relations with them. I had done the same thing in Russia and Ukraine, and the rewards were enormous—valuable business connections, lifelong friends, and a beautiful wife.

But I didn't establish these relationships in hopes of a payoff down the line. I became friends with Russians, Ukrainians, and, later, Iraqis because I enjoyed them and had a deep interest in their history, customs, and culture. (The Middle East was a prime focus of my undergraduate degree.) I often wondered how any American could be plopped down in the mythic city of Baghdad and not be utterly fascinated by the people and their surroundings. Yet many Americans in Iraq distanced themselves from the locals, possibly out of a rarely spoken contempt for a country classified as "third world" or because of a deep-rooted, internalized fear of a conquered people who were sometimes hostile, who dressed differently, who spoke another language, and who professed a different religion. Most American contractors in country, however, simply weren't curious and didn't possess a strong desire to interact with the Iraqis; they were in theater to do a job . . . no more, no less.

As a consequence of their attitude, I was among the very few who managed to establish close friendships with a wide array of Iraqis, men who were key to the success of our operations. As time passed, it became increasingly obvious that my relationships with these good people greatly benefited the company and contributed significantly to the AISG success story.

Indeed, I came to believe that this camaraderie was essential to the achievement of our goals. I don't know how long the Iraqis would have faced death for a foreign company whose management was aloof and uncaring. Side by side we risked our lives, looking out for each other, developing our own jokes and language, daily confronting a deadly enemy. And the Iraqis stuck with us, in part because they knew they had at least one friend in the hierarchy.

However, after weeks of confrontations, I felt the need to walk down a street without having to worry about who was behind or ahead of me. You get used to constant danger, but it still takes its toll on your nervous system. Also, I missed my wife and children. So I put in for leave and arranged to meet my family in Greece, a country full of ancient ruins and friendly faces. As we toured the Acropolis and Parthenon, where no armed Wahhabis, Sunni Islamic fanatics, lurked, I could feel my muscles relax and the knots in my stomach loosen. For a day or two I forgot that Iraq existed. Then we ran out of time. After Greece, I took a plane to Kiev for a brief trip to make Spetsnaz bodyguard arrangements for Baghdad.

The day I returned to Fort Apache from Kiev, Antony, our British security specialist, shot himself in the foot with armor-piercing AK rounds. I was inside; and when I heard rifle fire, I came running out to the driveway just as he emerged from a BMW, violently shaking his right leg. "I was just trying to walk it off," he said through clenched teeth as we drove the streets of Baghdad to the U.S. Army combat service hospital (CASH) in the Green Zone. "It reminds me of getting blown up in Africa in the Legion."

Antony was a thick, dark-haired man, a refrigerator with tree trunklike arms and legs. He was a physically strong and vibrant man, and it pained me to see him lying on the ground, face contorted in agony and blood rushing out of his foot. The entire top was blown off, or rather burned off, by two AP bullet blasts. (At 3,000 feet per second muzzle velocity, these Russian-made, armor-piercing 7.62mm bullets give off an intense jet of heat from the business end of a Kalashnikov.) Antony—who had been ripped open by a landmine in the French Foreign Legion in Rwanda just before the Hutu-Tutsi genocide in 1994—lost two-thirds of his right foot to amputation and never again returned to Apache.

Welcome back to Iraq! I thought as we left Antony in his hospital bed at the CASH and headed home. The sun had yet to set on my first day back in Baghdad.

The primary reason Antony accidentally shot himself in the foot was AISG's first paying client, a Louisiana-based construction company. Its management team had moved into Fort Apache after fleeing a rocket attack on the roof of the hotel across the street from where they were quartered.

During this attack, I had been in the hotel having dinner with J. D., the client's in-country manager. J. D. was a balding, bespectacled .357-magnum-carrying gunslinger from Texas who was ready for whatever risk came to him while working in the combat zone. He was ready, that is, until the locals rocketed their new house further up the Tigris from Apache. After that, he didn't travel much outside the U.S. Army–protected Green Zone.

When the rocket impacted the hotel, it wiped out the rug merchant's shop on the roof and seriously disturbed our lamb and scotch dinner. In addition, the nearby Hotel Lebanon got burned down by a massive car bomb fifteen minutes later. J. D. and the ex-British spy, Robert, from the M&I building site survey, moved into Fort Apache the next day. They left their rooms in the Karrada district, as well as the high-end haunts of Western journalists, and came to us for safekeeping.

The U.S. contracting world in Iraq had just gotten a lot smaller. We were about to undertake the impossible: reconstructing, according to Western standards, a country that was still, for the most part, a third-world nation of villages without electricity and running water. And we were going to do it in the middle of a war zone, with insurgents shooting at us as well as at the military. To complicate our job further, the existing power and water infrastructure had been substantially degraded during the more than twenty years of the Iran-Iraq war, the Kuwait invasion, and a decade-plus of UN sanctions. The biggest flaw of all in the preintelligence estimates was underestimating the state of degradation that Saddam had brought on the country from the heyday of big oil prices in the 1970s.

Now with J. D. and the Parsons people starting to retreat into the Green Zone (Fort Apache was just a transit point into a trailer park near the Palace), there was often no American quality control of the billions of dollars in U.S-contracted projects. For this reason, the dollars were not forthcoming, and the work crawled to a halt.

With money tight, contractors had to establish secure construction sites and logistics in the middle of bombings, mortars, rockets, beheadings, and ambushes. Foreign nationals who did nothing but deliver food to the U.S. Army were being kidnapped and killed. With all this going on, the field of DoD contracting in Iraq was open only to the very bold.

A few weeks after J. D. and crew moved into Apache, the son of the subcontractor owner flew in from Baton Rouge to check out business in Iraq. To protect his son, the subcontractor rented some high-speed bodyguards from us, including Antony.

The morning I got back in Iraq—and unbeknownst to me—J. D. and Robert took off with the owner's son without Antony and his security team. J. D.'s car broke down and the whole crew—like bandits in an old cowboys-and-Indians movie—had to take cover in the median of BIAP road. J. D. used his cell phone to call their Iraqi driver and tell him to come pick them up in another car.

When the driver arrived, they abandoned the broken vehicle on the side of Airport Road and piled into the rescue car. By the time they got back to Apache, Antony was fuming. So the professional soldier stomped off to take Robert to another meeting and shot himself in the foot out of pure frustration. More focused on his anger than the mission ahead, he climbed into the back of the BMW with the safety off his AK, standard operating procedure for all the high-speed knuckle draggers. He must have brushed the trigger on his body armor grenade loops, launching two rounds into his foot.

As a result of this incident and further clashes involving the freewheeling J. D. inside Fort Apache, our clients found other lodgings. They had overstayed their welcome at our compound, but we were working on getting them their own safe house with AISG-provided security in our neighborhood. J. D., however, rejected that offer. Instead, they moved into a huge mansion directly across a dirt road from the dykes walling in the Tigris River, two bridges north up from the 14th of July Revolution Bridge at the Green Zone.

I asked Amer—our first new employee after we formed AISG—if he would go with me to the client's new location to deliver some documents. J. D. had not used Ahmed for Internet, and their IT system had crashed at the mansion, so we couldn't just e-mail the cost estimates for a Parsons bid due the next day. I planned to take along a security guard and suggested that Amer do so as well. I instinctively trusted Amer, and he eventually climbed the corporate ladder to be our ranking Iraqi employee.

He said, "OK, I know the place. You drive through a little village area of small houses at the base of the bridge. This is a dangerous route. *Inshallah* . . . I know a better way to go, back behind the village and to the villa."

Having driven to the new villa numerous times, I said, "Yes, it will make more sense to try another way. This area is so exposed, I feel nervous there. Let's try. I'll follow you."

"Good, I will get two SUVs ready. You will drive one and I will drive the other."

On our way to deliver the urgent documents, we headed out in our two-car movement to the client's Tigris River villa. I followed Amer. We got to the base of the bridge where the village interjected itself between us and our destination. By then the sun was setting. We had left late because I had argued long and heatedly with some of the other American managers about the risk factor. They warned against the venture.

I said, "Hey, how can we be a security company if we're afraid to go to our client's location?"

They had no response to that argument. It was also easier for them to drop their objections because I was going and they weren't. With the rise in violence, almost all the Americans had even further restricted their travel.

But everyone was fearful, including Amer, who would later prove his courage in a wild shootout. With Amer in the lead, we began to navigate a warren of streets farther away from the river to approach the client's villa from the backside.

Right behind the villa, across a low field, stood a mosque. As we turned down the street in front of the mosque, hundreds of people appeared as if from nowhere, milling around in front of the temple. This crowd blocked the road. Amer took a sharp left—the only turn away from the crowd, though it was away from our destination. We looked up at the building to the right and realized that he had taken us down a dead end. Men holding rifles ran along the top of the building, an extension of the mosque, pointing at us in the fading light and talking into walkie-talkies. Everyone expected the RPGs to come out next.

Amer froze in the lead car when he came to the dead end. I slammed my Galloper in reverse, stomped on the accelerator, and spun the four-wheel drive around and sped away into the now dark warren, just missing the crowd surging toward us. From above I'm sure we looked like cockroaches scattering when the kitchen light came on. I shouted into the handheld radio to Amer: "Get out of there! Follow me!" Somehow I retraced the several turns on the unlit roads and went back the way I had always gone to the client's villa.

We delivered the paperwork, and after leaving the villa, the security guy riding shotgun—a Mexican-American former army sergeant who had served in Bosnia—said emphatically, "I am never going back to that house."

I went back several more times, but each time I was increasingly aware that this was not a safe place. Sure enough, trouble struck. Al Atifiyah, where the villa was located, was a Baghdad district that served as a sort of border zone between Shia- and Sunni-dominated districts. No other Westerners lived there. The massive residence featured a fabulous view of the slow-moving, ochre-colored river, at this point about two hundred yards wide and constrained from seasonal flooding by concrete levees on both banks. To compound the risk, behind their house stood the mosque where we confronted the crowd, the stunted yellow-white minaret clearly visible from the back windows of the villa. The mosque, I found out, was Wahhabi. The Wahhabi Islamic sect in Iraq is a small Sunni minority, less than 1 percent, but it's a major source of support for the foreign al Qaeda-type terrorists operating in Iraq. Osama bin Laden claimed to be a Wahhabi.

From the beginning, we warned J. D. and Robert about the clear dangers of the location, even before they moved into the house. Subsequently, they had a bomb threat, and small-arms fire hit the back balcony of the house. However, they stayed on, seemingly oblivious to the rising danger. The company owner's son, on a brief visit back in country, thought his security guards shot the house themselves in order to get a pay raise.

They never accepted our security services for the house either. The company's main local partners were members of a powerful Shia family from the area where the house was located. A week prior to the event that sent these U.S. citizens fleeing back to America, the Shia family had placed a big sign in front of the house, displaying in bright letters the name of their construction firm. They mistakenly thought the mere name, known throughout Iraq, would offer protection.

According to a post-action assessment from U.S. intelligence at the CPA, the Wahhabis came after them. About midnight, the Islamist insurgents launched three rockets out of homemade PVC tubes at the front of the house and fired small arms into the front and back. This was a planned and coordinated attack. The bad guys missed once with a rocket and hit the neighboring house's diesel fuel tank, which exploded, burning up two cars in the driveway. The other two rockets impacted on the front arch of the house, just missing the massive windows looking out over the river—the offices and living quarters of the Americans.

The consequent explosions did very little structural damage to the massive brick edifice. The Iraqis built almost all their buildings very solidly from mud brick, as they have been doing for millennia. The rockets were antipersonnel, meant to kill people, not destroy structures. The Kurd security force (which J. D. had poached from us during his earlier stay at Fort Apache) opened up on the insurgents from the roof and put a lot of lead down range, but the bad guys escaped in their car. The Pesh Merga, just like almost all the Iraqis, were great at pulling the trigger, but not so good at aiming.

During the firefight, Robert called me on my cell phone (J. D. was on vacation), shouting that they were under attack. I could hear prolonged rips of automatic rifle fire in the background. I hung up and immediately called the two U.S. Army quick reaction forces (QRF) telephone numbers I had programmed into my cell phone. The First Cavalry Division said they had a patrol in the area. The imagery almost overwhelmed me: "The cavalry to the rescue!" I fielded several calls over the next ninety minutes, including those from Corps G3, the U.S. military operations center for all of central Iraq. The problem was, we were using two different cell phone systems. Our client had one and the army used the other; but I had both. In order to call one phone system from the other, you had to make a not-too-reliable international call through a U.S. exchange.

A patrol quickly arrived in the general area, a force consisting of three Bradley infantry fighting vehicles and—since I had told the army our people had taken two casualties—a medic M113 armored personnel carrier. One Pesh Merga was wounded by the blast from the diesel tank, and the other was an Arab translator who had slipped and fallen down the steps while running around like a chicken with his head cut off. I had the brigade tactical operations center (TOC) in my right ear (on the CPA-provided MCI cell phone system) and our client in my left ear (on Iraqna). I was frantically trying to effect a linkup in the pitch black of a moonless Baghdad night.

The army had come down a different route from the one I advised, because the road that ran parallel to the river, which I used practically every day, was not on the map. Confronted with the heavily congested neighborhood—

intersected by tight, twisting lanes beside the Wahhabi mosque—the unit decided to send out dismounted infantry ahead of the rumbling multiton tracked vehicles. Because they took the road behind the Americans' house instead of the street in front of it, everyone was confused. Talking on two cell phones five miles away—and assuming they had followed my directions—I could not visualize from their ongoing descriptions where they were located.

The TOC kept asking if our client could hear the high whine of the Bradleys without realizing that the patrol had dismounted to press forward to the military grid coordinates I had given them. The grids were on my computer from a security survey we had run for the house. (The client had rejected our recommendations as too expensive.)

The soldiers on the ground were extremely nervous. I could hear increasing concern in the chatter on the radio net blaring in the background. As everyone grew more frustrated and tense, the TOC asked me to have our client come out of the house and onto the road with a flashlight. Robert continued to say he could not hear the forty-ton steel-tracked Bradley vehicles, and a thought kept niggling at me in the back of my head: *These guys have the wrong grid.*

Meanwhile, I was walking Robert out into some serious exposure: he was starkly silhouetted by the neighbor's still-burning cars as he moved away from his "safe house." Or maybe I had given them incorrect coordinates. Then the soldiers appeared out of the inky, moonless darkness, and I heard on the cell connect an American voice tell my client: "We're from the 1st of the 5th Cavalry." I could breathe normally again.

Our client abandoned the river house shortly after

daylight, and the two Americans—Robert and Ron, a stocky Native American engineer originally from Canada— were on separate planes back to the States within seventy-two hours.

———————

Fort Apache was growing by leaps and bounds, but Parsons owed us over $2 million for delays in a project we undertook with Namir's construction company outside Baquba. The site was right on the Iranian border; and when I went with the first survey of the camp location as an extra shooter, I could see the purple-blue outline of the Zagros Mountains at the horizon, on the other side of the Iranian border.

AISG had had some serious delays in finishing the camp for Parsons. The weather was definitely a challenge. This was true desert—hot as hell in May with constant wind-swept sands that caused me to shed copious tears the entire time we were checking out the site. From that time on, I carried sand goggles whenever we left Baghdad proper.

To compound the problem, there was so much explosive ordinance lying around Saddam's Iraq that this contract called for seven years of continuous environmentally friendly destruction! Iraq most likely had the fourth-largest quantity of explosives in the world after America, Russia, and China. And this was in a country with less than one-tenth the population of the United States.

Namir's people were getting shot at en route to the camp. Threatening notes were left on the doors of their homes by insurgents. And they were being kidnapped left and right. Did Parsons care? Apparently not. They didn't pay us for work done, and when they did pay us, it was often months late, despite the fact that our contract called for net ten days on delivery of invoice. There was also a serious disconnect between Parsons site management and the multibillion-dollar construction giant's Iraq headquarters. The HQ management hardly ever traveled from the safe zone of BIAP's Camp Victory out through the badlands of the Sunni Triangle and on to the Baquba site. Yet their project managers at the camp were allowed to exercise unchecked and arbitrary authority.

Because of Parsons' failure to pay, AISG was forced to economize. This was painful, dangerous, and damn near fatal. But necessity is the mother of invention. In this case, the process built value for the company since we started to cut out several layers of middlemen that burdened so many U.S. contractors in-theater with added expense. One of our biggest internal costs was the payroll for our Pesh Merga guard force at Apache, run by a Kurdish warlord named Peshraw, who was also the intelligence chief in Baghdad for the Kurdish Democratic Party (KDP). KPD was one of the two power-house parties that dominated separate regions of Kurdistan. Peshraw was a serious operator who had become rich providing guard services to the U.S. government through Custer Battles at highly inflated prices. Therefore Peshraw decided that he should get the same prices from us as he did from Uncle Sam. His monthly toll was killing us financially, since we had forty of his men living and working at our compound.

He was charging us $900 a month per scantily trained man, including a number of boys—and we had to feed and house them. This was in a country with a per capita monthly income of less than $200. I had been dealing with Peshraw since the Custer Battles days, when he provided the convoy security force for SGD. The Pesh Merga were all good guys, aggressive and loyal. Not so well trained, but they put on a good show. None of them could shoot straight, as we found out at the river house attack. Nevertheless, Peshraw had great pride in his "army" and thought that it ought to continue to make him millions of dollars.

The first time I met with the Kurdish warlord, I was impressed. He was a six-foot hulking, balding tough guy, with a large head that was completely flat in the back. He had taken Frank and me to a famous Baghdad restaurant— the Ramaya on River Road paralleling the western side of the Tigris. It was the only restaurant in an unsecured area of Iraq that I ever went to. But I assumed Peshraw would not endanger Frank and me, to say nothing of himself.

Of course this was January 2004, and the insurgency had not yet made Baghdad as dangerous as it became in later days. We sat down to the usual lamb dinner and (surprisingly) wine. Peshraw—ostensibly a Muslim but like many Kurds an imbiber of alcohol—drank scotch from a bottle he brought with him.

As the drinks began to flow, I asked Peshraw a series of questions about Iraq. Most of his answers were predictable, but the one that most impressed me was his response when I asked, "Will the Kurds side with the Shias in the new Iraqi government?"

He answered in precise English, "We will side with the Sunni Arabs because we are Sunni."

"That is shocking to me," I said, "after all that Saddam and his Sunni supporters have done to your people."

"Yes. Halabja where they gassed five thousand Kurds. And the *Anfal* ["spoils of war"] campaign when Saddam's army killed over one hundred thousand Kurdish and forced hundreds of thousands more from their homes and into the mountains. I was lucky. We got most of my family out, and we settled in Sweden. I came back to Kurdistan to be with the American invasion."

"Then how can you now possibly support a Sunni Arab leader over a Shia?"

"You must understand that the Shias have no love for us either. They will want to be ruled from Iran, where they have killed the Kurds as Saddam did. In the end, the Sunni must support the Sunni."

"Your country is so complicated. How must we understand all this?"

"Remember this: in the end, we will stay allied with the Americans. That is our protection."

I thought, *Maybe he's just selling me—an American—with that statement.* But I had a hard time believing that the Kurds would not stand with the newly empowered Shia over centuries of repression by Sunni Arabs. After all, what they wanted was an autonomous Kurdistan. We would see about that. Peshraw struck me as primarily motivated by self-interest. But that statement stuck in my mind, and I remembered it four months later when I started negotiating with him over the cost of his guards at our compound.

After discovering that some of his Kurds had left his service to work for our clients at the doomed river house, Peshraw told us, "I will have anyone that breaks rank with me hung upside down and I will drain the blood from him." In actuality he did catch a "deserter," one of the few real warriors formerly in our guard crew. This huge Kurd had massive scars all over his body from wounds received in numerous battles with Saddam's forces, the Iranians, and maybe the Turks. Peshraw had the deserter jailed in Irbil, capital of KDP Kurdistan, most likely on specious charges. These people played rough, and the game between Peshraw and AISG had just begun.

Because of our Parsons-generated cash-flow problem, I was assigned the task of squeezing him to reduce the price for his forces. After four months in country, I was confident enough to speak in a straightforward manner with the high-level Kurd chieftain—since he must have known by then that I walked the talk.

"Peshraw, how are you?" I asked him as we sat in my office at Fort Apache.

"I am good, Carter. I am glad to see that you are still over here. I wondered what happened to you after Custer Battles."

"I miss your men who were with me at SGD. Is everyone good?"

"You know, after you left we lost four of those guys in an ambush outside Fallujah."

A whole SUV of his Pesh Mergas got killed. I had heard that the ambush was so overwhelming that the Kurds shot their weapons straight up through the vehicle roof, not at the bad guys attacking them.

"I am so sorry. Yes, I heard. Please give their families and the other men at SGD my best wishes. As you know, what we want to do now is establish a partnership with you, where we provide everyone with a percentage of the profits that AISG earns. We will sell your guard services. But what we need to do now is understand what your costs are, so we can know how high to mark them up, how much profit to add."

"What! No one knows my costs. No one has ever even asked." He looked at me with surprise that I had the chutzpah to raise such a question.

"Well, I am asking now because that's how we must go forward together. So please tell me: what are your costs?"

We were alone in my office. He was well practiced at intimidation and had his sidearm, as did I. But I remained cool and outwardly friendly.

"OK, it's $600 a man. You know I give them a vacation in the north [Kurdistan] every month. Plus, I must pay out big money to their families when they are killed."

He stuck by these figures and didn't budge an inch.

Of course, we discovered that he was paying his men about $200 a month—less in some cases. We never had any evidence that he paid large death benefits. And a significant percentage of his men were Baghdadis (the capital included at least a hundred thousand longtime Kurdish residents)—thus no vacation to the north!

In addition to the exorbitant cost, his men had been guilty of drunkenness, theft (they were always stealing food even though we paid them well enough to buy their own groceries), and dereliction of duty. So we decided to fire the guard force and bring in our own America-allied Kurds. The problem was that we had no money to pay off what we owed Peshraw, since Parsons had not paid us. So we were forced to negotiate a payment plan with the warlord. I was business development, not yet management, so I was not involved in the negotiations until the end when the payment terms were already settled. By that time, Peshraw had already scared the living hell out of Pete Baldwin, our negotiator, by bringing his machine gun–armed bodyguards to the meeting, as well as a younger brother who kept his hand on his loaded pistol in a constant threatening manner.

I had been watching this progress from the sidelines with growing concern and anger. The settlement arrived, and the younger brother was coming over to collect the final signature on the IOU from AISG. At the same time, we had a change of the guard, with Peshraw's forty guards leaving Fort Apache and our new Kurds coming in thirty minutes later. At least that was how it was supposed to work. We realized this was a dangerous transition. For at least half an hour we would be without a guard force. And we didn't know what to expect from Peshraw.

At this time, just three other Americans were living inside Apache, and only two of them were worth a damn for security purposes. There were also thirty Filipinos, both women and men, and, fortunately, three Ukrainian Spetsnaz bodyguards led by Sasha, who would later fight by my side in front of the Green Zone. We only had two Iraqis available to help in the security transition: Amer and Khalid, the former fighter pilot. Because I was the only one who could communicate well with the Spetsnaz, it fell to me to seize the security situation and post the Ukrainians and the Iraqis at the gates just prior to the changing of the guard and the arrival of the warlord's brother, the Junior Intimidator.

At the foot gate where Peshraw's Kurds were to exit Fort Apache for the last time, I posted Amer and Sergei, a thirty-six-year-old, six-foot-six-inch Slav from Zaporozhye who had fought at the bloody Battle of Baku in 1990. I then walked the one hundred yards to the front vehicle gate with Khalid, Sasha, and Max, a six-foot, part-Chinese Ukrainian from Kiev who ran one hundred kilometer races and could bench-press

350 pounds of free weights, after I taught him how. Once we got to the entrance, I posted Khalid out in the road with an AK-47. The retired colonel was obviously uncomfortable playing the role of a mere guard standing in the street. So as not to be visible from the road, the Ukrainians and I stood inside the entrance behind the chest-level, layered-steel sliding vehicle gate.

Junior showed up shortly thereafter with two bodyguards, carrying drum-fed AK-47s and bandoliers of ammo strapped to their chests, looking as if they were ready for a prolonged firefight. The bodyguards were small in stature, as were Kurds in general, somewhat smaller than the Iraqi Arabs and definitely smaller than the average Ukrainian. These two knew me from running the roads at Custer Battles, where I had briefly helped train them for convoy protection. In contrast, Peshraw's brother was a tall, aristocratic Kurd with an arrogant tilt to his chin.

"Do you really need to bring in the bodyguards?" I asked Junior as he slid by me with his two gunslingers trailing a few feet behind.

He stopped when the bodyguards hesitated. As he turned back to respond, I could see confusion on his face—as if I had told him he could not go in his own house. He obviously had been sure his display of firepower had intimidated us completely. In addition, Peshraw was in the driver's seat because we owed him a huge sum of money and because he had an "army" of several thousand, one of the largest private security groups in Iraq, while we were few in number. So the confrontation took on added significance for him, particularly because forty of his guards were lounging around, still inside Apache's walls near the foot gate, not a hundred yards away. They were well within earshot. Junior had to prove that he was in charge.

Not on this day, brother. As he tried to mumble that he needed his people, the bodyguards started to move by me through the gate. Sasha stepped up behind me and stuck his meaty fist clutching an AK like a Mattel toy in the face of the lead bodyguard, who weighed maybe 150 pounds. Max moved up next to his fellow Kievan and looked menacing— cocked, locked, and ready to roll. The warlord's two security men quickly decided to stand out in the street—a smart move.

We later paid off the IOU out of Fallujah receipts, and Fort Apache never saw the cast of Peshraw's, or his brother's, shadow again.

The new Kurd guard force had its problems, and we could not guarantee the quality of the protection or the supply as we could with Peshraw's organization. We went through hundreds of Kurds and the odd Arab as we sought mature, physically fit men who could handle a weapon and would be loyal. AISG could not guarantee supply of security men from Kurdistan even though we tried by sending the driver Abu Hind north to round up some cousins. Only a few showed up, and most of them left homesick not long after arrival. Therefore we began to recruit in the city, primarily through Amer, a Baghdadi Kurd. But we needed about forty; and as the company grew, the Fort Apache guard force eventually expanded to over one hundred men.

The problem within the Baghdadi Kurds reflected in microcosm the essence of the tragedy of Iraq, if not all premodern societies—that of political fragmentation along bloodlines. In the case of the Kurds on our security force, the fracture came along clan lines. One clan supplanted another clan, and this led to a firefight inside Fort Apache— on one side, the new reigning clan, on the other the old, newly fired clan. Their clash resulted in the worst day of my time in Iraq—until the killings in the Western Desert began several months later.

Understanding the clan structure was the key to dealing with Iraqi workers. We hardly ever hired by individual resume, but by familial relations, thereby recognizing the overriding importance of bloodlines in the Middle East. Almost all of our local workers somehow came through Amer, Brahim, Ahmed, or Abu Hind. Yet each of these men went to different sources for new employees. This diversity of competition cut down on the threat of a single clan having company-wide control.

The company employed thousands of Iraqis, and we never had an internal-insurgent incident the entire time I was in Baghdad. That's how tightly the clan-based society controlled the individual employee. We showed trust and respect to our first Iraqi managers, and they trusted and respected us. This trust resulted from leadership by example and was never a given. Each succeeding day brought a new challenge to that critical relationship between those of us who were American and our Iraqi employees and partners.

Yet jobs were few in the city, and control over jobs meant power—not to speak of money—so the leaders of the clans inside our work force struggled for dominance. Until now, we had maintained a balance that kept the peace. But with the wholesale firing of a group of Kurds for various transgressions such as drunkenness, absenteeism, and minor theft, only one clan came to dominate the guard force. Apparently the new clan in power had worked hard to get rid of the other, now-fired clan. This power struggle extended back to the Kurdish Baghdad neighborhoods and had created a great deal of bad blood between the two groups. Bad blood in Iraq often meant spilled blood was on the way, as we soon found out.

It began as all days begin in wartime Baghdad with the exception of the few rainy months in winter: the sun shown brightly in an azure sky with nary a contrail to disturb the purity of its arcing blueness. One of the stranger aspects of the world-renowned city was that no commercial airliners flew over it, just the occasional jet fighter and the near-constant buzz of low-flying U.S. Army helicopters leaving and returning to the Green Zone at all hours of the day and night. The air had a bite in it from the organic micro-elements blown up from the huge alluvial plain created by the Tigris and Euphrates Rivers.

That day I was working in my office, putting together another proposal. Having moved up the chain, I was now in charge of the bid department; and we had submitted one hundred bids in less than thirty days. The Iraqis still looked at me as a man of action, I guess because I was the only American they knew who drove around Baghdad by himself.

As I was concentrating on my laptop, I looked up for a moment and there stood two of our Pesh Merga guards, sig-naling me through the glass door with hand signs shaped like a pistol. Realizing this meant trouble, I jumped up and ran out the door. The Kurds led me around the corner to the tiled front porch of the main house where I spotted our assis-tant director for security, J. P., a short but muscular former

110

paratroop officer, surrounded by angry Kurds on the porch. One towered over J. P., gripping his arm. Even-angrier Kurds gesticulated in the walkway in front of the raised porch.

When I saw J. P. in the grips of the agitated sergeant of the guard, I ran up and knocked the man off, shouting, "Get the hell away from him!" I then noticed our security director, Woody, standing tall, all six foot four of him, on the back edge of the porch, behind the twenty or so angry Kurds. Woody, with prematurely gray hair and a thick moustache, was as low key as you could get. He must've taken up his rear position to be able to get the drop on anyone if things really got out of control.

After I got the Pesh Merga off J. P., I looked out in front of the porch and saw a bunch of Kurds in a drunken frenzy. I started shouting, "Get out! Get out!"

Suddenly I realized that these were the Kurds we had fired earlier in the week, some of the many we had hired and fired after we stopped using Peshraw's people. Somehow they had gotten back into the compound!

They had a leader and I knew him: Mehmet. We had run the roads together, so he looked at me and then directed his crowd to leave. Everything seemed back under control. I asked J. P., "Why are these men here?"

J. P., who was responsible for the guard force, replied, "They are here to get paid."

"Why did you tell them to come or allow them to get inside Apache? We have no money to pay them! You should have warned us." Parsons still had not paid us, and so we had no money yet to pay the dismissed guards. Even after we had fired Peshraw's men, we continued to have money problems because of Parsons' continued failure to pay us in a timely manner.

After it appeared that everything was stable and the angry men were leaving, Mehmet, their leader, approached Woody, J. P., and me, standing together in the parking lot. With Amer translating, Mehmet said, "I am sorry that we have caused this problem, especially to you, Mr. Carter, my friend. I hope you can still respect us."

Tensely I replied, "We will get you and your men paid. I am sorry for the delay, but this angry crowd is no answer."

Returning to my office, I got back to work, thinking, *That was almost a catastrophe.* Thank God they didn't have any guns. Little did I know then that during our confrontation Mehmet and his crowd had gotten within one man of breaking into our armory and stealing enough automatic weapons to arm all his clan. One of the invading Kurds had punched the armorer, but he had held strong until the rest of the on-duty guard force had arrived. Apparently one of the guards had let them through the foot gate and into the compound because he didn't know they had been fired.

In reality this was more of a clan struggle, with the winning clan persuading Woody and J. P. to get rid of the other clan. For example, one of the dismissed Kurds was Fatah, a most excellent warrior who had accompanied me on the road to Taji. His dismissal had nothing to do with his behavior, just his allegiance to the wrong group.

I had just sat down at my desk again when all of sudden: *Brrrraaaaaaap . . . brrraaaap!* The sound of AK fire on full automatic shredded the silence, echoing from every angle inside the cavernous walls of Fort Apache. Over fifty rounds were fired. I couldn't tell where the sound was coming from, so I ran out of my office next door to the main house. I climbed the stairs up to my second-floor bedroom to put on body armor and grab my own AK, an Iraqi-made *Tabuk* that I had zeroed near perfectly at thirty meters in just two bull's-eye-tight, three-round shot groups. Even the Spetsnaz snipers were impressed.

As I debated where to deploy myself, AK fire erupted from two places simultaneously: near the man gate by the main house and from the other side of the compound. I considered going to the nearside man gate in order to control anyone trying to get in, but decided instead to head up on the roof, which was my designated position in the event of an attack.

To get to my position, I needed to exit through a glass door near my bedroom onto a second-floor patio that adjoined House Two, where my first-floor office was located. Then I had to climb a ladder up to a four-story tower in the middle house—the highest point in the neighborhood. Our Special Forces guys had painted an American flag on the flat top of the tower, invisible to everyone except the U.S. flyboys constantly zipping above Apache. We definitely wanted the heavily armed choppers to know we were an American operation.

According to our defense plan, I was then to climb down a shorter ladder to the lower adjacent roof of House One where the Filipinos lived. There I was to give them security supervision, since none of them had had military training. As I ascended the tower, the shooting stopped and I realized how exposed I was. During the climb, gripping the hot metal handles seared by the Iraqi sun, I instinctually pointed my AK up the ladder toward the guard looking down over the side at me.

When I got to the top I handed him my AK, muzzle first, thereby interfering with his control of his own rifle. You never point your weapon at someone unless you are prepared to shoot him. There were two Kurds stationed at Apache's peak position as I started to cross over to the other side of the tower to go down to House One. Below, our guards were scattering about; and Woody, walking in the parking lot toward the vehicle gate, looked up at me on top of the tower. I glanced back and saw another Kurd climbing behind me, shouting at the Pesh Merga who had just handed me back my AK. For a brief moment I wasn't sure if the Kurd was shouting at me or at the Pesh Merga.

I stopped, turned around, and met the Kurd on the roof at the end of the ladder. I recognized him, although I could not place his name. The recognition was unusual, for the guard force was constantly in flux. He was a taller Kurd in his early twenties with dark curly black hair. He had been with us almost from the beginning and had accompanied me on many missions, usually with an irrepressible smile on his face. I noticed immediately that he was unarmed and that he continued shouting in spitting, vehement Kurdish, completely unintelligible to me. He was directing his rage at the guard on the tower, a short toad of a man, who remained silent.

Yet the shouting affected me, so I began to shout back, "Shut up! Shut up!" as if the Kurd would know what I meant. In my frustration, I almost threw him off the roof, but something held me back. My shouting, however, did serve a purpose: it alerted the Filipinos, huddled together, terrified in their safe room deep in House One. Mar, the former head chef for the president of the Philippines—the money was better in Iraq than even at the Malacañan Palace—said to the others crammed in the room, "Mr. Carter is on it. Everything must be OK."

Finally Azad—I later remembered his name—stopped

shouting and went back down the ladder. I turned, still not realizing that the guards on the tower where I stood were the ones shooting tens of AK rounds down at the fired Kurds, after they started hurling insults at them from below. Thankfully no one got hit.

I crossed over to House One and took up my position above the vehicle gate where the Iraqi police had arrived in a couple of blue and white Isuzu Troopers. The crowd of angry, drunken Kurds still mingled on the outer edge of our t-walls (Texas walls). This was the first time the IP had come calling at Fort Apache. They were the security detail for interim Prime Minister Iyad Allawi, who lived only a few blocks away.

I looked down from the roof and saw Woody striding purposefully toward the gate. He looked up at me and said, "Cover me."

"Will do, Woody," thinking I had heard that line somewhere before.

He disappeared around the corner of the t-walls, and I couldn't really "cover" him from my position. So I climbed down from the roof through the Filipinos' TV room and walked out the gate to where the crowd had gathered. A lean IP major of military bearing talked with Woody and Mehmet through Amer's translation. I stood next to Woody and held my AK with one hand by the pistol grip hanging down by my side. Right away, one of the other fired Kurds, an older man in a black suit with no tie, charged Woody from the side, apparently trying to knock him over, a grave insult in Iraq. Just as he got to me, I grabbed him with my free hand and somehow threw him back on the street. I never raised my weapon, although I would have been justified to have shot him.

No one rushed anyone on the streets of Baghdad.

Everyone, including the IP major, looked on approvingly. The discussion ended. The police left, and so did the drunken Pesh Merga. We borrowed some money from Brahim, who was now getting rich selling arms to the company, and paid off the fired guards the next day. That evening, I fired the two guards shooting from the roof. End of story: but it took me days to shake off the fear of a shooting among the guards, our friends and allies, inside our own walls.

When an external test did come, our patchwork guard force reacted immediately and effectively. Once more, I was working in my office. Dark night had fallen on Baghdad. We had finished the communal meal a couple hours before.

Crack! A single shot rang out. I thought, *OK, an accidental discharge.*

Then *crack, crack, crack*—disciplined, single-shot, aimed fire sounded out at the vehicle gate. Woody had started training the guards inside Apache with realistic AK-47 BB-gun mock-ups that improved individual shooting skills in a neighborhood-friendly way. The training showed this night.

A second or two later, a loud rending sound erupted from the far corner machine gun on the main house roof. This was the deeper-throated rapid *bud-bud-bud-bud* of the PKC medium machine guns we had mounted at all the over-watch corners of Fort Apache's roof line. These were serious bullets, heavier than the AK round. The guards were firing at someone in a serious way.

A car—earlier identified to our guards by the patrolling IP as "a bad-guy vehicle"—drove by our gate and took a pot shot at those standing by the vehicle entrance. Big mistake. The Pesh Merga immediately started to shoot back, happy to have a live enemy to target. The car could only go one way, and that was along one hundred yards of concrete blast walls forming a shooting gallery.

Then the bad guys made a worse mistake. They turned right at the corner heading up the street, giving our machine gun a direct line of sight stretching out over three hundred yards. Down the whole length of the street the tripod-mounted, belt-fed machine gun pumped round after round into the car, firing well over sixty times.

The car somehow kept going but was stopped at an IP checkpoint a short time later. Even in Baghdad it was hard to hide a shot-up sedan carrying three shot-up men with most of the windows blown out. The Iraqi police reported back to us that two of the occupants were dead and the driver was alive, but barely. They all had weapons and were known bad guys; whether criminals or insurgents, I don't know. But they often overlapped in Iraq.

Shortly after the brief but loud and repetitive shooting ended, I went out to check on the guards at the vehicle gate. The Kurds were hyped up, especially the sergeant of the guard who had a pistol in his hand (the same guy from the pay revolt). This was a sign of his elevated office. But these simple soldiers had very little experience with pistols. The next thing I knew, the sergeant accidentally shot off a 9mm round, thankfully straight into the road but less than five feet from my leg! Obviously Fort Apache's indigenous security force still had a ways to go. However, after that night, no one ever tried attacking Fort Apache again.

Slowly but surely we were learning our way through

dangerous times in Iraq. Baghdad was growing more unstable with the rising insurgency. Fort Apache in turn reflected the surrounding capital city. Most importantly, we were successfully building a large supply of loyal Iraqis from all sects and ethnic groups, with all sorts of in-demand skills and life-risking courage. Even during the clan firefight inside our walls, neither I nor any of the other non-Iraqis felt threatened directly by the fratricidal Kurds. Now that we had gained security and control in and around our own house, we could venture out successfully to provide the same protection to others anywhere nationwide in the Iraq combat zone. This capability was to prove highly bankable as the country tumbled into full-scale insurgency warfare.

FIVE
Low Profile

Ka-boom! The side of the Humvee and the soldier in the turret disappeared from view in the explosion not fifty yards in front of us as we sped down Airport Road. We were heading to check on Max, who had been shot in the stomach in an ambush on the road to Fallujah. Not fifteen minutes before, I had been having lunch in Fort Apache's formal dining room, enjoying one of Mar's orange-cream-and-crackers cakes. The cake topped off a four-course meal—including one of the Filipino chef's special soups. (His repertoire included over fifty different recipes.)

Woody had rushed into the room and said, "Stay seated, Carter. I have something to tell you."

"OK," I said, putting down my fork. I could hear the bad news in his voice.

"Max has been shot. He's at the air force hospital at Camp Slayer in BIAP. We need to go see him. He'll be OK, they say."

J. P. met us at the main house double-doors, and we dashed across the parking lot and jumped into a tiny Kia sedan. Throughout the morning and the night before, rockets and mortars had exploded periodically, echoing from every quadrant of the city. Just after dawn a massive car bomb's explosion at the Green Zone's airport checkpoint rattled the window of my bedroom. From the roof of our house you could see the black, oily mushroom cloud pouring into the sky from the checkpoint where Sasha and I had gotten into a firefight not one mile from Fort Apache. Machine-gun fire rent the air, the racket from a firefight that lasted several minutes not far from the car bomb. The day before, we had watched from the main house's rooftop as the U.S. Air Force fired 30mm chain-gun rounds in an almost laserlike continuous green flow from a circling AC-130 Specter gunship. The target: Haifa Street, Baghdad's "mini-Fallujah" just north of the Green Zone's main gate. The city was rattling as we prepared to leave the protection of our compound to head down the "Road of Death," as the airport highway was now known worldwide.

I turned to J. P. as he slid behind the wheel and Woody folded his long frame into the passenger seat. "Is this the only vehicle we have? It doesn't have tinted windows."

Woody stared for a second at me, and then put on his white prayer cap with geometric patterns stitched into the side Islamic style.

"All the other vehicles are out on missions or broken. No one would suspect Americans to move in this car."

We were having serious problems maintaining our vehicles because of the constant abuse of the potholed Iraqi roads, ill-trained drivers, and a shortage of mechanics. And since Parsons had still not paid us, we had little money to improve or even sustain our fleet.

"All right, let's go."

As J. P. cranked up the car, I figured we didn't look too bad: J. P.—a very short, swarthy man with a full black beard— was behind the wheel. Woody, with his tanned square face and gray-silver hair, could pass at first glance for an older Iraqi (but only because he was sitting in a moving car). And I with my desert tan and brown beard would get past a quick glance. Above all, we were driving this beat-up Kia sedan. We were definitely low profile! I relaxed a little.

We zoomed from behind our blast walls and out of the vehicle gate into a blue-sky, sun-drenched day. J. P. was already driving like a mad man. He steered us down Al Kindi Street, with its shops and restaurants always crowded with people, and headed toward the nearest Green Zone gate. That was Checkpoint 12 where we could get on a bypass to the airport without actually going through the U.S. Army security stop.

The bypass entrance was manned by a hodge-podge of Iraqi security types. They were standing around in civilian clothes under a tree, scoping some vendor stalls selling gum and sodas. Just a few weeks before, on May 17, a car bomb had killed Izzedin Salim, the president of the Iraqi national Interim Governing Council. The assassination was claimed by Abu Musa al Zarqawi, the pseudonym of the Jordanian terrorist mastermind affiliated with al Qaeda. As we flashed our badges to the Iraqi security, we could still see where the massive blast had left scorch marks and a crater in the road.

To access BIAP road, we needed to pass through a short tunnel that always had water flowing in the bottom from broken pipes. The Kia hit the stream fast and splashed a car-high wave onto a rusty Jeep Cherokee next to us. The Jeep was driven by an Iraqi whose window was open in the scorching heat of the Arabian summer. The dirty water covered the poor guy. He started to shout at us through his window. I thought, *Lord, that's all we need, a case of road rage.*

As we sped out of the tunnel, the Jeep followed. We entered a busy traffic circle, and the wet driver pulled right up beside us. He gesticulated angrily down at us from his SUV, which towered over our little sedan. I looked back up at him and put the palm of my hand out, motioning him not to get any closer. We continued to mask our weapons from view: J. P. and I had AKs, and Woody had his WWII-era Tommy gun, a heavy caliber .45 submachine gun famous from the days of the Untouchables. Finally the Iraqi figured out that three strange European-looking characters driving the streets of Baghdad might not be the best people to shout at. He fell away as we entered the highway to BIAP.

J. P. revved the little Kia up as fast it would go, and we hurtled down Airport Road at about ninety miles an hour. We drove under overpass after overpass, going around or between the slowly flowing Iraqi traffic. The U.S. Army had continued the policy of clearing the shoulders and median of trees that could provide cover for an ever-increasing number of insurgents. The highway now featured several attacks every day, primarily on high-profile contractor convoys and U.S. patrols. There were drive-by shootings and sniping from the homes along the highway. But by far the most common attack was the roadside bomb.

At the last underpass before the gate to the airport, where the wounded Max lay, we came up on a three-vehicle Humvee patrol providing security for the highway. J. P. hesitated, trying to decide whether to fall back and follow the slow-moving convoy or move to pass. The rear tactical vehicle's turret gunner motioned for us to pass, just as the middle Humvee shifted toward the shoulder before the underpass and into a well-timed explosion. The improvised explosive device (IED) must've been remote controlled from afar because there was no one near the bomb in the wide-open, desert-like shoulder. We felt its impact on the little Kia, which swayed abruptly from the concussion just fifty yards away.

J. P., who successfully ran the roads of north-central Iraq for several months during an earlier struggle, made a radical move. He stomped on the accelerator and thrust the car into the median at about fifty miles an hour for a sharp U-turn to get us out of the kill zone. The median, which stretched almost forty yards across, was surfaced in deep sand and littered with hundreds of thick palm stumps, left over from the army's ongoing tree-clearing project. This was near where J. D. and Robert had taken cover when their car had broken down. I had a brief vision of them trying to hide behind the palm-tree remnants.

"Watch out for the stumps," I shouted from the back seat as we went airborne from bump to bump. When we hit the sand, I thought for sure we were going to get stuck. Sand spewed out from the Kia's front end as our little car dug into the ditch. Through pure momentum we emerged on the other side.

"I got it!" rejoined J. P. as he did his best Mario Andretti impression.

When we jumped up on the opposite side of the highway, we were all shaking with relief. Woody looked back at me, eyes wide, and said, "That was a near one. We had better head back to Apache. This is not a day to move around Baghdad."

"Damn. What about Max?" I asked.

"Tomorrow will be a better day. He'll be all right at the air force hospital."

Inshallah, we all quietly prayed.

We never did find out what happened to the soldiers in the bombed Humvee. The next day we drove out the same route to the hospital. Max was in good spirits after surgery and was already trying to hit on the nurses in his quickly improving English.

I was relieved to see Max and to realize that he was in better shape than I could have hoped. At this point I was curious to know how he had been wounded. After talking with Max, Brahim, Amer, Sasha, and Sergei, we determined that the following had happened on the road to Fallujah.

By way of background, I should say that Woody and J. P. had convinced Parsons that AISG could deliver anything anywhere in Iraq. So Parsons started to give us the most dangerous jobs. One of these turned out to be the delivery of brand-new Ford F-350 pickup trucks to Paladin, an American military base on the far western side of Fallujah.

The Sunni city was by then a no-go area. Insurgents had killed, dismembered, and hung from a bridge the Blackwater security contractors, and attempts by the U.S. military to pacify this "City of Mosques" had subsequently failed. So Max and the others, providing security for the pickups, had entered the lions' den.

To compound the risk, the local trucking company we'd hired had not followed instructions. We explained to them that new American trucks would provide the insurgents with targets too tempting to resist. They had to be inconspicuous, out of sight. Yet at the start of the journey the three transports stood lined up with two F-350s each on the side road between the man gate for the main house and House Four. There hadn't been enough tarp to cover the six new Ford trucks sitting on the flatbed transports. So anyone driving alongside the car-haulers could have seen the cargo. And only Americans used brand-new American-made pickups in Iraq.

Parsons had been pushing hard as usual. The Pasadena-based company had failed several times prior to move the urgently needed vehicles to Paladin. Their subcontracted transport company had failed to show or, when it did, balked at the clearly U.S.-only cargo—an invitation to murder in the Sunni Triangle.

In spite of the trucking company's failure to follow our instructions, Woody and J. P. had decided to press ahead with the delivery anyway. The low-profile principle had been discarded—with predictable results.

The group set out from Apache in the late morning across Baghdad, heading west to Fallujah. The convoy included four security cars—three Suburban "urban battlewagons" and the Caprice taxi, driven by Brahim—and three car haulers. The cars were carrying one American (against my expressed advice), Zinc, a junior AISG security man and former air force policeman who was technically in charge of the convoy; fifteen Iraqis; and three Ukrainians (also against my advice, since these were high-end bodyguards, not materials and equipment protection). Sasha was in the lead SUV with Zinc. Amer was driving the second Suburban with Max. The three flatbeds carrying the Ford pickups followed with Brahim's taxi shifting among the trucks as the column moved down the road. The convoy trail vehicle was an SUV with Sergei in the back manning a machine gun. All the security vehicles' teams were rounded out with the additional Iraqis, almost all Kurds.

When the vehicles reached the capital's densely populated outskirts, the U.S. Army had blocked the highway. After a brief discussion on the handheld radio net, they had decided to take an alternate, parallel route, and exited off the highway and up onto an overpass where scores of Iraqi passenger cars intermixed with delivery trucks. Our seven vehicles were strung out over the two hundred yards of the bridge spanning the six lanes of the superhighway below. Civilian cars were interspersed among the AISG vehicles, further extending the convoy.

On foot, a man wearing a red-and-white-checkered *shmag* approached the driver's window where Brahim the Shia sat trapped in traffic in an insurgent-infested Sunni neighborhood. The man asked menacingly, "Are you going to Fallujah?"

Brahim looked at the bearded man and told him in Iraqi Arabic, "No, by Allah. Get away from the car or you will be shot."

"You go to Fallujah?" the man—an *ali baba* (thief or insurgent, as they often overlapped) and possible Wahhabi jihadist—insisted again.

Not only did all four heads in Brahim's Iraqi taxi 1989 Chevrolet Caprice turn toward the *ali baba*, but so did all of their weapons; and all the weapons in two of our other security vehicles with the convoy. The security element had some nice-size medium machine guns, such as the belt-fed PKC firing a large 7.62 by 54mm round. The AISG men had torso body armor on, except some of the drivers, who refused the protection because the Baghdadis felt that the added bulk made them look out of place on the road and obstructed their driving. Our secure movement strategy called for a team heavily armed but as Iraqified as possible: totally low profile. The convoy trucks, on the other hand, might as well have had a neon sign blinking, "Bound for Americans!"

Brahim shouted at the *ali baba*, "Get away from the car now, or my people will kill you."

The man grunted, turned, and loped back to his beat-up, four-door, dust-covered Toyota where two other men sat. All of a sudden, AK-47s flashed inside their car. This AISG crew was stuck—completely surrounded by other vehicles. To make matters worse, people were milling about in dead-stop traffic strung across a bridge after an IED investigation had blocked the main highway west. The white-bright sun glared down, and khaki sand whipped about in the constant wind. The convoy was deadly vulnerable.

After the exchange between the *ali baba* and Brahim, Amer, driving the SUV in front of them, drew first blood, prematurely triggering the ambush on the road to Fallujah. Upon seeing the rifles in the bad guys' car and after watching one of them just having approached Brahim, Amer charged out of his car and started shooting with an AK at the Wahhabis. Very few Iraqis other than Wahhabis wore beards, just moustaches. The beard, therefore, was indicative of bad actors, but native-born bad actors. In traffic you would not stare at a man with a Taliban beard, just as any intelligent American wouldn't blatantly stare at a group of Hell's Angels if they pulled up next to your car at a stoplight on their snarling Harleys. This was especially helpful to me, with my Talibanesque beard, as very few Iraqis possessed the nerve to stare at me long enough in traffic to see the foreigner inconsistencies in my general appearance.

Another old Japanese-type sedan pulled up on the bridge in support of the first Wahhabi vehicle but did not have time to do anything but turn around as quickly as possible and leave the kill-zone. Several of the AISG security men had opened up on the follow-on sedan. As soon as Amer began firing at the first vehicle, Sasha, Max, and several of the Pesh Merga deployed from the lead two security SUVs. Lying prone on the road or resting their weapons on the hoods of their vehicles, they laid down a devastating fire line along the length of the bridge.

Brahim told me later, "*Aiya*, yes. Traffic clears, we move out. No one move in the car that Amer shot up. Ukrainya Max got shot by sniper from roof three hundred meters away. No one else from *Ikhwan* [Brotherhood] hurt." Brahim smiled at the memory of the escape from the ambush.

In the rear convoy's SUV, holding a PKC machine gun, Spetsnaz sniper Sergei explained in Russian: "The second vehicle fled in front of me the wrong way down the ramp and back under the bridge over the blocked Fallujah highway. As the car sped away, it was being shot at several times by Max, Sasha, and all the Kurds. I realized this: in the flash of all of this happening, I could not put the machine gun on it before the terrorists cut under the bridge. But I will tell you this: the back window was blown out and the front window looked like Swiss cheese from the bullet holes." The *ali baba* had tried to rob the wrong convoy.

"Then," Amer continued the story, "the U.S. Army shot

several rounds in the air, including from the big [25mm] cannon of a Bradley. Their checkpoint blocking the highway was just in front of the bridge. A couple of Humvees appeared. The American soldiers secured both ends of the bridge and then took Max to the hospital. We headed back to Apache."

Max had received a through-and-through wound from an AK round across the front of his abdomen just below the waistline of his body armor, but he returned to work three weeks after surgery by the U.S. Air Force. Through Woody's Special Forces connections, we called Spec Ops headquarters in the Green Zone to do something about the building where the sniper who shot Max had been positioned. The word came down through the ex-Green Beret's Old Boy network that Delta Force hit a week later, taking some bad guys down in the ten-story apartment complex. We delivered the now properly covered Ford trucks without incident to the U.S. Army base in Fallujah three days after the ambush.

That was how Max had been shot—an avoidable injury had everyone followed the established rules for AISG missions. And because of that wounding, we had almost been killed en route to the hospital to see Max. We had to make some changes to the way we were conducting our operations before anyone else got hurt.

Once we got back to Apache, after being turned back by the IED, I sat with Woody and J. P. in the company ops center under the thirty-foot ceiling.

"Woody, you remember that I operated Secure Global Distribution for Custer Battles?"

Woody, who had run the ops center for CB at BIAP, nodded. "Yes, I remember."

"We never used Americans that looked like Northern

Europeans on our convoys. And in reality, we rarely used Americans at all. I have a lot of respect for your camouflaging techniques, but you know what I think about today."

Woody, the shaken security chief, said, "Yes, we shouldn't use Americans because they attract attention. But I don't think that Zinc even got out of the car."

"Right. But Max and Sasha did get out on the bridge. They probably would have been all right—a classic counterattack with Amer charging the near ambush, before it even triggered—but the problem was that big Europeans Sasha and Max in their heavy, army-green flak jackets attracted attention. As a result, Max was shot from three hundred meters away. And then there's the issue of the Fords being exposed on the car haulers."

"I know," Woody replied, "we will never operate like that again."

J. P. chimed in. "We should only use Kurds for convoy security. We can even train the Pesh Merga to be drivers like we discussed before."

I summed up the argument. "Hey, it's less expensive, doesn't attract attention, and fulfills our mission as an Iraqi-focused company."

From then on, that was company policy, carved in granite, never to be violated.

The failure of Parsons to pay out invoices was a continuing problem, with several damaging results for AISG. We were constructing man camps for the ammo-demolition program in Ashraf (near Baquba), Baiji, Tikrit, Al Hadr (fifty miles south of Mosul), and Camp Victory (BIAP)—and with very mixed results. Fallujah was initially included but that fell by the wayside, because even Parsons, a giant international construction firm, could not pretend to the U.S. government that it could operate there. So AISG reconned the site at Paladin, but no further construction activity occurred at that camp.

Parsons had its internal management problems, but so did AISG. Because of late payments by Parsons, we went without paychecks for August, September, and part of October. Needless to say, morale was affected, especially among the site supervisors we had hired for the Parsons projects who had come primarily for the money, not as much for the mission, as had the founding Americans. They were also a greater security burden for us than the other expats who were all prior military—thus more alert and adaptable to the high-threat environment. Transporting these construction managers around Iraq further exposed the risks of not operating completely low profile.

Woody, our low-profile security guru, was always trying different types of vehicles so as not to be predictable. The CPA banned tinted windows in order to make it easier for the military and police to see inside of cars. This made sense unless you were an American trying not to be seen. AISG kept on using tinted windows; but because of the ban, this practice actually increased our profile, since only DoD badge holders could get through checkpoints with tinted windows. As the security situation continued to deteriorate, we eventually went to curtains for the back seat and tinted windows for our follow-on-security, urban SUV battlewagons. Curtains were legal. And you wanted the interior of your trail security vehicle to be invisible. We believed this invisibility served as a deterrent to attackers, who never knew just how many people were behind the curtains and tinted windows and how heavily they were armed. Almost all of the AISG security men were spoiling for a fight, but were disciplined enough not to go looking for trouble in the Iraqi war zone. On the other hand, it didn't matter to them if their battlewagon looked like a security vehicle. The AISG *esprit de corps* meant we would run the streets of Baghdad always—no one could stop us.

What Woody now came up with was a Kia van with heavy curtains. The problem was that you had to keep the curtains open a bit to see out for area awareness. On the way back out of the Green Zone, we picked up one of our new site managers, a large beefy man named Jerry, to transport back from a job site to Apache. Thus on the way home in the van, we had the obviously non-Arab Jerry, a fully healed and part-Chinese six-foot-tall Max in ammo-laden tactical gear, three Pesh Merga, and me riding along heavily armed. We were a force to be reckoned with. However, if in the world of the combatant contractor you had a choice between being better armed than your adversary or maintaining a low profile and slipping away unawares to your destination, you opted for stealth every time. We had concentrated way too many high-profile people in a vehicle that did not conceal the occupants.

We weren't without support when we hit the road. When you drove up on Checkpoint 12 and the CPA entrance, you encountered the toughest gate guards in the world, backed by tanks and snipers and special ops troops with helicopters and uplinks to satellites and attack jets. In addition, they had a battalion each of precision 155mm cannon and 298mm MLRS rockets. The Infantry Division manned the gates. This division was Audie Murphy's unit and the most decorated U.S. combat division in WWII. The Third had taken over the regiment where I served in the army, the 15th Infantry. The division had made it first into the center of Baghdad in April 2003 and now had returned for another yearlong tour of duty. The grunts on the gates performed with élan, never knowing when the oft-bombed Green Zone checkpoints would have another suicide ride—packed with TNT—roll up to where the troopers stood out in the open on the downtown Baghdad streets in front of all the CPA gates.

For the most part, however, you were on your own. You settled disputes on the highway with bullets or dollars or words. When you got into a fender bender, you didn't wait around for the Iraqi cops or the Third Infantry Division to mediate.

A case in point.

Packed into the newly curtained minivan, Jerry, Max, three Pesh Mergas, and I were driving along the road to BIAP after leaving the Green Zone when I happened to look down at the inside lane as we swung around the corner to the right. I saw a Mazda hatchback with a patchwork paint job move sharply toward us as it gained on the AISG van, heading into the tight corner turn. I couldn't see into the car, though, because of the downward angle.

I warned the Pesh Merga driver, "*Sirchow, sayyawra!* ["Attention" in Kurdish, and "car" in Arabic]." Scree-eech! The Mazda tagged our van, scraping the left front panel of the hatchback.

The AISG driver looked back at me, sitting on the back bench of the van, and said something in Kurdish that probably meant "Their fault."

According to Baghdad-lawlessness rules, yes. However, according to international driving laws, you cannot cut off the inside lane ever. So we were in the wrong. I urged, "*Yella, yella* [go, go] Fort Apache."

Then I turned to the others and said, "We will go back home and take care of it at the gate. This isn't my first fender bender at this turn. It's a famous spot for conning foreigners. They'll follow, and we just pay them off at the gate—whether we're in the wrong or not. Good public relations. It's usually not expensive. Iraqi car repair costs only in the tens of dollars."

Just as I finished my speech, Neoshad—an atypically large, fat Kurdish security man—leapt up out of the front right jump seat and crossed in between me and Max. The forty-five-year-old Neoshad—a minor war chief, as I found out later—was shaking his drum-fed RPK at the rear window toward the Mazda, which I assumed was following us for payment. Neoshad was shouting, "*Aw-gov!* [Stop]" out the closed back window.

Max cried, "*Smoo-tri!* [Look out!],", as Neoshad dove to the floor, spinning his body and AK around toward the rear.

I looked back and saw two men in the speeding Mazda. They were both wearing what looked like police-blue blouses. I turned to Neoshad crouching beside me. He stuck out his pointer finger and thumb, and wagged his hand.

I allowed our driver to drive on, then thought better of it, and said, "*Awgov.*" Maybe these were real police; and no matter how obviously we had them outgunned, we probably should hear what they had to say. So I told the driver to stop. Sure enough, when they got out of the car they looked like IP officers. They held pistols below their hips, pointed down at the asphalt.

134

All three of us showed them our DoD badges, letting them know that according to UN-recognized law of the CPA, no Iraqi security man could impede our passage. Knowing this, I turned to the driver, assuming the incident was over, and said, "*Yella*, Fort Apache."

Having said that, I noticed that the head IP—if that's what they were—did not move away, even with my Kurd driver's AK pointed at his belly.

These were only "possible" IP, because, as I well knew, you could buy Iraqi police uniforms at any bazaar. These two had no badges on, but they did have IP-issued, Soviet-designed Makarov 9mm pistols. In addition, they were driving around in a civilian car, and they had targeted us for the minor scraping.

I understood that these men did not want us to leave. On the other hand, we sat very much exposed on the side of the road in the middle of violence-torn Baghdad, drawing unwanted attention from the hundreds of cars passing by in the late-afternoon rush hour.

The dressed-like-IP man at my driver's window just shook his head and said, "*La, la, la* [No, no, no]."

I realized then that I would have to be a little more aggressive. I stepped across the back of the van to get in the face of the man standing in the street beside my driver, while his partner stood behind him to the rear between our two vehicles. As I moved diagonally across the jump seats, something dawned on me: I was about to put my head in the face of a man holding a pistol. With this thought in mind, as I crossed to where he stood, I pulled out a fully cocked Colt .45 1911 automatic with a muzzle hole the size of an eye from a quick-draw holster strapped to my right leg. Putting the .45 up next to my ear as my head squeezed between the side of the car and the driver's seat, I said, "*Yella!*"

The possible-IP now stared right down the barrel of a man-stopping "horse pistol." My finger rested on the trigger and my thumb rested on the slide safety. I was ready to click and pull in sequence, shooting the man in front of me, if he made a wrong move.

He shifted his eyes from the barrel into my steady gaze, dropped his head, and walked back toward his vehicle. I almost felt sorry for the con man, cop, or whatever. To ensure no possible wrongdoing on our side, I holstered my .45, got my wallet, and put $60 out the open window. The second IP-appearing man saw the money, stopped, and scowled, making no motion to accept. I pulled back one of the three twenty-dollar bills—he realized what was next, and grabbed the forty that remained. This was plenty to fix the little self-inflicted scratch the con men had hoped to use to waylay us. After the face-off, we never saw or heard from them again; although every day for a couple weeks I feared while on the road that they would reappear with reinforcements to bushwhack my car.

As often as possible I moved around the city as a lone American. I tried to utilize Clausewitz's most-difficult-to-achieve principle of war: surprise. I realized that very few Americans drove alone through Baghdad in the summer of 2004. Very few bad guys would be looking for that profile in the tens of thousands of vehicles tooling around the metropolis at any one time. I got rid of the Galloper and started driving the AISG taxi for business calls inside Baghdad, as well as on the way to BIAP. The commonplace Caprice, white with orange panels, had all tinted windows to the sides and rear. I'd pull the eyeshade down, leaving just a slit for me to see out. A Shia Hussein medallion with several loops of beads hung from the rearview mirror. The back pitch-black tinted window had an Ali—the Shia hero caliph—in rapture, painted on a glow-in-the-dark sticker. (I once got pulled over by a U.S. patrol at the border fence between American and Iraqi-secured areas of the Taji Iraqi army base because some food contractor at the KBR chow hall reported a taxi driving around inside the wire with heavily armed men and a "Saddam" sticker on the back!)

Woody had really spent a lot of time with Brahim getting the cab just right. People used to hail me for a ride all the time on the streets of the capital. When available, meaning when AISG did not have other missions or all the other rides were not broken because of lack of payment by Parsons, I would take a trail car. The second vehicle would have one Iraqi, most often, Brahim—driving something different, such as an SUV, an old Mercedes sedan, or a plain Caprice, just in case of breakdown. Thus, I continued my plan to complete all missions successfully without personally having been directly shot at or bombed by the bad guys. I established this record while putting over ten thousand miles on the Iraqi roads. Mostly I traveled in the Sunni Triangle and/or in the besieged capital where on my map of the Triangle the two overlapped at the Abu Ghraib suburbs.

SIX
In Memory of Namir

Things were actually beginning to look up for AISG. In fact, during the first three quarters of 2004, we were among the few companies doing business in Iraq. In that chaotic period of post-invasion reconstruction, the only work being done nationwide—and especially in the Sunni areas where we primarily operated—was by DoD contractors. Most Iraqis were sitting on the sidelines, stunned and fearful, waiting to see what the American presence would bring after the downfall of Saddam.

Therefore, because everybody with a job was employed directly or indirectly by the U.S. government, it was easy for the Neo-Saddamist Sunni insurgents or the anti-American Shia militia of Sadr to attack and intimidate our employees and subcontractors. All the bad guys had to do was to see which Iraqis got up every morning and headed out to work.

At that point I was chief business development officer for the company; and as we took on more and more jobs involving high risk, we won more and more contracts with

NATO, USAID, Contrack Int'l (an Egyptian contractor that the CPA awarded $350 million in road reconstruction), and Fluor Amec, one of the largest publicly traded construction companies in the world.

Our first big contract after Parsons was with NATO, and the fact that we could win it and fulfill its terms gave us the confidence we needed to persevere in what was a dangerous yet highly competitive market. The contingent of NATO officers and men—primarily from Britain, Italy, and the United States—took over the Palace originally built by Saddam for Jordan's King Hussein as a reward for supporting Iraq in the Gulf War. The spectacular headquarters stood on the Green Zone's Tigris River bank between USAID and the American embassy, which was occupying Saddam's ornate Republican Palace. So NATO was located on prime real estate, but the six-story-tall concrete building—with its pale, faux sandstone façade and pointed arches—was highly vulnerable from across the river. The organization hired us to construct security improvements such as blast and privacy walls, drop-arm vehicle gates, a bulletproof receiving booth at the entrance, and sand bags along the windows facing out toward the Tigris. The river was trapped at this point to about two hundred yards wide between concrete dykes, not enough distance to prevent a handheld RPG launching from the lightly patrolled Baghdad neighborhoods on the far side of the waterway.

We completed the NATO job with minimal disruption and concluded that we were in Iraq to stay. Following that job, we received a USAID contract, repayment for my good deed in steering the U.S. Army to the River House that hectic night when it was under siege, which taught us that we could do business in this war-ravaged country without running substantial risks and incurring devastating losses.

One day I got a call from an unknown number on my Iraqna cell phone, which only worked inside Baghdad. I answered on the third ring:

"Carter, how are you doing? It's Ron."

Ron, who had been with Robert during that attack, had returned from his house in Thailand to work in the war zone once again, this time as head construction engineer for AID's residential compound, just up the Tigris River from the massive Republican Palace. Ron was a Canadian American who grew up on a Chippewa tribal reservation, moved to Toronto, and earned a B.S. in civil engineering. Having built a power plant in the wilds of radical Yemen, he knew almost all there was to know about international construction carried on in hazardous circumstances.

We spent the next five minutes catching up. When he told me he was back in Baghdad, I couldn't believe it.

"Man, I'm surprised to see you so soon after the River House incident. I admire your courage."

"The job is sweet," he said. "And I am not going to leave the safety of the Green Zone," he laughed.

"Where are you located?"

"I am over at USAID, and that's why I called. I need a realistic bid. The guys we've worked with aren't cutting the grade."

"What kind of job?"

"It isn't huge. You'll be paving our residential area. Laying down brick pathways, to start. Do you think you can handle it?"

"No problem," I told him.

However, it turned out there *was* a problem. None of the top Iraqi skilled laborers normally employed by Namir or by our other subcontractors would show up for work—and for two good reasons. First, if they were spotted working anywhere in the Green Zone, they were immediately identified as collaborators with the United States, and bad things happened to collaborators and their families. And second, the USAID compound was under constant bombardment by the Sunnis insurgents or by the Shia militia of Sadr. Rockets came looping in at all hours, launched from just across the river; and while no one inside the compound was killed during these attacks, the noise, the flying debris, and the near misses proved to be major distractions. So we ended up with tradesmen absenteeism that would have choked any organization.

Those who did show up for work—whether out of desperation for money, or having a strong dose of courage—were rarely qualified to do the jobs they were hired to do. Namir and the other AISG subcontractors laying concrete and ornate brick sidewalks among the staff bungalows were pulling at their hair.

Another problem our subcontractors faced was the difficulty of getting Iraqis into the Green Zone. (We learned to do this so well that USAID hired us to provide gate guides for all non-Western logistics and construction people headed for the residential compound. At the gate, you had to have a forceful DoD badge holder, whether Gurkha, Ukrainian, Lebanese, or American. These security-cleared guides would meet and identify personnel and vehicles entering the compound, then escort them into the high-security area.)

A couple of weeks after we began pouring concrete and laying bricks, 127mm Soviet-designed rockets began to fall less than one hundred yards from the residences, primarily aimed at the next-door UN compound, though landing perilously close to where Ron lived. As the incoming rockets became common, Ron holed up in his one-bedroom house, and when he had to leave, he geared up in a Kevlar helmet and level-6, extra-heavy bulletproof torso vest with steel-alloy back and front plates.

When the rockets started to drop in among the bungalows of the compound, blowing great chunks out of our sidewalk into the air, Ron called me again. "Carter, didn't you talk about having access to some t-walls and anti-rocket roof protection?"

He was talking about major bucks, so as soon as I hung up, I collared Ken and told him what Ron had said.

"We need to get the anti-rocket program together to pitch to USAID."

"Let's get on it," Ken said.

I knew all about t-walls (Texas walls). We had already installed them at Fort Apache. No car bomb could topple, much less destroy, U.S. Army-approved 3000 PSI reinforced steel concrete t-walls, if correctly installed by cabling together the giant "teeth." Cabling kept the wall of overlapping inserts locked together, thereby allowing the entire length and weight of the barriers to absorb the shock, not just the individual Texas wall. Outside the U.S. military, AISG was the first to cable and install t-walls in Baghdad.

Namir was wary of their use, since they were known to be American-made.

"With these, what do you call them, t-walls? Everyone will now know that you are an American company."

"Can we hide it?" I asked, and the others agreed this

143

might be an option. During this discussion, Namir and all the company's Americans looked out the bay windows of the middle house's second floor and watched a thirty-ton crane lower the three-ton blast barriers into place among power lines and pink-flowering trees.

"Better to have the protection than not," I said. "A car bomb or an RPG without the t-walls would be devastating."

Namir pondered the risk, maybe thinking about London, where he and his family could retreat anytime. Then he smiled and said, "*Na-am*, yes, let us put them up for your safety."

After alerting Ken to Ron's call, I contacted Joseph, a Maronite-turned-Baptist preacher from Beirut. Joe was a former bodyguard for the president of Lebanon and was now in-country general manager for a Lebanese-owned construction company.

"Hey, Joe, can you get me t-walls?"

"You know I can," he said. "I'll send Gabby over to hook you up." Gabby was a bald, Christian Lebanese who looked like a thug and talked too much. He was Joe's right-hand man until kidnapped in Mosul later on. Together with Joe's company, we proceeded to put in place—with all Iraqi-local transport, heavy cranes, and labor—over four hundred tons, at ten tons per delivery truck, of life-protecting Texas walls.

Next, we had to pitch the anti-mortar and rocket system—a cable mesh and light-steel plate overhead, suspended above a building or trailer by steel girders. The design was expensive, but effective up to 107mm rockets, as tested by the U.S. military during the ill-fated mission in Somalia in the early 1990s.

However, the larger 127mm rockets pounded the Green Zone practically every day. We went into the sales meeting with Ken and Fernando, the deputy mission chief for internal administration controlling the residential compound, who obviously resisted employing American contractors in the mission.

"Here are the brochures for the system," I said. "It will take us about forty-five days to install over all the 110 residences and office buildings for about $1.2 million. If you have the budget, we think . . ."

Blam! Blam! Blam! Blam! Blam! And then another bone-jarring *Blam!* Rockets impacted the compound just outside the walls of the aluminum office building where we were sitting.

Good timing for the sales call. The incoming rockets hurt no one, but they blew out areas that our sidewalk workers had just left. However, the State Department never authorized the purchase of our protection system by USAID, even after our engineers back in the United States strengthened the cables to protect against 127mm rockets. The system worked quite well in computer-modeling simulations.

The t-wall alleys we did install formed a maze cutting across and between the Iraqi-built adobe brick bungalows and office buildings in the twelve-acre compound. This reinforced-steel concrete labyrinth contained the blasts of the odd mortar and rocket detonation, thus effectively protecting from collateral wounding. To be blown to bits, you had to be in the wrong spot at the wrong time, not just in the general area. The walls actually saved some USAID workers' lives beginning the day after being installed. Yet the overhead protection would have further diminished the remaining threat.

I had come up against USAID people before. Shortly after we had created AISG, I was invited to a USAID farewell party by a couple of colleagues from Custer Battles days, John and

Kurt, two forty-one-year-old former West Pointers and army artillery officers. Both guys were unscathed by the Custer Battles implosion. They were business development experts, and I saw the party as a sales opportunity for me.

After arriving, I found out that the drinks and hors d'oeuvres were honoring a USAID official who was leaving Iraq. All over Baghdad, people were talking about AID's failure to put crews in the field to "reconstruct" Iraq. Whereas AISG trucks were delivering goods all over the country, USAID trucks feared to leave the Green Zone. In addition, USAID personnel couldn't get work crews to work outside the friendly confines of the Green Zone—largely because USAID operatives wouldn't dare expose themselves to the danger. As a consequence, a key power plant—one necessary to restore electricity to much of the nation—remained unbuilt.

USAID wasn't the only offender. All the U.S. and UN agencies sent hired guns to do their dirty work. Even the U.S. Army Corps of Engineers hired Gurkhas. Others used Filipino commandos or Fijian infantry. Across a t-wall canyon from USAID, the UN relied on U.S. soldiers to protect its much-reduced presence in Iraq. The organization asked for U.S. protection after Sergio Vieira de Mello, then the world body's much-respected top Iraq official, was killed by a massive truck bomb allowed into the UN perimeter under a flawed protection scheme. Up until that moment, the team of international bureaucrats had histrionically refused the repeatedly proffered U.S. security assistance, stating that such aid would compromise the UN's neutrality. After the assassination, the UN displayed no such scruples.

When I arrived at the party, I found my way to the patio, which was alive with low chatter and the clinking of ice against glasses. John and Kurt waved me over, and John, noting the "taxi" I had driven, said, "Nice car, Carter. I like your low profile."

"Yeah, the taxi is the way to go now," I said, still pumped up from the adrenaline rush of driving alone through the Baghdad night, where American soldiers and their Iraqi allies did battle regularly with the insurgents. On my way over, explosions and shooting rocked the city's darkened streets, as was the case night after night.

Kurt introduced me to a tall man standing nearby and identified him as the number two administrator in Iraq for USAID. This was his going-away party.

Having just risked my life to come to his party, I couldn't resist the temptation to needle him, obviously one of the guys who decided that his agency wouldn't come to the larger party, the one taking place day and night all over Iraq, where lives were on the line as we worked to put Humpty Dumpty together again.

After chatting with him for a minute or two, I began to needle him. "It's tough to get people out in the field now, isn't it?"

He was outraged. He knew what I was getting at.

"We are not soldiers!" he barked. "I will not risk the lives of my people to reconstruct a power plant."

I nodded. "I guess what we need now are more 'Seabees,' the U.S. Navy construction battalions so effective in Vietnam and WWII who would shoot back when fired upon."

"I know who the Seabees are!" he said between clenched

teeth. He looked daggers at John and Kurt and said, "Where did you get this guy from!"

Then he wheeled and stomped off—another retreat from engaging an enemy. His last in Iraq.

I looked at Kurt and John. "Looks like I struck a nerve."

I had some small sympathy for these nervous bureaucrats. We were experiencing some of the same difficulties. The Baquba camp—located in the insurgent battlefield fifty miles northeast of the capital near the Iranian border—was a real struggle.

Meanwhile Namir was going crazy trying to fulfill the number one priority for Parsons—well-constructed mobile homes. The construction company owner asked Woody and me, "Can we not get the U.S. Army to escort the trailers?"

Woody told him, "That's one way. Our Pesh Mergas are ready to go. But the truck drivers won't leave the factory unless we provide a heavily armed escort like what the U.S. Army would bring. That's not our style. And besides, we can't afford it. Our guys have already been shot at on the way to Al Hadr [deep in the Sunni Triangle] hauling these huge trailers. The bad guys know that anything that big can only be destined for U.S. use. These mobile coffins are the highest profile cargo in Iraq."

The owner shook his head sadly. "Even now that we have gotten the factory working again after rockets blew up the main building, we still cannot deliver. This is so painful."

"We'll see what we can do," Woody said.

Trying to push Woody to get the job done, I said, "You know Parsons isn't going to pay unless we deliver the trailers ourselves. That's in our contract."

A day later, after a visit to the Green Zone for a look

at the USAID project, I rode back in Namir's car with Haider, a short, gentle Sunni Arab engineer who was Namir's right-hand man. On the way, we continued our seven-month-long discussion about democracy in Iraq. Namir was the ideal Iraqi to me. He was outward looking, a strong Muslim in his personal life, but secular in his public existence—focused on business, not the politics of religious primacy. He never joined Saddam's Baath Party, even though it kept him from the highest pinnacle of wealth. A Sunni, he was married to a Shia. He represented the best in this misunderstood country.

"Namir, you know that in Islam you can find the call to democracy," I prodded.

"How is that, Carter?" he responded pleasantly, surprised that I had ventured onto this terrain, which he held to be his own. His family name, *Al Mufti*, means "a professional jurist who interprets Muslim law."

"In *Ijma*, there is a claim in Islamic jurisprudence to the demand that the Muslim rulers stay within the popular will of the people. The early leaders were forbidden to stray from this popular consensus even as it evolved."

Haider, surprised at the turn in conversation, asked Namir, "What is he saying?"

"He speaks of *al-Ijma*."

As we pulled into Apache's gate, he carefully responded, "You make an interesting point, my friend. I will have to think about this further. We will discuss this later."

The next day my cell phone rang late morning. It was Haider. He spoke in a rasping voice. "Namir is dead, Mr. Carter," he said.

"Wha-at happened?" I said, suddenly in shock.

149

"He was killed on a bridge over BIAP road. We're not sure what happened. He is at the Yarmouk hospital morgue. We are on the way there now."

"OK, please call me when you know more," I heard myself say, as if at the bottom of a deep well.

Namir had gone out with a U.S. Army patrol to inspect damage to chain-link fences on the BIAP highway over-passes, fencing his company had installed under an army security contract. The fences were built to keep people from jumping or throwing things off the bridges onto the six-lane airport highway. A lot of the damage was the result of explosions. Namir was with his driver in a smallish Renault sedan, perfectly low profile for a multimillionaire. We kept trying to give him extra security, but he knew better than we did that increased security would bring unwanted attention. His sister, a prominent medical doctor, was kidnapped on the way home from her hospital in Baghdad, and only was returned safely weeks later for $40,000.

However, in this specific instance, Namir misplaced his faith in our Big Green Machine, the U.S. Army. In so doing, he violated a key principle of Iraq low profile: avoid hanging out with "the Big Target." These troops from BIAP escorting Namir were some of the most ill-trained for their mission in Iraq. They were Air Defense Artillery (ADA), not ground-pounders trained in Ranger tactics. The ADA captain had taken his three-Humvee patrol onto the overpass and stopped at the bridge's peak. The army officer was briefly delayed, receiving further instructions on the radio inside his armored vehicle.

Namir's driver, Abbas, a gaunt man with perpetual dark rings under his eyes, survived the suicide bomber because he stayed inside the car. He told me later at Apache through Amer's translation, "Mr. Namir got out of the car to find out what was going on. We were sitting behind the third Humvee lined up on the bridge. Mr. Namir stepped out on the road, as a Caprice taxi rolled by and approached the lead army vehicle. There was a huge explosion from the taxi. He was tossed to the ground. Then I don't remember much after that. My head hurt for many days."

A couple of hours after Haider's first, brief report, I called him and asked for an update about Namir, as well as to pass along our condolences to his family.

"How is everything? We are so sorry over here at AISG. It is hard to believe; he was just here yesterday. How is his family?"

"Carter, the doctor at the Yarmouk morgue told us that Namir died from American bullets!" Haider said.

Having heard that rumor already from Woody and J. P. just a few minutes before—and knowing that it was common for the Yarmouk morgue to stir up anti-American fervor—I exploded.

"That is a lie! J. P. met the American officer with Namir who had tried to treat our friend's chest wounds sustained from the suicide car bomb. *Entehari!* You and I are going to drive out to the airport right now and see the huge hole in the bridge where he was killed by the car bomb."

"Let us not go there, Mr. Carter," the Iraqi engineer pleaded.

"No, we must. No American bullets killed Namir. A suicide car bomber killed him. You tell the family, please."

"I will," Haider said.

"Also, you tell that doctor at the morgue that I will

personally come over there and kill him if he continues these lies!"

The company was in shock. I gave an impromptu speech to the other Americans, telling them that we would be measured by how we responded to the death of this great man—our mentor, financial partner, protector, and brother—killed by the insurgents. I told them we had to carry on to make his death meaningful.

Meanwhile, we were trying like hell to get paid by Parsons. I had now taken over collections for AISG. And I was dogging the giant corporation to get the huge amount of money they owed us—a couple million dollars. With Namir gone, the company had no source for the short-term loans necessary to cover our $100,000 a month payroll. We were hovering on the brink of bankruptcy. So the next day after Namir's death, I went out to Parsons HQ at Camp Victory in BIAP with Ken, from whom I was taking over collections.

During the ride back from the BIAP collections call, Ken—hard-hit by Namir's death—was suddenly overwhelmed by his job as AISG construction director. He was never really suited for the position, since the only construction background he had was a Special Forces engineering course. This prepared him to win the hearts and minds of some stone-age Filipino village through worthy clinic-building and clean-water systems. But it didn't equip him to run a multimillion-dollar construction and logistics business with over six project sites stretching the length and breadth of war-torn Iraq.

"I can't believe it. Namir is dead," he said as we approached the third overpass from BIAP's main gate, the spot where he died.

"Look," I said, "you can see what the explosion did."

The powerful car bomb had contained some type of shape charge, a chemical round focused to explode with maximum force in one direction. Fortunately for all the other people on the bridge, the directional cone of the explosive was pointed downward, not out to the side. The hole the bomb tore into the concrete, steel-reinforced bridge was almost the size of the SUV in which we rode. You could see the rebar hanging down from the jagged opening like strands of steel hair.

Ken shook his head. "Those Air Defense Artillery guys didn't even block off the ends of the bridge when they stopped up there—and with Namir following them."

"Incompetent," I said. "They just set everybody up like bowling pins—themselves and Namir. They were down on their knees, begging some suicide car bomber to come creeping up and knock them off. How many car bombs have struck in Baghdad during the last two days?" (Namir was killed on a Sunday—September 12, 2004—three years and a day after 9/11—different battlefield, same Islamic fanatics. They had ruined a bridge and killed a good man in Iraq. They had ruined the Manhattan skyline and killed thousands in New York. Different battlefield, same war.)

"Ten car bombings in forty-eight hours, my count," Ken said, "if you include Namir's. Several happened within a short time of his killing."

"That's a record, I think. Hope we're not seeing the beginning of the kind of craziness we saw in Beirut in the 1980s," I responded.

During the Lebanese civil war, suicide car bombs were invented and used frequently to inflict mass casualties.

Unfortunately it turned out we were indeed seeing the start of a trend that would continue for years to come. You had to forgive the soldiers with Namir; they were caught in a radical, new escalation of violence. They were just trying to allow the Iraqis to continue their lives unimpeded by not blocking the bridge.

Ken's cell phone rang. He answered, and tears welled up in his eyes. "Woody just called to say American soldiers shot and killed Brahim's wife and the baby she was carrying!"

Ken broke down in tears as I simply said over and over again, "This cannot be happening."

And sure enough, it wasn't happening. Brahim's wife had miscarried at home in her bed, losing her baby, but was all right otherwise.

Late that afternoon Ken and I arrived back at Apache, I noticed the guards and other Iraqis looking at me strangely, as if they were seeing me for the last time. I went and got Amer, my first source of information on what was happening in Apache and in Baghdad. As usual, he was hanging out with the other Iraqi drivers in the compound parking lot.

"Amer, what's up my brother? *Shakoo Maku*?" I asked the Shia Kurd.

"I am so glad you are back, Mr. Carter. You remember Nora?"

"Yes."

Nora was a young Shia Arab woman from Baghdad whom we had hired as a translator for the office staff. She had lived in the United States for a couple years and was quite fluent in American English. Today we found out that she was a sower of discord.

As Amer told me what she had done, my mouth fell open.

"The woman, when she was supposedly translating for Mr. J. P., told the guards that the company was going bankrupt. That Mr. Namir's family was going to come to AISG and seize every piece of furniture and equipment. That there would be no more pay. Take anything you like, she told the men. For example, when I came back after being on the road to Baquba, I found one of my cousins working away to remove that air-conditioner box from its window mount. I had to hit him on the head to stop it. Nora even said that you—Mr. Carter—were leaving and weren't coming back."

"Where is she?" I asked.

"She's gone home."

"Make sure she never comes back. Don't worry, I'm not leaving, and there's money on the way from Parsons and USAID," I told him.

When we got back inside Apache, we found the place all but spinning out of control with rumors that the company was folding after Namir's sudden death. During our collections meeting earlier that day with the Parsons managers—who knew and respected Namir—they had quickly reacted to his death by granting our request to expedite AISG's overdue payment. I was confident that money was on the way. But Ken, J. P., and the other Americans apparently had never known a time when they didn't receive a regular paycheck. Consequently, they were severely stressed, as were their wives back home. Now with Namir's death, they were close to panic.

We had hit bottom. Could the company survive Namir's death? No one knew, but I realized that because of this terrible tragedy, I would have to run the company and make it succeed. I knew that Namir would have wanted me to do exactly that, not run away from the enemy, which would be a betrayal of my country and his. He didn't run away. Neither would I.

SEVEN

Catering to Fallujah

Sergei said to me in Russian, "Put this on. Do not balk. You are my client. It will protect you."

Sergei was a two-meter-tall Ukrainian with hunter's blue eyes embedded in a lean skeletal face. He took his job seriously. He handed me an army-green Kevlar helmet across the middle seat of our up-armored orange and white Suburban taxi with tinted windows.

We always told our clients that we didn't bullet-proof the windows, just the vehicle walls and doors. That way you could shoot through the thin glass instantly, without needing to open a gun-port first. Of course the real reason was because bullet-proofing was too expensive, and the hardened glass was impossible to find in Baghdad.

Looking over at Sergei, sitting beside me in the SUV—the entire convoy was running blacked-out with no headlights on in the early darkness of a late fall evening—I detected a genuine note of concern. He was holding a Dragunov sniper rifle with a light-intensifying, high-powered scope, and I thought, *We are going to get hit. The first convoy always gets hit. Just be ready.*

But I didn't say that. Instead I said to him—a sniper, who had shot at least one man long-range during prison riots in Ukraine—"OK, but you know this will be the first time I have ever worn this damn thing. It makes me look *kak soldat!* We increase our risk."

"You are right, boss, but this time is different. We go into battle."

Sweat gleamed on his pale white face, reflecting the outside light on a star-bright, moonless night. Tension ran high in the urban battlewagon. Brahim was driving; and a big Kurd with an AK—Jaafer, a good kid who later got caught up in steroids trying to compete with Sasha at weight lifting—sat silently up front. Slava, a mature, middle-weight Judo master who had served in the Soviet army, sat in the back of the SUV, also wearing a Kevlar helmet. He was baby-sitting two extra AK-47s, a couple of boxes of grenades, two thousand rounds of good-quality Russian AP ammo, and a PKC medium machine gun, hanging on a thick bungee cord aimed out the back flip-spring window. Everyone, including Brahim, wore body armor.

We were the lead vehicle of a twenty-five truck convoy, passing by Abu Ghraib prison on our way to reconnect the Iraqi national Ministries of Defense and Interior with the Baghdad-to-Fallujah logistics route. These days battles raged everywhere. At night you could see arcing tracers and continuous flashes on the western horizon and hear the artillery fire, tank fire, aerial bombing, and strafing from the capital, barely twenty miles away. Over four thousand Iraqi soldiers and policemen were fighting side by side with over eight thousand

U.S. troops in the second and decisive battle of Fallujah fought during the first four weeks of November 2004.

How did we get involved? The phone had rung at about 3 a.m., Baghdad time. I had told all my people that the cell phone is always on, so I wasn't too surprised.

I answered groggily, "Hello."

"This is T. J. I am with the PCO [The Project and Contracting Office]. We have a situation in Fallujah, and we need your help. Your company has done business there?" It came out rapid-fire, with a harsh, crystal-clear Midwest accent.

"Yes," I hesitated. We had made truck deliveries and had done the recon at Palladin. So it was technically true. But that didn't mean we could go into the insurgent stronghold and do business tomorrow.

"You will be a good American if you help us with this. We've already lost all three of our key Iraqi contractors, and our U.S. general contractor needs help desperately. Can you get cranes, bulldozers, backhoes, generators, cable, air conditioners, kitchen equipment, food, water, sewage sucker trucks, etc., shipped into a camp for five thousand at Fallujah?"

Coming out of a deep, dreamless sleep, I was trying to process the words. Was this opportunity calling, or an invitation to disaster?

"Look, whether or not I can help, I am already a good American," I mumbled, while I turned the proposition over in my head. We knew about the ongoing battle. Everybody in Baghdad knew. The bad guys knew. If we went rolling down the highway with that kind of heavy equipment, we would be advertising our intentions and our vulnerability.

"Look, my general contractor will be back with you ASAP," the guy said. "Just let me know if you can do it or not?"

The camp was supposed to house and feed all the interim Iraqi government of Iyad Allawi's combatants fighting citywide, in the soon-to-be former "Emirate." As I later found out, T. J. was making his last call, taking his last chance. No established DoD or local contractor would step in to take care of the new Iraqi army and commando police, who were fighting and dying in the battle for this radical Sunni city. Fallujah was the linchpin of America's current strategy in Iraq. Subdue the insurgency there, and al Qaeda would have to reconsider its presence in Iraq.

However, the U.S. command now faced a classic problem in logistics, one that plagued Napoleon, Robert E. Lee, and George Patton: keeping supply lines open—in this case to a besieged city. For the army and marines, this was the biggest urban battle since Hue, when, in 1968, we destroyed the Vietnamese imperial city to save it. And now, if what T. J. was telling me was right-on, we were about to have a repeat of what happened in the first battle of Fallujah, when the American-trained Iraqi soldiers ran away. This time they were about to collapse, not from fear, but from lack of food.

I looked up at the ceiling in my room, hoping for an answer. Then I heard myself saying, "Yes, we can do it."

Laudes, the DoD-designated general contractor, called a few lost and precious days later. Laudes consisted of three Americans managing the in-country project, subcontracting various tasks to Iraqi companies. The Iraqi subcontractors had performed well at several new army camps, but they had run lickety-split from Fallujah as the critical battle heated up. Laudes was on the verge of contract failure.

Larry, the New York-born owner of the company, whose primary residence was in Paris, called me in for our first meeting in the kitsch baroque-gilt sitting room of the Palace that now housed the U.S. embassy after the closure of the CPA and the reestablishment of Iraqi sovereignty. First, we discussed our capabilities. Our people had been to Fallujah several times. AISG had tens of potential subcontractors. As we sat around a low table, Larry—sixty years old and a former U.S. Navy aerial navigator—analyzed our $12 million bid. The written proposal included 145 different cost line items required to supply, build, and operate a camp housing 2,500 and feeding 5,000. Deliverables ranged from main distribution boxes for one megawatt generators, cranes and backhoes, commercial kitchen equipment, down to bottled water, bread, eggs, and wages for the cooks needed to prepare up to 15,000 meals a day.

"We're going on a site survey tomorrow," I said.

"Can you have food there day after tomorrow? The Iraqis haven't been fed a decent meal for over a month. They watch every day as the U.S. soldiers receive hot rations, while they get cold canned food and no fresh bread or fruit. This is killing morale."

"Yes, we can get there tomorrow. If you give us the opportunity, we can cater hot meals to the Iraqis until the commercial kitchen is ready." (I didn't know then that establishment of the commercial kitchen would take seventeen days.)

"OK, you need to link up with the marines outside BIAP for the run-in to the camp. We'll get you connected. By the way, you're the first company that offered to do a site survey before you had a contract. This is a good sign."

"Standard operating procedure at AISG for all our project proposals." I grinned. "We may not want the job."

He understood what I was saying.

"Our marine Humvee escort is to hook up with you outside the back southwest gate of Baghdad International Airport."

I thought to myself, *Outside the gate! So they'll be there, and we'll just roll, right?* No problem? I knew better. Sitting outside a gate in an Iraqi no-man's land was a very bad idea. But we tried it.

The next day we entered through the airport's Checkpoint One—the eastern, Baghdad-side main passenger gate—where we faced a lengthy and disorganized search that delayed our departure. Our complement included a 1989 red Caprice, a blue 1999 Suburban, and my usual up-armored, long-distance taxi Suburban. Iraqis were driving and riding security in each vehicle, so we couldn't use the nonsearch gate for DoD badge holders. Iraqis could not receive DoD badges. And where was our marine escort?

Theoretically moving from one safe area to the other and leapfrogging to Fallujah via BIAP looked great. In actual practice it wouldn't work. I came to that conclusion as our leader's recon element to the East Fallujah Iraqi Camp (EFIC) passed by the guard towers of the southwest gate and crossed into green Iraqi farmland between the capital and Fallujah.

Sure enough, no marines in sight. We were in no-man's land, and we couldn't go back in the gate without a major hassle, since this was a DoD-only entrance. In the distance we could see an Iraqi police fort situated in the median of the four-lane highway stretching out to merge with Highway 10 just before Abu Ghraib prison. But with low-slung Sunni Arab villages scattered among the date palms and sugar-cane fields intersected with canals, we had the distinct feeling the police fort only controlled the small section of the highway upon which it stood. We were alone in true no-man's land on the eastern edge of the insurgent-contested Al Anbar province. The highway was empty with no other traffic at all. The BIAP gate behind us might as well have been a stone wall instead of an entrance into the biggest airport in Iraq. Anyone observing us from the nearby tree lines would know we came out of a U.S. military-only gate. I put the three vehicles in a triangle, bumper to bumper, and told everyone to get in the center with security facing out. At least if we got hit we could put up a fight.

Finally, after almost an hour of anxious waiting, the marines came rolling out of the gate. Our escort consisted of four Humvees, up-armored with steel plates and bullet-proof glass and turret-mounted M-2 .50 caliber heavy machine guns and Mark 19 40mm grenade launchers. These artillerymen, with no cannon in country, had converted to what every soldier worth his salt started out as: riflemen. These fit and alert young troops—the oldest couldn't have been thirty and the average age was probably twenty-one—ran security on the highway between the battle zone of Fallujah and the capital. No one except the military now traveled on what had been one of the busiest stretches of road in Iraq. These marines had faced near-constant shooting and roadside bombs while supporting the coalition siege of the "City of Mosques."

As the lead vehicle pulled up beside us, I looked in the side window and saw a laptop glowing in between the front seats. Everyone was linked. This was a high-tech, wired, and battle-ready military operation.

As the second lieutenant in charge jumped out of the Humvee, I asked, "Hey, where have y'all been?"

"We've been looking for you inside the gate. Just intersperse your vehicles in between mine. Let's move out."

"Will do. How will we communicate?"

"Just watch my hand signals and follow my Humvee."

"Here, Lieutenant, take a radio. We'll talk on this." I handed him a Motorola walkie-talkie, and he took it. We did a brief radio check and off we went to Fallujah.

Lesson learned. Watch out for yourself and your people. No one else will. The U.S. military obviously had too much on its plate to worry about us, a bunch of civilian contractors operating with irregular forces on the battlefield. Their message to us: just stay the hell out of the way of the U.S. troops. We should never have waited outside the gate. I knew better.

We rolled out and on down the highway, passing by the police fort with a six-story guard tower and a few random vehicles in its sand-covered parking lot. Otherwise it appeared empty. Just before we merged with the main highway, I glanced to the left and saw the frame of what looked like a U.S. military Humvee, stripped silver and nearly melted into the tarmac of the highway. I found out later from a former Army Ranger medic who had been at the ambush that the level-six fully armored civilian Hummer had been hit by an RPG. The armor would withstand an RPG but not the windows, and that's where the round hit. This was probably an armor-piercing, rocket-propelled grenade with a five-pound shaped warhead that shot a molten jet upon impact, burning through the bulletproof glass and scorching all four men—killing two and severely wounding the others. The molten jet's complete force and heat were contained inside the armored Hummer, with the only exit for the explosion the six-inch-wide grenade entry hole.

The partially melted remnant was a security vehicle for the last convoy that had set out to supply the Iraqis fighting in Fallujah. As the convoy of fifteen or so supply trucks—with three contractor security vehicles and their USMC escort—passed by two villages set back about two hundred yards from the road, an insurgent launched an RPG at the lead Hummer. The consequent explosion stopped the convoy, and security dismounted to help the injured. The other vehicles should have kept moving, escaping the kill zone as quickly as possible, because thirty to forty insurgents then opened up on the halted column with automatic rifle fire. An American security company, EODT, had some well-trained ex-military troopers; and they gave as good as they got, if not better. Plenty of targets had been running along the roof line of the villages shooting at the supply trucks; but a marine major who happened to be with the escort unit kept shouting, "Don't shoot! Don't shoot! You might hit civilians!"—as if anyone in the middle of a preplanned ambush was an innocent bystander. What was left of an armored car on the side of the road, destroyed in that ambush, ran the subcontractors off and was the reason why no one was supplying EFIC.

I didn't have time to think about all that, as we zipped along the empty highway, but I knew there had to be a better way. I didn't want to end up like the EODT Hummer.

We pulled off the highway just before entering downtown Fallujah. We were not far from the bridge where the Blackwater contractors had been hung, their bodies mutilated. This event had triggered the first battle of Fallujah in April when the United States had failed to oust the entrenched insurgents. The security escort led us onto a two-lane road paralleling the eastern edge of the city where we could hear periodic explosions and rips of gunfire. After about three miles, we pulled onto a sand road that led to a derelict bunker bordering an opening in a low dirt protection berm extending to the left and right several hundred yards. The marines, recognized immediately, blew right by a couple of Iraqi army guards in former U.S. Army "chocolate chip" desert pattern, camouflage fatigues. We followed.

With me in the Suburban taxi was my construction manager, Carlos. Ken, J. P., and the other Americans had fled from AISG after Namir's death. Only Pete Baldwin, Woody, and I remained from the original group. Baldwin had made me his number two man, in charge of company operations, with the promise of taking over AISG completely in 2005. After giving me this assignment, he went back to the Philippines where he had spent more than half of our first business year. So for all intents and purposes I was now running the company. The best man I had working with me was Carlos.

When he first showed up on the scene in late summer, I immediately saw that he was the most qualified man to run our construction department. Dark-haired and thickly built, he was fifty-three years old, a civil engineer from Honduras. At the time I was only the office bid director. Ken was still in charge and still out of his depth.

When he first arrived, I asked him, "Carlos, you have a

degree in civil engineering. What kind of projects have you worked on?"

"Well, I ran a $100 million bridge-building project for USAID in Honduras, connecting the Contras on the Nicaraguan border. Their camps were on the other side of a swampy river delta from Tegucigalpa, the capital and my hometown. So we had to get them supplied."

"That must have been dangerous."

"Yes, I used to carry a .45 pistol and get in shootouts with bandits on the highway through the wild swamp by the river. One time, the gun battle went on for several minutes. But either I got him or I had more bullets, because he stopped shooting and I kept on."

Carlos was a proud man and would tell me that he should be running the bid department, not me, because of his extensive government proposal writing experience. I told him, no, he should be running the much more important construction department. He just smiled.

When we entered the East Fallujah Iraqi Camp that first time, he was tightly gripping a .45 pistol he had bought from an Iraqi, since the company only issued weapons to trained security men. The area enclosed by the berm included several abandoned one-story, flat-roofed stucco buildings that surrounded what appeared to be a couple of parade fields cut into the sand. This had been an army barracks under Saddam, and we now had to build anew amid the detritus of his collapsed military.

As we inspected EFIC, Carlos gasped. "The camp is in total destruction. There are supposed to be air-conditioned tents with electric lighting and raised flooring for two thousand, five hundred men here, over seventy 40-man tents.

There are just four standing, and none of the shelters are properly erected or have power. None of the generators is functioning. Where are we going to put the kitchen? The port-a-johns installed by the earlier contractors are jammed up with water bottles. There is crap everywhere, in almost all the buildings."

"Yes," I said, "the Iraqis don't know how to use the Western-style toilets and toilet paper. They want to use the water bottles to wash their hands afterward, as cleanliness is very important to Muslims. They then throw the one-liter plastic bottles down the hole. So when the sucker trucks come by, the bottles jam up the hoses. The workers have to fish the bottles out of the tanks by hand first. Obviously the contractors couldn't get this done. There are over one hundred port-a-johns and not one is available for use."

"Look at all the trash! It's piled in heaps everywhere," Carlos said, as a couple of the very few visible Iraqi soldiers emerged from one pile with something vaguely edible in their hands. "Where are all the soldiers? This place is like a ghost town!"

"I know. I expect to see tumbleweeds blowing by. The troops are in the city fighting. They're going from door-to-door clearing houses. I heard they found a courtroom with a special area for chopping off heads in accordance with the *sharia* [Islamic law] rulings of the *Mujihadeen Emirate al Fallujah* [holy warrior princedom]."

We definitely had our work cut out for us.

After completing the site survey, our marine escort returned to take us to nearby Camp Fallujah, headquarters of the First Marine Division, the oldest and most decorated division in the Corps. Their area of operations included the battlefield of Fallujah, and they were responsible for making sure EFIC functioned, and—more importantly now—survived.

We entered the command operating center (COC) for the division, situated in a sunken, two-hundred-seat auditorium and occupied by Americans manning radios and standing around in clusters discussing the ongoing battle. A twenty-seat conference table sat on the theater's stage, with a large tactical map extending its length. The map was of the First Division's area of operational responsibility (AOR). It extended from the edge of Baghdad and beyond Fallujah, past Ramadi and into the Syrian Desert of the vast Al Anbar province—the Wild, Wild West of Iraq and the heartland of the Neo-Saddamist and al Qaeda-fueled Sunni insurgency.

Several marine officers sat around the table. The lead officer, a full colonel, stood up as Carlos and I took a seat and said, "EFIC is failing because the Iraqis cannot keep it supplied. We have to ensure consistent logistical support. I understand this is why you are here?"

"Yes," I answered. "There's been a linkup problem with the supply columns. They have to have your escort to come into the camp."

Another officer, a captain, jumped up and said, "You [meaning contractors in general] have not been at the linkups on time, or have not shown up at all."

"OK," I said as I looked at the tactical map. I had already made up my mind. "We don't want to meet at BIAP. It is not feasible to pass through the airport with Iraqi trucks and personnel. The search time is prohibitive. Is this your AOR boundary?"

I pointed at a dashed line I recognized from my days as

an infantry officer. The line crossed Route 10, the main highway to Fallujah that paralleled to the north of the route we had taken from the airport earlier that day.

"Yes. This is the dividing line between us and the First Cavalry Division [the famous U.S. Army unit with the distinctive horse-head emblem, then responsible for security in the capital]."

"Can we then meet at this checkpoint, just on your side of the boundary?"

"That is 39 Alpha. We can link up there. Do you want to coordinate escort from the First Cav? We can help you with that."

"Not unless we have to. We try to stay away from the U.S. military because it attracts unwanted attention. We understand that we have to have your escort to Fallujah, and we really appreciate that. Your guys today were outstanding. Thank you. We will just flow all our trucks and subcontractors to 39 Alpha and then convoy with your folks into EFIC."

I didn't realize at the time that this position was right in front of the high walls of the notorious Abu Ghraib prison.

"Good. What time do you want our escorts to be at the checkpoint?"

I noticed that he did not say "times," meaning only once a day and no opportunity to vary the schedule for security purposes. *Keep it simple*, I reminded myself. This escort issue is the key to success. We can't supply without solving it.

"Can we do it twice a day? That way, we can flow cargo and people in and out in one day so our people and their trucks don't have to spend the night at EFIC. This would really help our turnaround times. Can we do 11:30 a.m. and 5:30 p.m.? Then we can serve a hot lunch made in Baghdad and give the vehicles time to off-load before they head out. Your outbound escort could then bring in the additional trucks waiting at the checkpoint to head to the camp."

The marine officers murmured among themselves for a minute. Finally the colonel in charge said, "Let's do it. This is critical to our success. We have to have the Iraqis continue the fight."

This would be my destiny over the next seventeen days: to be at Abu Ghraib prison twice a day at the exact same times to ensure that our supply convoys linked up with the mandatory marine escort. First, though, we had to get food to EFIC the very next day, as I had boldly promised Laudes at our meeting in the Palace the day before. I wasn't exactly sure how we were going to pull that off. But even before I could finish those supply arrangements, contract negotiations abruptly intervened.

Shortly after returning to Fort Apache from Fallujah, Larry from Laudes called me on my cell phone. "You want a mobilization fee of $2 million on the $10 million two-month contract?!" (They had negotiated our price down $2 million, mostly by reducing our cost for bottled water and limiting the number of meals we had to provide.)

"Yes. As you know, Larry, this is a cash economy. We can't get credit from suppliers, so we have to pay up front for food, security, equipment, everything."

I was ready to compromise on the mobilization fee, but I had a hunch this would not be necessary. Nevertheless I had rarely been so nervous on a business call. I held my breath between sentences to keep calm.

"How do I know when we give you the money that you will not default and walk away with the cash?"

In that situation, Laudes would have no recourse since there was no contract law operational in war-torn Iraq, just as there was no civilian criminal law for Western Coalition contractors. The only law applicable was their home nation's legal system according to the Transitional Administrative Law (TAL) put in place under UN mandate by Paul Bremer as head of the CPA. For American law to apply here there had to be a U.S. Attorney for Iraq. No such office existed.

"You have my word of honor that we will fulfill the contract" (or die trying, I almost added). I held my breath once again.

"OK, come by tomorrow and pick up the money after you sign the contract."

This was my biggest close ever. I jumped up and down in my office as I clicked off, knowing that this money and this contract would save AISG. Little did I realize that the $2 million Carlos and I picked up the next day in the parking lot of the Palace—packaged in blocks of one thousand $100 bills shrink-wrapped and labeled with U.S. Treasury bar codes—would barely make it through the first three weeks of the EFIC project. Almost half of it went to pay down debt and salaries and to buy much-needed equipment for Apache after the lean eight months of working for parsimonious Parsons.

No one at AISG could believe it—that we were going into Fallujah on a large-scale construction, life-support, and security contract. First things first: we had to find food and water as soon as possible for delivery tomorrow. We turned to the suppliers for Fort Apache. Under ordinary circumstances, we had three of them. So we began the internal bidding process that made us the most competitive DoD life-support contractor in the Iraq war zone. But I only had one available in the short time left. This was the man who, with his brother and partner, would become U.S.-dollar millionaires off our DoD life-support contracts.

"Ghassan, can you get me hot meals tomorrow for two thousand, five hundred?"

The dapper Shia medical doctor turned entrepreneur and high-quality grocer replied, "Twenty-five hundred! Who is that for? Where are they located? It must be the American army with two thousand, five hundred!"

"It's for the Iraqi soldiers fighting in Fallujah. They haven't been fed a decent meal for almost forty-five days. They are eating out of the garbage in some cases. This will be huge for your company. Can you do it?"

Ghassan pondered the numbers, smiled, and then seemed to grow larger in size and stature. "What time do you need it by? How are we going to get all the food there? That is quite a lot. I don't have the trucks to do it."

He only had a few one-ton delivery vans.

"We'll get Crazy Amar to do it," I said. "He has a transport with a full forty-foot bed. He'll be drunk and/or on drugs, but he'll go anywhere."

We had used him before on the Parsons contracts. No one else would go to Fallujah for us now on such short notice, not with that epic battle raging in the city and on the minds of all Iraqis.

I then went to Ahmed—who, as an AISG subcontractor, would end up making almost as much money as Dr. Ghassan. I asked him, "*Ahooya al asghar* [younger brother], are you ready to go to Fallujah?"

Ahmed cracked a smile, then saw that I was serious, and

asked tremulously, *"Ahooya al akbar* [older brother]. . . to Fallujah? When? Why?"

"Bacher, tomorrow. I need you to go with me and set up the satellite-linked Internet so we can communicate with the camp. You know that has to go in first. We have a big new contract to take care of the Iraqi soldiers in Fallujah."

"Well, at least it won't be to Taji again!" Ahmed laughed.

The next day I didn't get a chance to see the AISG loaders pack Amar's truck with the hot-chicken-and-rice meals and fresh bread before we set out for EFIC. I was at the Palace parking lot picking up the $2 million mobilization fee from Laudes. As soon as I arrived at Apache and had discreetly deposited the forty-five pounds of cash in our company safe, we moved out to make the first rendezvous at Checkpoint 39 Alpha. The first linkup allowed a window of time, 11 a.m. to 2 p.m., because the marines said they would have "a lot of patrols" going back and forth. But this was the last time we could depend on that flexibility.

By the time I arrived, the trucks were loaded. They numbered only four, including the tractor-trailer with Crazy Amar at the wheel—the only man in Baghdad with the guts to drive a truck into Fallujah for the U.S. Army.

I shouted up at the cab, *"Marhaba* Amar!"

The door creaked open and empty water bottles and food wrappers fell out on the residential road, now turned into a logistics staging area for the Iraqi army fighting in Fallujah. "Mr. Carter! *Wallah-kum-salaam!"*

I was careful not to look too closely at him because I didn't want to appear as if I was checking his sobriety. After all, this was the man who drove and owned this truck, now loaded with hot meals for the Iraqi troops—the first they will have had in over a month. I asked, "*Schlownig, Ahooya* [how are you, my brother]?"

"*Oni ja-az*! [I am ready]." Grinning a near-toothless smile, he then lifted up one of the ubiquitous in Iraq AK-47s he had stashed next to the driver's seat. I admired his bravery, at the same time acknowledging doubts about his sanity. He was making big money: $2,500 a trip for the thirty-five miles to EFIC.

I looked up and down the line of trucks and three SUV security vehicles, including my taxi in the lead, and shouted what I'd always shouted back in the army: "Mount up!" Then I circled my right hand above my head and tomahawked the direction of travel. Roger's Rangers first standing order: "Don't forget nothing!" but the second directive of the founding document of what are now the U.S. Army Rangers (Airborne) included keeping "your hatchet scoured." This was going to be our first movement to Fallujah for the Iraqi government.

We headed out BIAP highway and onto the outer ring road, just cruising along, with Sasha and his team, including Max, in the rear vehicle. I was with Sergei, Slava, and two Kurds—a sharp young driver and a true Pesh Merga, an older but stout-looking fellow whom I had seen earlier around Apache—in the front seat. We were armored up and loaded for bear.

We were flying down the Baghdad to Ramadi highway, just about on the edge of Baghdad proper. All our trucks traveled in a row with one-hundred-yard flex-spacing between each, allowing traffic to weave in between, as necessary, not blocking the flow. We were exercising tactical dispersion so that no two would get caught in one explosion.

The drivers were doing just what we had taught them. All seven vehicles were on the hand-held radios, with backup walkie-talkies in each cab. All the trucks had armed Kurds riding shotgun for the Arab drivers.

We approached a gray-market fuel bazaar, the last pit stop in Baghdad. I had passed this way before and remembered it as a place where we had almost gotten into big trouble, so I grew doubly alert as we came up fast on the bazaar, flowing out into the six-lane freeway not far opposite the no-exit village.

All of a sudden two men with rifles emerged from the gas can–bearing crowd and stepped out in front of our speeding Suburban. One of the men raised an AK in the air, pulling the trigger: *Bud, budda budda budda*! This meant "Stop!" in Iraqi police terms, although we all knew instantly that these were not police.

My driver swerved toward the two fake IP to run them over. You have to love the Kurds! I was situated perpendicular to the two ali babas as we rolled along at ninety miles an hour. From the back seat I could see them look at our SUV again, seeing through the windshield the two fierce-looking Kurds sitting in front. That brief crucial moment slowed down in my mind. Combat speed had kicked in again. The one who fired his weapon lingered longest as we caught each other's eye through the front glass. I raised my AK up above the dashboard, aiming to shoot the man through the windshield. He saw the muzzle and disappeared back into the crowd.

The convoy blew by the spot, and we never had a problem there again. Neither did any of our subcontractors rallying to the linkup in Abu Ghraib. These intrepid Iraqi small businessmen transported almost every possible piece of cargo necessary to provide basic comforts to human beings. But you can imagine that at the minimum, all Iraqi transport out of the only main road from the capital to Fallujah was potentially subject to a criminal blockade and looting. But with this first run, we created order from chaos. The word got around. No ragged band of desert pirates would be able to stop the AISG supply wagons.

Our small convoy merged from a curving on-ramp onto the super highway surrounded by an encroaching desert before the narrow flood plain of the Euphrates. We drove on, bypassing the BIAP to Abu Ghraib highway, where the destroyed Hummer still stood, too far for us to see. (It was towed away a few days later.) Ahead I saw the thirty-foot-tall yellow walls of Abu Ghraib prison. But first there was a sign in Arabic that said, "Stop here or you will be shot by the U.S. military." This left a gap of three hundred yards before you could get to the impromptu checkpoint strung up with Texas and Alaska walls (shorter but stouter than the three-ton t-walls). This was Checkpoint 39 Alpha that I had chosen the day before as our organized rally point after a brief map recon at the First Marine Division COC.

My Arabic-reading driver stopped instinctively, and I realized why after spotting the halt sign. Otherwise the massive highway, six lanes including four asphalt shoulders stretching more than fifty yards across, was eerily empty, like a moonscape. To the right and left, about one hundred yards from the shoulders, stood the edges of two villages dense with date palms, lush light green and khaki. The palms cast dark shadows into countless hidden areas among the fortresslike brick homes. These were studded with observation turrets peering over the surrounding irrigated fields and out into the nearby desert. This was the always uncertain border between "sown" and "unsown" in the three millennia history of the Bedouin nomads who raided the farmers inhabiting the Valley of the Two Rivers. The peaceful farmers were the "sown." The plunderers were the "unsown."

With the U.S invasion, the ancient border was blurred, but this classical conflict was still evidenced in the ongoing battle of Fallujah. The civilized world of human rights (sown) versus the anarchic Salafi jihadism (unsown).

I got out of the Suburban, noting that the U.S.-controlled prison walls and the flanking hamlets resembled the ambush area a mile back on the southeast split to BIAP. An army Humvee, bracketed and fronted by gray concrete blast walls, sat in the highway about the length of three football fields from the stop sign, pointing its grenade launcher in my general direction. I said to Sergei in Russian, "No weapons out, but accessible in the vehicles. Post lookouts at all angles, scanning 360 degrees around the convoy. [I circled my hand above my head.] I have to walk to the checkpoint."

The big Ukrainian, who stood out as a towering white-haired Cossack amid the khaki of Iraq's featureless flatness, replied, "Da, Boss, but I keep my AK, slung on my back."

I nodded yes and went looking for Ali, an English-speaking Kurd—an academic I was turning into a warrior. I wanted to communicate with both the Arabs and the Kurds through the same translator.

"Ali, get me a count of all our people. I have to walk up to talk with the military. The marines should be waiting for us in a few minutes. Please tell everyone to be ready to move when I return."

He looked even smaller than normal; his shoulders were hunched as he stared out at the villages and the prison and replied, "Yes, I will. *Inshallah*."

"*Shukran* [Thank you]. Then tell Sergei the count."

I turned to walk back down the line of seven vehicles and set out into the open area to walk alone up to the few camouflage figures milling about the lone Humvee. We had learned a lot about checkpoints in Iraq in the last year or so. In this high-threat location, the army had put over three hundred meters between the checkpoint and anyone approaching. At the same time, they risked minimal collateral damage by posting just enough soldiers at the front edge of the hasty checkpoint to communicate and protect themselves. If under attack, the checkpoint soldiers could signal for nearby reinforcements and over-watching fires from the USMC snipers and machine guns of "Fort Abu Ghraib."

One of the few Americans who later traveled under my protection to Fallujah said, "You cut quite the figure out there, hatless and all alone in your blue jacket, calling out, 'DoD, DoD!' But only as you got close to the troops. You never looked left or right, not even at those hostile villages. You stayed focused on the U.S. soldiers. This has got to be one of the most dangerous sections of road in Iraq."

I replied, "I was scared every time. But why stare at the imponderable in the villages? That would only make me trip over my own feet."

After walking across the windswept highway—only ten miles from the center of an ongoing urban battle—I greeted the soldiers with a smile, happy to have made it to the other side of the Checkpoint 39-A security buffer. The soldiers were surprised to see us.

"DoD contractor!" the Egyptian-American army translator said. "We don't see many of you since the battle began."
He was a civilian contractor, outfitted in U.S. military body
armor, helmet, and battle dress uniform (BDU)—but with
no insignia.

"Yes, we're here to feed the Iraqi army in Fallujah.
Have the marines contacted you about us? American-Iraq
Solutions Group? We are supplying EFIC. The marines are
supposed to be here now for our escort."

The American Arab said, "You need to talk to the NCO
in charge." As if on cue, a GI emerged from the armored
Humvee.

The lanky sergeant said, "My command told me on the
radio that the marine escort will be here in fifteen mikes
[minutes]. You can move your vehicles up to the center and
wait. The vehicles will need to be searched also."

"Who are you guys? I thought we would be dealing
with the marines. It's great to see army out here. Thank you
for your help."

"We're a transport unit converted to military police and
now attached to the First Marine Division force protection
for Abu Ghraib."

I headed back to our caravan as a few bedraggled-looking
Iraqis walked past. They were trying futilely to get further
down the military-controlled highway. We mounted up. The
army men directed us across the shallow sand median and up
the opposite three lanes. As we cruised the few hundred yards
to the center front of the prison, Alaska walls stood in the
median between us and the yellow walls. To our left, open
sugar fields waved to a horizon interspersed with Sunni Arab

hamlets. They had put our convoy in that lane to protect Abu Ghraib from us!

"Hey, these Iraqis have weapons!" the soldier searching our vehicles called out.

"Yes," I said. "They all have company badges and weapons permits. They are convoy security." I was making it clear that this was no big deal—standard operating procedure for DoD contractors in Iraq. No one was going to disarm my Iraqis.

Just then, four Humvees arrived from the marine artillery unit, also converted to infantry duty, the same unit that had met us outside BIAP—same battalion, but different company. Same professionalism also exhibited. This time I was not heading into EFIC, but just ensuring a smooth linkup for our initial food delivery. Once with the marines, the convoy—carrying the first hot meals and fresh bread in almost forty-five days for the Iraqis fighting in the Sunni city—could not get lost. Attacked yes, but not lost.

I stood by the front of the little convoy and waved at them as they roared past, weaving into the marine column, which was staggered on the road ahead. (From that day forward, for seventeen days in a row, twice a day at the same time, I took the same highway walk to Abu Ghraib as we catered to Fallujah.)

The next evening our first full resupply convoy departed Checkpoint 39-A—with me in the lead vehicle now wearing a helmet—and after going through the same search and waiting for the marines. The twenty-five-vehicle convoy, stretching over half a mile, passed out of the outskirts of Abu Ghraib, the greater city surrounding the namesake prison, and into the brief piece of desert between the far suburbs of Baghdad and Fallujah, formerly a city of three hundred thousand, now with less than five hundred families and several thousand insurgents, dead or alive.

Once you left the mid-route Checkpoint 39-Alpha's search lanes and security buffer, you felt like you had passed through an airlock into another type of atmosphere. The first evening-turned-night on the way to EFIC was so black that a feeling of otherworldliness almost overwhelmed me. The marines drove slowly looking for signs of the enemy through their light-intensifying optics that turned the dark into a greenish day—a huge tactical advantage over the night-blind insurgents. The trip of only ten miles seemed to last forever. I couldn't see anything through the tinted windows, other than the glimmer of lights from the scattered farmhouses and the shadows of larger buildings outlined by starlight.

When the supply column finally rolled into EFIC, I took off my helmet. I slapped Brahim driving, Sergei, Slava, and the Kurd up front each on the shoulder and congratulated them in their various languages. We had a lot to do that could prove to be insurmountable with the camp, but our Baghdad-bazaar-supplied convoy carrying enough food, fuel, and water to take care of over four thousand soldiers for two weeks had just reconnected to the world the Iraqi army fighting for its life in war-ravaged Fallujah.

As we stood in front of the trucks, off-loading the still-steaming lamb and chicken kebab with rice and fresh flat bread, a dust-covered, weary Iraqi army officer approached me and spoke with tremendous emotion, struggling to make himself understood in English: "You the one who has brought this food to us. Thank you, thank you for my men in Fallujah. They will be happy. We thought everyone forgot us."

"We're honored to serve," I said as I noticed the thousand-yard stare in the man's dark eyes, the look you get after prolonged battle. "You're brave men. We salute you for your courage."

Ali ran over and quickly told me, "This is Major Hisham, and he is the commander of the battalion we are now feeding."

The major then hugged me and trotted off to make sure his men were fed.

Without our supply effort, the Iraqis would have almost certainly broken and run. They were on the verge of doing just that when we showed up. This group of almost five thousand men formed the core of the new Iraqi army and security services that would grow to three hundred thousand-plus over the next two years. Without the success of these men in this critical battle that killed at least one thousand hardcore al Qaeda terrorists, the chances of creating stable Iraqi government control of their own country would have been next to impossible.

These men not only denied a citywide safe haven in Iraq for the Salafi jihadists but also laid the foundation for a democratic government in their homeland. The Second Battle of Fallujah would be the Battle of Yorktown for the new Iraq.

EIGHT
Prime Contractor

The camp we hoped to find operational had turned out to be a pile of rubble, garbage, and human waste. So we had a camp to build. And while we were building it, we had to resupply the basic needs of the Iraqi soldiers, especially the hot meals—prepared every night into the early morning for daily delivery. The Iraqis at EFIC ate so well that they cried when we turned over the camp to a Kurd-operated Iraqi general contractor, per DoD plan. The only time the marines were ever solicitous of me and my operation was the day AISG pulled out of the Fallujah camp in March 2005. The "Devil Dogs" contract officer representative for EFIC and his staff ate at the same chow hall with the Iraqis. Our chefs did a helluva job there.

One of our suppliers cooked his food in the ever-dangerous Sadr City. We started out with 2,100 meals, just feeding the ones rotating into the camp from operations in the city. The other two thousand or so would be fighting in Fallujah. Initially I had hired two prime food providers:

Dr. Ghassan and Basha, the elegant, hawklike brother of Namir's wife.

On the morning of the third day we supplied Fallujah, I saw Basha walk by the glass door of my office in Fort Apache. I was no longer in a room with a one-window view of the narrow alley between House Two and Three. I was now in the executive suite in the central house. When I saw Basha, I immediately thought trouble. I cracked the door and asked, "Basha, my brother, where is the food?"

"The restaurant called . . . *Amriki Ja-ish* has a battle with Sadr in front of it. That crazy man! They cannot move. Food is ready to ship."

"OK, we have thirty minutes till we depart. How far is the food?"

"Mr. Carter, you know I want this. *Inshallah*. It is only twenty minutes away, but *Ja-ish* stay all day, maybe. Many bullets fly just a little ago. We already attract a lot of attention for making so many good meals. I have lamb kebab, the best rice, cooked ripe tomatoes! They all say this must be for the American Ja-ish. I already have the fresh bread here at Apache, baked this morning!"

"Excellent. No, this is for the Iraqi army, as you know. I'm sure that you'll do right for us. We will never forget that you fed Apache on credit when Parsons did not pay, and after the great man's death. I have faith . . . you know I miss Namir every day. How is his wife . . . and two children? Please tell them I asked."

I believed in my soul that I could trust Basha, a Shia Pesh Merga—now a merchant warrior. Namir's wife was a Kurd Shia even though he was a Sunni. You had to love the Kurds in Iraq—they were pure and loyal and, in large part, competent fighters who would pull the trigger and not run.

I looked at my Iraqna cell phone for the time. (I hadn't worn a watch since my tour in the army, where they practically mandated it for infantrymen.) We had less than twenty-five minutes to departure, so I went out to the Apache parking lot and side road—now serving as a logistics staging area—to check again on progress. Vehicles stretched almost the full length of the neighborhood byway, lined up between the tall facades of flat-topped mansions, including the home of the minister of electricity.

Three trucks alone carried thousands of water bottles, our bulkiest item after the construction equipment and materials. The contract mandated that we provide them with five liters of water a day! As I said earlier, the Iraqis wanted to stay clean. In addition, the shower trailers at the camp were nonfunctional, except for two 8-showerhead facilities that the Navy Seabees had reconstructed. (Yes, they were on the scene, but in a very limited way, unlike in World War II and Vietnam.)

I turned the corner out of the Apache vehicle gate and saw the former Jordanian consul's residence, a grim reminder of the dangers we faced. The consulate had been abandoned a few weeks after the Amman embassy was suicide car-bombed. The explosion killed more than forty. This was one of the first uses in Baghdad of the car bomb, the most feared weapon of the terrorist insurgents. The consulate residence now stood empty, no longer proudly flying the flag of the Hashemite Kingdom. During the first three months of our company's existence, we could see the bright stripes and Islamic patterns waving in the wind from practically every vantage point facing eastward in Apache.

I looked down at a delivery van that belonged to Ghassan, standing by the alley that divided the school's property and our little square of the Harithia neighborhood. This was too small a conveyance for the more than two thousand meals. We needed a bigger truck.

"Ghassan, where are the meals?"

"We have bread, Mr. Carter! The chicken and rice meals will be here in a few minutes."

I looked down at my cell phone: fifteen minutes to go if we wanted to make the linkup twenty-five miles away. And we would be cutting it close since we had to fight Baghdad traffic. Apache was located in the center of the city with its five million people, and there were almost that many cars jetting erratically about the streets—old Japanese, German, and Korean beaters, most of them imported after the fall of Saddam.

Walking back up the internal Apache parking lot, I saw Amer frantically scuttling about.

"My brother, what's going on? You know the meals aren't here. Yesterday the food got rejected because Crazy Amar carried the meal boxes uncovered and out in the open, with flies and all. The bread at least was accepted after Laudes initially rejected the entire food delivery, out of hand." We were already—on day one from our receipt of the mobilization fee—in deep dung with the general contractor.

"I have to get you two more drivers. The new American security guys took drivers for the presentation with Iraqna—the two I had planned for your other security vehicles. Brahim will drive your *sayyara*,"

AISG was bidding to be the security firm for the monopoly Baghdad cell phone provider, Orascom—the largest market cap local firm on the Cairo stock exchange. The company's brand in country was Iraqna. Joe Morris, Pete Baldwin's nemesis from Custer Battles, had just reappeared on the Iraq scene. Somehow the former West Pointer had escaped sanctions, even though he was publicly listed as being banned from all DoD contracting. Morris now headed our number one competition for the marquee commercial security job, calling for over one thousand, five hundred men.

After checking my satellite phone and cell phone, I again made sure that all my vehicle security men were set. I checked to be certain the drivers all had walkie-talkies. And I chatted a bit with everyone and said, "*Sirchow!*" to the Kurds, both convoy security and Apache guards.

Tension vibrated in the air, as we prepared our convoy to drive through the rising and random violence of the capital—and on to the raging battle's edge in Fallujah. I looked at my digital clock and noted the departure time had come and gone. We were now five minutes into the hour I had planned for movement. At that moment up sped a white two-ton truck with metal rails and fencing in the back bed. The food had arrived!

"Ghassan, you are the man!" I shouted. We had double ordered, from Basha and Ghassan, to ensure that we had enough to feed the troops. This was expensive, but my goal was always redundancy on key items that were time sensitive, and everything seemed to be time sensitive in the war zone. For the entire time we catered to EFIC, I double ordered, just to make certain at least one load would show up in time for the lunchtime trek west.

Ghassan shouted back happily as he replaced the driver of the two-ton, also carrying a Kurd AISG guard with an

AK: "I will drive the truck and my brother will drive the van with the bread!"

"Here," Amer said to him, "take another guard for your brother's van."

We lined up and headed out across the city. The security vehicles, including my Suburban taxi, pulled out of Apache. Now the convoy had only forty-five minutes to make it by the Green Zone's Checkpoint 12 to BIAP highway to the Ramidi-Fallujah-Abu-Ghraib bypass out Route 10, and on to Checkpoint 39-A and our marine escort. The marine command had already emphasized that if we were not there on time, they would have to leave without us. This was about twenty-five miles in all—doable but iffy.

The eight-vehicle convoy pulled out of our neighborhood and onto Al Kindi Street, a shopping area busy with cars. However, it was relatively secure because of a constant Iraqi police presence that even allowed outdoor cafes. Our column turned on Damascus Street as we headed west toward Mansour and went around the traffic circle. I looked to my right and saw the looming Saddam Tower, its glass cupola glittering in the still-bright autumnal sun. From Mansour we dropped onto BIAP road about a mile from Checkpoint 12. Once on the freeway, we stepped on it, getting up to over seventy miles an hour on the first inner-city part of the superhighway. We arrived at Checkpoint 39-Alpha at 11:25 a.m., taking just over thirty-five minutes. This would be near-record time and a relatively uneventful convoy run into Abu Ghraib.

However, I feared that the next convoy for the first 5:30 p.m. rendezvous would be a lot trickier. This was to be the first full-scale logistics movement including construction equipment, supplies, and labor—maybe the most tempting target to roll down this highway since Saddam ran the country.

After the convoy linked up with the marines and delivered lunch, I returned to Baghdad with Sasha in the Suburban taxi. As soon as I got back to Apache, I called Big Joe, our Lebanese subcontractor, on his cell.

"Joe, where are my construction workers? You said that there would be three busloads of them here to head with us to EFIC at 4:30. There is only one bus here now, and they don't come from you but another subcontractor."

Joe was normally laid back, but I heard a note of urgency in his voice. "Carter, they will be there. They are just delayed. We will have over 150 men at AISG this afternoon. Carpenters, electricians, plumbers, laborers, cooks, just what we need to build and operate the camp."

"Good, but your company is our prime construction sub because you said you could deliver everything on the list. We have no time to waste. Laudes is all over us already. We will need over three hundred men from you."

"OK, no worries. I have even put in a call to my shock troops from down south. These Shia warriors built the camp for me at Umm Qasr [the Iraqi naval base at the head of the Persian Gulf]. We will not fail."

"Are you coming out to EFIC today? I need you there running the construction effort on-site. My American supervisor isn't ready yet. You'll have Mel [AISG's lead Filipino engineer] to work with on-site until my man is in place. He's flying here in a few days."

"I will be at the checkpoint at 5 p.m. We have a lot of vehicles flowing there per your instructions. I'll see you there."

A truck here and a truck there, one with a diesel generator, another with four-wheel drive—all appeared on the side road of Apache as the afternoon drew on. We had to supply two weeks' worth of nonperishable food and dry goods as emergency stock at the camp, and Iraqis were running around cross-loading as more foodstuffs arrived. These amounted to over one hundred tons of various Iraqi preservatives, lamb, and chicken in cans, and fifty-pound sacks of rice. Everything we were bringing into the camp came from the bazaars of Baghdad. We imported nothing and were unique among all DoD contractors in that respect. However, this policy made for some unpredictable results. As I watched the chaotic ebb and flow of deliveries with deep concern, our time window once again slipped away.

Ahmed came walking up to me in the parking lot. So at least my communications guy had shown up about five minutes from departure, alleviating that stress point. I knew that if Ahmed was with me, we would be all right with any Iraqis along the way. The aristocratic Sunni commanded respect everywhere for his bearing, business acumen, and fearlessness.

Our primary method of communicating with the outlying camps was via Internet. Satellite phones were expensive, and you had to be outside in line of sight with the orbiting "bird." Ahmed would take a dish, buy the bandwidth from Dubai, line up and acquire the satellite, resolve the IP address, and hook up a multiplug interface, and we could get five laptops online at dial-up speeds running off a tiny 5 HP gas-powered generator. So before we had heat and light in the office, we had Internet connectivity. The IT guru had done this already at eight different camps in Iraq for AISG and our clients. It usually took him less than an hour from start to finish.

Time was up. No worker buses from Joe, but we had all the foodstuffs gathered and we had our initial construction management team ready. With our eleven vehicles (we would collect fourteen more from our construction and service subcontractors at the halt sign next to Checkpoint 39-A), we headed back out of town via BIAP highway. As we left our neighborhood, cars intermingled with the convoy while the IP standing and watching traffic just stared at us, recognizing my taxi Suburban in the lead. They must have gotten the earlier word from the special police guarding the interim prime minister's nearby house that AISG was mounting up a large movement.

As we rolled down the ramp toward Abu Ghraib prison, I noted that the sun was already starting to set in the late fall sky. The temperature was dropping also. Iraq in winter time is cold and rainy. Although scorching hot during half the year, Baghdad is at the same latitude as Atlanta, Georgia: 33 degrees north, and in the temperate zone.

There were already six trucks at the halt sign before the checkpoint. I could make out Joe's tall form moving about among the vehicles gesticulating vigorously in the Arab manner—hands flying about and rapid-fire words with aggressive intonations that to the American outsider appeared to be the start of a fight. But this was just their way when excited, whether about something negative or positive.

"Joseph, where are my construction workers that were supposed to be at Apache today?" I asked as we shook hands in a brisk wind blowing across the desolate highway.

"Man, I don't know about these Iraqis! They all promised to be here. We are paying top dollar! And, look, I should have twenty trucks here right now. Maybe they are just late.

It is difficult to get out of Baghdad with all the IED-created traffic jams."

"This ain't going to be easy, Joe. You have to kick ass. Already we figure that of every twenty-five contractors we have used before, five will agree to come to work at Fallujah, and only one will actually show up! I am glad that you and your team are here. We'll get it done."

"The good Lord willing. What do we do now? Shall I walk with you to the American army?"

"No reason for both of us to make the walk. I'll go. Just get me an accurate count of all our people and what equipment is going in when I get back, please. Hopefully more vehicles will flow in. I'll ask if the marines can wait."

I turned from the convoy and set out across no-man's land. When I got to the other side, the sergeant who approached me was a different guy from the one I had dealt with the last couple of days, although the same Egyptian-American translator was still working the post.

"How are you doing, Sergeant?" I asked with a smile in the approaching dusk. "You guys must be the shift change. What unit are you all from? I don't recognize the patch."

"We're military police from the Kentucky National Guard. We've been running this highway from BIAP to Ramadi for seven months now," replied the stocky, balding staff sergeant who had to be at least forty years old.

"Wow, seven months! You must've seen a lot of action."

"Well, every one of my vehicles has been hit by at least eight IEDs that exploded right next to them. This Humvee right here has caught eleven. You'll never see us riding around with our windows open. That armored glass does wonders for the longevity of passengers."

I thought this guy must be an insurance salesman in his real job back home. Nonetheless these "weekend warriors" exuded quiet courage and workmanlike competence in what they were doing out here in the wilds of Iraq. The marines had not yet arrived and wouldn't for an hour or so. I was glad, since the delay gave us more time to collect additional laggards still rolling into our rally point from Baghdad and elsewhere.

When the marines finally showed up, I went to Joseph and said, "What's the final count?"

"We have 25 vehicles and 112 men. We have four 50 KVA generators, 100 full propane canisters, a twenty-ton crane, seven sucker trucks, three water trucks, 10 one-ton spools of heavy cable, 8 fifteen-man tents, one field kitchen for our workers, two office trailers, two portable welding shops, and one 30,000-liter diesel fuel truck. I also have enough food to feed my 100 workers for 10 days without resupply."

"No backhoes? You know we have to trench the power cables. What about kitchen equipment? That is first priority."

"I know, I know. We'll get it all; I promise."

"Joseph, we only have two weeks to get this camp up and running—meaning housed and fed from a commercial kitchen. OK then, let's go to Fallujah, *Ahooya*."

The next day, we set out to do it all over again, just as we did day after day for the next couple of weeks. The fourth convoy to EFIC pulled up on the first significant overpass from the Green Zone to BIAP in the complex, modern highway system of Baghdad. It reminded me that Iraq was once a rich nation. Immediately to our front at the peak of the six-lane, concrete-and-steel road were two blown-up brand-new SUVs and the remnants of a taxi Caprice and a thirty-yard radius, black-scorched circle burnt into the bridge. This was the remnants of a USAID diplomatic convoy heading to BIAP. Two Americans were killed.

BIAP highway was now closed to vehicles. The U.S. Army had just begun to block the road, and I was not going to stand around in the aftermath of a car bomb and negotiate passage. We had to turn around and go back through the city! The convoy once again had grown, and my up-armored taxi SUV led twelve vehicles—thirteen of us in all.

Abu Hind was now driving for me because Brahim had to obtain weapons for the new security guys, already hired in anticipation of winning the Iraqna contract.

Abu Hind was only forty-six, but he looked at least fifty-six. He said, "I know different way. *Makoo mishkala*, no worry," as he turned the Suburban around and the entire column followed.

I counted the vehicles and looked each driver in the eye during the U-turn on the bridge, which was still smoking from the explosion.

I said, "*Shukran . . . Sirchow*, Abu Hind, you are my hero, once again!"

While loading the caravan, we didn't even notice the explosion. We heard major ones at least once a day. Everyone was so focused on preparing for the mission that no one thought about what lay just ahead.

We drove back toward the Green Zone to cross over the median before Checkpoint 12. Once across the median we could get back up to Mansour Circle and Saddam Tower, then move along on a parallel boulevard that ran by Yarmouk Hospital, with its infamous morgue. Masses of cars choked the crossroads we were aiming for. Everyone, including my convoy, was fleeing the car bombing on a main thoroughfare late on a business-day morning.

We cut the side of the median and headed straight for the turn. We had to take precedent. I was leading thirteen vehicles, stocked up with critical supplies for the Iraqi soldiers fighting and dying in Fallujah. We had to link up with the marines in fifty-five minutes! The Iraqi drivers saw us coming and got out of the way.

This was normal driving in Baghdad. Abu Hind took us across the road and up a side ramp by an Iraqi commando police post. I showed the commandos my DoD badge, and they let us through. As soon as we turned up the parallel road, I looked back and saw that the column was split. Ghassan's brother, a balding, less-impressive version of his sibling, had allowed someone to get in front of his food van, and now several cars blocked his van from crossing BIAP road.

Sasha was sitting next to me in the Suburban. I had put Sergei in another vehicle since his aggressive presence was beginning to get on my nerves. (Eventually, fed up with his bullheadedness, I banished him to the Syrian border for several months.) Anticipating my next move, Sasha looked at me and said, "*Nyet*, do not get out of the car. No . . ."

"I have to, Sasha. We've got to get to Fallujah. No time, *moi Brat*," I said in Russian while opening the door and stepping out into the highway—without my AK because I didn't want to appear inflammatory. I was just a businessman trying to get his job done. Of course I did have my .45 and torso body armor.

I jogged across Airport Highway, just out of sight of the army men at Checkpoint 12, and about five hundred yards from the destroyed USAID vehicles. Ghassan's brother saw me motion to him, and he gunned the white and green delivery van forward down the slope of the median. I looked and saw that there were hundreds of cars backed up in three directions, all trying to go out one of two other directions. I stepped to the front of the longest line, put up my left palm open, and at the same time placed my right hand on my very visible horse pistol, full cocked in the quick draw. Traffic stopped, I waved the food van forward, and eight of our other vehicles followed. I glanced back and saw Sasha trotting up, hauling his RPK drum-fed light machine gun with a bipod dangling from the muzzle. The six-foot-two hulk had on a bright-green, full-size with groin protector, level-five-plus flak jacket of a military combatant, with two fighting knives and a smoke grenade hanging off the vest. No ifs, ands, or buts—if you saw this guy coming at you, you knew he was about war. Sasha waved the Kurds in my trail security car back into their vehicle as several began to dismount.

Then I felt the pressure. Hundreds of cars stared down the ramp at me. All of a sudden, I felt very exposed and squinted my eyes back up at the masses. At that squeezing, my left contact lens popped out of my eye and fluttered away in the wind, to land in the middle of a dusty Baghdad traffic jam. I could only see out of one eye now, and that one was irritated by Iraqi dust and unfiltered exhaust pollution from hundreds of cars exhaust pouring out in the little valley created by the slope to the BIAP highway underpass. The car hiccupping immediately to my front held a family, an older woman wearing a cream *hijab*, a grizzled man in the front seat with a red-and-white-checked *shmag* wrapped around his neck, and boisterous children in the back. They were all crammed into a beat-up white Toyota. I quickly ducked my head down below the Toyota's hood and searched the ground in front of the car's bumper for my contact. As I looked, I heard Sasha's scrunching footsteps behind me in the sand, as well as the gunning engines and honking horns of the angry denizens of a city suffering from a suicidal insurgency.

There it was. The light blue lens, matching the color of my eyes, glinted up at me. I grabbed the plastic disc just as the last convoy vehicle swung in behind the reestablished column. Sasha and I ran back to our car, and off we went through the city, by the Yarmouk morgue entrance and onto Checkpoint 39-Alpha.

We guided these food convoys every day out of Apache, and we were never once late for the linkup. This period included a couple of days when our convoys were shot at by the U.S. Army—warning shots, but an M-16 bullet going by your car is a heart-stopper. The real action had now shifted to the Abu Ghraib assembly area, as construction equipment, crews, and vehicles flowed to link up with our two daily convoys in and out of Fallujah. The one piece of equipment that we could not seem to find was a backhoe. Joe had sent two of them already out to EFIC, but neither worked. We had a thirty-foot boom, tracked excavator onsite, but our electrical crews couldn't get in between the alleys of the tents without the much smaller backhoe. Finally Carlos found one—a small pickup truck with a scoop mounted on the back. It would have to work.

Laudes was attacking us every day because we hadn't found this very basic piece of equipment. But for some reason there was a shortage in the capital—an anomaly compounded by the lack of flat beds to carry the bulldozer/excavator variant with which we were all familiar. The one Carlos bought fixed that problem.

I came out to inspect it and so did Amer, who was always there in the beginning of EFIC to ensure that the convoys started moving. I had asked him—now recognized as the top Iraqi in AISG's employ—to act as a backup to Carlos in making sure the trains ran on time.

"Amer, please get the driver and one shooter for the back-hoe and have them fuel up and then head over to the convoy."

"Roger," he answered, using the American military lingo prevalent at AISG. Later we found out that he ruled the Iraqis he brought in with an iron fist, beating the hell out of one kid who disrespected his stepfather in a pay dispute. Amer was a serious operator.

We got ready to move out. The boom-excavator truck had been on the other side of Apache in the lane between House Four outside the walls of Apache and the man gate for the main house. The convoy assembled in a line along the edge of House One and the abandoned Jordanian consulate residency. This was a distance of over two hundred yards, blocked from visibility and sound by the walls of several brick and stucco flat-roofed mansions.

I looked down the line of trucks and saw no backhoe. We drove the SUV around the other road through the back alley and still no excavator. I went around the front side of Apache on the road running from the Baghdad Zoo Park to the Al Kindi shopping and café area. Amer was standing there talking with the guards.

Highly stressed now, I whipped open my car door and jumped out on the street and barked, "Where is the back-hoe, Amer?"

"I told him to go over to the convoy and get his radio and shooter. But I just saw him drive off that way." The Kurd pointed toward al Kindi. "I can't see him now. He went to Abu Ghraib by himself."

"Amer, why didn't you make sure he made it the two hundred yards to the convoy? Can you think now that that little truck with a construction boom sticking up in the air, driving down the road with no security, isn't going to get stolen—at the very least? Am I the only one doing my job here?!"

I shouted the last sentence right in Amer's face. The guards with AKs, all of them related to him in some way, stood around us in the street. Thirty or so men sitting around the corner in the convoy, ready to go to Fallujah, heard my angry tone. No one was getting out of here alive unless we performed, and that included Amer, the Iraqi strongman of AISG.

Amer's head dropped and he said, "I am sorry; we will go find him now."

"No, we will just hope he makes it. You get back to making sure the evening convoy is ready, *Ahooya*. No worries. We'll get it done."

As the convoy motored along the highway beyond Baghdad's western ring road, the U.S. Army blocked our passage—an IED. Everyone was rushing toward a bypass that always appeared after the highway was closed. There on the bridge, sky-lined by the boom, our little backhoe, the last piece of equipment for the Laudes contract, trucked along, dead set on getting its little, lonely self to the edge of the battle for Fallujah. When we caught up with the backhoe and folded it into our security buffer, I thought, *We are truly blessed; I cannot believe this.* Once again, we were just in time to link up with the marines at the prison, and to avoid defaulting on our agreement with Laudes, the EFIC prime contractor.

For their part, Laudes was way behind schedule. Larry was feeling pressure from the possibility of failure. So he in turn bore down on us and on me in particular.

It was three or four days since our first meeting with the project general contractor, and as I walked across the camp we were building, I saw one of the EODT security men still running camp security for Laudes in Fallujah. I knew then that Larry must be near.

I rounded the corner and asked the American-hired warrior carrying an M-4 with a laser aim point, "Where's Larry?"

"Hey, Carter. He's up there on the hill." He pointed toward a circle of six or seven men, all in desert-battle dress uniform with helmets, except the Laudes CEO. The powwow was taking place on the edge of an orange mud berm, overlooking the camp's entrance. What should have been Sector Three of the five thousand–man camp was instead a giant mud field, miring the remnants of three 40-man tents.

I heard Larry talking, and then a British voice kicked in, from a thin man with a single star on his visor—a UK brigadier. One of the other men was a two-star U.S. Army major general. Various staff officers massed around including two majors I recognized from the First Marine Division COC meeting two days before.

Larry pointed at me as I approached and said, "That's the man who is going to fix it!" as I heard the Brit trail off with "This is a disaster . . ."

The U.S. general turned to me and said, "How are you going to reconstruct this mess and supply this camp? EFIC is critical to the effort of building a new Iraq and to the battle now securing Fallujah."

I replied, "You keep the roads open, and AISG will supply whatever is needed."

Laudes was under the gun. We were under the gun. Now it all boiled down to this: we had to get the kitchen operational.

"Carter, what about the kitchen?" Larry asked for the fifteenth day in a row.

"Look, Larry, I am getting damned tired of catering to EFIC myself. We're working it hard. The guy you offered disappeared. But the word is, we have a source, and we'll have the equipment we bought hauled to the camp by tomorrow. Then we need two to three days to set up."

"You have two days to be cooking, or that's it!"

I went out to EFIC that day and found Joe and Charlie, newly hired to run the camp for us. From Cleveland, Ohio, Charlie had put in twenty-eight years as a union master carpenter and, ten years earlier, had married my wife's neighbor back in Kiev. Tanya and I attended his strange civil wedding, where the officials made every attempt to replace the Cross with the Trident of Ukraine—symbol of the newly independent nation. Charlie was a hard charger and knew how to do most construction work with his own hands. The key, however, was Joseph's work force on-site, which now numbered over three hundred men.

Dr. Ghassan had found a newly opened kitchen store and bought everything in stock and on the display floor. We'd scoured Baghdad, and that was all we could find. What should have cost us at inflated prices in Iraq about $60,000, rang up at over $110,000. It was just enough, and now Joseph's men had to install the brand-new ovens, microwaves, fans, refrigerators, stoves, sinks, plumbing, and, last but not least, power and lighting.

As we stood outside the building that was to be the kitchen, I told the two of them, "Charlie and Joe, I just talked with Larry. If we don't have the kitchen cooking, at least partially, by the day after tomorrow, then we're fired and we can all go home."

Joe—now no longer acting like a California surfer-dude—answered, "That's a tough one. We have to get the electrical work done first. This is an industrial facility to feed five thousand men. This is heavy-duty work. We're just now finishing sanitizing and painting the building. We're getting ready to install the equipment."

"Where are the electricians?" I asked in frustration. "That's the choke point. Where are they? We have been talking about this all week. Joe, you told me you'd have the kitchen equipment—that's seriously delayed us. Now we have to get this monster working."

"OK, Carter, I'll get the electricians. They are working on wiring the tents and setting up the generators. We have a shortage of them. They'll be here."

"When will they be here? What does that mean?" I snapped at him, not wanting to dance the dance anymore. Now I had to be an American manager and get it done or die trying.

Joe leaned forward and said, "F_ _ _ you!" Then he saw the look on my face. I was standing there with Charlie, a dark-haired, strapping craftsman with the athletic moves of a pro shortstop. I'd throw the Lebanese the hell off the site right then and there if I had to. He then smiled and said a bit softer and in a humorous tone, "F_ _ _ you. I'll go get them."

The next morning, I called Charlie on his satellite phone. It took me about ten tries, but we finally connected. Larry had just called to remind us of the seriousness of his deadline. Not a pleasant conversation, but my discourses with the man rarely were.

"Charlie, how're we doing on the kitchen? You know we have to have it cooking tomorrow for lunch."

"Well, it doesn't look good. We have that marine bird colonel acting like the contracting officer representative and watching over our shoulders with the USMC FM [field manual] for food preparation, making sure the kitchen meets U.S. specs. Like we're on an American base!"

"Charlie, my brother, you get that kitchen working tomorrow. I don't care if it's only to boil rice. You get it going or we are dead! Do you understand? We will be fired! There will be no tomorrow! Laudes is looking for a way out, and they'd love to blame it on us. Do it!"

I shouted over the satellite phone, so loudly that I blew the speaker out and my friend at EFIC could not even understand the gibberish, only the urgent tone. A couple of the new American security men came running out of House One, thinking there was an emergency at Apache.

Charlie got the message. The kitchen opened for lunch the next day. A full dinner was served the next evening. EFIC was fully functional now that it had a kitchen. The Iraqi soldiers could always find a place to sleep, but to eat a full, hot meal—now that was life support! Two days later Checkpoint 39-Alpha closed down for good, and the highway was reopened to all traffic. EFIC was up and running, and Fallujah was pacified. The Iraqi Fallujah Brigade had held its own. These brave men would be the nucleus of the new Iraqi army.

I will never forget the look on the face of the Iraqi major in command of a battalion of 350 men—fresh from battle— as he thanked me over and over again for their first hot meal in more than a month. Out of his dust-covered face peered eyes brimmed with tears of gratitude and exhaustion.

Laudes, however, was toast. Larry had gotten sick and fled back to Paris. They were finished, and the Pentagon contracting office was glad to see them go. On December 22, 2004, AISG took the place of Laudes and became the prime contractor to the Iraqi government and the U.S. Department of Defense for East Fallujah Iraqi Camp. What a Christmas present! We could now compete directly for DoD contracts like Halliburton, Bechtel, or Lockheed Martin. We no longer had to rely on a middleman for payment—a process that always caused delays, just like with Parsons. The U.S. government would pay, often slowly but without fail. The same could not be said about other contractors. In addition, this status gave us authorization to obtain directly Department of Defense badges for our people with authorization to travel freely in and out of Iraq and U.S. bases worldwide and to carry weapons in the war zone, including assault rifles. AISG was now a full-fledged corporate member of the Coalition with greater access to the billions of dollars in U.S. funding for the reconstruction of Iraq. The company was on its way.

NINE
Projects

There were two reasons why we became the prime contractor for this project and others. First, AISG had guts. We would rush in where others feared to tread, not because we were fools and they were angels, but because we knew how to minimize our risks and fortify our courage with good sense. In the end, we were the only approved contractor left who would take the job. The competition was simply too afraid.

Second, with few exceptions, we employed Iraqis and bought from Iraqi suppliers. Once we established our local contacts, we could hire workers and put together a supply shipment in a few hours, as we did those first days servicing the camp at Fallujah. No other contractor could have cooked and delivered two thousand–plus meals in less than twenty-four hours. And no one else could have bought so much kitchen equipment and built an entire kitchen in no more than a couple of days. The military thought we were near-miracle workers. Everyone in the organization knew we were conscientious with the capability to operate anywhere in Iraq and the right Baghdad connections.

What we provided at Fallujah was characterized as "life support." That meant meals, kitchens, sewage and refuse collection and disposal, electrical power, water supply, latrines, and possibly—depending on the contract—housing, armory operations and supply, barbershops, road maintenance, a bakery, and laundry ops. This included convoy and personnel security along with local site static guards. In World War II, the military supplied its own kitchens, food, and cooks but often contracted construction of its own permanent facilities. GIs, however, provided all security on the battlefield for troop facilities, personnel movements, and logistics. In addition, ground troops carried canned C-Rations, often described as "better than starvation, but not much better." We contracted to supply hot meals, prepared from scratch, whether delivered to the camp like Domino's Pizza or prepared on-site by contracted cooks and later by our own.

Once we became the prime contractor at EFIC, AISG was able to bid against the big firms, especially in life support for the growing Iraqi security forces. Our main competition was ESS Technology, Inc., a multibillion-dollar company that was not performing well on the smaller projects primarily because of the security situation. We ended up replacing them in two camps, Mosul Public Safety Academy (MPSA) and BIAP Area Four, where the Iraqi Special Forces trained. The competition we posed forced them to tighten up their ship, and they substantially raised their performance level—a textbook illustration of how the free market operates.

Our chief strength was our ability to mobilize and turn on

a dime while providing our own organic security. All other life-support primes outsourced their security to firms such as Blackwater, Dyncorp, Triple Canopy, Control Risks, or Falcon. The other prime contractors like KBR and ECC—they loved those three-letter names—needed weeks to crank up a project and bring in the necessary people, equipment, and materials from outside Iraq. For these reasons, several of the Iraqi camps they serviced were in the same shape as Fallujah before we got there in mid-November.

AISG's next project—won from the Project and Contracting Office (PCO)—was to do essentially the same thing on the northeast side of Mosul—a city then seething with daily gun battles in the streets. As was the case at Fallujah, no one had done a lick of work on the camp in Mosul. It had been bid much earlier, but the winner had never showed up to do the job. In effect, the PCO had asked us to step in and save the Mosul project on a sixty-day contingency contract.

With the camp in shambles, the Mosul Public Safety Academy was about to train special police commandos for the Iraqi Ministry of Interior. Both cadre and trainees needed to eat. We contracted to build a kitchen and supply and cook the food as well as construct latrines, a septic system and water supply for the cadets, and eventually upgrade the showers.

As soon as I had gotten the word that we would get the contract, I called Joe. "We've landed a big job in Mosul," I said. "Isn't that great! Are you ready to go?"

"Carter, you know that Gabby [his thug-looking Lebanese deputy] just got kidnapped up in Mosul. We can't go up there. The owner won't let us. We are about to do a lot of work in Kurdistan. We will continue to work the NATO and Fluor jobs for you. No worry."

I was shocked and said, "You promised us that you would do this. I based our bid on you being our prime sub, just like EFIC. This will come back to haunt you."

I hung up the phone and thought, *This is a disaster.* Then I thought again. It was also a great opportunity to expand our capabilities and build AISG into something more than a project management firm or a general contractor. We were being challenged to become a company that had assets and employees. We could do for ourselves what Joe was doing for us.

Still, I resented the fact that Joe would do this to us. Where was the love, the brother-in-arms spirit that I told myself informed our organization? I was even more disillusioned when I found out later that Joe had gone behind our backs to try to become the prime contractor for Fallujah.

So I gathered up Carlos, Mel, and all our subcontractors and called Charlie in from EFIC, which was now humming along as the result of his nonstop eighteen-hour workdays, his ability to do any construction task himself, and his tough-love leadership.

As we all sat around the conference table in my glass-enclosed office, I began, "Carlos, Joe has pulled out. Can we do this job on our own?"

Carlos immediately answered, "Yes, we can. All we have to do is get an electrical engineer up there to set up the generators. There is some construction, but you can handle that, right, Charlie? The kitchen is a matter of the equipment and we have access to that. Ghassan? Basha? Ahmed?"

Ahmed, who was now our chief supplier, answered first. "Not a problem. There are new shipments in from Jordan. I can have a full kitchen setup here by tomorrow." He was talking like an American entrepreneur.

Abu Amar, another cousin of one of Amer's cohorts and a new supplier, stepped up and said through Ghassan's translation, "I am here because we are ready to source food, materials, people, and equipment from Irbil in Kurdistan."

"Can you get us a crane? We need to be able to set trailers. We'd hate to have to take one with us all the way to Mosul."

Carlos said, "You know Mahmoud from Mosul. He says he can source anything in the city itself."

"Great," I said. "I know him. He's the boom truck operator that we call 'Mahmoud the Great.' He drove me out to EFIC many times. If he says he can do it, then we should believe it. He'll drive my vehicle up there."

"All right then," I continued, "we're going to do this. Carlos, please give everyone the new bid list. We need everyone's quotes by close of business tomorrow. Ahmed, you get ready to go with me, in three days, to set up the Internet satellite hook-up like always."

There was an engineering map of Iraq on my office wall, and I kept staring at it. We didn't want to drive directly to Mosul, because that route would take us right by Tikrit in Saddam's home region. I had made that run to the much-favored capital of the Sunni Triangle under the Baathists. It was the brightest, whitest, and most spacious city I saw during my time in Iraq. Yet on the way back, our two-BMW caravan was pursued by a carload of unknown men whom we had detained at the first highway checkpoint south after they began following us at over one hundred miles an hour.

Going to Mosul by way of Taji, Balad, Samarra, and Tikrit on friendly Route 1 was not a good route. It was called "the roadside-bomb freeway." The usual route for personnel was to go to Kirkuk and then drop in from the northwest, but this wasn't an option for a convoy carrying hundreds of tons of foodstuffs, fuel, generators, and other equipment, and followed by several buses, vans, and SUVs full of skilled labor and security men. Kirkuk was dangerous and so was the stretch of highway into Mosul, lined on either side with Sunni tribal areas. Even in September 2006, leaders of one of the main tribes west of Kirkuk—the three hundred sheikhs of the al Ubaidi—were calling for "the reinstatement of Saddam Hussein or [continued] al Jihad, if not." No, we had to go a different route.

Amer came into my office, and I said, "*Ahooya*, go get Neoshad, please. He is the one that you said knew where the police academy in Mosul is located."

A few minutes later, the portly Kurd—who had been with me on many trips and was now one of the top Pesh Mergas at AISG—knocked and came into my office. For our mission, Woody had printed up a detailed map of Mosul and its twin city, Nineveh, a name from the great empire of three thousand years past. I pointed at the topographical map and asked, "Is this road a good one from Irbil?"

Neoshad answered, "Yes, that is good road. Much business from Irbil to Mosul. I am from Irbil, you know. If we go that way, I know hotel and parking area for night stay."

Thus I planned the movement of men and equipment to

Mosul, drawing on my training as a field officer planning military maneuvers—and with some of the same considerations. I decided to split off the leaders' recon from the main body of the convoy. We would travel—linked by satellite phone and radio, but separated by several hours—until our three-vehicle group caught up with the main eighteen-vehicle supply-and-security convoy. Both segments would pass near Baquba, northeast of Baghdad—the most dangerous point until Mosul itself. I knew this stretch of highway from our job with Parsons. We would be traveling a great distance—over five hundred miles.

OK. Now we had the route. We were going to go via Kurdistan and then drop down from the mountains into Mosul. This plan would avoid the badlands and ensure a safeway station for our convoys in pro-American, highly secure Irbil, a city of over five hundred thousand. Having gone that far, we only had to get by Khalis outside Baquba. But Khalis was one of the most dangerous small cities in Iraq. Our people had drawn enemy fire there while driving into the camp we had almost completed for Parsons. Namir's brother was finishing construction of the Ashraf camp only three months late—a near miracle given the problems he had faced. I was now trying to collect money owed by the huge construction management firm.

With an expanded capacity to do business, we started out on the first leg of our journey to Mosul, traveling in two separate convoys as planned. The main convoy left Apache at first light, and our leaders' recon left around 11 a.m. The leaders' recon group consisted of my vehicle and two trail security Suburbans with Ahmed's ultra-low-profile

1980s Toyota hatchback squashed in between us—the days of the red Jaguar were long gone. The plan was to link up at the internal Kurd-Iraq border north of Kirkuk.

In our group, Mahmoud the Great drove, Neoshad rode shotgun, and Sasha held the machine gun in the back. Sergei and Max rode in the rear Suburban. Charlie sat beside me. He was going along to mobilize MPSA, as he did EFIC. The middle SUV had two new Ukrainian Spetsnaz, including one who was six foot eight. These two would remain behind with Charlie at MPSA as his bodyguards.

The first leg was from Baghdad to Kirkuk. As we passed through Kirkuk's twisting streets leading to the highway to Irbil, Neoshad, now sitting in the front right seat of my Suburban taxi, started pointing out the window at the people and saying, "Kurdi, Kurdi!"

What I saw were dense concentrations of poverty and open ditches flowing with sewage. The side streets were knee-deep in mud. The low, brick, and off-white stucco shanties leaned into each other forming a maze of garbage-littered alleys.

Neoshad, a Kurd chieftain, saw my face and said, "Saddam *muu-zen*, *muu-zen*, bad, bad. Kirkuk Kurdi!" After the forced exile of the genocidal Anfal campaign in the mid-1980s, the dictator, in his plan for ethnically cleansing Kirkuk of non-Arabs, had allowed those Kurds who remained to live in hovels in the ghettos on the edges of one of the first Western oil-company towns in the Middle East. British oil moved in after WWI. There was fabulous wealth in the liquid carbon that flowed under the city's streets. This wealth made the degradation of the Kurds in Kirkuk all the more evident. In this respect, Saddam had done to these people what Stalin had done to the Ukrainians during the farm collectivization and *de-Kulakization* in Ukraine and southern Russia in the early 1930s. This kind of oppression was a hallmark of totalitarian regimes.

I was apprehensive about the police commandos we would encounter in Mosul. At Fallujah we had had several confrontations with the police commandos, whom Charlie called "gorillas." The Ministry of Interior men helping to secure Fallujah were stone-cold killers. They shared the camp with the more numerous Iraqi army troopers. From time to time, these rugged, combat-stressed enforcers would stomp up to the kitchen and demand food. We would deny them if it was outside of our feeding hours—they could always get *chai* (a heavy tea brew loved in the Middle East), but no food.

They would threaten our cooks, but we had thirty Kurd security men who feared no Iraqi policeman. So the confrontations welled up and always had to be defused by an American. On one occasion, Charlie had kicked a group of the commandos out of the food tent for loudly complaining that no one was still serving chow. Later that evening one of them shot his pistol at the tent. These were dangerous men. So I had the feeling that the police commandos in Mosul might be trouble as well.

For this reason, I put a monster-sized Spetsnaz and an English-speaking Ukrainian up with Charlie, mostly to deter internal challenges to our authority. There are two types of bodyguards: those who deter violence with sheer size and those highly capable of maiming or killing anyone who poses a real and immediate danger. Deterrence and reaction—these are the two active goals of physical security.

As I looked back at Sasha, I noticed that Ahmed's car was dropping back, and Sergei's SUV had passed him to keep up with us. I got on the walkie-talkie and called Ahmed. "What's up back there, *Ahooya al asghar*?"

"My car is not working well. I think the engine is dying," he crackled back over the Motorola.

"That's what you get for being too low profile with a piece of junk for a car. This is not a good place to break down. Stop the car, and we'll tow you. You get in my car."

He rolled to a stop on a long stretch of two-lane highway known for accidents and insurgent attacks. The spot was between two Kurdish-controlled areas—a sort of chaotic border zone. The dusty green shrub-studded desert of Iraq stretched out below to the far western horizon. To our right rose the foothills of the Zagros Mountains, extending deep into Iran. The snowcapped peaks loomed in the far distance. (Several months later, after I had left Iraq, Max was killed in a head-on collision after his recently fired and rehired driver decided to take advantage of the straight road and pass in the dark coming back from Mosul on their way to Apache.)

We dropped off the Toyota just on the other side of the Pesh Merga frontier post for Ahmed to pick up later. We had now crossed into Kurdistan proper—for all intents and purposes, a separate world from the war-torn Arab parts of Iraq. Sasha had already been up this way, when Joe had asked me to send a security team to Irbil to recover Gabby, after he had gotten himself kidnapped in Mosul. Sasha and Max had escorted Gabby to the airport for his flight home after Joe's Lebanese construction company had paid the ransom. Therefore as soon as we crossed into Kurdistan, Sasha took a nap. I didn't join him, despite the fact that I was exhausted from lack of sleep and stress. Sleep alleviates stress; but in Iraq, if you're not careful, you may never wake up.

About an hour later we came up on a huge multi-laned, backup of trucks of all types and sizes. There must have been over five hundred vehicles stopped, waiting in line. This was the customs post just prior to Irbil. The Iraqis made a practice of putting their export/import controls not on the wide-open border but near the cities, at key cross-roads where the road system funneled all highway move-ment to one checkpoint. Thus, the customs post for the Jordanian and Syrian borders stood over 350 miles inland at Fallujah, the gateway to Baghdad and the transportation axis for the entire country.

I stuck the sat phone out my car window and speed-dialed Amer's number. The phone rang and Amer answered. I immediately asked, "Where are you?" I knew he was near because he had checked in just an hour before.

"We are in the middle lane waiting in line. Where are you?"

"I am getting out of the car to find you. Stand by." We had pulled off to the side of the highway at a vast open bazaar and truck stop that offered everything from food to fuel to whatever else you might want, provided you were willing to probe the deeper, shadowy parts of the market.

After I moved in and out of the shifting lines of heavy trucks, all the drivers noted my approach with pleasant, and sometimes surprised, looks. I saw Amer sitting in his SUV at the head of his eighteen-vehicle column. Everyone was noticeably happy, knowing we had at least completed the first leg. The AISG Kurds sang their songs, while the Arabs stayed near their vehicles, knowing that they were no longer in the Arab world.

"Amer, my Kurdish warrior, why are we waiting in line?"

"I was just holding fast for you to get here," he said as he jumped out of his Suburban packed with heavily armed security men.

"I'll be right back. Please go to your car, and we'll get moving."

Five minutes later, Amer returned and said, "We go that way. See the open gates to the right. You first, Mr. Carter, and then the convoy will follow. Go where the Kurdish police tell you."

Off went this brave Iraqi friend, who always said to me, "You bring your family to Baghdad. I will be their bodyguard."

Next thing I knew, the convoy was snaking out of an opening in the outside line of trucks with Amer walking in the lead. The trucks fell in right behind us. We drove up to the border post, broken into search lanes, and just kept on rolling as the uniformed Kurdistan border patrolmen waved at us in welcome.

This was a different world. After we drove the thirty miles into Irbil, we put all the trucks in the parking lot of a service station whose owner Neoshad knew. Except for a few security guards who stayed with the convoy, eighty of the Iraqis who were not from Irbil went to a well-kept workers' hotel. The Ukrainians, Charlie, Ahmed, and I went to a three-star hotel that reminded me of Brussels. Neoshad knew the owner here also. The scene was one of contrast—the twilight zone just on the other side of a frontier of a country with a war going on. Guests in business attire sat in the lobby in overstuffed chairs smoking and drinking coffee, discussing the happenings of the day just like in Europe or Marrakesh. Our group, on the other hand, came stomping in with boxes of ammo and machine guns. The jack-booted Ukrainians temporarily stacked the weapons on the maroon-and-off-white Persian carpet as we checked in with the very friendly staff. They seemed neither frightened nor surprised at our appearance, though some of the guests seemed uncomfortable.

After registering, eight of us went out to dinner at a nearby café. We felt as if we were on R&R in this war's version of Switzerland—high snow-topped mountains and all. Irbil seemed ten thousand miles from Iraq.

The next morning we linked up at the parking area and headed out into Mosul. The leadership recon vehicles left first, reduced to three vehicles with the breakdown of Ahmed's beater. The main convoy left shortly after we did, but the trucks moved much slower than our SUVs, especially our one forty-footer, Crazy Amar's ride. Once again he was the only tractor-trailer owner/operator in Baghdad who would go to the dangerous north for the Americans. This time he really scored: $4,000 for the trip. But the unstable Arab then left out with no warning to head back from MPSA without us and got arrested by the Kurdish police outside Irbil. I had to send Amer to the jail a week later to get him out.

Because the trucks moved so slowly, we hoped we would arrive about an hour prior to the main column. As we entered Mosul, the third-largest city in Iraq, our Baghdadi drivers started to peer around uneasily and drive more aggressively—even more so than in the capital. The road turned and split several times in the midst of bazaars and squares, and I couldn't always tell where we were by the map. But I tracked the odometer and noted the general direction. We were on the right track.

I told Ahmed, now sitting in the back next to Sasha, to ask Neoshad, "OK, where is the camp? We're on the main Nineveh highway, and we should be looking for the split northeast about ten kilometers up the road."

Neoshad answered hesitantly. Ahmed translated, "It has been a while, but he thinks we are on the right road. It is not far, if this is the camp he remembers, the old police academy."

This answer did not reassure me. Neoshad had been much more positive in his knowledge back at Apache. I looked to my left, and there stood several police in full riot gear, including helmets with Plexiglass face guards. Then I noticed they were on every major street corner amidst the four- and five-story gray concrete buildings, some with neo-gothic modernist facades in what appeared to be business and government centers. These serious-looking men were reinforced at every major intersection by green Stryker armored infantry vehicles from the U.S. Army.

These were the first American troops we'd encountered since we'd begun this looping five-hundred-mile journey. (There had been no visible U.S. presence at the Irbil customs point.) I thought, *Man, these police commandos are in it deep; they are going to be a handful in camp, no doubt.*

After the fall of Fallujah, there had been a burst of insurgent activity in Mosul, where many of the bad guys fled after their safe haven *al Emirate al Fallujah* capitulated in flames and tank fire. Every house had at least one hole in it. I had watched as a battalion of 155mm heavy artillery—some of the little cannon left in country—had reduced a building in Fallujah to rubble.

Mosul was attractive to political refugees from Fallujah because it had a substantial Sunni Arab presence in an ethnically diverse metropolis. However, the city also had a substantial Kurd population, a fact that made us feel a little bit safer. As we passed out of Mosul-Nineveh into the foothills of North Iraq, Neoshad nearly jumped out his seat as he called out, "Pesh Merga! Pesh Merga! Pesh Merga!"

He pointed at the approaching checkpoint. When the highly alert Kurd security men saw us in the back of the SUV, I shouted, "*Sirchow!*"

They smiled and waved us forward; we did not stop. My Kurd chieftain riding shotgun for me said, "It is near, it is near" in ragged but intelligible English.

I turned toward Ahmed sitting in the very back of our vehicle facing to the rear next to Sasha, and said, "The camp?" After a rapid-fire exchange in Arabic, Ahmed answered, "Yes, it should be up the hill, toward Dohuk. You know that is in Kurdistan?"

"Yes, I didn't realize from my map recon that we're this close. Do you think we can supply from the direction [due north]?"

"Yes, it would be much cheaper than Baghdad," he said.

"Maybe we should have come from that direction, furthering our loop around Kurdistan to the north. That ride through downtown Mosul was not a good one. There is no other way for the convoy to go now. I'm sure they will get through this time but maybe not the next time."

Our three-SUV battlewagon convoy moved rapidly through heavy traffic, bypassing slower vehicles, slowed mainly by large black scorched areas marking the boulevards of the city of three million at war with itself. It was about three o'clock on a midwinter's day—we could see the snow in the Zagros Mountains rimming the far horizon of the high Euphrates valley. Our body armor kept us warm against the chill.

We pulled up to a gate just past the first Kurdish checkpoint. The road beyond the gate ran straight up to a complex of buildings squatting in orange mud. I looked back down to see the conurbation in all its hues, much darker than the pastels of Baghdad. We were about a mile and a half outside the city limits.

"Neoshad, this is it? *Huna, al maddrassah al shurta?* This is the police academy?"

"*Na' am*, yes," the big Kurd said with relief as several blue-shirted Iraqi Arab guards came to surround our vehicles. I checked the longitudes and latitudes from my satellite phone. The numbers came up true. I had thought for sure we had farther to go. Then a couple of U.S. Special Forces soldiers came walking down the road from the hilltop, covering about five hundred yards to the main gate from their camp within a camp. There was an "A" team of ten men and two officers situated in a low area in the middle of the camp. I could tell MPSA was a serious American priority because of the presence of the talents of the philosopher kings of the U.S. military—hearts and minds with a quick trigger and an accurate aim.

Above the Green Beret camp, ensconced in five-foot-tall, sand-filled concrete barriers, stood a fortresslike building with a central adobe brick tower two stories tall. This was the former Saddamist commandant's quarters and offices, now empty and trashed. We asked and received permission to set up our ops there. It was a perch safe from the insurgents who attacked one night two months later and were either killed or run off by the Spetsnaz men, including "Big" Sergei, who I had left there with Charlie for security problems. Sergei number two (we eventually had three Sergeis from Ukraine including "Old" Sergei who was with me in Fallujah) was not only physically intimidating but also proficient with a sniper rifle. His precision shooting forced the insurgents to flee before the Apache attack helicopters I had called arrived at the scene. Word got around the neighborhood, and they left us alone after that one attack.

We all dismounted in the parking area in front of the MPSA commandant's buildings and across from the razor-wire enclosed Special Forces compound. The convoy with Amer in charge arrived about one hour later, as planned. There were over forty AISG workers and management. I walked down the hill with Charlie to the proposed chow hall, now a refuse-filled shell. Ahmed was already there, setting up the VSAT Internet dish. Once the camp was online, we could leave. As I returned up the hill, Amer came striding toward me.

"Mr. Carter, the guards we brought with us do not want to stay. Some are asking for more money; some just do not like the area. I am sorry to say these men are Kurdi."

We had to provide sixteen security guards and one security manager to comply with our DoD prime contract. Fourteen of these men with us at MPSA were Baghdadi Kurds we had dragooned into service from Fort Apache. AISG was paying top dollar, but Mosul made them nervous. They were far from home. It was understandable.

"Who's in charge?" I asked impatiently to the crowd of men carrying AKs, knowing full well that almost all of them had run the roads with me several times. The Kurds could not even look at me without sheepish grins on their faces. Then I knew this was mostly about money, though a few were afraid as well. The near mutineers gathered around me. Of course, I had four Spetsnaz and Charlie standing behind me and Amer.

"*Sirchow! Sirchow!* Here's what I offer. We will increase your salaries to $900 a month for everyone. [They had been promised $800.] This is a big increase over what you are paid in Baghdad. You will all rotate every twenty days back home, for ten days rest. Who will not stay and confront Saddam, here near Kurdistan?"

A babble rose in the crowd as I stared hard at each familiar face while Amer finished his translation. I then went over and started grabbing the arms of the Pesh Merga I knew. I laughed and laughed, but squeezed each strongly. We would be leaving the camp's kitchen, our workers, and Charlie practically naked if these men were to return home.

"OK, they all agree to stay." Amer uttered in relief. "They will follow you to hell, Mr. Carter, I think."

"Where is the crane? We need to off-load Crazy Amar's truck, which carried the trailers."

"Mahmoud went out and said that he would be back in a couple hours, so he should be here now."

Mahmoud arrived soon thereafter with a thirty-ton crane, more than enough power to lift the trailers. The Mosul-born Kurd even said he would have a precious backhoe later that evening. The markets of Mosul were open for business, and things were cheaper than they were in

Baghdad. However, we ended up supplying the six hundred or so police commando trainees with food from Dohuk, Kurdistan. We also routed our Apache-loaded convoys on through Dohuk on their last leg from Baghdad into the camp. We never shipped through downtown Mosul again.

Instead we took the 550-mile trip from Baghdad that hooked up parallel to the Turkish border and dropped in from the Kurdish-held mountains. The elite national Mosul Public Safety Academy was back in business, and we were pleased that we had solved the logistics issue locally by buying our supplies in Dohuk.

———————

After the Mosul commando police academy, we picked up two more DoD-funded camps, one at BIAP serving the Iraqi elite of the elite Special Forces, and another out on the Syrian border at Al Walid. We had found a niche for the United States Department of Defense in the Iraq war zone: life support and convoy security for the Iraqi security services, whether Ministry of Defense (MOD) or Ministry of Interior (MOI). Of course, our field of operation was in the Sunni Triangle, and this fact opened up the competition a little more. There was low-hanging fruit for the big boys like ESS. This company fed the entire Marine Corps and saw little reward in capturing smaller contracts in some of the hot spots of Iraq—Baquba, Tikrit, Baiji, Mosul, Fallujah, Abu Ghraib, and every district of Baghdad.

The BIAP contract proved to be our biggest business challenge. After I took over company operations, BIAP was the only camp that did not undershoot our cost projections.

This was ostensibly a sweet spot, not fifteen minutes from my old office at Terminal C, and in the safest place in all of non-Kurdistan Iraq. However, we were too close to the Palace; and we were forced to feed U.S. Special Forces trainers along with their Iraqi trainees. The Iraqis were happy with a steady diet of greasy chicken and rice and fresh bread. The Americans were not, and we were criticized by visiting dignitaries for "not taking care of the boys."

Then we had the goat cook scandal.

There was a big feast celebrating something with the Special Forces. So they asked for lamb. We caused a spot shortage in the Baghdad bazaars with our demand to feed almost nine hundred hungry soldiers with the traditional meat, so our suppliers supplemented the lamb with a little goat. Goat took longer to cook, and if you're not used to the tangier, stringier meat, it can cause stomach problems. Thirty men—including a few Americans—made brief trips to the hospital.

We had to explain, apologize, and increase our oversight of Dr. Ghassan. But after we left BIAP upon successful conclusion of our contract, I know that the troops were sorry to see a Saudi food giant running the kitchen instead of AISG.

The competition stiffened when we competed against companies in the world market. However, we had already proven ourselves at EFIC and then MPSA. Both of these camps were in shambles when we took over because DoD contractors had withdrawn or defaulted. We had a track record as a company that would take on any job and finish it on time.

The PCO had offered up a series of thirty-day wartime contingency contracts to place Iraqi forces along the critical

Syrian border. At the time, not one Iraqi security post was functioning along its more than 350-mile length from Jordan to Kurdistan and Turkey. Parsons had abandoned the work. They had awarded the first contract to us, because we were the only company that could mobilize and be on-site within two weeks. We did it with no time to spare. The commanding general of the PCO now referred to AISG as "a rising star" for the Pentagon's multibillion-dollar contracting authority.

Meanwhile, I had other corporate responsibilities. For one thing, I had to collect money from the Iraqi Ministry of Defense and Ministry of Interior—our clients for the Fallujah camp. We were burning through mountains of cash, feeding almost five thousand, including our three hundred workers who were getting the tents and A/Cs wired, building multiple chow halls, and cleaning up after the MOD grunts and MOI troopers, who were in turn clearing the urban battlefield, house by house.

In addition, we had won the Iraqna cell phone provider protection contract and were already spending money mobilizing the one thousand, five hundred men required for this job. And we were also hiring expatriate high-speed security managers. We now had twenty-plus Americans, including a retired SEAL commander and two retired Special Forces lieutenant colonels. These additions made Fort Apache, with its blast walls, nearly invulnerable to direct attack.

We were the size of a combat infantry company, if you included our live-in, 110-man Iraqi security force, and the Ukrainians, the Gurkhas, and the newly arrived Fijians and Jordanians (DoD badge holders all). Where my position on the roof was once lonely, it now had too many guns.

The only problem with this arrangement was that Baldwin had wanted the multimillion-dollar contract so badly that he allowed the Egyptians at Orascom (Iraqna's parent company) to hammer down AISG to such a low-profit margin that he couldn't cover the insurance costs for the Iraqna ex-pats. This ended up being borne by my DoD contract revenue.

The Egyptians are feared throughout the Middle East for their negotiating skills. Pete Baldwin, with Woody at his side, haggled for several days in the board room of the tallest building in Cairo, a shining glass anomaly in the ancient mud-brick city. The Orascom Telecom chairman and president manipulated the AISG CEO into signing an unprofitable agreement, in part because the Iraqna executives knew that Baldwin was terrified that Joe Morris, Pete's nemesis at Custer Battles, would win the contract. In addition, we started mobilizing and paying people months before AISG actually won the contract. So the monthly payments coming in from EFIC were flowing out of the company safe like water from a leaking pipe.

Finally after many days of nagging the U.S.-run Project and Contracting Office in the Green Zone—and through them putting pressure on the Iraqi government—we received an MOD check from a Baghdad bank account, filled out in Arabic that turned out to be worth several million dollars!

After getting back to Apache with the check in my notepad, I went across the hall from my office, through the glass doors into our accountant's office, and said, "I have good news and bad news, Atul. We got paid for EFIC . . ."

"Great, that is great!"

Atul was a short, portly Indian of Brahmin blood who

had just earned his accounting certification from California. He had worked with Baldwin in Atlanta and was now responsible for transacting all AISG payments. He was the only accountant we knew who would come out to Iraq on minimal start-up pay.

"Well, hold up, brother," I said. "This is a check made out to the Rafidain Bank in Arabic. I'll have to get out my dictionary to ensure the figures are correct."

"OK," Atul said. "Let's get with our Iraqi moneyman and see what we can do."

It turned out that one of our local moneymen had connections with the Iraqi Central Bank. First, we had to get the check certified by the Rafidain—government controlled and one of the most prominent banks in Iraq and the Middle East. Then, because the check was made out in Iraqi dinars (the MOD did not want this to be easy for us to cash), we would have to take it to the Central Bank to pick up the tens of pounds of U.S. dollars.

Abu Zein, our Baghdadi money-handler, said, "One of the officers must go to certify the check."

"Yes, I'll go with you," I replied.

"This is not the right answer, Carter," Atul said. "I must go, as you will draw too much attention."

Abu Zein agreed. We needed to do this ultra-low profile. So Atul, Abu Zein, and his son would go with one bodyguard, Tony, a former Christian Commando in Lebanon's civil war and now a U.S. citizen and recent AISG employee. Tony, a sturdy six-footer with pitch-black eyes, was by far our best security man and soon to be my great friend.

"I want to take a pistol," Atul told me. "I may need to protect myself."

"Atul, you remember last time," I said. "You don't know weapons."

When Ken had tried to force me to take Atul on our leaders' recon to the Parsons Baquba camp, Atul showed up with an AK for the trip into the Sunni Triangle. I had refused to take him with me.

Tony, standing nearby, spoke up: "Let him take it. He'll feel better."

We went to the security office and picked up for him an Iraqi-made 9mm pistol—all we had, since the sidearm shortage in Baghdad continued. He had to pull the slide back before he could fire the first bullet, because I made him carry the weapon without a round in the chamber. This would be very tricky for a novice in a confrontation, but the greater risk was an accidental discharge that wounded himself or someone else. Of course, Atul had no holster—an even more acute supply problem. He stuck it in his belt, and as he stepped into the SUV the heavy automatic slipped down his pant leg and clattered on the street.

The complicated process of cashing the first check included walking from the Central Bank down a mile-long Iraqi pedestrian way and carrying over $4 million in a rucksack hanging from Tony's broad shoulders. When they came back with the money, I congratulated them on their safe return.

"Atul, you're so brave. What a story. You are the man! Thanks to you, too, Tony. Outstanding!"

"Let me go return my weapon," the accountant said, justifiably proud of his achievement.

I sat down at my desk, and several minutes later a couple of Kurds ran up to my glass door and shouted, "Mr. Atul shot! Mr. Atul shot!"

I didn't hear the gunfire through the sandbags and thick walls, but I thought to myself while running over to the security office: *Atul has shot himself.*

When I got to House Three and went into the foyer of the mansion, I saw Atul lying on the floor, with one of our new silver-haired Special Forces Vietnam vets bandaging the Indian's leg. One of the young Iraqis who served in our not-yet-seasoned guard force was turning in his weapon, a still-loaded AK, and somehow accidentally pulled the trigger. Two high-powered rifle rounds penetrated the A/C wall unit between the makeshift armory and the security office. One of the rounds went straight into Atul's upper leg as he turned in his pistol after the heroic check-cashing mission.

To his credit, Atul kept his cool. I shouted to get a car to take him to the hospital. We then started to carry the small man out the foot gate to the waiting car. First, I thought, *Better check on the car before we expose the wounded Atul on the open street.* When I jogged out the narrow entrance between the towering t-walls, I saw an Isuzu sedan full of our armed Iraqis waiting for Atul. Not a DoD badge-holder among them.

How were they going to get him into the Green Zone CASH? Then I realized they were going to take him to an Iraqi hospital. The Iraqis knew this South Asian was not an American so they naturally thought of him as one of them. I turned back to the house and grabbed Max and one of our now-numerous retired Special Forces men so we could get Atul to the nearest U.S. military hospital, perhaps the top gunshot-trauma, first-response unit in the world.

Had Atul gone to an Iraqi hospital, the insurgents probably would have come for him and either kidnapped him or killed him. That's how insecure the hospitals were in Iraq. We would soon learn more about that problem while operating in the Western Desert. Meanwhile, Atul recovered completely without even a limp. Life as a corporate accountant was more dangerous in Baghdad than it was in Atlanta!

TEN
Death on the Highway

I was in shock. After a long series of successful runs—from Baghdad to Fallujah, from Baghdad to Mosul—we had been lulled into a false sense of security. Not officially, because at the top we always prepared for the worst—took the same precautions, avoided danger spots, went fully armed, and provided our workers with security forces. We constantly reminded each other that we were surrounded by terrorists, who would kill us as quickly as they would kill our military if they caught us off guard. However, when a group as large as ours successfully dodges the bullet time and time again, someone is bound to let down his guard.

One day I got the news I had dreaded from the beginning.

"Ar Rutbah?" I asked. "That scrub town? It's over a hundred kilometers from Al Walid. . . . That's right; we're sourcing from there—a bit here, a part there. But no security? How the hell did that happen?"

We had just lost our first people—two dead, ambushed as they were leaving a bazaar in the Sunni Arab city of Ar

Rutbah, located in the no-man's land of the Great Syrian Desert. Ar Rutbah was the most isolated town of any size in Iraq. It was over sixty miles from the population-empty Iraqi west border and at least two hundred miles farther to the nearest big city: Ramadi, capital of Al Anbar Province, heartland of the Sunni–al Qaeda insurgency.

This was the Badlands of Iraq. Up until then we had been able to low-profile our way through Iraq with no dead, some wounded (like Max), but no one killed in action. Al Walid reminded me of an Arabized and seedier version of "South of the Border," a tasteless tourist trap with a Mexican theme on the North Carolina/South Carolina border. In Al Walid you found a hotel, a truck stop, and a restaurant and that was about all.

Amer, heated up from the exertion of running from the ops center with the bad news, answered, "They took no security to Ar Rutbah. They left their guards with the fuel truck at the service station. These were Pesh Merga mostly, yes. They would be perfect here. Only one vehicle attack as they leave bazaar. Leith, the engineer you called 'The Lion' for his courage to leave his home and go to Syrian border, and two cooks shoot the bad guys. Drive them off. Put many holes in their car. Leith called me from the camp. The two cooks are hurt and now at the hospital in Ar Rutbah."

"The hospital at Ar Rutbah?! We have to get them out of there. I'll call the camp and find out what is exactly going on."

"Yes, that hospital is dangerous. We need to get them from there. No wounds very bad but not good town. It is dangerous. *Erhabeen!*" The Kurd warrior spit out the last word, meaning "terrorists," in Arabic.

"You remember that trip to Al Walid," I asked, "when I

went first and you led the follow-on convoy just like Mosul? There is a lot of emptiness up there. That night in late December was one of the coldest times in my life. Man, did the wind blow off the desert."

"Yes, I tell the convoy guys that you go with Mr. Carter and he will take you places that you have never gone in your own country, like Al Walid! I was never there before."

"You are my brother forever, Amer, *shukran jazeelan. Sirchow*! Keep me updated, like always. Please ask Tony to come over when you go to the security office."

Amer and Tony were like two bulls in the same stock-yard. They feuded about respect, with Amer, the Kurd, always feeling that Tony, the Lebanese American, did not consult enough with him, a "sheikh of Baghdad" (my phrase) and top Iraqi at AISG. I loved their debates and would deliberately provoke them while I adjudicated from behind my desk. These two men knew what I was doing and half-enjoyed themselves. But I could tell my request to see Tony in the wake of this grim news riled Amer a little, particularly since these days Amer provided the guard force and Tony managed it—fertile ground for differences to arise. Yet despite their rivalry, they eventually became friends, and brothers in the Ikwhan: Shia Muslim and Maronite Catholic.

Tony was the perfect warrior for Iraq. A burly six-footer with stylish sideburns, he was trained by Israel's elite *Golani* brigade and fought for the Christian Commandos during the long fifteen years of the Lebanese civil war. Then he served as a security manager responsible for personnel vehicle movements at the U.S. embassy in Beirut toward the end of the kidnappings heyday in the early 1990s. As a result, Tony became a U.S. citizen and served in U.S. Army military intelligence. He knew the Arabs because he was one himself; yet he was completely American in his loyalties. Over time Tony and I became great friends, out of mutual respect, I guess.

I had an edge on Tony, super-security man: I knew Baghdad and he did not. When he first arrived in country, I had already been there almost a year. He had been at Fort Apache maybe a month when we took the company's armored BMW to Baghdad International Airport to visit our newest project: feeding and supplying the Iraqi Special Forces. The Iraqis were being trained by their U.S. counterparts on the edge of the massive airfield. As we drove out of the gate, with me at the wheel, Tony was sitting next to me as my shooter. He was not sure what was going on, because here was the number two company executive driving himself around town. He had heard from the Iraqis that I was the only American who cruised around Baghdad all by himself, although this had changed with the kidnappings increase and Namir's death in September of '04. From that point on, I almost always took a couple Iraqi bodyguards with me. I rarely used my Ukrainian Spetsnaz, and never traveled with Americans, because they attracted attention. Now with Tony, I had the total package, an American who was also an Arab.

As soon as we got on the highway to the airport, the undercarriage of the BMW started to make a strange noise. We both thought that the car was going to break down, and no Triple A was going to show up to tow us. This was a first-line fear—ending up on the shoulder of Baghdad airport road, scene of hundreds of attacks. So we had to drive very slowly to the project and back. Not the best plan, very nerve-wracking. Then we got caught up in a random IP checkpoint that blocked us from getting back to our compound. I then took us around the back way, and Tony said, "You're the man," surprised because he had no idea where to go. Even the bravest man had trepidations about being in a strange city where people were actively trying to kill you.

A few weeks later, Tony saw me in my office and came wandering in. I had learned early on that the Iraqis felt respected if they knew your door was always open to them. Over time, I became a sort of safety valve for issues that percolated up in our growing workforce. I usually did not leave my office until after 11 p.m. every night; and Tony started to stop by around then, usually with Iraqis from our security force in tow, bringing some issues.

"You know, Carter, whenever my guards have problems, they always ask to see you, not their chain of command."

"Well, that's probably because I kind of represent the institutional knowledge around here," I said. "Most of these guys have been out on the road with me, so they know who I am."

"That's true, but they also say that you're a hard ass and that you've been there, done that, and are ready to do it again. That's why they respect you."

So as time went on, Tony and I formed a real bond, especially evident when he took me over the deep end into the dark depths of what it was to make war Middle-East style.

"I had an older brother," he said, "the best of all of our warriors in Beirut, killed right in front of me by the Syrians." Tony began to unwind. "We were on a recon patrol in the hotel district, where we fought room-to-room with the

Palestinians and Syrians. A sniper shot him not ten feet from me. But I couldn't get to him. I got wounded once in the leg trying. He was just across the street. I could see his body twitch with every bullet's impact."

"That must have been so painful," I said, trying to find my balance in this conversation.

"Yes, it took me several months, but I killed enough of them to get it out of my system. I used to keep count of the number. I stopped keeping track when I had killed over a hundred men."

"That's messed up, Tony," I gasped.

"You have to understand, that was the man I loved most. They shot him so many times as he lay there for hours, that after I finally got to him after dark his body was in pieces. I picked them up and put them in a garbage bag to take home."

Knowing what he had told me about himself and what I had observed in Tony, I felt completely safe in his hands.

When Tony came to my office a few minutes after Amer had left, I said, "Tony, as I am sure you know now, we just lost two men in an attack at Al Walid. I think I ought to send you and Sam up there to see what the hell is going on." Sam was a former Navy SEAL and Vietnam War combat veteran working in our security department. Maybe I should have gone myself, but the company was overloaded with projects, and they could not afford for me to be away for two days. Including the Syrian border, we were then managing camps (EFIC, MPSA, and BIAP Area Four) with almost nine thousand Iraqi security troops, and three construction projects in the Green Zone (NATO, USAID, and Fluor-Amec). I was also closing out the Parsons camps, which meant negotiating payment from Parsons and settling subcontractor costs with Namir's brother and Joe. They had completed projects under the $6 million contract that included building camps in Baquba, Camp Victory (BIAP), Mosul, and Baiji. We also were working on bidding new work with the PCO every day. I was driving around Baghdad virtually every day, hammering business and making collections.

"Well, Carter," Tony answered, "they have shut down the highways for the elections. We can't get up there even if we tried now. The marines don't want to move either. As soon as they open the route, Sam would be a good choice to go with me. He has seen some serious action in Vietnam. We at the Christian Commandos respect the SEALs."

I responded, "Why won't the Marine Corps move? These brave Iraqis are working for a DoD contractor. The least the marines could do is mount a patrol and go to the Ar Rutbah hospital. The nearest base is Korean Village. It's right outside the city. What do you know about what happened this morning?"

Tony—who had been military intelligence NCO at the 10th Mountain Division—quickly briefed me. He was in the AISG ops center when the Al Walid camp first reported the incident via satellite phone. Further information was pouring in fast, in a rapidly developing situation. What he told me was chilling. "A resupply convoy with a security truck with five armed guards left Al Walid and first went to the truck stop next to the border crossing. Leith then took off by himself with two cooks to go to Rutbah. Leaving town, they got caught on the highway and were attacked. Apparently, one of the cooks mentioned to a storekeeper in Ar Rutbah that they were working for the border patrol. They were then targeted and attacked by one vehicle full of insurgents on the highway. Our men fought back, driving off the bad guys. The two cooks were wounded and went to the hospital. Leith caught a ride back to the camp.

"The details are still sketchy but we think that the two men at the hospital have been killed by the insurgents, who took their wounded to the same hospital. One of the cooks is a member of a Sunni family from Ramadi who have tribal connections with the sheikh in Rutbah. It appears that our two men's bodies are now out in the street in the middle of town and everyone is afraid to touch them."

After that horrific summary, I made a series of phone calls to the Project and Contracting Office, the Al Anbar Area of Operations Marine liaison at the Palace, and then out to the camp. Just prior to the satellite call, I had been instant-messaging with our people up there, and they alerted me that the army captain who was the contracting officer representative had just arrived at the camp. The Coalition-Police Advisory Training Team (C-PATT) was the U.S. command responsible for the border patrol academy. This small team of two or three officers lived at the hotel next to the Al Walid border point where the marines had based a motorized platoon of about thirty men.

After being handed the satellite phone, the young army transport officer answered, "Hello" and then faded away to silence.

"Captain, you know what happened to my men. They are down at the hospital in Ar Rutbah. Please get the marines to retrieve them. This is their area of operational responsibility."

"The marines are not going to go down there. The elections are going on, and the highways are shut down."

"Look, I know that you as an army officer, if you had the people to do this and if it was in your area of responsibility, you would go down there."

"Yes, I would. But you know about that platoon at the hotel FOB [forward operating base] in Al Walid. We had problems even getting them to listen to the radio frequency for your people at the camp. They have their own mission, and we're not necessarily a part of it."

"I will tell you this, Captain. There will be hell to pay if no one goes to recover my people. I have already been talking with senior commanders in the Palace. You go over there and get those marines to move!"

Sensing my growing agitation, the captain, whose commanding officer I had met with back at the Palace, responded over the crackling satellite link, "All right, I'll do it. They won't go out in the night, and the sun is already going down. [It was midwinter and the days were short in the high desert.] I'll get them to go in the morning, first thing."

To their credit, the marines started out the next morning and tried to enter Ar Rutbah. They were turned back by insurgent fire. The First Marine Division ended up launching an all-out assault with aerial bombing before retaking the town, supposedly won over by the Special Forces almost two years before during the 2003 invasion. Plumes of black smoke rose above the town from the bombing. This took several days and was never reported in the press—that's how far away Rutbah was from the Baghdad Palestine and Sheraton Hotels, the dwelling places of Western journalists, who were afraid to travel the countryside. This was an investiture and battle unreported by the international press—only by the Jihadist Web sites, a forewarning of what was to come. At the time, the only word in the press was that thirty marines and one sailor had died when their transport helicopter crashed near Ar Rutbah on 26 January; this had occurred during the period of the operation to recover our people from the insurgent-infested caravan way station. Meanwhile, the bodies of our two men lay in the street. Finally, the family of the man from Ramadi recovered both bodies a couple days after the marines got control of the town.

We later learned that during the ambush, one of the cooks had been wounded in the back, the other in the hand. During the fight, the two brave men had killed a couple of bad guys and had wounded two more with their AKs. Our men were then stuck there with only the shot-up vehicle they were in—which had broken down after the attack—and without the extra security vehicle our company policy mandated. They needed to find transportation. Fortunately, cars stopped on the highway to help, and Leith was able to catch a ride back to the camp. The wounded men were taken to the nearest hospital, where death awaited them. The two wounded insurgents were also at the hospital, with other gunmen, when our guys arrived for treatment; and the Neo-Saddamist and al Qaeda allies snatched our Iraqi men, one Shia and one Sunni, from their beds at the hospital and shot them dead in the street.

Once the deaths were confirmed, we needed to take care of the families. The company would give them each a $10,000 death benefit. It was only right that we meet with the families first to hand-deliver the money.

I told them, "I am so sorry for what happened to Mohamed [the Shia cook who had started out as a security man before going for the bigger salary of a cook]. He died like a lion, though. You should be proud of him. All of us at the company are proud to have had the opportunity to work with this man of honor."

Then I sat back, not knowing exactly what to expect as Tony translated to the father, his two brothers—one of which also worked at AISG—and the wife, dressed head-to-toe in a black abaya, including the full-facial screen of the truly pious Muslim woman in mourning.

The father spoke, "We know Mohamed was doing what he thought was right. He always said that you were a good company that treated him right. Thank you for your efforts on our behalf. He is now with Allah. We are proud of him."

The calm acceptance of the situation brought home to me further how present their God was to these believing Muslims. *This was the fate of Mohamed, to die in Ar Rutbah. We had to continue to move forward.* That was the sentiment I gathered from the father's speech. I walked down to the other end of the black-lacquer conference table where the woman sat in all black and gave her the packet of money. Mohamed's wife immediately gave it to the father. This made me uncomfortable, but that was their way: the extended family of her dead husband would take care of her and their children.

Tony alone dealt with the other cook's family several days later; I was in the Green Zone making collections at the Ministry of Defense when the father appeared at Apache without warning.

By now, AISG had become a large contractor. We had secured a growing number of DoD projects, the Iraqna security contract with VIP bodyguards for the Egyptian ex-pats, security for the movement of money (a million dollars a day in receipts), and the furnishing of guards at over twenty villas. We had over two thousand, five hundred people working for us. Fort Apache was no longer Woody and I running around with our pistols out. The lot we acquired from the elementary school next door in late 2004 easily accommodated three 40-foot tractor trailers in between our freezer trucks, refrigerator vehicles, mechanics' area, manager's trailer, and security huts.

We needed this infrastructure to service all our camps. The refrigerated vehicles were especially necessary because we transported fresh meat nationwide. The Iraqis would not eat a packaged meal like an MRE, even if it was *halal* (prepared according to Islamic law). In fact, we almost lost a lot of money on a contract Carlos signed while I was at Al Walid because the contract mandated *halal* MREs for the Special Forces at BIAP Area 4. We had to get them airshipped from Fort Lauderdale, Florida, but the Iraqi soldiers wouldn't touch them. So we had to ship frozen chickens and fresh lamb throughout the Sunni Triangle in the heat of a Persian Gulf summer.

Our neighborhood school served as polling station for the January 30, 2005, national assembly elections. This was the first free election in the thousand-year history of Iraq, and for that matter, Mesopotamia. With an almost 60 percent turnout of registered voters with eight and a half million people casting ballots, this was a success that I so wished Namir could have seen. I wish he could have witnessed election day itself, the laughing and shouting Baghdadis sticking their dark purple stained right index finger in the air—proof they had voted—as they passed by our security gates. And this was in the face of threats of amputation, torture, and beheading from the near ubiquitous insurgents.

I had ordered extra t-walls to block our side streets further from the explosions and firefights we all thought would break out during the election. The night before election eve, I had gone out to check the guard and found a tall, lean U.S. Army lieutenant colonel in full battle gear standing just inside our far drop gate next to the school's front. I could see the silhouettes of two Bradleys in the darkness, with the forty-ton troop-carrying tracked vehicles blocking the ends of the street bordering the school's entrance. He had a bodyguard of three soldiers from his unit, but other than these, he was alone in the Baghdad street on a walking inspection of all his sector's polling stations.

As I stretched out my hand in greeting, I said, "How are you doing, sir? I am Carter, and I'm a senior manager here at American-Iraqi Solutions Group. This is our checkpoint."

He shook my hand and said, "Yes, we know about you. I'm Tom MacDonald, commander of the 1st of the 9th Cavalry. This part of our sector has been very quiet. In part, I suspect, due to your presence here. We have been up mostly on Haifa Street [they called it the 'Fallujah of Baghdad']. Now that we have that sector under control, we can spread our wings a bit further."

"It's great to see you here. We very much appreciate your service to the country. I love to see the Bradleys. I had four of them about fifteen years ago at 3/15 Infantry when I was a platoon leader. You and I must be about the same date of commissioning. It's good to see an old man like me out on the streets. Just to let you know, we're on full alert now and we have over a hundred men to protect our part of the polling station's security zone."

Later that night, I woke up about 4 a.m. to check perimeter security. I knew this would be near the time when the guard force's attention level would be the lowest—just before dawn. Grabbing my AK, I put on a dark brown suede jacket against the winter cold with level-four steel-plated body armor on underneath. I had shifted to steel from polymer, because, although the polymer or ceramic weighed less, the steel alloy was thinner and therefore easier to hide. My appearance only indicated a thick jacket as I headed out into the side street for the 250-yard walk down by the logistics staging area to our Gate Three, where I had briefly chatted with Lt. Col. MacDonald earlier that night.

Tony emerged from the darkness of the alley between the six-foot, brick-walled truck park and the seven-house block.

I glanced over at him and said, "*Sirchow*," as several of the guards moved in to form a wedge around me as we all headed down to the far gate.

All of a sudden, *crack, crack, crack, crack* . . . *zing, zing, zing*, and then the two sounds merged in a sort of elongated *craaaa-eye-kkk* as several bullets flew about ten feet above our heads. Ducking, I looked over at Tony, and he looked back at me with a grin on his face and his eyes somehow gleaming brightly in the dark.

Excited, he said, "Those are bullets!"

No one had a direct shot on us since these were shots fired from an area on the other side of a couple three-story residences across the street from the school. Nevertheless the night was alive with gun battles and explosions. The next night, however, was relatively quiet, just like the following day of the election, when the army shut off all vehicle travel in Baghdad and elsewhere. There would now be a sovereign legislature for Iraq—the National Assembly—put in power by an election where the majority of the voters participated at a higher rate than in America. We all smiled for several days after this. The U.S. mission in Iraq, seen as faltering at that time, gained new life. We felt a strong resurgence of optimism at the grass roots of the effort—among the several thousand Iraqis of all sects and ethnic groups who worked with us.

Not everybody was happy. For the election, we had blocked off a part of the street on the front side of Apache, further restricting our neighbors' vehicular movement. This angered one large family up the street who was originally from Ramadi, the heartland of the anti-American insurgency. One of the men from the clan shouted at our guards when he saw the new t-walls cutting across the street. As soon as it was dark, a bullet shot from the Ramadis house zinged down the street, hitting high up on one of the offending t-walls. This was not an attempt to kill any of us, just a single "honor" shot. Nevertheless Tony took a patrol of our guards down the lane and to the front of the shooter's mansion to let the Ramadi clan know that we knew. His presence told them there would be consequences if it happened again.

Life went on at Fort Apache as AISG rapidly expanded. We ran convoys every day, and sometimes twice a day. The company was moving hundreds of tons of supplies to Fallujah, out to BIAP, Mosul, and the Syrian border. The convoys had almost gotten routine.

About midnight in late February, Ahmed showed up at my bedroom door. This was unusual but not unheard of, since the welcome mat was always out at my room and office. I answered the door and met the unusually disheveled Baghdadi. He always looked dashing and professional. His black hair was askew, and he had dirt on his face and clothes.

"The Mahdi army got us. They made us all lay face down on the road. They thought we were al Qaeda!"

"What! I knew you were on the highway coming back from Al Walid after you had gone out there to fix their Internet. I put you in charge of that convoy. How did you end up in Sadr City?"

"No, you know that part of the Baghdad-Ramadi highway on the northwest corner of the city just as you enter the capital? It is a Shia area. [This was Khadamiya.] The American army blocked the highway. We sat there for hours. So we decided to take the convoy through the side roads. When we entered the Shia area, there were hundreds of Sadr's Mahdi army people all over the place. They saw the weapons of our security men and thought we were the bad guys. I thought for sure they were going to kill us right there when they made all ten of us lie down in a row on the road, face down in the dirt."

"Wow, is everyone all right?"

"Yes, I kept telling them that we are not *erhabeen* [terrorists], but that we are with the Americans. I showed them our AISG badges. Finally, they started to listen. The main Sadr leader then called the Iraqi police, who let us go—over three hours after Sadr's men had stopped us."

"So the Mahdi army let you go because you were with the Americans! That's interesting; I thought they didn't like us."

"They just want to kill the Wahhabi and Saddamists. They know that without the Americans, the Shia would have no power. They are not your real enemy like al Qaeda."

"Thank God no one was hurt. Stay here tonight. There is a spare room in House Four. You don't need to go across town to your house and risk getting caught by the curfew [that started at 10 p.m.]. You've had enough excitement for today, *Ahooya*. Thank you very much for being there with the convoy. Without your leadership, the situation may have gotten ugly."

AISG was rocking. We had successfully completed over ten prime contracts for the Pentagon in Iraq. We now set the standard for quick mobilization among contractors. As a result of our work in the insurgent hotspots, the Iraqi security troops were getting fed and supplied. And as Napoleon said, "An army travels on its belly." This was the key for the U.S. victory (and exit) strategy: get the Iraqis securing their own country. They were better at identifying the enemy than we would ever be.

In all, the total business I obtained and my team executed was climbing toward $50 million. I could see the company doing $100 million and beyond. And I had gotten a tip that we were going to get a piece of the operations contract for the huge Taji Iraqi army base—the crown jewel of the U.S.'s new Iraqi security services training program. The original contractor was struggling to provide life support to the almost twenty thousand soldiers training at my old hangout of Taji.

Fort Apache had become a small city with a continuous ebb and flow of hundreds of Iraqis, Filipinos, Gurkhas, Jordanians, Fijians, Ukrainians, and Americans. We were probably the only DoD contractor that had such a huge contingent of armed Baghdadis in our midst. All of the managers and guard officers carried sidearms, and we had over one thousand, six hundred armed guards, all carrying AK-47s during their shifts. My office became a way point in the company flow.

One time, about 9 p.m., fifteen Iraqis from convoy protection flowed into my glass-encased office, led by Amer with Ali, the academician-turned-convoy-commander. Both were Kurds, as were most of the other men, including some from the north who had been with us since AISG's beginning.

I asked Ali as he sat down, "This has to do with Neoshad, yes?" Amer had already told me what had happened.

"Yes, Mr. Carter, he abandoned the convoy in Irbil."

At that moment, the portly Kurd chieftain walked in. I asked him quickly with Amer's translation: "Neoshad, my old friend, how could you leave your post? I brought you over to convoy protection after you were fired in the clan struggles from the guard force. [Woody had dismissed Neoshad several weeks before from the guard force because he could not get along with the captain of the guard.] We trusted you to command the security of the convoy. All your men are here, and they do not want to ride with you again. You abandoned your post."

"I could not communicate with Ali. I thought that he did not respect me enough."

"Then you should have complained here and not taken off with a company security vehicle and left the ten-vehicle convoy. I'm especially concerned that you were responsible for the security of a Filipino engineer. You need to go home now, and I will think over whether you should stay with the company. This is a sad day for me."

Amer nodded with approval as all the men filed out. The several who had driven with me on the roads stopped by to greet me with the traditional four kisses, two cheek-to-cheek on each side of the face. This was mandatory in their culture. If you really wanted to show respect during one of the kisses, you pressed your lips on the shoulder. I can remember that when the captain of the Al Kindi–Fort Apache police district came to visit me, I greeted him with the traditional cheek bussing. He was startled and responded, with Tony translating, "You are the first *franji* [Westerner] that ever greeted me the 'Iraqi way.'"

One of my most important lessons on leadership in dealing with Arabs in general and Iraqis in particular was from Lawrence of Arabia. I read the *Seven Pillars of Wisdom* by T. E. Lawrence while in Baghdad. In this beautifully written and densely intricate book, the author pointed out a key practice of the sheikhs: your door is always open and late into the night for the complaints, suggestions, information, and chitchat of your people.

Our Iraqi staff would wander in to see me at all hours with information about terrorist activities. This happened several times, and we reported it through the Special Forces Old Boys network to Special Ops in the Green Zone. Their base was less than a mile from us; we could hear their helicopters fly over us at less than fifty feet as the "door kickers" hit targets in the capital city, night after night. The report was that we had provided actionable intelligence from time to time. That was about all we ever heard back from the secret operators.

Ahmed came into my office once, very upset looking. He started to complain right away. "The police are so corrupt! So corrupt! I cannot drive on the streets. I was driving my Jag and a police captain in Mansour demanded $100 from me or there would be 'problems.' Just like the old times!"

"What! Do you have his name? We will report him to the Palace. The American police advisors need to know."

"I have his phone number. But I do not need trouble. What if he finds out that I told on him?"

"He won't know. But if good Iraqis like you don't report this corruption, then who will? I see you don't want to do this. Go home and tell me tomorrow, *Ahooya*."

He returned the next day and gave me the cell number. I took it to the inspector general's office at the U.S. embassy. One step at a time: the only way forward.

With the big Iraqna contract taking on great importance for the company because Pete Baldwin, AISG president, had finally closed the deal with the Egyptians, he decided to make the security department an independent entity—outside my authority—in early 2005. Baldwin brought in Van, a retired Special Forces lieutenant colonel, as senior vice president in charge of the new security company. As a result, I had less and less visibility over the security side. This would lead to trouble.

After the split-up of the company, Brahim and Amer came into my office together, leading a young Iraqi. This was unusual, because although I never saw open hostilities between the two Sadr City Shias, the original AISG Iraqis stayed clear of each other. They had their different lanes.

Amer began, "Brahim wants to report that one of the new Iraqis is demanding kickbacks from all new employees."

I had hired Brahim to work with us as a troubleshooter after Van had recently fired him from the security department for reasons unclear to me at the time.

Brahim said, "Yes, the new guy, Sabah, brought in by security to be head Iraqi for the guard force, is asking for $50 from every new security man. This boy here will tell you; he had to give."

I listened to Amer translate as the young Baghdadi repeated the same story Brahim had just told. I kept thinking that all these new guys over at security don't have the necessary feel for the Iraqis. There was only Woody over there. He had been pushed to the side and currently ran the ops center, now hooked up with Iraq-wide vehicle tracking capability and monitors for security cameras watching every gate at Fort Apache. Tony, our only Arabic-speaking American, was no longer working with convoy security, but only on special missions and the guard force. I had begun to fear that the security department was out of touch and bad things were going to happen. I also worried the company might be getting ripped off. I no longer had any control over security after the AISG split.

After Amer finished his translation, I said, "We will get to the bottom of this. Go tell Van about the kickbacks. This man sounds like a bad man. If he is a bad man, then he is my enemy just as you said he is yours. He is hurting the company."

Both the AISG old-timers—men who had been with me through it all, protecting me and the company at all times—nodded. Brahim then said, "You are our sheikh. Sheikh Carter!"

"Yes, Sheikh Carter," agreed Amer, the Kurd chieftain.

"We are *shoohk* together, my brothers. *Ikhwan!*"

This was a high honor. Sheikh not only meant chief but also had religious connotations to my Iraqi friends. No honorific title for a foreigner could be higher.

———————

Tragedy struck a couple weeks later on June 12, 2005. The weather had turned hot. Summer had arrived and Iraq was on fire. The heat wrapped you in a blanket of white-hot radiation. The sun—*shamas*—cooked the earth like a broiler. Once again, the long, empty highway to the Syrian and Jordanian borders marked with orange-hued sand dunes of the high desert proved deadly.

U.S. and Iraqi military operations on the Syrian border and in the Upper Euphrates Valley forced the insurgents to the interior of Iraq, where over twenty men with rocket-propelled grenades and machine guns ambushed one of our supply convoys, killing eleven of the company's men, including three bakers returning home on leave. The cooks were burned alive inside their vehicle; and two truck drivers were captured and executed two days later, their bodies left on the side of the highway near insurgent-controlled Hit, a town about fifty miles from the attack. The lead convoy protection escort put up a fight, but in the end all the security men lay dead, with bullets in the backs of their heads. The rear security vehicle fled the attack without firing a shot.

Tony came back from the ambush kill zone after retrieving the dead men's bodies and walked into my office and said angrily, "They shot at us when we drove up. The bad guys. They finally stopped shooting, and we got to the corpses. There were bullet casings all around them; they fought hard, including Ali, whom you trained to be convoy commander. Bear, the big Gurkha, lay next to the Iraqis. The scene looks like the insurgents hit the lead truck with an RPG from the nearby overpass. That stopped the convoy, which then tried to turn around and flee, but the big transports were unable to escape. It was tough to see the carnage, even for me. The wolves had already gotten a hold of the bodies."

Later that day, my cell phone rang. I answered, and on the other end a British voice said, "Associated Press, we were at the Yarmouk morgue and saw several dead men including a Nepalese that the morgue workers said were from your company."

"Yes," I said, "one of our cargo convoys was ambushed, and we are investigating the incident now. It was west of Ramadi. I cannot give you further details, not because I am trying to hide something, but because we are just now getting additional info."

The logistics route from Baghdad to Al Walid was now cut. How were we going to supply the six hundred Iraqi border patrolmen and our thirty employees stuck in the middle of the desert at the Al Walid base, not a stone's throw from hostile Syria? Mission failure was imminent—for us and for the border police. As a consequence, we might also face the collapse of our DoD contracts. The death of so many good, brave men hit me hard—I knew them all.

ELEVEN
The Sunni Solution

After the insurgents killed our eleven men, the highway was effectively shut down to convoys. But we still had a contract to supply six hundred border patrolmen—the Desert Wolves—living and working at the Al Walid base. This base was the only operational frontier post for the Iraqi security services along the entire border with Syria. For this reason, it was key to the success of our efforts in Iraq. The Coalition plan was to expand from there, reoccupy the abandoned-by-Parsons forts, and build new ones to stop the infiltration by terrorists and insurgent support out of Syria. Since we possessed the only viable operation on the border, the Coalition's training team planned to give us the sole logistics contract for the expansion. The proposal was already on the table and funding was on the way.

So how were we to service the site with our supply route shut down? The answer to that question came from a surprising source. It all started when I had tried to collect an overdue bill three months before the ambush.

Almost every day for over two months—from late March until mid-June 2005—I had haunted the contracts office at the Iraqi Ministry of Defense, attempting to pry loose the money owed to us from the Fallujah job. Talk about a labyrinth. The bureaucracy the Iraqis had created was as difficult to stumble through as a house of mirrors.

To make matters worse, at the first meeting I really screwed up. Dr. Ziad Cattan, the third-highest official in the Ministry of Defense, was known for two things: his pomposity and his open hostility to weapons—a curious position for a major figure in the MOD. Unaware of his feelings, Tony and I walked through the front door of the Ministry armed. *Al wizarat id-defa* (the defense ministry) was housed in one of Saddam's grandiose concrete palaces located in what was now the Green Zone—the U.S. Army–secured home for the new Iraqi parliament and key security ministries.

The place was brimming with employees, supplicants, and armed guards. Our driver, Abu Hind, stayed behind with the car with my body armor, AK, and grenades. Tony and I walked right past Iraqi army security as if there was no stopping us. We had on our DoD badges, and in we went, minimally armed, according to our usual protocol. I had only a pistol. Tony had a modest submachine gun. After all, who knew what could happen with all these Iraqis walking around, armed with AK47s and pistols?

Tony and I marched up the wrought-iron staircase and straight through a dark-mahogany double-door into the assistant secretary general's office. At least I had my .45 Colt concealed under my jacket, but Tony was flaunting his weaponry, with three-inch-thick, heavy-plate body armor and a mini-Uzi only partially tucked under his T-shirt pulled over the flak jacket. The man could intimidate with the best of them.

Ziad—a man who looked like he was used to being in charge—stared over his large desk, noted Tony's armor and Uzi, and asked, "Who are you?"

"I am with the contractor that did the life support for Fallujah," I said. "I am here to talk with you about the money MOD owes us."

Ziad exploded, "You are with a *company*! I thought you were U.S. government! Go outside my office now." The words echoed off the walls of his meeting room.

We were being thrown out before we even had a chance to engage the man who signed all payment approvals. It took me weeks of trying every day before I could get in to see Ziad again. And I was admitted only after I hammered the U.S. senior advisor to MOD, Mike Smith, to get me in to see the Iraqi bureaucrat. Mike, a middle-aged former army man turned DoD civilian, was a good guy; but the Iraqis were now sovereign, and he had only so much sway over a partially U.S.-funded ministry that Ziad and the minister of defense himself were evidently in the process of looting.

When I finally got some action, it was because of a Byzantine tour through a series of offices that eventually led me to Major General Mohamed, the contracts officer for life support at MOD. Mohamed was immaculately dressed, a chain-smoking man who spoke English well and was obviously cultured and educated. General Mohamed's office was down a chaotic hallway from Ziad's. Petitioners milled around, clutching letters and invoices, stoic and bewildered. I joined them, and day after day sat quietly by Mohamed's desk, hoping like the others to win his help. While I waited,

I studied my Iraqi Arabic with the coaching of his staff, who began to see me as their pet American.

Eventually my patience paid off. Somehow the general came to respect me, perhaps because he saw that I was making a genuine effort to learn his language. Mohamed and I began to exchange pleasantries and eventually got down to the business at hand.

"We need to be paid," I said. "When do you think I can see Ziad?"

"You might try dropping your price," Mohamed said, with the trace of a smile. "That usually catches his attention."

Knowing that Iraqis love to bargain, I had built some wiggle room into the contract, so I quoted a new price.

"I'll see what I can do," Mohamed said.

After about twenty sessions at his office over forty-five days, one of his minions walked in and said something to him in Arabic. Mohamed grabbed me from my Iraqi language studies and pulled me down the hallway. "Quick," he whispered, "we must catch Ziad before he leaves on vacation."

At that moment, Ziad bolted out of his office door, a much larger and more imposing man than he appeared to be sitting behind his desk. He saw me and the general approach, and, before we could speak, said in crisp English, "We will get you through a commission, now that you have renegotiated your price, and you will get paid."

"Thank you, Dr. Ziad," I replied, honestly grateful. I understood that the Ministry of Defense in a war for survival had more important things to do than pay overdue bills.

On our way back to his office, Mohamed smiled. "You see, I am going to help you."

I looked at him and said, "I love you. Thank you."

The problem with trying to collect our overdue bill for $2 million through General Mohamed was that with the change of government in April, the Shias had taken control of the Ministry of Defense. Mohamed was a Sunni. In a world run by Shias, one could not have a Sunni controlling defense contracts. At least that was the reasoning of General Mohamed as to why the government axed him in early June 2005.

In reality, he carried an even greater liability: he wasn't in on the scheme with Ziad, an Iraqi businessman married to a Polish woman, and the minister of defense, Hazem Shaalan. They together allegedly moved a substantial portion of their government's oil revenues abroad, using fake contracts to buy a billion dollars in arms from former Warsaw Pact nations. (FindLaw.com: "$800 Million Stolen from Iraq Government in Corrupt Arms Deals," October 22, 2006, and numerous other articles in the mainstream media.) That's why they got rid of our general.

Aware that Baghdad was no longer a safe place for him, Mohamed prepared to leave for Amman, Jordan. There were threats on his life from the insurgents, the criminals, and probably even Shia militias, for he was a former Baathist who had held power under Saddam.

Immediately after his last day at MOD, I attended a business lunch at the general's house in the Green Zone. The general's guests included me, Abu Sally al Qubeisi, a scion of one of the greatest Bedouin and Sunni families in all Iraq, and Abu Aziz, one of my Lebanese managers who served as Tony's commander in the Christian Commandos.

In war-ravaged Iraq, you couldn't talk about business without also talking about politics, culture, and military strategy.

Besides, I was extremely curious about General Mohamed and what motivated him. So I began to question him.

Since he had been a director of intelligence for the Iraqi air force, I asked him about Saddam, and he told us about confronting the dictator.

"I was giving a brief in 1996 about how the Americans would attack next, and the president interrupted me.

"'You are talking about the F-117 stealth?' he asked.

"'No, I'm talking about the B-2 stealth.'

"Saddam said, 'Impossible, you must be talking about the 117.'

"I said, 'No, this is the B-2, a newly deployed bomber much more powerful than the F-117, a fighter bomber.'

"The room—filled with all the top military officials in Iraq including the minister of defense and the commanding general of the air force—let out an audible gasp.

"No one had ever seen anyone tell the tyrant no before. Afterward, the minister of defense and my commanders all came up to me with congratulations on surviving the confrontation and for having the courage to stand up to the man. I shrugged it off, saying that it was only a technical point, not political. But that was the type of fear and stupidity that Saddam's reign of terror instilled in normally brave men."

"Were you not afraid?" I asked.

"No. It was not the first time I had told him no. But always over just technical matters. In hindsight it does seem humorous that grown men would be afraid to correct an error of fact."

"Do you think this attitude figured in why you didn't become commander of the air force?"

"Probably."

At this moment, Abu Sally al Qubeisi broke away from our discussion to pray. He sought the *qibla*, the direction of Mecca. Qubeisi, a short, rotund man with a kind face, was diligent about praying five times a day. His face bore the true mark of the devout Muslim: a circular, raised callus the size of a fifty-cent piece in the middle of the forehead, earned by touching his head to the ground in obeisance to his God.

I said to Mohamed, "Hopefully he will pray for us."

The general, who quoted from the Prophet Mohamed often, corrected me: "His prayers will be for himself . . . There is, however, one prayer for friends. Maybe he will say that."

"That is a little different for us." I made the plunge for the first time in Iraq. I quoted from Christ to a Muslim: "Jesus said that there is no greater sacrifice than to give one's life for another. This is the soldier's prayer, in that if he dies for a righteous cause, he will go to heaven."

General Mohamed nodded approvingly. The thinking Muslim who follows the Qur'an has respect for the words of Jesus Christ. They regard Him as the last of the prophets before the Messenger of Allah, Mohamed, put the final seal on the revelations the Almighty allowed to humankind.

"You know why I want to help you, Carter?" Mohamed said. "Because you are helping my country."

"Thank you. I want to be of help," I said. "Of course, I'm a businessman and I'm here to do business. But that's not why I stood alone in front of Abu Ghraib prison seventeen days in a row, twice a day at the same time, in order to feed the soldiers in Fallujah. A man doesn't put his life on the line for money alone. The enemies of my country, of peace, are the people we're fighting."

"For what you did at Fallujah, you're a hero. We all recognize that," Mohamed said. "I try to explain to my brethren that they see two enemies, al Qaeda and the Americans. Let us fight one and not the other. Otherwise, we will lose all. Let us not choose the men who pervert Islam and blow themselves up along with our women and children. This is the real enemy."

Qubeisi returned to the coffee table from prayer and said, "Let's talk business now."

From Carlos's accounts-payable reports, I could already see trouble brewing. In continuing to supply Al Walid four hundred miles from Baghdad, we were now seeing our transport costs rise. At the same time, we were incurring increased security risks. Our Iraqi subcontractors, acutely aware of the climbing death toll in Al Anbar, understandably charged us more as a consequence. By the time of General Mohamed's business lunch, we had already lost our two men trying to resupply Al Walid from Ar Rutbah.

Coincidentally, a few days prior to our lunch, I found out that Qubeisi had a house in that city and that he and General Mohamed maintained a storage area for vehicles they were importing from Jordan. This really piqued my interest. I wanted to see if these two men had the connections to get us supplied in the Sunni Triangle—an area where we had already lost two men, a place the marines could not penetrate after a week of trying. If we could do peaceful business with the locals of Ar Rutbah, then we had a gold mine. And more important, perhaps, we would have pointed the way for all of Iraq.

I carefully explained our problem to them. They asked a couple of questions. Then General Mohamed spoke for both of them. "I believe we can help you. As you know, the Shias have been the enemies of the Sunnis for more than a thousand years. But they have not been the enemies of America. Some Sunnis blame the Americans for everything that has happened recently, including the gift of their country to the Shias. Others, however, harbor no such animosities. With those we can maybe do business."

Qubeisi nodded in agreement. "I believe we can do business together. Give us a few days to see what connections we can make. Then we will meet again."

Shortly thereafter, Mohamed moved out of the U.S.-protected Green Zone and back into Baghdad proper as he prepared to leave for Amman. Mohamed owned two houses in the capital, because he had two wives. Why Mohamed practiced polygamy helped me to understand the traditional reason for multiple wives in Islam. As he explained it to me, "My best friend was killed during an air battle I fought with him over Iran during the Iran-Iraq War. For a decade after my friend's death, no one would marry the widow. I loved my friend and wanted to care for his wife. So I married her, and now have a small boy in addition to my children from the first wife." From my study of Islam, I knew it had started as a religion carried forth in continuous warfare by the Arab nomad Bedouin. Because they fought countless battles, there were many widows left alone in their childbearing years, the source of future warriors and protectors of the tribe.

With two houses, he was doubly exposed, since he had to travel from one to the other—and, as noted, he had several enemies. Before he departed for Amman, the only time he left one of his houses in Baghdad was to see me to talk about business. On those occasions, he always drove up to

Fort Apache in a low-profile station wagon or a beat-up Toyota sedan. He now operated just like us, but with no bodyguards or visible weapons.

———————

At this point, we were also providing logistics and running the kitchen for Camp India, an Iraqi army base named by the U.S. military and located in Abu Ghraib—the home city for the infamous prison and one of the hottest spots in Iraq. The insurgents in Iraq rarely mounted small-unit assaults involving twenty, thirty, or forty men with coordinated fires, as did the Viet Cong on many occasions. However, the insurgents had done it at least twice at the gates of the prison, not very far from our new camp. About five days after we took over our share of the base, mortar rounds fired from an adjacent, huge cemetery with lots of cover and concealment landed not more than two hundred yards from my people. The attack killed five Iraqi construction workers employed by another contractor.

I left Baghdad to visit Camp India and traveled directly through Abu Ghraib, with heavy traffic flowing all around us. When our two-vehicle convoy arrived, Tony—already at the camp, setting up security at our newly established position—had put up a sign in English and Arabic at the entrance to our compound within Camp India: "Abu Ghraib welcomes the Wildman!" Wildman was my radio call sign in the army and at Apache.

Tony opened my door and asked me as soon as I got out of the car, "Will you talk with your team here? After the mortar deaths, I think the guys would appreciate it."

All the workers, cooks, security men, mechanics, electricians, carpenters, plumbers, drivers, and laborers lined up in the dining tent, with the head chef at the beginning of the line. I shook everyone's hand and then said, "On behalf of the company, I want to thank you very much for your courage in coming to work out here. It is very dangerous, and what you are doing for yourselves and your country will not be forgotten ever. We will succeed together. You all honor me and the company with your trust and hard work."

Tony finished translating and shouted, "Let's eat!"

Later, while making a convoy-run out to the camp from Fort Apache, Tony watched as insurgents fired a rocket-propelled grenade from the back of a pickup truck maneuvering through traffic. The grenade destroyed a truck carrying t-walls, blast protection used only by Coalition forces. This happened right where I used to walk alone on the highway to link up with the marines for supplying Fallujah. All the camps in the combat zone and their exposure wore me down, but this latest incident was foremost in my mind.

Right after this incident, General Mohamed, Qubeisi, and I met again in my office to hammer out the specifics of a deal that would enlist the Sunni tribes to help us execute our projects safely. So I asked them, "Can you connect us with the sheikh of Abu Ghraib to provide us with security and intelligence to ensure that our convoys are not attacked?"

I knew the sheikh was a Sunni. Except for Baghdad, the Sunni province of Al Anbar that stretched hundreds of miles of empty desert west of Fallujah and onto the frontier at Al Walid was the most dangerous area in Iraq.

Mohamed translated Qubeisi as saying, "My family is

good friends with the sheikh as is General Mohamed's. We both know him personally."

"How should we move forward?" I asked, trying not to sound too excited.

"We will contact him and go to his house to discuss these matters," Mohamed said. "But most likely it would involve his people doing the security for your convoys."

"Great," I said, noticing that Qubeisi was warming to the subject.

I then asked, "Where are the al Qubeisis from?" I was very interested in their patch of Iraqi geography. I later found out the man reputed to be the most prominent Sunni religious scholar from Iraq was a Qubeisi. Dr. Ahmad Qubeisi was so powerful that after the U.S. invasion, he purportedly controlled who would be the imam at Abu Hanifa, one of the most prominent mosques in the world and the founding institution for the school of Islam to which about half of the world's billion-plus Muslims subscribe.

The three of us stood and moved to an engineering map of Iraq on my office wall. We were alone, with Mohamed translating.

Qubeisi pointed on the map to the vast area of western Iraq running from Hit on the edge of the Euphrates valley through Fallujah to the southeast and Ar Rutbah in the western emptiness of the Iraqi portion of the Syrian Desert.

"This is where my family calls our homeland. There are thousands in my clan. We have been smugglers and free Bedouins from time immemorial, recognizing no borders. Not here, and not in Saudi Arabia, Syria, or Jordan."

He indicated the entire northern half of the great Arabian Desert—over thousands of square miles of desolation north to Damascus and west to the Red Sea and Egypt's Sinai Peninsula. Modern political borders did not exist for these nomads.

I don't know where it came from, but I said, "I have just finished reading Lawrence of Arabia's book, and he talks about the Beni Hassan tribe in this border area. Are they related to you?"

Qubeisi, a portly man always dressed in worker's city clothes belying his close tribal roots, smiled so widely I thought I could see his rear molars from the side. "My grandfather was killed by Lawrence!" he said.

I didn't know how to respond or what to think; I just looked at Mohamed for guidance and said, "Wow." I was worried that the mention of Lawrence would turn him against me.

Qubeisi then boomed out, "Lawrence was a great man! My grandfather was a great man!" Apparently he was quite proud of the connection with the English officer. (During World War I, T. E. Lawrence organized the Arab Revolt that proved to be the death knell of the Ottoman Empire's six centuries in the Middle East.)

I turned to Mohamed and asked, "How can we control this area and end the insurgency?"

Mohamed shook his head and smiled.

"Remember, my brother, no one has ever controlled this area. Even under Saddam. He put his main customs posts for the western borders at Fallujah, five hundred kilometers from the frontier. Al Anbar is just a piece of the Arabian Desert that recognizes no border, just the byways of the Bedouin."

"We have a camp on the Syrian border. This is an area where we need help. It's an expensive and dangerous route for our convoys to travel. Maybe you can help us with supply from Ar Rutbah?"

"Yes," Qubeisi said, "but better yet, let's get goods from Syria, just across the frontier from Al Walid."

The thought of supplying the border post from Syria struck me as a delicious irony. Of course, we were doing the same thing at our police commando camp in Mosul, where we supplied from Dohuk, Kurdistan, less than thirty miles away. But Kurdistan was friendly territory; Syria was the enemy, the safe haven and transit point for neo-Saddamists and al Qaeda terrorists operating in Iraq.

I asked, "How much will this cost to supply Al Walid?"

"Give us a list of your requirements and we'll get back to you in a couple days."

In the interim, the June 12 ambush on the Baghdad to Al Walid highway had taken place. Tony had gone to recover the bodies from the wolves. We determined that a gang of bad guys—forced down from the border areas by the U.S Marine operations in the Euphrates Valley—had gathered in the southwestern part of Al Anbar and ambushed our convoy, killing the eleven men and stealing or burning four of our forty-foot supply transports. On hearing the shocking news from Amer and then discussing it with Tony, I had immediately called General Mohamed to ask him and Qubeisi to come to my office. Fortunately Mohamed was still in Baghdad—he was planning to leave for Jordan in just two days.

Meanwhile, Sam delivered the news that, as of that day, AISG security could not provide convoy protection for our supply movements to Al Walid. Mission failure stared us straight in the eye. The Desert Wolves on the Syrian border would run away when food ran out and leave that section of

the border—the main point of entry for insurgents and terrorists—open to invasion. This would be a major setback for
an emerging Iraqi security force, and therefore a severe blow
to the hope for a U.S. victory and exit strategy. Closer to
home, AISG would never recover its "can-do" reputation.

After my urgent call, Qubeisi agreed to meet us on a
busy corner of Al Kindi Street—Fort Apache's neighboring
business district—near the newly reopened bridal shop
where haute-culture mannequins stood draped in classic
full-length white in the picture window. General Mohamed
met us at Fort Apache and we drove to meet Qubeisi in our
armored BMW. Qubeisi quickly stepped into the car out of
an evening crowd that filled the sidewalks in spite of the
insurgent threat. Hardly anyone noticed the transaction or
the lone American in the back of the German sedan.

Once we got back to the office, Mohamed immediately
said, "Qubeisi and I are truly sorry for this—how do you call
it?—ambush. Tell us what happened. We want to help."

I finished the story with the most recent news: "The two
truck drivers kidnapped during the melee following the
rocket-propelled-grenade attack were found today shot to
death and thrown on the side of the road in Hit. You can see
their death poses on an insurgent Web site along with the
company IDs of some of the men killed."

"This area where the attack happened, it does not surprise me," General Mohamed said. "This crossroads of
Route 4 and Route 10 is the site of many such robberies and
lawlessness in the past.

"During the early 1990s a Saudi prince hunting hawks
was stripped naked and killed with his retinue not far from
this location. And the ambassador from Jordan, then an ally

of Saddam's, had his vehicle stopped, also not far from the site of your men's deaths. The diplomat and his travel staff were robbed, had their car taken, and were left in the open desert on the side of the road. The police never captured the thieves."

"It also seems to have been in a gap of U.S. forces from Ramadi to the east and Ar Rutbah to the west. Evidently, none of our military was within thirty miles of the ambush," I noted.

"This area has never known the law," General Mohamed said. "You really have several threats facing the Coalition in Al Anbar: al Qaeda, Sunni nationalists—including Baathists—and the lawless tribes. Of all three, the most intractable will be the tribes, the Bedouins."

"Thankfully, the suicide bombers—*entahareen*—are not Iraqis," I said.

"I don't know if we should be so sure about that." The Sunni general held a hint of pride in his voice. "These Iraqis from the Western Desert, such as the al Qubeisi, accept no control. The mere existence of foreign, non-Muslim troops on the soil of Arabia stirs murderous intent and frustration in the Bedouin. These are men bred to believe you are not a man unless you have stolen from the neighboring tribe, and you are not a real man unless you have killed raiding your neighbor. This is the nomad code of the Arabs going back to before Islam."

"We need to supply Al Walid now from Syria. How soon can you start?" I asked Qubeisi, probably a bit too abruptly.

"Tomorrow," he stated matter-of-factly. We were over five hundred kilometers from our supply destination across, most likely, the most treacherous badlands in the world.

This route was soaked with blood and dangerous as hell. We discovered that the Sandy Group, another DoD security contractor, had had twenty people slaughtered on the same stretch of highway only three weeks prior to our ambush.

OK, I thought to myself, *now it's time for negotiations*. We still had a business to run, and all the replacement trucks, including a forty-foot freezer unit, were going to cost a pretty penny. But we were doing $4–6 million a month ever since I took charge of company operations in October '04. Nevertheless I stated, "We are sending out for sources in Jordan also. But we want to go with you first. However, others will bring supplies also."

"I require authorization to cross the border with Syria," Qubeisi enjoined, "and company badges."

We sent Qubeisi off to get his picture taken for his AISG identification and weapons card. Mohamed and I continued the negotiations. We sat directly across my desk on the second floor of a Christian pharmacist's square flat-roofed adobe mansion, with the office windows sandbagged to the roof. (The newly established life-support/construction company, with staff and living quarters, was now crouched behind fourteen-foot blast walls just across a side road from the original Fort Apache.) I wrote a letter to generic Coalition forces listing our DoD contract numbers for the border project and stating that Abu Sally al Qubeisi was working for us and should be assisted in crossing back and forth over the Syrian border. I placed all my contact info in the letter and signed it.

When Qubeisi returned smiling with his new photo badge and weapons permit listing his pistol's serial number (you don't travel the roads of Iraq without at least a sidearm), I gave him the letter.

Mohamed said, "Let me translate for you," and took the letter from Qubeisi, who listened and then turned to me with a smile on his face: "*Enta athini al sharaf.*" I had given him honor, trust. This he respected, for the passport letter I had given him was risky for us. But I knew that it would either hold true or the U.S. military would call me. This letter alone would not keep him from being searched at the border.

"I will require $50,000 for the first resupply filling your biweekly list for Al Walid. We will need $25,000 up front and the rest upon delivery," the Arab businessman said through Mohamed's translation.

"We will pay you upon delivery for all items based on your price list provided along with the goods delivered. The agreed mark-up for you on your cost is 35 percent, and it is that high because of security risks," I firmly stated.

The Arabs looked somewhat shocked by my counter-proposal, then rapidly spoke between themselves, looked at me, and waited a bit of time. I sat silently attentive, pondering the next move. We sipped on our chai. (I only had Lipton's, but you put enough bags in and you can get a passable facsimile of the strong Iraqi brew.)

Finally, Mohamed, after a burst of quick Arabic with his business partner—they had an agreement to share in any profits from AISG—said, "OK, let's do it."

I said to both as they left to make arrangements for the mission, "*Allah haleaky!* [God protect]."

We had not only found our way out of a potentially terminal situation, but we had gotten a good deal—if they could deliver. For the last six months, we had been paying $65,000 to $70,000 every two weeks to supply the six hundred border patrolmen, and our thirty-man crew, with required food,

274

water, tires, vehicle spare parts, razors for the barber shop, and lubricants for the armory—all the life support required for the base. This amounted to about $7.50 per man, per day.

Now I had to figure out how to get $50,000 out to Al Walid. They only had a few thousand in petty cash.

Shortly after the Sunni meeting, Ahmed, my Iraqi super-star entrepreneur, walked into my office here to help save us. I said immediately, "Ahmed, my brother, where have you been, hanging in Amman with your family? I have not seen you in several days." He had moved his family to Jordan for safety's sake.

"Yes, I heard about the ambush. Terrible, terrible, terrible . . . I remember the Kurd convoy leader, Ali, who went to Mosul with us. Do you remember that trip? My car broke down and you towed it across the border to Kurdistan, and we stayed that night in the Irbil hotel."

"Like it was yesterday, bro," I answered.

"Came back to help. We resupply from Jordan, as we discussed before," continued the Iraqi millionaire from contract revenue that he knew me responsible for obtaining for AISG.

"Great. Let's do it. But while you're en route, please drop off some money to the camp for me—$50,000."

"OK, I'll do it, not a problem." Ahmed, a pensive Sunni Baghdadi, agreed after a moment's delay, most likely realizing this could help a competitor. But he knew the deal. This mission had to succeed.

True to his word, Ahmed dropped off the money at Al Walid. About two o'clock in the morning the very next night, the ops center called on my cell. "Sir, there is someone trying to get back to Baghdad from Al Walid now."

"What the hell, can't they wait till tomorrow, or the next convoy?" I asked, confused.

After a brief interval as I lay back again in my bed, I realized that this was Qubeisi making his delivery. I quickly got back on IM with the camp and also called the satellite phone there. The marines went out into the town of Al Walid proper, and retrieved Qubeisi, waiting at the desolately empty parking lot of the border point's lone restaurant, the only hangout in the one-horse town of Al Walid. You could even see the fast-food joint's parking lot during a clear day from the border post guard tower. His three-truck caravan was filled to the brim with food, water, and other perishables to feed the border patrolmen living in the middle of a desert where during the day it was well over 120 degrees in the present month of June.

We had done it. A Sunni had saved the mostly Shia border patrolmen of the Shia-dominated interim Iraqi government, securing the lawless Sunni province of Al Anbar's border with Sunni-majority Syria. Qubeisi continued to supply Al Walid long after I left Iraq.

TWELVE

Homecoming and the New Iraq

The ebb and flow of events and people in and around Baghdad had become the rhythm of my day-to-day life. I felt almost at home in that exotic Middle Eastern battleground—reason enough to take the next flight back to Maryland. Besides, I had promised my wife and children that I would be gone one year at the most. Now, like my father in Vietnam, I was rolling into eighteen months in a combat zone, broken up here and there by a couple of weeks' vacation with the family. Almost one million Americans who served in the military or with the U.S. government in Iraq signed on for one-year tours or less. I was tired of the stress that comes with danger every minute of every day, and I was ready to return to a world where I didn't have to worry about the man or woman or child walking beside me along Main Street. However, I did feel guilty about leaving the men who worked under me to the mercy of someone less experienced in the fine art of staying alive, a discipline I had mastered.

I had become one of the "old guys," with institutional

knowledge of contract battlefield operations. Most of the Pentagon contractors out on the ground were old enough to be the fathers of the soldiers patrolling the country and manning the checkpoints. So the contractor combatants provided the kind of "seasoning" essential to the success of the overall mission of our troops, which was to subdue the insurgency and reconstruct Iraq.

Being a contractor combatant in Iraq was a tough business. We faced the usual problems of an international business—a multinational workforce, the mastery of a foreign language, an alien legal system, and a strange culture. At the same time, AISG shouldered the additional burden of being undercapitalized from the beginning. And most of all, we faced the constant threat of violence from insurgents, deadly weaponry, the occasional and inadvertent hostility of our own military, and the ever-present thought of serious injury or death.

As the chief operations manager and a shareholder in the company, I had to think not only of my own life but also of the lives of two thousand, five hundred AISG employees. In addition, the insurgents harassed, assaulted, and killed the family members of those who worked for Americans, so I had to worry about several thousand additional families and about our subcontractors and their families, at least the ones living in the war zone.

We also had to protect our clients. One of my main sales points had been that we never lost anyone's cargo nor allowed the death of a client or—until later—the death of an employee. These successes, stretched over a year-long period of service, were rooted in a solid strategy and our trust in the Iraqis we employed.

Then, at the beginning of 2005, things began to unravel.

Pete Baldwin again became involved in running the company as he began to focus on the Iraqna security contract he had obtained. Baldwin, however, was managing from afar as he still spent most of his time on an island in the eastern Philippines. He divided AISG into two independent companies: security and construction / life support. The latter was to be my only responsibility. I no longer had direct control over the security that linked and integrated all our camps scattered nationwide, even though security had been my main operational focus up until then. Van would be assuming those responsibilities.

On paper, my security background could not compare to Van's, a fifty-six-year-old retired Special Ops lieutenant colonel who had founded "Blue Light," the predecessor to Delta Force, the most elite direct-action troops in the world. In practice, however, our excellent security had been grounded in Iraqi loyalty and performance. We operated with minimal American involvement in project operations. We were heavily armed, were Iraqified, and maintained the lowest of low profiles.

This MO put maximum stress on relying on the locals. Step by step, I had gained the loyalties of Namir, then Amer, Brahim, Abu Hind, Ahmed, and every security man who had run the roads with me. I didn't seek their friendship and trust just to ensure more effective business operations. I was interested in their lives, their families, and their hopes for Iraq and its people.

In addition, they noted my actions. They all knew I had driven one of them to a hospital in the dead of night, the most dangerous time to be traveling Baghdad streets. They knew I had put my life on the line to rescue them from the

Iraqi police. And they knew that my door was always open to any one of them for whatever reason. Few Americans bothered to learn their culture and to speak to them in their own language. Our success rested in part on the sense of brotherhood that we all nurtured.

My concern for their future safety as I prepared to return to the United States was partially mitigated by the knowledge that Tony, who had arrived in late 2004, would still be there. With his Arabic language skills and warrior-chief ethic, we had arguably the best contractor combatant team in Iraq. If Tony stayed on, he would look out for my Iraqi friends and the overall security of the company.

The team I built successfully fulfilled over fifteen U.S. Defense Department prime contracts. We supported the nascent Iraqi security forces and secured the hotspots of the war zone without one failure—a record that testified to our effectiveness. And this was during a period when American taxpayer-funded contractors were failing left and right, struggling with the growing insurgency, often breaking contracts and running from danger.

However, with the change of control in the company, chaos began to spread in our security work force. Maybe it wasn't anyone's fault. Maybe we had grown too large to operate without the law of averages nailing us. Maybe in a war people have to die.

The tragedy of the deaths of the two cooks at Ar Rutbah was the result of a security breakdown. If those men had kept their security team with them instead of sending the Pesh Merga back to the base, a few bad guys—just one carload—would never have attacked them.

Then there was the loss of an Egyptian engineer who

was covered under our Iraqna cell-network security contract, killed by a random car bomb near the Green Zone in March 2005. His car happened to be in the wrong place at the wrong time—tragic but unpreventable in this war, where death might be a man, woman, or child coming toward you smiling, a walking bomb.

The killings on the highway could have been significantly reduced if our new American security leadership had enforced proper training, tactics, techniques, and procedures. Sam, the retired SEAL—who became number two in the new security company—had a local sheikh on the payroll from the area west of Ramadi where the ambush occurred. But we never contacted him for an intel update on the highway before the doomed convoy moved out. So we never received a warning that the insurgents were increasing their presence in that area.

Furthermore, another contractor, the Sandy Group, had lost an entire team near the same location just twenty days earlier. This was information available to security contractors at the American embassy in the Green Zone. Pete Baldwin's security team never got it, didn't even look for it. When you are fighting a war, you have to know the strength and location of your enemy. A failure to get timely intelligence can lead to disaster, as Lee found out at Gettysburg.

Also, under the new organizational structure, the discipline in the convoys had broken down to the point where, on the way from Al Walid to the ambush site, the convoy's rear SUV's machine gun was not even loaded. So, when the shooting started, the vehicle turned tail and ran. To make matters worse, the guy manning the satellite phone gave out inaccurate grid coordinates. As a consequence, the quick-reaction

Cobra gun ships flew to a spot over one hundred miles from the ambush site. Had the Cobras arrived in a timely fashion, the bad guys would have faced an impossible task in pillaging our convoy and killing AISG men.

To make matters worse, there was no lead recon car for the convoy during the four-hundred-mile journey. The vehicles just joggled along, blind to what mile after mile of hostile territory would bring. In effect, our new security people were on their knees begging to be attacked. After all, this was the most dangerous work undertaken by AISG. The ambush exposed the lack of effective American leadership in planning and preparation for our weekly convoys across the Sunni badlands to the Syrian border.

You can't learn the intricacies and dangers of doing business in Iraq from an island halfway around the world. Thus, after Baldwin had taken control, the security department had declined, and at a deadly cost.

My good friend Ali, a Baghdadi Kurd, had been killed in the ambush. He had never wanted to be a security guy; I hadn't wanted him to either. I had wanted him to be a translator. That's why I split the two jobs of convoy commander and security commander—one to talk with us via satellite phone, and the other, a competent warrior chief, to direct the guard force.

Ali served as the security manager on the fated convoy and died failing to do a job that his fellow Iraqis knew he was incapable of handling. Bear, the Gurkha who commanded the convoy, could barely communicate in English with Ali, who spoke the language fluently. Bear was a competent warrior from Nepal, but he was unqualified to manage such a sensitive operation, if only because no American could understand him. The sole justification for his presence was his DoD badge, which the convoy did not require for delivery to an Iraqi base. When I ran security into Fallujah, Mosul, the Syrian Border, all over Baghdad, and elsewhere in the Sunni Triangle, our logistics convoys operated successfully with an Iraqi-only crew. Now, with Baldwin's security team not having the connection with the Iraqis necessary for our low-profile approach—nor did they focus on convoy security but were wrapped up in the cell-phone company security contract—I had lost a mind-numbing number of friends.

The lack of American leadership within an organization I had risked my life to create hurt me deeply. My frustration began to boil over. I couldn't take it anymore. AISG was now stable business-wise. I had successfully negotiated a potentially huge contract to undertake life support for Taji, the crown jewel of the Pentagon's exit strategy. With Qubeisi, we had saved the border contract. With his blessing, we now could go anywhere in the Sunni Triangle. Our network of Baghdadi suppliers was unmatched by any other American contractor. However, the new security management team rarely, if ever, ran the roads with our Iraqis—they never built the mutual respect from shared risk that underpinned our success. As time went on under the new leadership, the bonds built through shared risk and open communications began to unravel.

This breakdown in discipline—which occurred at the height of our potential as a profitable business—left me frustrated and helpless. I hated to abandon my friends to incompetence and neglect. But I felt like I was beating my head against a wall as no one in the security leadership was listening to me.

Following the ambush, I told Baldwin once again that he had to strengthen security by putting me back in charge, after ostensibly hiring Van to allow me to focus on business and not be distracted by security; otherwise he accepted the risk that we could continue to lose good men in increasing numbers. He refused and said that AISG was stronger with the divided roles, as Van was the better security manager, not me. I then strongly recommended that he give Tony a greater role in security management. He agreed to that. With this final effort done, I felt a little better about wanting to leave Iraq. In addition, I knew that Carlos—a Honduran civil engineer with a $100 million in U.S. government contract experience—could keep the machine running. Tony was watching over security. With those two in place and with the company now able to pay competitive salaries, I concluded that Pete could replace me with any number of competent managers.

Well aware of my growing discontent, Pete presented me with a buyout of my minority ownership and profit share. I accepted and headed to Maryland via London from Amman and out of the Iraq combat zone—back home to my wife and children. When I landed in Baltimore, the decompression began.

Back home in Maryland, I was able to step back and objectively evaluate what I had been through. With a master's in history and with my own experience and knowledge of Iraq and Iraqis, I was able to make some sense out of U.S. policy in that war-ravaged country. I read cover-to-cover the books by the expert observers, including Kenan Makiya, Rashid Khaldi, Shams Inati, Albert Hourani, Fouad Ajami, Edward Said, Anthony Shadid, Khidhir Hamza, Zaki Chehab, and Ahmed Hashim, along with T. E. Lawrence, Bernard Lewis,

Gilles Kepel, L. Paul Bremer, W. R. Polk, Bob Woodward, John Keegan, and Michael Gordon.

What I read convinced me that I had a story to tell, one that had never made it to the network news. The books that focus on the war in Iraq were, for the most part, written by people who had come to the subject with a built-in bias and had constructed an artificial war to reflect their own ideological perceptions. If they had been to Iraq at all, they had stayed no more than a few days, talked primarily to people who supported their bias, and then had flown out of BIAP unsure of where they had been. Had they remained there a year and a half, 24/7, as I had, they might have been able to overcome their prejudices and depict Iraq and its people more accurately.

For example, they found unrelieved despair among the Iraqis where I found an abiding sense of hope. They found nothing but hostility toward Americans where I found friendship and admiration. They found death where I found rebirth. I couldn't help but believe that such books were written out of ideological zeal. I not only found these works to be narrow in focus, but I also found a number of factual errors, which convinced me that much of their research had been gathered at a hotel bar inside the Green Zone. At this point, I decided to write my own account of the war and the Iraqi people.

Our experience working with Iraqis of all sects and ethnic groups was successful because it was grounded in trust and pride of performance. The thousands of Iraqis who worked with AISG risked not only their own lives but those of their families. As I looked back on my eighteen months in country, I asked myself, *Why were they able to do that?*

The answer may surprise many Americans, who have been

285

conditioned by the media to see the struggle as hopeless: the insurgency is not strong enough to intimidate the vast majority of Iraqis, who want to move forward with us into a future of peace, freedom, and relative prosperity. If the polls show that Iraqis want us out of their country, that's because the questions have been carefully worded to evoke what seems to be a groundswell of anti-American sentiment. Of course, Iraqis look forward to a time when foreign troops no longer walk their streets. On the other hand, few eagerly anticipate a future when the current violence will erupt into full-scale civil war, with perhaps hundreds of thousands dead on both sides.

In addition, they remember what life was like under Saddam Hussein. They suffered great hardships under his regime, particularly during the economic boycott when he refused to allow the UN to determine whether he still had weapons of mass destruction. During that period, the UN Oil-for-Food program allowed Iraq to sell enough of its oil on the world market to ensure basic human needs for the population. Saddam had access to billions of dollars that never reached his people, all the while telling them they were suffering from UN-mandated sanctions. The deprivation the Iraqi people suffered as the result of his greed and deception alone justified his removal from power.

He also used poison gas on his own people and on the Iranians in a war of aggression initiated by Baghdad, a conflict that cost over six hundred thousand soldiers their lives. This genocidal dictatorship annihilated hundreds of thousands of Kurds and Shias. In fact, Saddam wiped out an estimated one hundred thousand Shias following their ill-fated uprising during three months immediately after the liberation of Kuwait by U.S.-led forces in 1991.

After the successful removal of Saddam from power, the U.S. Congress appropriated $20 billion for the reconstruction of Iraq. Yet these funds, allocated specifically for the projects we were servicing, flowed as slowly as a glacier through the newly formed bureaucracy. Such regulations would have been difficult enough to follow if you were serving the government in Washington DC; but they were all but impossible to deal with in a country under siege by an insurgency using urban guerrilla tactics. No one understood this problem better than I did.

That's why I was hired by the Department of Defense—to tell them how to improve the system. They were particularly interested in what I had to say because I had effectively employed Iraqis to rebuild their own country. Given this experience, I pushed for the Defense Department to establish an Iraqi central contracting registry to allow for vetted local companies with the proper competence and proven loyalties to offer their services in fair and open competition for business with both the U.S. and the new Iraqi governments. I told them the Iraqis themselves were capable of reconstructing their own infrastructure. I pointed out that they had the technical skills and the work ethic to take on any job.

After all, if you believe the evidence in Jeff Stein's *Saddam's Bombmaker*, you understand how close the Iraqis came to developing a nuclear weapon. With that understanding, it's easy to believe that Iraqis have the ability to build dams, roads, and power stations. All they would require is a nonhostile environment in which to get the job done.

In talking to officials at the Department of Defense, I emphasized that I wasn't speaking as a scholar of history with a specialty in Middle Eastern culture. I had lived with these people under the most dangerous of circumstances, and I knew their capabilities. Nothing reveals character more readily than flying bullets, unless it's unremitting danger day after day, month after month, year after year.

I also told them the main problem with our news coverage of the war was the failure of editors and anchors to cover the weakness of the bad guys. Why do I say the insurgency is weak? Not only because I had gone head to head with them in helping to destroy their only chance for an Iraq safe haven in Fallujah, but also because the vast majority of Iraqis have time and time again resisted terrorist threats, whether it be to carry through on elections or to work with U.S. contractors. Whenever we had jobs available and advertised for labor through our clan network, Fort Apache saw lines of applicants stretching hundreds of yards, all the way to Al Kindi Street.

The chief tactic of our enemy in Iraq is to instill terror in the hearts of the Iraqi people. But it hasn't worked. Iraqis aren't paralyzed with fear, and their courage is evidence enough that our greatest chance of success is to count on their will to survive and prevail.

Terrorism is a function of what military scientists call "asymmetrical warfare"—an action, such as a car bomb, meant to have a greater impact on the targeted people than the number killed by the bomb itself. So where is that impact felt the most? The car bomb's effect fits perfectly on the TV screen. Thus it takes only one car bomb in one localized area to ensure that the blood-soaked scenes of mayhem and destruction appear regularly on the evening news back in the United States.

The Vietnam syndrome is well known by the enemies of America. The media led the way in forcing a U.S. withdrawal from Vietnam, a war we were arguably winning if you read the latest research and analysis in Lewis Sorley's *A Better War*. The communists did not take over South Vietnam through an internal popular revolt but via the North Vietnamese blitzkrieg assault down Route 1, an attack American airpower could have handled. But Congress cut off funds. We pulled out of Vietnam. And the result was mass murder in Southeast Asia, followed by the boat people leaving in droves.

Do we really want our Iraqi friends to surrender their country? Are we ready for hundreds of thousands of Iraqi boat people washing up on our shore, swarming across our porous borders—people who sided with us and whom we will have abandoned as we did our friends and allies in Saigon? The results in the wake of our withdrawal from Vietnam were catastrophic: retaliation, executions, and mass murder. The same will surely happen in Iraq.

In the war on terror, the insurgents' *schwerpunkt* (point of decision), to use Liddel-Hart's term, is the press, American and European. In the United States, this is fertile ground. Just how fertile you can measure by the anti-war posture of the mainstream media as recorded by the *Pew Research Center for The People & The Press* in a study published on November 17, 2005. The Pew poll found that among "top" American journalists "only 28% thought the U.S. should have invaded Iraq in 2003, as opposed to 48% of the public."

The continuous flow of negative information, evidenced by books with such over-the-top titles as *State of Denial* and *Fiasco* (I have read both cover to cover), reinforces the chaotic images Americans see on the "small screen"—innocent Iraqis slaughtered in the marketplace, mothers wild with grief over the loss of a small child, caskets draped with an American flag. In spite of these tragedies, I have seen streets crowded with Iraqis shopping, defying terrorist threats, a 60 percent turnout in the national election, and children talking to U.S. troops while parents watch with smiles on their faces. This is the Iraq I knew, and I believe this Iraq will prevail over the war-sick, bleeding nation the networks give you every night.

But what about car bombs? Haven't they proven themselves invincible? When media types argue this, they show their ignorance of military affairs. The car bomb, unlike the roadside bomb, is a weapon that has failed to be militarily effective. Time after time, car bombs have targeted police and army recruiting stations in all areas of Iraq. Yet Iraqis continue to show up and sign up for the security services. Currently, Iraqi forces under arms exceed three hundred thousand volunteers—all their security forces need given the time—under American guidance and protection—for proper training and unit development. News reporters and TV anchors have omitted this success story from their coverage of Iraq.

So the car bomb is really intended to be a weapon of psychological warfare. At a very low cost to the insurgents, this tactic, covered extensively on U.S. TV, gives the impression that the war is out of control. Sitting on a sofa, in Poughkeepsie or Chicago or San Jose—eating burgers and french fries—Americans cannot understand how the Iraqi government could be making progress when such barbaric scenes appear on the screen nearly every night. They don't realize that this war is being fought in the minds and hearts of Americans as well as in the streets of Baghdad and Fallujah and Mosul. The Iraqis want to keep what they've got—freedom from Saddam Hussein, a government they can control, and peace in the streets. A growing number of Americans want to pull out because they believe the grim message the car bomb conveys, that our presence in the Middle East has caused this fratricidal strife and that if we pull out, the killing will stop.

The car bomb merely requires a junk car, a thousand pounds of easily obtained explosives, and one jihadi—usually not of Iraqi origin but from one of the many surrounding hopeless nations—ready to enter "paradise" and greet those seventy-two black-eyed virgins. Hundreds of al Qaeda jihadis are drawn to Iraq, eager for martyrdom, and operating with local Sunni support.

Because the U.S. newspapers and TV commentators habitually misrepresent the war, and because some at the Pentagon fail to understand the mess in the Middle East, the car bomb has now become a highly successful strategic weapon, similar to nuclear bombers, missile subs, and ICBMs. At the moment, these small-scale explosions threaten to become surrender-inducing assaults on the will of the American people, despite the fact that we are making significant progress in almost every aspect of our mission there.

Many people argue that the war in Iraq is crucial to our national security. They maintain that by moving the battle against Islamic terrorists to the Middle East, we have forced the terrorists to fight the war on their soil rather than on ours. After all, American soldiers, all volunteers, are fighting the same militant wing of Islam that produced the 9/11 hijackers who attacked the World Trade Center and the Pentagon. Also, U.S. troops are fighting this war side-by-side with Iraqis, happy to be free of Saddam and fearing the other brutal regimes so prevalent in the Middle East, a couple of them hoping to metastasize into vulnerable Iraq.

The fact that many see the original invasion of Iraq as unjustified does not change the reality that this is now a war we must win. If we don't, our failure will follow us to our own shores. In the beginning, I was opposed to the war, primarily because I saw the possibility of another abandonment and another bloody aftermath. I didn't think Americans had the will to fight such a war, not after what had happened in Vietnam; and I didn't want to see young Americans give their lives on behalf of a failed cause.

Out of frustration, I wrote a letter in late 2001 to my hometown newspaper—the *Washington Post*—attacking its endorsement of war against Saddam. My letter stated that when the children of the *Post*'s owners serve in the military, then they will have the credibility to urge war. (The *Post* didn't publish it.)

Some have criticized our strategic plan, arguing that we don't have enough troops in Iraq. This criticism is unjustified, even when voiced by retired generals. Time has proven that we have just enough troops to maintain the rotation and training cycle necessary to sustain an occupation force that could extend out more than three years. With only 460,000 in the entire active-duty U.S. Army (less than half the size than when I left in 1990); with 185,000 in the Marine Corps; and with our security obligations in Afghanistan, NATO, Japan, Korea, the Horn of Africa, and elsewhere, where would we go to get more ground troops?

With over 600,000 troops, why can't we put more than 140,000 in the Iraq war zone? The main reason: in Iraq we primarily need combat troops, people who pull triggers and kill bad guys—Special Forces, infantry, armor, helicopter crews, and military police. The standard tooth-to-tail in the U.S. Army—meaning combat troops versus combat support and service support specialists—is 1 to 10. In reality then, we have, with the National Guard and Reserve forces, less than two hundred thousand door-kickers, those trained for infantry and police work. These patrol and fight the insurgents directly, as is required for close-quarters, low-intensity warfare in urban terrain. Therefore one can see that the Pentagon planned correctly—possibly out of chance—for a sustainable rotation of troops to cover the contingency of a multiyear insurgency and the long-term demands of creating an effective Iraqi military once we overthrew Saddam.

This is also where the contractor combatants came in—to fill the gaps for a maxed-out military in areas that did not require U.S. government–funded soldiering skills. KBR, much maligned in the press for its connection to Vice President Dick Cheney, successfully assumed a critical role in supplying and feeding the troops in Iraq at great cost in human terms. I was constantly awed by the sight of KBR trucks—obviously American—moving in long convoys along the shot-up highways of Iraq, delivering the bread, hotdogs, water, and mail demanded by a U.S. force dug in for a long war. The risks these KBR employees took are reflected in the hundred or so of the company's civilian employees killed in action.

I do believe that critics were right when they faulted the U.S. strategic war plan for our failure to know what to do with Iraq after we owned it. The plan called for major U.S. construction companies to rebuild Iraq immediately after the invasion. Planners anticipated that this reconstruction would provide jobs and develop infrastructure with proven contractors who had done billions of dollars in international construction work.

After a ragged start, due primarily to the ad hoc nature of the CPA, this plan became well-developed administratively with open and fair bidding in accordance with high-standard U.S. government contracting rules reflected in the nearly two thousand pages of the Federal Acquisition Regulation. At the same time, that plan was budgeted as if this massive reconstruction would take place in a relatively peaceful and orderly environment, not in an active war zone. Once Iraq turned violent, the plan broke down. For example, the security costs ballooned from an estimated 7–10 percent of contract value into more than 20 percent in most, if not all, cases.

Our government should have planned for an extended low-level insurgency where the Seabees—the armed construction battalions of the United States Navy, could have led the way and undertaken extensive and massive rebuilds of infrastructure. They effectively led the project management office in Vietnam, concluding over two billion dollars (1960s dollars) in construction projects, utilizing many of the U.S. prime contractors (or their predecessor companies) that underperformed in Iraq. (To date, the Seabees have been employed primarily as convoy security in Iraq.)

The Seabee-created indigenous construction units included over two hundred thousand Vietnamese workers, laboring away in the midst of a major ground war of much higher intensity than in Iraq. I ran into a Seabee battalion commander at Baghdad International Airport's Area Four, the Iraqi Special Forces training area where AISG provided life support. He told me that elements of his six hundred armed construction specialists and their large-scale construction equipment were scattered across the globe from Guam to Baghdad. I asked him why there were not more Seabees in Iraq. He said, "We are not here to build. That's for the Iraqis to do."

The Seabees are a significant force comprising eight active-duty and twelve reserve battalions. After a couple of years of initial struggle, they and their support command (Naval Facilities Management) successfully controlled all U.S. construction funds and contracting theater-wide in Vietnam. This is a documented model that the United States could still replicate in Iraq.

In my opinion, the greatest weakness of our intelligence-gathering agencies was their failure to ascertain the degree to which the infrastructure in Iraq had deteriorated following three crippling blows: the Iran-Iraq War, the Gulf War, and the decade-long UN sanctions. For example, even before the current war, oil-rich Iraq imported gasoline because most of its refineries were in disrepair and no longer functional. Prior to the U.S. invasion, the non-Sadr City areas of the capital may have enjoyed a full day's electricity, but the outlying provinces, especially the heavily Shia south, often had just four hours a day, if any at all. All of this deterioration, amplified by unrealistic preinvasion expectations, further undermined the impression of American competence. How could the most powerful nation in the world not keep the lights on? They weren't on even before we showed up.

The other failure of our prewar intelligence was the inability of U.S. forces to pinpoint weapons of mass destruction in Iraq. In October of 1998, five years before the invasion, the Stockholm (Sweden) International Peace Research Institute *Fact Sheet* titled "The UNSCOM Experience" reported that there were, among other banned items, the following WMDs known to exist but not accounted for by the Iraqi government: 4,000 tons of chemical warfare precursors; 750 tons of VX nerve-gas precursors; 31,000 chemical warfare armaments; and 40–70 chemical-biological warfare-capable missile warheads. Although Saddam's minions claimed these were destroyed, they never produced a shred of evidence to document this destruction—not in 1998 or by March 2003 when the last UN inspectors pulled out before the invasion. The VX alone is enough to kill hundreds of thousands of people.

After 9/11, the desire of Americans to operate as if we lived in normal times gave way to reality. After watching those planes hit the Twin Towers on news show after news show, we wisely decided to recognize the danger and take appropriate steps, however inconvenient. We were no longer *Festung Amerika*, protected by wide oceans from the violent chaos and suicidal fanaticism rampant in the Middle East. America was now target number one. Once the Taliban ceased to rule Afghanistan in late 2001, the leaders of al Qaeda fled to other safe havens. Many ended up in the lawless Northwest Frontier of Pakistan, others in Iran. Both locations, however, restricted their operational movement.

One leader, however, went to Iraq, where Saddam was gloating publicly over the success of al Qaeda in New York City and northern Virginia. This leader's nom de guerre was Abu Musa al Zarqawi. There is clear evidence that Osama bin Laden had funded, at least in part, Zarqawi's operations in Taliban Afghanistan. He would eventually orchestrate attacks against American and Iraqi forces in Baghdad and surrounding areas. He was number two on the international Most Wanted list, considered by many to be more dangerous than bin Laden. With the blood of thousands on his hands, he was killed on June 7, 2006, in a U.S. air strike.

Zarqawi came to Baghdad—a city so well controlled by Saddam's secret police that not one single effective U.S. spy operated there. Almost no accurate information leaked out to Western intelligence services after UNSCOM departed in 1998, and this dearth of intelligence was not for lack of trying or financial resources.

Zarqawi made his way to the far southeastern corner of Kurdistan, occupied at the time by the terrorist organization Ansar al-Islam, another known al Qaeda affiliate. This enclave was, in theory, a Coalition-protected area, free from Baghdad's control. In reality—squeezed up against the closed border with Iran—it sat well within striking range of Iraqi security services. Interestingly, the Iraq-supported and U.S. State Department-listed Iranian terrorist group, the Mujahideen-e-Khalq, was located at Ashraf, where we built the ammo-destruction camp for Parsons. Ashraf was not far from Ansar's territory, albeit outside the U.S. and British airpower-protected zone of Kurdistan. In 2004, Zarqawi publicly declared his fidelity to bin Laden and changed the name of his group to "al Qaeda in Iraq." Connect the dots.

The National Intelligence Estimate, partially declassified in September 2006, declared that Iraq was "a cause celebre" for jihadi terrorists. This designation was viewed by those opposed to the war as an example of how the Iraq War had exacerbated the terrorist threat. In reality, it illustrates the success of what I call the *Field of Dreams* strategy: build it and they will come. The United States has picked the battlefield with this enemy and drawn out the anti-American terrorists lurking in every dark corner of the Middle East and even in Europe. Every time another Western European jihadi is reported dead or captured in Iraq, that represents one less potential terrorist who could get on an airplane and fly to the United States without a visa.

It is naïve or disingenuous to think that the Iraq War created the jihadi threat to the United States, an example of a post hoc fallacy, erroneously assuming a causal effect. Our justified support for Israel's existence, the presence of American troops in the holy land of Saudi Arabia (watching out for any further Saddam aggression), the destruction of the Taliban, and the non-*Salafi* (pre-eighth-century Islam) nature of our world-influencing culture clearly existed prior to the Iraqi war. The Salafi fanatics had plenty of reasons to escape from their hopeless lives, seek martyrdom, and hate the U.S.A. After all, the 9/11 attacks occurred before the U.S. invasion of Iraq.

The people the U.S. strategy has drawn to Iraq are beyond the pale of international law or human rights, as are the Neo-Saddamists continuing to fight for a return to a Sunni Arab totalitarian hegemony, i.e., imposed minority rule. They are outside the Geneva Conventions and the Law of Land Warfare.

There are several categories of combatants covered in the Conventions: those in uniform or who have some other defining insignia "visible from afar . . . carrying arms openly . . . conducting their operations within the laws and customs of war"; civilians accompanying armed forces, such as combatant contractors, carrying an identity card issued by the armed forces stating their position; and *Levee en Masse*, where inhabitants take up arms to protect their unoccupied home area against an invader. Note that all must comply with the rules of land warfare, which include bearing arms openly—that is, not concealing them on the approach of the enemy.

Therefore the fight against al Qaeda and neo-Saddamists in Iraq is a struggle against war criminals operating outside civilized norms. The murderers who targeted and blew up thirty children as the little ones received candy from U.S. soldiers at the grand opening of a sewer-pumping station deserve no quarter and are guaranteed none by international law.

Before I left for Iraq at the beginning of January 2004, I studied *Just War Theory*, as defined by Augustine and Thomas Aquinas. There are several elements that define a Just War, including *Just Cause*. Just Cause for this conflict is engaging the aggressive, genocidal actions of a totalitarian dictator who used weapons of mass destruction on his own people and that of a neighboring country, then celebrated the 9/11 attacks while allowing a known al Qaeda–affiliated leader to pass through his capital and seek sanctuary within his country's borders.

The other primary elements of a Just War include a wise ruler, a good cause, pure motives, declared as a last resort, probability of success, and whether or not the war is an overreaction to the offense it seeks to redress. Arguing that all of these are present in the case of the Iraq War would be futile. The debate could continue until the twenty-second century.

More importantly, the United Nations Security Council—the designated arbiter of what is and isn't a Just

War per Article 42 of the UN Charter—decided in an unanimous decision (15 to 0) to make the United States the legal "Occupying Authority" for Iraq after our successful coup de main, which removed Saddam from power with minimal civilian casualties. This is a definitive and binding statement of the international community's recognition of the legality of U.S. actions in toppling Saddam's regime and taking control of the country that he had so exploited during his thirty-plus years in power. The insurgency that followed this declaration by the UN has therefore consistently violated international law in waging illicit war, first against the legitimate Occupation and second against the UN-recognized, democratically elected sovereign government of Iraq.

The insurgency in Iraq would collapse if the Sunni tribes turned against the nihilistic killers of al Qaeda and the proponents of a violent return to the minority sect's ruling status in Iraq. This is the sea in which the insurgents swim, whether in Al Anbar, Baghdad, or other areas of Iraq where Sunni Arab communities are located. The Sunni Arab leadership in large part has seen political benefit in turning a blind eye to the Neo-Saddamist forces allied with al Qaeda. The Sunnis seek to leverage that threat against the popular weight of the Shia and Kurd supermajority, which constitutes 80 percent of the Iraqi population. Now, following the bombing of the Golden Mosque in Samarra, the Shia giant has angrily awakened and is exacting revenge on perceived supporters of the insurgency. Once the terrorists cease sending suicide bombers to target large gatherings of Shia civilians, then the Shia death squad and vigilante killings of Sunni Arab men will end, as the majority sect is confident of its power to govern in the new democracy. It is up to the Sunni Arabs. They can stop the mad cycle of killing by allying themselves with the Iraqi government in the struggle against the terrorists.

The strength of the U.S.'s mission lies in its ability to maintain the support of the Shia masses. Upon this support rests the success or failure of our efforts in Iraq. Therefore, as with the demand of Kurd and Shia leaders for the demobilization of the Sunni-dominated, genocidal Iraqi army and the removal of the brutal and primarily Sunni Baathists from government, the Sunni Arab community must recognize their minority status. Apparently, such recognition will continue to require force of arms because, as General Mohamed, my friend and former director of Iraqi air force intelligence, would say, "The men of the [Sunni] Bedouin tribes of the Western Desert will die before they accept foreigners in their country." Along the same lines there is another common saying in Iraq: "Some Sunni men cannot sleep with their wives if the Shias rule." In other words, many Sunni males consider Shia rule a reflection on their manhood and are rendered impotent by the very thought of it. Unfortunately for these loveless Sunni men, the Shias hold power, constituting a 60 percent majority in the new democracy.

This intransigence on the part of the Sunni Arab tribes provides the sustaining strength for the insurgency, especially the key suicide bombers of al Qaeda who are, as I have said before, the "strategic weapon" of terrorists holed up primarily in Al Anbar province, a place never subdued, even by Saddam's totalitarian regime. This vast, barren, and underpopulated area has never known law, not for thousands of years; so we have to calibrate our expectations of what the U.S. and Iraqi military forces can achieve there.

Baghdad has now become the center of gravity for the war, a war that is now the focus of an international terrorist movement whose agenda is to create violence and promote chaos. Baghdad is also the holding pen for the media. The capital is a free-wheeling metropolis of more than five million people, driving around in hundreds of thousands of cars. After the destruction of Fallujah, the last significant safe haven in Iraq for the insurgency, the terrorists' only hope is to break the American will to remain strong in Iraq by car bombings and other urban terrorist tactics. Well aware of the nation's unwillingness to stay the course in Vietnam, al Qaeda hopes the media can again break the will of the American people.

The Coalition has now "fixed the enemy" in the capital. This confinement to Baghdad makes confrontation much easier than chasing and battling insurgents in Mosul, Kirkuk, Ramadi, and other major cities with substantial Sunni populations. This is exactly what we did with Fallujah, attracting and then annihilating the jihadists in the self-proclaimed Salafi "Emirate." Military forces fighting an elusive insurgency need to find the enemy, fix him in place, and then destroy him. In the end, the focus on Baghdad will work out to both Iraq's and America's benefit.

Unfortunately, the forces of Moqtada al Sadr, operating from the teeming Shia ghetto in eastern Baghdad, have now careened out of control. The Iraqi government, with substantial U.S. assistance, will have to bring Sadr's militia to heel. The Mahdi army has metastasized to the point where it can be compared to Hezbollah in Lebanon, a state within a state. Hopefully, Moqtada will see the light and disarm; but before that happens, most likely we will see more bloodshed.

As I think of this problem, I remember when Ahmed—caught by Sadr's militia in a Shia neighborhood in Baghdad—was about to be executed along with nine of our men. Moqtada's people finally realized they were with the Americans, not the *entahareen* (the Sunni terrorist insurgency) and the militia set them free, returning their weapons. I therefore have to believe that most of Sadr's bombast against America is political posturing, since he knows we liberated his people.

Nevertheless, the Shia death squads—vigilantes attacking the perceived supporters of suicide bombers—feed off the anarchy brought by the Mahdi army control in Sadr City. The comparison between these vigilantes and the terrorists blowing up women and children in mass-casualty car bombs does not favor al Qaeda. By not supporting the war aims of their nation's democratically elected government, the Sunnis in Baghdad reinforce the perception that they do not hold their brethren accountable for the daily atrocities and are now suffering a fierce backlash.

The United States must continue to support the Shia majority. Such support is key to victory in the Iraq War. We must do this because the Shias are fighting to preserve the liberty they have gained by the toppling of Saddam and their participation in free elections. They are fighting to remain free of the opportunistic jihadi forces that also threaten the United States and that are now trying to hijack the Iraqi people's newly won freedom. After hundreds of years of repression, the Shias are ready to rule, though they are not yet well practiced in the nurture of democratic institutions. The fear of a coup by theocratic, coreligionist Iran—which kept us from supporting the Shias when they rose up after the Gulf War in 1991—is misplaced. The Iranians can never infiltrate Iraq in sufficient numbers to pose any real problem.

Fort Apache was in the same neighborhood as the interim Iraqi prime minister's residence. One day two men drove up to our gate guards and asked, "Where does Iyad Allawi live?" That brief phrase, spoken in Arabic, told our security men that these were Iranians. They immediately detained the two and Allawi's bodyguard picked them up a few minutes later.

The point of the story: Iraqi Arabic is extremely difficult for other Arabs to master, but for a native Farsi-speaking person it is nearly impossible. Iranians cannot travel in Iraq clandestinely if at any time they are required to speak. Consequently the country cannot be overrun with Iranian spies. The Arabs and the Iranians have centuries of mutual enmity exemplified by the hundreds of thousands of Iraqi Shias who went to their death fighting their fellow Shias in the Iran-Iraq War.

In the end, the vast majority of Iraqis—Shia, Kurd, and most secular Sunni Arabs—want America to succeed in helping to establish a peaceful, democratic Iraq, fully integrated into the world economy. The popularly elected government in Baghdad has requested us to stay, as did Japan, Germany, and South Korea. The Americans running the greatest risk in this mission are the U.S. troops in Iraq; and they are reenlisting at historically high rates. These brave men and women know better than the American people at home the importance of their mission to individual Iraqis. Our military operation in Iraq is built to run for years. The American economy has absorbed the cost of the war and has still grown at historically high rates. The present and grave threat to America evidenced by the 9/11 attack arose from the religiously inspired suicidal and genocidal tendencies rampant in the Middle East. We must be there to eliminate the source of that threat. Why turn back now?

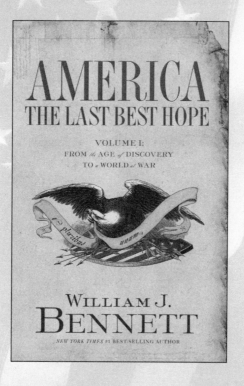

AMERICA
THE LAST BEST HOPE

VOLUME I:
FROM *the* AGE *of* DISCOVERY
TO *a* WORLD *of* WAR

WILLIAM J.
BENNETT

NEW YORK TIMES #1 BEST-SELLING AUTHOR

From the bold, brilliant mind of best-selling author William J. Bennett comes this thrilling account of the virtues and vices of our great country and the many brave men and women who have made it the powerful nation it is today. A sweeping tale of human initiative, struggle, and victory, Bennett uniquely captures what is unique about America.

ISBN 978-1-59555-055-2

THOMAS NELSON
Since 1798

For other products and live events,
visit us at: thomasnelson.com

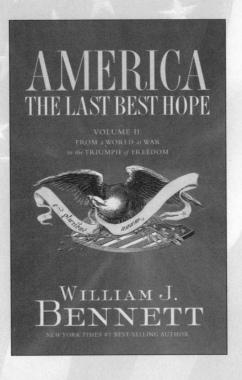

AMERICA
THE LAST BEST HOPE

VOLUME II:
FROM a WORLD at WAR
to the TRIUMPH of FREEDOM

WILLIAM J.
BENNETT

NEW YORK TIMES #1 BEST-SELLING AUTHOR

Respected scholar William Bennett reacquaints America with its heritage in the second volume of *America: The Last Best Hope (Volume II)*. This engaging narrative slices through the cobwebs of time, memory, and prevailing cynicism to reinvigorate America with an informed patriotism.

ISBN 978-1-59555-057-6

THOMAS NELSON
Since 1798

For other products and live events,
visit us at: thomasnelson.com

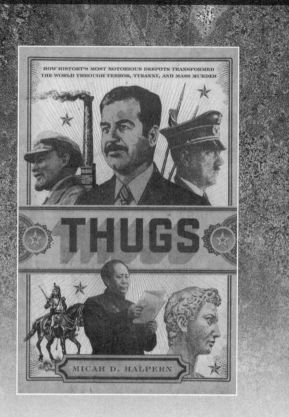

*From Hitler to Hussein, Napoleon to Pol Pot,
Alexander the Great to Idi Amin, this is a
trenchant look into the lives, politics, and horrible
deeds of history's most notorious world leaders—
and how they shaped our world for the worst.*

ISBN 978-1-59555-073-6

THOMAS NELSON
Since 1798

For other products and live events,
visit us at: **thomasnelson.com**